Implementing and Configuring SAP® MII

 **PRESS**

SAP PRESS is a joint initiative of SAP and Galileo Press. The know-how offered by SAP specialists combined with the expertise of the Galileo Press publishing house offers the reader expert books in the field. SAP PRESS features first-hand information and expert advice, and provides useful skills for professional decision-making.

SAP PRESS offers a variety of books on technical and business related topics for the SAP user. For further information, please visit our website: *www.sap-press.com*.

Manuel Essl and Uwe Oehler
The Developer's Guide to SAP xApp Analytics
2007, 452 pp.
978-1-59229-148-9

Jo Weilbach and Mario Herger
SAP xApps and the Composite Application Framework
2005, 293 pp.
978-1-59229-048-2

Jan Rauscher and Volker Stiehl
The Developer's Guide to SAP NetWeaver Composition Environment
2008, 365 pp.
978-1-59229-171-7

Abesh Bhattacharjee and Dipankar Saha

Implementing and Configuring SAP® MII

Galileo Press

Bonn • Boston

Galileo Press is named after the Italian physicist, mathematician and philosopher Galileo Galilei (1564–1642). He is known as one of the founders of modern science and an advocate of our contemporary, heliocentric worldview. His words *Eppur si muove* (And yet it moves) have become legendary. The Galileo Press logo depicts Jupiter orbited by the four Galilean moons, which were discovered by Galileo in 1610.

Editor Meg Dunkerley
Developmental Editor Kelly Grace Harris
Copyeditor Kevin Kent
Cover Design Jill Winitzer
Photo Credit Image copyright Dainis Derics. Used under license from Shutterstock.com.
Layout Design Vera Brauner
Production Editor Kelly O'Callaghan
Typesetting Publishers' Design and Production Services, Inc.
Printed and bound in Canada

ISBN 978-1-59229-256-1

© 2010 by Galileo Press Inc., Boston (MA)
1st Edition 2010

Contents at a Glance

Contents

5   Display Templates: Let Your Data Speak   153

6   Business Logic Transactions: Intelligence in Action   231

9 Advanced Techniques for SAP MII Composite Application Development 383

10   Implementing SAP MII Composite Applications 427

Appendices 447

Foreword

When we started Lighthammer Software Development in 1998, we had no idea that the vision we held for ubiquitous access to manufacturing information would quickly transform itself into an entirely new market for "enterprise manufacturing intelligence" software. The original concept for the product was code named "Morning Coffee" – this quite vividly describes the intent of the software – which was to enable manufacturing personnel to have access to a breadth of operational information each morning to prepare themselves for their daily production meetings. Having spent some time as a supervisor in a steel mill, I knew the importance and value of up-to-date knowledge, and after a few years in the software and integration industry, knew the challenge and complexity of obtaining that information. The products are an evolution of that original vision, since expanded to include not only visualization and analytics, but also the integration of manufacturing systems with each other and with the rest of the enterprise.

What I find most fulfilling of all is the incredible community of customers, implementers, developers, and experts that have formed around what is now known as SAP Manufacturing Integration and Intelligence (MII), and the value that has been created for this community as a result of the many innovative and successful applications of the technology around the world. As this ecosystem grows, the opportunity to expanded value creation grows with it. In our networked and connected world, the importance of sharing knowledge and best practices becomes a key link in unlocking the potential within the participants businesses.

This book represents the hard work of two of the ecosystem's leading experts, Abesh Bhattacharjee and Dipankar Saha, to bring their wealth of knowledge and experience in implementing SAP MII to the broader community. On behalf of the entire MII community, I thank them for their initiative and effort in making this book a reality.

In hindsight, we should probably have named the product SAP MIII – with the additional "I" referring to innovation. Software should not be the end solution itself – it should be an enabler that provides creative people with the ability to quickly deploy innovative business processes and ideas, particularly those that provide long term competitive advantages. It is in this spirit that I encourage you all to leverage the wealth of knowledge and experience presented in this book and to go forward and create!

Best regards,
Rick Bullotta
Phoenixville, Pennsylvania, USA
April, 2009

Foreword

Not quite long ago SAP announced their planned acquisition of erstwhile Light-hammer Software Development. Their product Lighthammer has evolved over the years to what we now know as SAP Manufacturing Integration and Intelligence. This was applauded all around by industry veterans and analysts worldwide with headlines such as "SAP discovers the Plant Floor." However, this was in line with SAP's "Adaptive Manufacturing" concept which envisions a manufacturing process that is capable of sensing and proactively responding to exceptions through the efficient use of available resources. It is here where SAP MII steps in to provide near real time shop-floor visibility to the enterprise and the availability of action-able intelligence.

From there SAP MII has come a long way. We have successfully delivered SAP MII 12.0 to the customers and SAP MII 12.1 is in ramp-up. Over the days, MII has only become better, providing better connectivity and visibility to the shop-floor and enhancing functionality to model applications that enable the end-user to better visualize the data and also take action in real time in response to unpredictable changes on the shop-floor. And all of this is done through a model driven develop-ment workbench that requires minimal coding.

This book couldn't have come at a better time, given that SAP MII is close to achieving maturity as a product. This is the first ever book on SAP MII and both Dipankar and Abesh have done an excellent job in presenting the various nuances of the product to the reader through ample examples and business scenario discus-sions. Both of the authors are very competent, having written a multitude of very well received SAP MII related blogs and articles on the SAP Community Network. The fact that they are also SAP Mentors only serves to reinforce the fact that they are amongst the leading experts in this field.

To get most out of SAP MII, use this book to find out how you can connect to the manufacturing shop-floor easily and provide rich data visualization for the end-users. Combine this knowledge of SAP MII with your creative zeal and passion for innovation to create the ultimate value for your organization or your customers.

Joachim Hechler
Corporate Officer, SAP A.G.

Michael Fiechtner
SVP, Manufacturing and SCM Development, SAP A.G.

Ramakrishna Yarlapati
SVP, Business Suite Core Product Development – India Centre, SAP Labs India Pvt. Ltd.

Acknowledgments

We want to express our heartfelt gratitude to the following people:

Our families without whose help and constant support this endeavor would have been just a dream.

Haimanti Bhattacharjee, wife of Abesh and a Technical Writer by profession, whose constant attention to details and zeal for perfection has made the book much more readable and presentable than the rough cut we produced.

Rick Bullotta, co-founder and CTO of former Lighthammer Software, ex-Vice President at SAP Research and SAP Labs LLC, and the chief architect of Lighthammer CMS that has evolved into SAP MII today, who, other than extending his helping hand at every step, has also reviewed this book for technical details ironing out whatever slips we might have made authoring it.

Parthasarathi Roy Chowdhury, Francis Simon, Salvatore Castro, Bob DeRemer, Jeremy Good, Thomas Mark Schuette, Pradip Ray and Sreelakshmi Chinnaraj of SAP; Rajesh Ray, Som Sarkar, Soumen Mondal of IBM and Manoel Franklin F. da Costa of Neoris; who have enriched the content at every step. Being our friends and colleagues, they did not for a moment hesitate to constructively criticize the contents when required while also helping us with facts, figures and other technical suggestions to ensure a much more fulfilling experience to the reader.

Ramakrishna Yarlapati, Vijay Seethapathy, Thilo Sieth, Mayank Bhatnagar of SAP and Anup K Ghosh, Asidhara Lahiri, Nilay Ghosh of IBM without whose encouragement and support the process of writing this book would not have been as smooth as it was.

SAP PRESS for believing in us and in our abilities to write a book on SAP MII, especially Jon Franke and Meg Dunkerley, editors of our book, whose constant help and watchful guidance at every step have ensured that our work is at par with the best in the industry.

Last but not the least, the SAP Community Network, without which we would just be one more developer in the crowd. We owe you.

Preface

It had always been a dream, one of our most cherished dreams, that we would author a book one day. We know our subject well enough being actually part of the SAP MII content development team currently and the SAP MII 12.0 product development team in SAP few years back, and we were happy dispersing whatever we know of SAP MII to our peers over at the SAP Community Network through weblogs and forum posts. We were happy helping out people in our own way and like all cherished dreams that seldom turn to reality we nurtured it at the back of our minds. Though SAP MII is gaining momentum among the SAP customers day by day, we have always felt that too little information is currently available, especially for the developers and consultants working in the implementation projects. So when SAP PRESS approached us to author a book on SAP MII last year, we realized it would be the best way to share our experiences and learning with the broader community.

The initial days and weeks passed in a haze planning what to cover in the book to make it a must-have resource for SAP MII developers and consultants. But finally a detailed plan was chalked out with our development editors in SAP PRESS and over a period of nine months this dream was carved out of our first hand experiences with SAP MII. What went into this book is what we know and what we have learned while working in various implementations and development projects on SAP MII. Apart from the general development know-how and tips and tricks for efficient development, it contains examples that we consider are typical, and should be shared with you so that you can use them effectively in the various implementation and consulting projects that you may work on.

This book is for you if you are a developer and want to get started on SAP MII to understand how to use it as a solution development platform for manufacturing composites. Also as an SAP manufacturing integration consultant, you may find this book useful to understand the positioning and effectiveness of SAP MII in ERP to plant integration and analytics scenarios with common use case examples. Moreover, as an architect, working on SAP MII implementation projects, you can use this book to understand the architectural and implementation approaches for SAP MII solution developments.

This book is a vision, a dream that turned into a reality and here, dear reader, we welcome you to share our knowledge and experience. We hope this book will help you to understand the various features of SAP MII and its positioning and guide you in the journey of mastering SAP MII.

This chapter explains the concept of adaptive manufacturing and how it is different from traditional manufacturing. It specifies and addresses the issues that traditional manufacturing plants are facing because of globalization, lack of decision support, and lack of visibility in the manufacturing processes. Finally, it explains adaptive manufacturing in terms of manufacturing synchronization and manufacturing excellence.

Introduction

This chapter explains the concept of adaptive manufacturing, including how to leverage a composition platform to achieve performance and responsiveness in your manufacturing operations.

From Traditional to Adaptive Manufacturing

Change is inevitable in the twenty-first century, both in everyday life and in the business world. Specifically in the area of manufacturing, enterprises today face tremendous challenges that force them to change the way traditional manufacturing processes operate in the industries. Some of the main issues faced by manufacturers today are as follows:

▶ Global competition is placing tremendous pressure on cost, quality, and responsiveness. Because of globalization, manufacturing nodes are pushed out to distant locations, leading to a loss of visibility and control by the direct management.

▶ The business and the financial impact of production exceptions cannot be monitored or controlled at the enterprise level because of a disconnect between manufacturing plant floor processes and the enterprise.

▶ Different plants use copies of master data, leading to compliance and quality issues. Often production personnel lack the information they need for decision support to meet their targets.

▶ Time-to-market windows are shrinking, regulatory requirements are growing, and the ability to maximize assets and utilize the workforce seem to be top priorities for management.

The business implications of these challenges directly affect the visibility and responsiveness of manufacturing operations, which in turn affect overall performance. Because of the disconnect between the manufacturing plant floor and enterprise, companies are learning about malfunctioning machines and production issues too late to take corrective action, which affects the visibility of actual production costs and other Key Performance Indicators (KPIs), such as yield, utilizations, and so on. This in turn affects the responsiveness of the business, most likely causing the business to fail to react rapidly and cost-effectively to manufacturing exceptions and to fail to balance supply and demand priorities. These factors finally end up affecting performance, resulting in constant rework, overtime, expedited orders, shortages, and budget violations, in addition to lower customer satisfaction, employee productivity, and general morale.

Considering the preceding factors, manufacturing companies need to plan new strategies and re-evaluate their operations management practices. Manufacturing operations need to be flexible enough so that they can quickly react to market changes, while companies also need to maintain better control over their manufacturing operations. The major problem for many manufacturing companies is that their manufacturing and enterprise business processes are not synchronized, giving rise to lack of visibility and loss of timely control.

At every level of the enterprise value chain, different information is required by different roles. For example, the management at the enterprise or Enterprise Resource Planning (ERP) level might want to monitor things such as production costs and the KPI for the actual production versus the target on a daily basis whereas the operations management on the manufacturing plant floor is more concerned about each shift of production and asset and resource utilizations. But if the different levels of manufacturing operations are not synchronized and not integrated to the enterprise-wide business processes, monitoring these factors in real time is almost impossible.

> **Example**
>
> Consider some real statistics: A typical manufacturing plant has between 10 and 50 shop floor automation (SFA) systems. So, a multi-site manufacturer could have between 40 and 700 SFA systems across its enterprise. In a customer survey conducted by some well-known analyst firms a few years back, less than 1% of the respondents indicated that their manufacturing data is automatically integrated with ERP with no manual intervention.

To address these challenges, SAP® is supporting a new concept, which is called "adaptive manufacturing." SAP's definition of adaptive manufacturing is straightforward: "Adaptive manufacturing is the ability to profitably replenish the supply chain, while dynamically responding to unpredictable change." This means that manufacturing operations must be flexible enough that they can be modified when needed, but can still continue producing in a cost-effective and efficient way.

Central to the SAP view of adaptive manufacturing is visibility responsiveness and a direct and powerful link among the manufacturing shop floor, the supply chain, the external partners, and the executive suite. Adaptive manufacturing is also highly focused on enabling and supporting business processes that operate in real time and on optimizing these processes to the mutual benefit of all stakeholders. The result is that adaptive manufacturing can be applied to a broad range of manufacturing companies and yield an equally broad range of results, including better resource allocation, improved shop floor yields, and a more productive workforce. In addition, adaptive manufacturing enables companies to set goals and milestones based on an accurate, a real-time, and a comprehensive view of the plant floor and its interactions with the supply chain and then to execute, modify, and rework these goals and milestones in response to rapidly changing market dynamics.

The two most important enablers of adaptive manufacturing are *manufacturing synchronization* and *manufacturing excellence*. Enabling these can make a manufacturing company an adaptive manufacturer. Manufacturing synchronization is defined as "electronically linking enterprise business processes and master data with plant manufacturing processes, to run from a single version of the truth." Manufacturing synchronization enables visibility across the supply chain, from the enterprise to the manufacturing plant floor. Manufacturing excellence is defined as "reliably producing to target with year-to-year cost reductions and quality improvement."

Manufacturing excellence enables a manufacturing company to produce cost-effective and quality products by quickly addressing production issues.

Because you now understand the concept of adaptive manufacturing and its enablers, you can take a look at how this can be achieved in practice using a composition platform to model and develop adaptive manufacturing applications with ease.

The Need for a New Integration and Composition Platform in Adaptive Manufacturing

Consider a real-life scenario in a manufacturing plant. A machine breaks down at the production line when a production shift is in progress. The operator shuts down the machine, informs the maintenance department by phone, and informs the product supervisor almost 30 minutes later. Upon learning about the machine breakdown issue, the production supervisor tries to find out if the required spare parts are readily available to get the machine up and running quickly and, if not, if overtime is required in the next shift to hit the target. Because no integration with the manufacturing plant floor exists—though the Distributed Control System (DCS) or the Supervisory Control And Data Acquisition (SCADA) system at the plant might have detected the machine breakdown—the information reaches the plant manager, who is at the enterprise level and is typically an ERP user, too late. Because he has no clear view of the alternatives, the plant manager finally decides to require overtime the next day and misses the due date of delivery. This failure results in the customer calling up the customer service executive and cancelling the order. After investigating the issue, the director of customer service sales learns about the machine breakdown almost 48 hours later. All of this is because of a lack of manufacturing synchronization between the manufacturing plant floor and enterprise and a lack of manufacturing excellence, which enables the manufacturer to have visibility and better control over processes.

> **Note**
>
> SCADA stands for *Supervisory Control And Data Acquisition*. It generally refers to an industrial control system along with a computer system monitoring and controlling an industrial process. Typically, a SCADA system consists of a *Human Machine Interface* (HMI) through which the human can interact with the system; a supervisory computer system that acquires data from the process and sends signals to it; and *Remote Terminal Units* (RTU) and a *Programmable Logic Controller* (PLC) that connect to the sensors in the process and convert the electronic sensor signal into digital data.

Distributed Control System (DCS) refers to a control system usually used in manufacturing processes in which the controller elements are not placed in a central location, but are distributed throughout the system with each component subsystem controlled by one or more controllers. The entire system of controllers is connected by networks for communication and monitoring. It is mostly used in continuous or batch manufacturing scenarios typically in process industries such as chemicals, pharmaceuticals, food processing, and so on.

The *Process Historian* is a specialized database system used for recording real-time process data such as digital or analog recordings of temperature, pressure, flow rate, valves, and motors on/off; product, quality information; alarms (out-of-limit information); and aggregate data such as average, standard deviation, Cpk, and so on. The data stored in the system as time-series data. You can retrieve both current and historical data and statistical data from Process Historians for monitoring and analysis.

Laboratory Information Management System (LIMS) refers to software applications used in the plant laboratory to manage sample information, record quality inspection results, analyze quality inspection results, and so on.

A *Manufacturing Execution System* (MES) comprises software applications used to support the primary production process in a production plant by managing and monitoring the work in- process, including manual and automatic labor and production reporting. It also automates management of recipes, schedules and manages priorities of production orders, tracks KPIs, helps with product or material tracking, and so on.

Now consider a scenario at a manufacturing company where the manufacturing plant floor systems are integrated with the enterprise business systems electronically. The DCS or SCADA at the manufacturing plant floor senses the machine breakdown automatically and sends a signal to the manufacturing intelligence system, which creates an alert for the production and maintenance supervisors to look into the issue. In addition, a maintenance notification is automatically created in the ERP system by the manufacturing plant floor intelligence system, which triggers a process for the maintenance supervisor to create a plant maintenance order and another for the production planner to reschedule the current production orders. The intelligence system searches for available work centers or other viable options and proposes them to the production planner, who makes a quick decision and moves the order to another work center nearby. In addition, the customer executive is notified automatically if a delay of the production is anticipated because of the rescheduling, and he can inform the customer and negotiate an agreeable deal.

As these examples show, the disconnection between manufacturing and enterprise business processes does not allow for "a single version of truth," which results in lower visibility and responsiveness. Because of this disconnect, manufacturing companies are seeking a platform through which manufacturing plant floor processes can be integrated with enterprise processes and provide real-time data synchronization and decision support.

A typical manufacturing plant uses various systems, including Process Historians, LIMS, DCS, SCADA, and MES, each of which controls or maintains various types of manufacturing process data or provides specific intelligence or analytics at various levels. Because these systems come from a wide array of different vendors and are based on different platforms, integrating them is a challenging task. As a result, data and intelligence are scattered across the manufacturing plant floor, and supervisors find it difficult to have clear visibility over the manufacturing execution process and take prompt actions in emergencies.

From this, you can see that a composition platform that integrates and delivers process intelligence over the manufacturing plant floor and enterprise business systems can address the challenge. A composition platform is typically a development platform you can use to model a business process or scenario integrating heterogeneous systems and applications into a coherent application. Ideally, the composition platform for manufacturing integration and analytics should be capable of integrating disparate systems in real time. Because the manufacturing plant floor uses different legacy systems and systems that use proprietary communication protocols, you need the platform to provide connectivity to LIMS, SCADA, Historian, and MES. The platform needs to support enterprise system connectivity by ALE/IDoc, RPC, and Web services and Messaging or the Enterprise Service Bus. After acquiring the data from the various sources, the platform needs to use custom business logic to process the data and create meaningful analytics to deliver intelligence and provide visibility.

SAP Manufacturing Integration and Intelligence (SAP MII) is such a solution. SAP MII provides a composition platform for developing manufacturing composite applications by providing near real-time data access from manufacturing plant systems and enterprise systems. It also provides a code-free, model-driven development environment to develop business logic and an analytics and visualization engine to enable intelligence and visibility on the manufacturing plant floor. Finally, as part of SAP, it provides built-in connectivity and integration content with SAP Business Suite products such as SAP ERP, SAP Supply Chain Management (SCM), and SAP Product Lifecycle Management (PLM).

What This Book Entails

This book covers the various features and functionalities offered by SAP MII 12.0 to enable manufacturing synchronization and excellence in the enterprise. The topics covered in this book enable developers to design and create manufacturing composite applications in the SAP MII platform and enable architects and consultants to understand implementation scenarios and architectural considerations using SAP MII.

> **Note**
>
> SAP MII was originally named Lighthammer CMS (Collaborative Manufacturing Suite) and owned by a U.S. based company called Lighthammer Software, which was acquired by SAP AG in 2005 and re-branded as SAP xMII (SAP xApp Manufacturing Integration & Intelligence). The first release of SAP xMII was 11.5, which ran on Microsoft Internet Information Server (IIS) and then later migrated to SAP NetWeaver® 7.0 in SAP xMII 12.0. More recently, SAP xMII has been again renamed to SAP MII (SAP Manufacturing Integration and Intelligence). This book is primarily based on SAP MII 12.0. The screenshots used are from SAP MII 12.0 SPS04.

Chapter 1 explains how SAP MII can be used to bridge the gap between the enterprise and the manufacturing plant floor by providing integration and intelligence services.

Chapter 2 explains the administration and configuration features of SAP MII with respect to user management, system management, and security services.

Chapter 3 explains the integration aspect of SAP MII and how it can connect to different manufacturing plant floor systems (by using the data servers) and enterprise systems like SAP ERP (using the message services).

Chapter 4 introduces the SAP MII Workbench and how you can use it to create query templates to work with the data from the plant systems.

Chapter 5 explains how to create the display templates for analysis and manufacturing plant floor visualizations in the SAP MII Workbench.

Chapter 6 teaches how you can use business logic services to create intelligent manufacturing composites, focusing on the modeling techniques and different action blocks to process data.

Chapter 7 explains how to configure animated objects to create more dynamic visualizations mainly for monitoring dashboards.

Chapter 8 explains how to create reports and web scripting to develop user interfaces and integrate composite applications into SAP Enterprise Portal.

Chapter 9 covers the advanced techniques for SAP MII composite development and provides a brief overview of the SAP MII Illuminator services.

Chapter 10 discusses various implementation scenarios for SAP MII and explains the specification, design best practices, and implementing ISA95/B2MML using SAP MII.

The **appendix** gives a brief overview of the new features available in SAP MII 12.1.

Summary

In this introduction, you have learned about the concept of adaptive manufacturing and how it can be implemented by a composition platform (such as SAP MII) to bridge the gap between the enterprise business processes and the manufacturing execution operations.

In the next chapter, you will learn about the various features of SAP MII 12.0 as an integration and intelligence platform for developing manufacturing composite applications.

This chapter explains the capability of SAP Manufacturing Integration and Intelligence (MII) as a manufacturing integration and intelligence platform, specifically covering the different components of the product and their features. It also covers the application architecture of SAP MII.

1 SAP MII: A New Composition Platform for Manufacturing Integration and Analytics

In this chapter, you learn about SAP MII's capability as a composite application development platform for manufacturing execution operations. You take a look at the data integration aspects of SAP MII (Data Services and connectors, data queries, Message Services, and so on) and see how the application delivers operational intelligence to the shop floor and other parts of the enterprise with a brief overview of the configurable display templates and business logic services.

1.1 SAP MII as a Manufacturing Integration Platform

Manufacturing synchronization is a key enabler of adaptive manufacturing and is supported by SAP MII as a primary feature, enabling you to synchronize your enterprise business applications with the manufacturing plant floor applications in real time. SAP MII provides bi-directional data access both in synchronous and asynchronous modes to enterprise and manufacturing plant floor systems. Its integration capability is unique because it provides specific data connectors to various standard manufacturing plant floor systems, as well as seamless connectivity to SAP ERP using the standard protocols such as SAP Java Connector, ALE, and Web service. Unlike the applications and systems such as the Process Historian, LIMS, SCADA, DCS, and MES, which have specific purposes such as maintaining process data, quality information, execution scheduling, and so on, SAP MII is an open platform that integrates the various systems used for manufacturing execution operations.

The major integration components of SAP MII are as follows:

▶ Data Services for manufacturing plant floor connectivity

▶ Message Services for enterprise connectivity

Data Services provides universal connectivity to manufacturing plant floor systems. This connectivity is accomplished by providing connectors for vendor-specific protocols for plant systems and standard protocols such as Java Database Connectivity (JDBC) to connect to relational databases such as MS SQL Server, Oracle, and so on. The data connectors come prepackaged along with the SAP MII installation, which you can configure easily to connect to any manufacturing plant floor system. In addition to the data connectors, SAP MII provides a configuration framework for data queries, which you can use to retrieve or write data to any of the underlying data sources. Different types of data queries such as SQL, TAG, OLAP, and so on are available for you to configure easily through SAP MII Workbench. You can configure data queries to retrieve or write the data to the manufacturing plant floor systems and process it as required. You can access the data queries by either HTTP calls (from external systems) or Java applets from web-based user interfaces. You can cache the data retrieved by the data queries in the SAP MII local database or fetch it at runtime, providing a real-time data synchronization of the manufacturing plant.

Just as Data Services in SAP MII enables manufacturing plant floor connectivity, Message Services provides the integration of enterprise systems such as SAP ERP with SAP MII. You can use Message Services in SAP MII for receiving the enterprise data in the form of asynchronous Remote Function Call (RFC), ALE/IDoc, or XML messages sent using HTTP Post. SAP ERP and other enterprise systems can send data such as production orders to be executed, work center capacity information, and material availability information. In SAP MII, you can define message listeners to receive the data and processing rules to process the data using specific business logic or a message category. Messages received by SAP MII using Message Services are stored in the SAP MII database when received, processed in a time-based way if a corresponding processing rule is defined, or just assigned to a category (for further ad-hoc processing). These messages can be sent to external systems by SAP MII either by using Data Services or by pulling them from external systems via Business Logic Transactions using Web services calls. A Message Monitor in SAP MII provides a technical overview of the messages received and the corresponding status. If the processing for a message is unsuccessful, you can reprocess it by selecting the message from the monitor. You can also define the cleanup rules to periodically clean up the buffered messages from the SAP MII database.

Along with the standard integration capability, SAP MII provides easy composition capability in Business Logic Services (BLS), which enables users to develop manufacturing integration composite applications by leveraging connectivity features. From the BLS transactions you can execute RFCs/BAPIs and Enterprise services/Web services to retrieve and update data into the enterprise systems. This serves as an integration platform between manufacturing plant floor and enterprise business. We discuss these features in later chapters of this book.

The key features of SAP MII as a manufacturing plant floor integration platform are described as follows.

▶ **Universal connectivity to real-time plant floor data**
  ▶ Provides an extensive library of plant system and application connectors
  ▶ Exchanges data with virtually any plant floor level system
  ▶ Utilizes standard APIs, communication standards (for example, OPC), and data access methods to connect to these systems
  ▶ Requires no modification to the existing plant floor systems
  ▶ Performs transactional exchange of information with SAP ERP
  ▶ Offers real-time accessibility to transaction data at the plant and enterprise level

▶ **Synchronization of SAP ERP and plant floor systems and processes**
  ▶ Extends the models, rules, and processes of SAP Manufacturing (ERP) for use in plant floor processes
  ▶ Uses standards-based communication structures to simplify the processing and interface requirements
  ▶ Provides easy development tools to help address requirements, information, and processes specific to particular manufacturing sites

▶ **A portfolio of Data Services**
  ▶ Provides single manufacturing data service for other composite applications
  ▶ Provides local data caching for vital information as needed to support 24x7 operation

▶ Exposes all integration level processes to enhance manufacturing intelligence applications

Now you understand the capabilities of SAP MII as an integration platform for manufacturing execution operations, you can take a look into its capabilities as an analytics platform to deliver actionable intelligence to plant workers.

1.2 SAP MII as a Manufacturing Intelligence Platform

After the manufacturing plant floor is integrated with the enterprise, you can provide intelligent visualization and analytics over the manufacturing processes and data. One of the key features of SAP MII is manufacturing analytics in the form of visualization (charts, reports, and so on) and statistical analysis (SPC, SQC, and so on). The manufacturing intelligence features of SAP MII include the following:

▶ Visualization services

▶ Animated graphics

▶ Business Logic Services

> **Note**
>
> SPC stands for *Statistical Process Control*, which is an effective method of monitoring a process characteristic by using a control chart. A control chart is a graph where the characteristic data is plotted along a time axis. It has a central or target line that signifies the average or the ideal characteristic value and two control lines as the Upper Control Limit and Lower Control Limit that specify the range within which the process characteristic value can vary. Using the control chart you can determine whether the process characteristic variation is consistent or not.

The visualization services in SAP MII are provided by an extensive set of display templates for different types of charts and by visualization controls such as line charts, bar charts, polar charts, gauges, area charts, regression charts, tickers, SPC charts, grids, and list view and tree view options. These display templates are standard controls for visualizations and analytics that you can easily set up by simple configurations and without writing any actual code. Each display template needs to be configured along with a data query for the end user visualizations in a web page. You can also modify the properties of the display templates dynamically during runtime by using simple JavaScript in the web page. The display templates provide many intelligent visualizations to the end users, such as color context and highlighting of special data in a report, Key Performance Indicator (KPI) monitoring, comparative charts, Six Sigma® analysis, and statistical quality analysis. The visualization templates are based on Java applet technologies and therefore provide dynamic and interactive features such as drill-down capability and auto-refresh to the end users.

Animated graphics are SVG objects, which you can configure easily in SAP MII to display animated dynamic visualization in any custom form. Some examples of animated objects in SAP MII are the 3DGaugeDial, the Horizontal Thermometer, the LEDMeter, and the PIDMeter. You can configure these graphics objects using the animated object configuration and Business Logic Services to provide dynamic custom visualizations over data. The animated graphics are a useful add-on to the standard display templates and make for an enriching visual representation of the manufacturing processes and KPIs. They are like widgets that you can plug into visual cockpits or dashboards, because they are rendered as graphic files (JPEG/PNG) and you can use them without any applet or Java Runtime in client machines.

Figure 1.1 illustrates the visualization capabilities of SAP MII, providing different types of dashboards and analytics components as native visualization controls and providing integration with other UI technologies such as SAP Visual Composer and SAP Enterprise Portal.

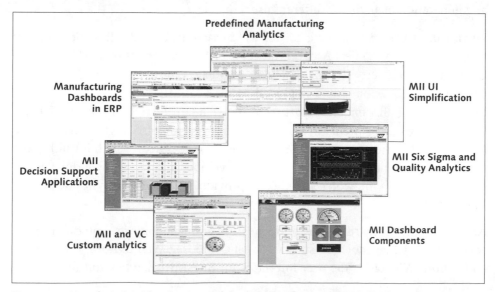

Figure 1.1 Manufacturing Visualization and Analytics Unification by SAP MII

The Business Logic Services are some of the most powerful services of SAP MII. With these services, business logic or process intelligence can be developed in a code-free modeling environment. SAP MII has its own business logic–modeling editor consisting of predefined action blocks; this editor enables you to develop business logic as a graphical tree-like flow model without writing a single line of code. The predefined action blocks provide almost all required common programming logic, data parsing, and system integration functionalities you need to develop business logic and provide manufacturing and statistical analytics functionality as well. This includes common programming constructs such as different loops, logical expressions, XML parsing, and data integration services such as data queries, enterprise connectivity using RFC/BAPI (JCo/JRA), Web services, and statistical analysis and calculations.

The Business Logic Services provide the real intelligence behind the visualizations generated by the display templates or animated objects in SAP MII. Whereas the data queries are templates to read and write data to manufacturing plant-floor systems, you use the Business Logic Services to manipulate or process data before or after the data queries. The statistical quality analysis functionality available in the Business Logic Services is also an integral part of the SPC/SQC analysis functionality provided by SAP MII. You can dynamically configure and render animated objects using Business Logic Services as well. The Business Logic Services also provide certain standard process intelligence features such as KPI update to SAP ERP and generation of alerts for different users or roles.

The Business Logic Services are created as transactions in SAP MII, which you can execute as a Simple Object Access Protocol (SOAP) Web service or an HTTP service or as an Xacute query by Java applets in web pages. Business Logic Transactions are XML files developed and deployed in the SAP MII WebAS and interpreted by the runtime BLS engine. Apart from the standard features in Business Logic Services provided as predefined action blocks, you can also develop new action blocks to use in the transactions. The Business Logic Services, which form the core of the SAP MII intelligence layer, can be developed in pieces or modular form. These can then be integrated together to provide a complete analytics or process intelligence.

Apart from the standard display templates and animated objects, you can also use several other UI technologies such as Visual Composer, Web Dynpro, Adobe Flex, and Yahoo! Widgets as the user interfaces for SAP MII analytics and intelligence dashboards. The Business Logic Services can be consumed in the user interfaces as SOAP Web services or XML messages using HTTP to provide or update the data.

Figure 1.2 illustrates the overall positioning of SAP MII in the SAP product suite.

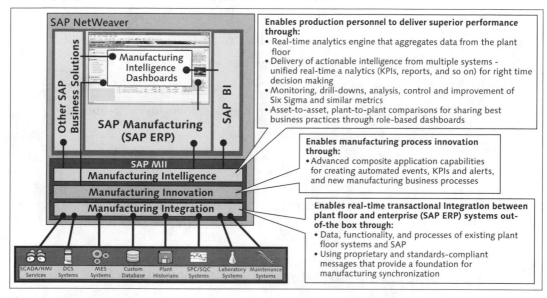

Figure 1.2 SAP MII as a Manufacturing Integration and Intelligence Composition Platform

So, SAP MII leverages its visualization templates and Business Logic Services to provide you with analytics for manufacturing execution processes. It is a powerful composition platform for providing manufacturing intelligence. A breakdown of the key features is as follows:

▶ **SAP MII delivers a real-time analytics engine**

 ▷ Embedded KPI engine with capability to browse plant floor sources and generate complex calculated metrics

 ▷ Analytics engine with capability to generate single view of Six Sigma analytics from disparate data sources

 ▷ Tight integration with embedded visualization services

 ▷ Easy maintenance of existing metrics or rapid delivery of new metrics

- ▶ **SAP MII delivers rich, unified analytics**
  - ▶ Rich analytics that can be rendered as iViews within the SAP manufacturing intelligence dashboards
  - ▶ Ability to add context to data from shop floor sensors or system through direct operator interaction (for example, reason codes or comments)
  - ▶ Customized visualization for specific teams, initiatives, or roles
- ▶ **SAP MII enables user-friendly visualization**
  - ▶ Ability to personalize delivery of metrics to support specific teams and roles
  - ▶ Library of visualization objects for rapid deployment of dashboards
  - ▶ Alerts to drive management by exception
  - ▶ Drill-in, drill-across capability to facilitate rapid identification, isolation of root causes, and resolution

Now that we've covered the features of SAP MII as a manufacturing intelligence platform, we can move on to the application architecture of SAP MII.

1.3   Application Architecture of SAP MII

In the previous sections you have understood SAP MII's capability as a manufacturing composition and platform for integration and intelligence. In this section you look at a basic overview of the application architecture of SAP MII to understand how the integration and intelligence functionalities are supported by the various components from a technical perspective.

SAP MII 12.0 runs on SAP NetWeaver 7.0 Java WebAS as a web application. It uses the standard services of SAP NetWeaver, such as Identity Management and Logging, and provides its own functionalities, including Data Services, Business Logic Services, visualization services, and Message Services by various modules developed using J2EE and deployed in the Java WebAS.

SAP MII is designed as a browser-neutral N-tier web application. Interaction with external systems is handled by SAP MII in a specific XML format. Almost all the functionalities of SAP MII are Java Servlets, which can be invoked as SOAP Web services or by sending an XML request using HTTP Post from an external system providing correct authentication. The contents developed in SAP MII are stored as XML or as web objects in the SAP MII database and published to the web folders of the WebAS as required. Though well-defined content and version management such as integration with NetWeaver Development Infrastructure (NWDI) is not yet available in SAP MII 12.0, it does allow easy importing and exporting of development content in the form of ZIP archives, which have to be transported manually between different installations.

Most of the standard data connectors are provided in the SAP MII installation itself. Additionally, you can use the add-on Universal Data Server to connect to OPC-based systems at the plant floor.

Business Logic Services form the core logic engine of SAP MII where you can model the application logic, and you can execute them from Java applets in web pages or as HTTP or SOAP Web service from web pages or external systems.

The user interfaces developed in SAP MII are web pages based on HTML and JavaScript with .irpt or .html extensions. The visualization components such as charts, grids, and SPC charts are displayed as Java applets embedded in web pages or can also be rendered at the server side and can be displayed as static images. SAP MII provides a lightweight portal along with the standard installation that you can use at the manufacturing plant floor itself to provide the visualization dashboards to the end users. Alternatively, you can install SAP Enterprise Portal and add the SAP MII web pages as iViews.

Figure 1.3 illustrates the high-level application architecture of SAP MII with different components, the integration aspects of it with the enterprise and plant systems, and the portal dashboards.

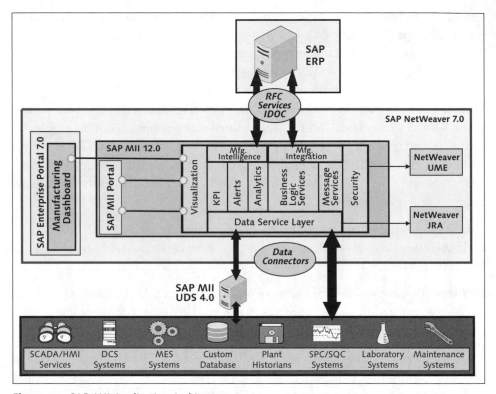

Figure 1.3 SAP MII Application Architecture

1.4 Summary

In this chapter, you have learned about the different capabilities of SAP MII to develop adaptive manufacturing composites integrating the enterprise business with the manufacturing execution operations. In the next chapter, you will learn about the various administrative and system configuration tasks available in SAP MII.

This chapter explains the general configurations required in SAP MII, such as user management and basic Java WebAS administration, along with system management and security services.

2 Administrating and Configuring SAP MII

As SAP MII is a development and a deployment platform for manufacturing composites running on SAP NetWeaver, administration and configuration of the server is an important and regular activity to ensure smooth operations.

In this chapter, you learn how to create users, assign required roles, and configure other aspects of SAP NetWeaver J2EE WebAS for running SAP MII. You also learn about the system administration and security configurations of SAP MII using the System Management and System Security menu options.

2.1 User Management and WebAS Administration in SAP MII

SAP MII 12.0 is installed on SAP NetWeaver 7.0 J2EE WebAS with a minimum support package stack level of SP14. You need to configure the sizing of the hardware according to the SAP NetWeaver 7.0 J2EE sizing guide, using the Quick Sizer tool available in the SAP Service Marketplace at *http://service.sap.com/quicksizer*. The usage type of the SAP NetWeaver installation is Application Server Java.

> **Example**
>
> A sample production installation setup of SAP MII 12.0 is as follows:
>
> Hardware
>
> ► Server Hardware—DB/CI - IBM 9119 server
> ► Number of CPUs—4
> ► RAM—6GB, Swap space—47GB
> ► System Disk—122GB

- Data Disk—200GB
- Clone Backup Disk—200GB
- Disaster Recovery Disk—200GB

Software

- Operating System—AIX OS 5.3
- Database—IBM DB2 - V9.5.1
- SAP NetWeaver Java SP14
- SAP MII V12.0.4
- JDK 1.4.2_08

This setup is for approximately 150 concurrent users.

The SAP NetWeaver J2EE engine on which SAP MII is installed might also have the SAP Enterprise Portal installed, which can be used as the portal for MII. If SAP Enterprise Portal is installed on the same WebAS as SAP MII, sizing must be done accordingly.

From SAP MII 12.0, the user management is handled by the SAP NetWeaver J2EE WebAS User Management Engine (UME). The following user roles are required and created by the MII installation:

- XMII Users
- XMII Developers
- XMII Administrators

You need to assign the users of SAP MII to at least one of the preceding roles. Assign the XMII Administrators role only to the systems administrators, the XMII Developers role to the developers who develop the composite applications using SAP MII Workbench, and the XMII Users role to all users running applications developed on SAP MII. These three roles are used in the development objects security by default, but apart from these roles, you can create project- or application-specific roles in the UME and can use them to assign security permissions to development objects.

To create new users and assign the MII roles, open the User Administration Screen from *http://<servername>:<port>/useradmin* and click on Create User or on Copy to New User, if an existing user needs to be copied. In the Assigned Roles tab, add the required SAP MII roles as mentioned previously or any other roles required, as seen in Figure 2.1. You can also use external Lightweight Directory Access Protocol

(LDAP) or Central User Administration (CUA) engines for the user management by connecting the SAP NetWeaver UME with it.

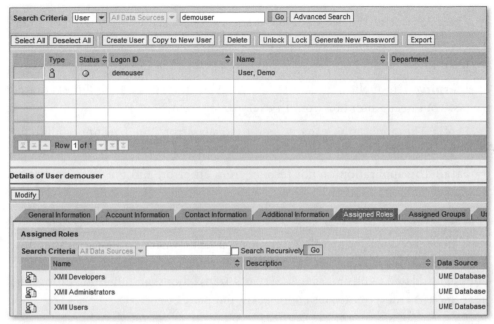

Figure 2.1 User Management for SAP MII

Logging and tracing functionality is also provided by the SAP NetWeaver logging service, which is used by SAP MII for logging purposes. You can view the system logs from the SAP NetWeaver Administrator (NWA). To view the logs, open SAP NetWeaver Administrator (*http://<servername>:<port>/nwa*) and navigate to ANALYSIS • DEBUG • LOGS & TRACES. The application ID for SAP MII is *sap.com/xapps~xmii~ear*, which you can use to filter the logs. By default, the tracing level is set to Error for the SAP MII application, which means only logs of type error are logged. You can change the tracing level if required for debugging purposes. To set the tracing level, navigate to SAP NETWEAVER ADMINISTRATOR • SYSTEM MANAGEMENT • CONFIGURATION • LOG CONFIGURATION. Select Tracing Locations from the Show dropdown list, then select ROOT LOCATION • COM • SAP • XMII from the tree view, and if required, change the log severity level to any other option available in the dropdown list, as shown in Figure 2.2. The trace severity level can be set to any one of the following options:

- ▶ **All:** Logs messages of any severity
- ▶ **Debug:** Used for debugging purposes, with extensive and low-level information
- ▶ **Path:** For tracing the execution flow; for example, used in the context of entering and leaving a method and looping and branching operations
- ▶ **Info:** Informational text, mostly for echoing what has already been performed
- ▶ **Warning:** The application can recover from an anomaly and fulfill the required task, but needs attention from a developer/operator
- ▶ **Error:** The application can recover from an error, but it cannot fulfill the required task because of the error
- ▶ **Fatal:** The application cannot recover from an error, and the severe situation causes fatal termination
- ▶ **None:** Logs no messages

Two trace locations are present under XMII as Illuminator and Xacute, as shown in Figure 2.2, for which you can configure the trace severity levels. Xacute logs all messages related to Business Logic Services Transactions, and Illuminator logs the rest, such as Query Templates and Display Templates.

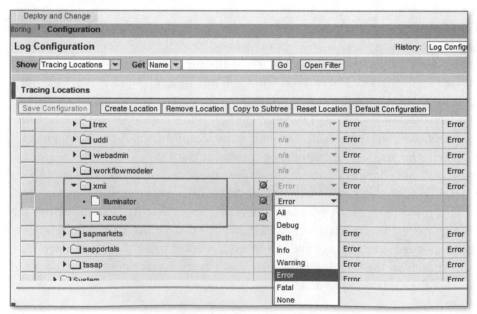

Figure 2.2 Trace Level Configuration for SAP MII

SAP MII uses RFC or BAPI interfaces to connect to enterprise systems such as SAP ERP. Both SAP Java Connector (SAP JCo) and SAP Java Resource Adapter (JRA) are provided in SAP MII for executing RFC and BAPI from Advanced Business Application Programming (ABAP) systems. SAP JCo needs to be installed separately in SAP MII 12.0 till SPS03, but from SPS04 separate installation of SAP JCo is not required.

In addition, SAP JRA is provided in SAP NetWeaver as an add-on to SAP JCo, which you can use for executing BAPI/RFC from SAP MII Business Logic Transactions. It is recommended you use JRA over JCo because it provides a number of advantages, such as load balancing, connection management, data buffering, and the connection properties are managed by the SAP WebAS in the case of the JRA, and thus, no user level configuration in SAP MII is needed by the user unlike SAP JCo. To use SAP JRA you need to install it as an add-on and then configure it separately for each ABAP system from where the BAPI/RFC will be executed.

The JRA library is available on the system where SAP NetWeaver has been installed under the following folder:

<Drive>\usr\sap\<SID>\sys\global\ra\sapjra.rar

To deploy it on the NetWeaver WebAS, you would need to use DeployTool, which can be started using the batch file provided under *<drive>:\usr\sap\<SID>\JC<XX>\ j2ee\deploying\DeployTool.bat*. After DeployTool has been launched, open a new project, give it a name, and browse to the Deployer tab. Select DEPLOY • EAR • LOAD MODULE, select the sapjra.rar file, and click OK. Select the sapjra.rar entry in the left pane to view its properties and browse to the Server Settings property on the right. Select the Auth Type as "Caller Impersonation." You can configure the other JRA properties now or later through Visual Administrator, as described later in this chapter. Connect to the WebAS you want to deploy the library to using DEPLOY • CONNECT and Deploy the Library using, DEPLOY • DEPLOYMENT • DEPLOY MODULE. Enter an application name, which can be any value of your choice, and when asked, select Yes to start the application. SAP JRA library should be successfully deployed into the server.

To configure SAP JRA in NetWeaver, use the following steps:

1. Open the SAP NetWeaver Visual Administrator from the following SAP J2EE Engine installation path: <DRIVE>\USR • SAP • <SYSID> • JC70 • J2EE • ADMIN • GO.BAT.

2. Log on to Visual Administrator.

3. Open the Services node on the left in the tree under the required server name, and select the Connector Container service.

4. Open the tree on the Runtime tab and select *sap.com/sapjra.rar*.

5. Under the Properties tab, specify the connection details for an ABAP system, as shown in Figure 2.3.

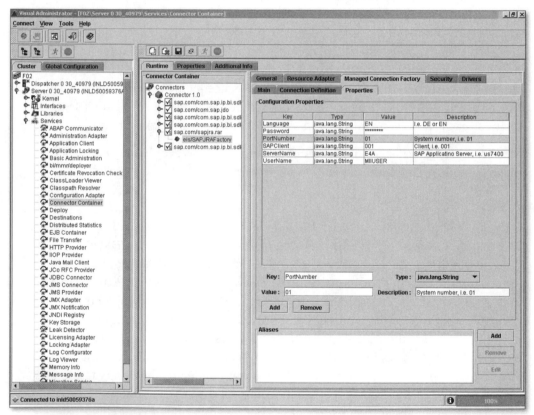

Figure 2.3 SAP JRA Configuration in Visual Administrator

You need to install Universal Data Server (UDS) or SAP MII UDS 4.0 separately in a server having either Microsoft Windows XP Service Pack 2 or later or Microsoft Windows Server 2003 Service Pack 1 or later. You can use UDS to retrieve data from Supervisory Control and Data Acquisition (SCADA) systems and historical data systems that support the industry standard OPC Data Access (DA) and OPC Historical Data Access (HDA) interfaces. SAP MII UDS also provides data connectivity to OLE DB-compliant data sources such as Microsoft Access and Excel. The various connectors for these systems are configured in the SAP MII UDS Admin Console, which is then used in the data servers configuration in SAP MII. You also need to deploy the different database drivers to be used by the data servers separately using the JDBC Drivers menu, which is explained further in Section 2.2.12 JDBC Drivers.

After you've got all that installed and configured, you can access SAP MII via the following URL: *http://<servername>:<port>/XMII/Menu.jsp*. The server name is the SAP NetWeaver J2EE WebAS hostname, and port is the corresponding HTTP port.

Now that you understand how to create users and configure the WebAS for SAP MII, it's time to move on to the SAP MII configurations using the System Management menu.

2.2   System Management of SAP MII

In SAP MII you can configure the system-wide settings under the System Management menu and enable the SAP MII administrator to manage and monitor the global configurations.

System Management in SAP MII mainly constitutes of the following tasks or menu options:

▸ System Administration

▸ System Jobs

▸ Scheduler

▸ Schedule Editor

▸ Active Sessions

▸ Custom Attributes

▸ Custom Attribute Mapping

▸ Configurations

▸ Projects

▸ Custom Actions

- PDF Fonts
- JDBC Drivers
- Applet Debugging

The next sections delve deeper into each of these tasks and to see how each can be configured.

2.2.1 System Administration

You can use the System Administration menu, as seen in Figure 2.4, to set global system property values. You need to assign the Admin and SystemEditor security services to a user, explained in Section 2.3.1 System Security, to enable access to the System Administration menu.

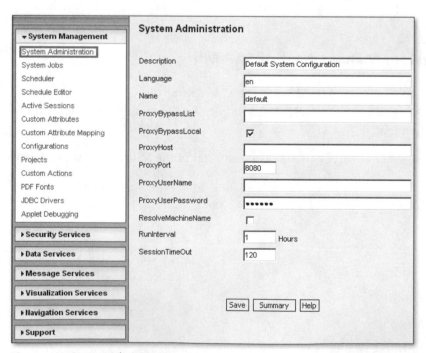

Figure 2.4 System Administration

The system properties explained in Table 2.1 are available for configuration in System Administration.

Property	Description
Description	A short text description of the configuration settings.
Language	Sets the default system language.
Name	A name that also acts as an identifier for the configuration settings.
ProxyBypassList	A comma-separated list of server names or IPs for which the proxy server should be bypassed.
ProxyBypassLocal	Indicator for whether the proxy server should be bypassed for servers in the same network.
ProxyHost	The hostname or IP of the proxy server.
ProxyPort	The port to which the proxy server defined above is listening.
ProxyUserName	Proxy authentication information, the user name to log on to the proxy server.
ProxyUserPassword	Proxy authentication information, the password for the user name declared previously.
ResolveMachineName	Indicator for whether SAP MII resolves and logs the machine name of the requesting system. If unchecked, only the IP is logged.
RunInterval	Duration in hours that defines the interval at which the message cleanup rules run (see Section 3.2).
SessionTimeOut	Duration in minutes after which idle user sessions are terminated by SAP MII.

Table 2.1 System Properties

The Language property in SAP MII System Administration is overridden by the logged on user's locale or language attribute, if set.

To enable localization features, SAP MII reads the language settings in the following order until it finds one:

▶ Locale attribute of the user, set in the SAP User Management Engine (UME)

▶ Language attribute of the user, set in the SAP User Management Engine (UME)

▶ The browser's language

► The Language property in SAP MII System Administration menu

► The Java Virtual Machine (JVM) language.

Note

If your organization accesses the Internet through a corporate firewall or proxy, we advise that you configure the proxy settings in the System Management screen. This configuration enables you to access any HTTP service or Web service on the Internet through SAP MII. For example, if you want to create a composite application that wants to geo-code a particular street address and in turn display the location on the map, you would need to access the Yahoo! geo-coding Web service and also the Google Maps service, and the proxy configuration in SAP MII is the only way to access them behind a firewall.

2.2.2 System Jobs

System jobs are tasks that run in the background at regular intervals and perform internal maintenance of the SAP MII server and content.

This menu option displays a list of the default system jobs running on the SAP MII server.

You find three default jobs running on any SAP MII server.

► **SessionLogger:** Runs every 30 minutes and logs system usage via the number of active users and the number of unique users.

► **SecurityObjectReferenceCleaner:** Runs once every 7 days; checks for and deletes invalid system and server permission roles, custom attribute roles, and users in the respective database tables.

► **TempFileCleaner:** Runs once an hour and cleans up the temporary files table.

2.2.3 Scheduler

The Scheduler menu, shown in Figure 2.5, provides overview and information about all the tasks that are scheduled by the user. It wakes up every 500 milliseconds to check for jobs that are ready to run and then executes them. Using the scheduler, any Business Logic Transaction can be executed periodically to do various activities, such as pull data from manufacturing plant-floor systems by data queries, execute a Web service or RFC, and calculate and update a KPI.

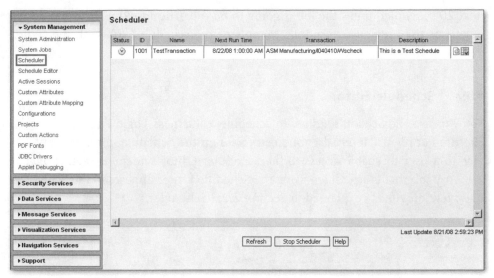

Figure 2.5 Scheduler View

The Scheduler screen displays the following information about the scheduled jobs:

▸ **Status:** The status of the job. The values can be Stopped, Pending, and Running.

　▸ Stopped: The job is currently stopped. Tasks that are not enabled have this status.

　▸ Pending: The job is scheduled and pending its next run.

　▸ Running: The scheduled job is running at the current moment.

▸ **ID:** The Job ID of the scheduled job.

▸ **Name:** The name of the job as set in the Schedule Editor.

▸ **Next Run Time:** The time when this scheduled job will run next.

▸ **Transaction:** The full path of the Business Logic Transaction that has been scheduled to run.

▸ **Description:** The description of the job as set in the Schedule Editor.

Other than the information just mentioned, the Scheduler also enables the administrator or any user with appropriate rights to view the Job Run Schedule (▣) and the Job Run History (▦). These functionalities are provided in the last column of the Scheduler view. The Job Run Schedule functionality displays a schedule of the next 20 scheduled times the job is going to be run. The Job Run History displays details of the previous execution attempts of the scheduled job with the status, duration, and details.

2.2.4 Schedule Editor

You can use the Schedule Editor to schedule a Business Logic Transaction to be executed at regular intervals. You need to assign the ScheduleEditor security service to a user to enable access to the Scheduler Editor screen, as seen in Figure 2.6. Any job that is scheduled using the Schedule Editor appears in the Scheduler overview previously explained in Section 2.2.3 Scheduler.

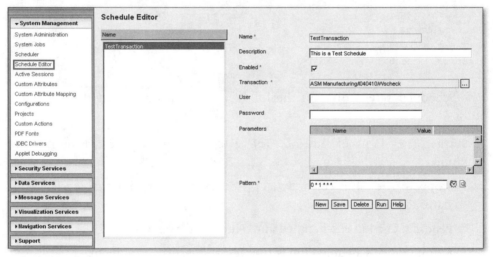

Figure 2.6 Schedule Editor

The parameters explained in Table 2.2 are available when you are configuring a new SAP MII scheduled job.

Parameters	Description
Name	The scheduled job's name.
Description	A description of the job, what it is supposed to do.
Enabled	When checked, enables the job to run periodically according to the cron pattern. The job is not scheduled if this checkbox is not checked.

Table 2.2 Scheduler Configuration Properties

Parameters	Description
Transaction	The Business Logic Services (BLS) Transaction that will be scheduled to run.
Run As Username	The user whose credentials are used to run the job.
Run As Password	The password of the user mentioned previously.
Parameters	The input parameters, if any, of the Transaction selected previously are displayed here. The user should ideally enter the values of the input parameters which would be used while running the transaction as a scheduled job.
Pattern	A cron pattern that determines the schedule of the job to be run.

Table 2.2 Scheduler Configuration Properties (Cont.)

You can create the cron pattern, which you use to determine the schedule, either manually or using the Build Pattern screen. The Build Pattern screen is invoked by clicking the Build Pattern (⬚) button and enables creation of cron patterns with ease.

The screen has four tabs (Figure 2.7) and enables users to create jobs that run at intervals of seconds, hours, days, and months. You can further fine-tune the job schedule by configuring the parameters in each of the tabs.

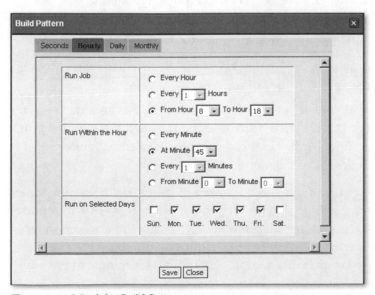

Figure 2.7 Scheduler Build Pattern

For example, we can create a job schedule that runs at the forty-fifth minute of each hour between 8:00 a.m. and 6:00 p.m. on all days except Saturdays and Sundays. The way to do this is shown in Figure 2.7. In the Hourly tab of the Build Pattern screen, choose the From Hour…To Hour option in the Run Job options. Select 8 in the "From Hour" dropdown and 18 in the "To Hour" one. Now in the Run Within the Hour options, select At Minute, and then 45 from the dropdown list. Lastly, in the Run on Selected Days options, deselect Sun. and Sat. and then click on Save.

We now want to discuss how you can create a cron pattern manually. The cron pattern consists mainly of the following fields, separated by spaces: Second, Minute, Hour, Day of the Month, Month, and Day of the Week. Each of these fields can take a single value, a wildcard, comma-separated values, or a value range. The values that each of these fields accepts are as follows:

- Second and Minute: 0–59
- Hour: 0–23
- Day of the Month: 1–31
- Month: 0–11, with a value of zero (0) for January
- Day of the Week: 1–7 with a value of one (1) for Sunday
- Other than the values just mentioned, you can also use an asterisk (*) to denote every instance of that field, such as every second or every minute.
- Comma-separated values (for example, 25,26,27) in the Day of the Month field denotes every twenty-fifth, twenty-sixth, and twenty-seventh of the month.
- A value range (for example, 2–5) in the Day of the Week field denotes Monday, Tuesday, Wednesday, and Thursday of the week.
- You should note that comma-separated values and value ranges can be combined together (for example, 5,10–15,20). In the Day of the Month field, this would signify the fifth, tenth, eleventh, twelfth, thirteenth, fourteenth, fifteenth, and twentieth days of the month.

With all of these options, you can also use a step modifier (/). The step modifier indicates which values can be used in the ranges. For example, 4–36/4 in Minutes denotes that the job runs from the fourth to the thirty-sixth minute every hour at an interval of 4 minutes, that is, every fourth, eighth, twelfth, sixteenth, twentieth, twenty-fourth, twenty-eighth, thirty-second, and thirty-sixth minute of the hour.

Now try to analyze the cron pattern that was created by the preceding example: 0 45 8–18 * * 2,3,4,5,6. A zero (0) in the first field means that job runs on the first second of every forty-fifth minute, which is the second field. The value in the hour field is a range 8–18, which denotes the hours from 8:00 a.m. to 6:00 p.m. The values for Day of the Month and Month are both asterisks (*), which means the job executes for every day of the month and for every month of the year. Lastly, the Day of the Week has a comma-separated list 2,3,4,5,6, which stands for Monday (2) to Friday (6), but not Saturday (7) or Sunday (1).

2.2.5 Active Sessions

The Active Sessions menu displays a list of currently logged in users and their details. You need to assign the Admin security service to a user to enable access to the Active Sessions screen.

The Active Sessions screen displays the following information regarding the currently logged in user:

- **Login Name:** The username of the logged on user.
- **Full Name:** The complete name of the logged on user.
- **Email:** The email ID of the logged on user.
- **Created:** The date and time of the first access of the user account.
- **Last Access Time:** The date and time when the user account was last accessed.
- **Expiration Date:** The date and time when the logged on user's session timeouts.

2.2.6 Custom Attributes

Custom attributes are custom variables that you can add to an SAP MII role or user. The values of these variables can be accessed at runtime in the Business Logic Services (BLS) as session variables and can influence the logic of the application by allowing different branches of logic according to the value of the custom attribute.

In the Custom Attribute screen in Figure 2.8, clicking on the New button brings up the custom attribute configuration screen.

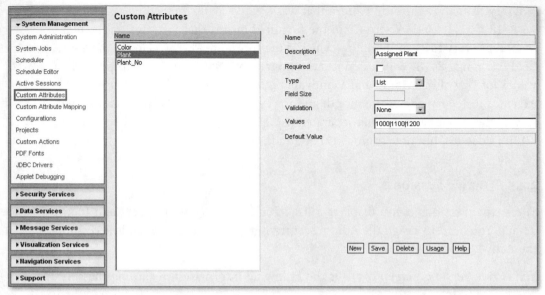

Figure 2.8 Custom Attributes Configuration

The parameters explained in Table 2.3 are available when you are creating a custom attribute.

Parameters	Description
Name	The name of the custom attribute.
Description	Brief text describing the custom attribute.
Required	Checkbox to denote whether or not the custom attribute is mandatory. If checked, the default value needs to be assigned in the custom attribute configuration. This value is mapped to all roles and users.
Type	This denotes the type of field that is displayed on the custom attribute mapping page for roles and users. Values can be Text, Date, List, and RadioButton.
Field Size	The length of the text box if the custom field type selected above is Text. Accepts integers between 1 and 1000.

Table 2.3 Custom Attributes Configuration Properties

Parameters	Description
Validation	Defines the validation type if the custom attribute is of the type Text. Validation methods are numeric and alphanumeric. Ensures that only text of the type set by the validation method is allowed as values for the custom attribute.
Values	Relevant only if the custom attribute type is Date, List, or RadioButton. A date format can be entered for date types whereas a pipe-separated (|) list can be entered for RadioButton and List values. The values of the pipe-separated list appear as the choices of the List or RadioButton on the Custom Attribute Mapping screen.
Default Value	Denotes the default value of the custom attribute. Relevant only if the Required option is checked previously.

Table 2.3 Custom Attributes Configuration Properties (Cont.)

Custom attributes are like user variables. When you want to assign particular values to a user and make them available when the user logs in, you should use custom attributes. A typical business case would be if you want to make visible to the user only those production orders for the particular plant and work centers to which he is assigned. In this case you can create the values of the plant and work center as custom attributes and assign them to the users. This value can then be read at runtime and passed on to query templates or BLS Transactions for retrieving data filtered on the basis of these values. One such example is explained in Section 9.6 Autobind and Session Variables in SAP MII.

2.2.7 Custom Attribute Mapping

The Custom Attribute Mapping menu enables you to map a custom attribute to a role or a user that has been created using the Custom Attributes screen (Figure 2.8). You select the role or user by selecting the relevant tab in the Custom Attribute Mapping screen, as seen in Figure 2.9.

To map custom attributes to a user, select the user in the Users dropdown list and the custom attribute in the Attributes dropdown. Click on the Add button to add the custom attribute to the user, change the default value, if it has one, and click on Save to assign the attribute to the user. All required custom attributes are assigned to all users by default with their default values. You can change the value that is assigned in this case by manually mapping the attribute.

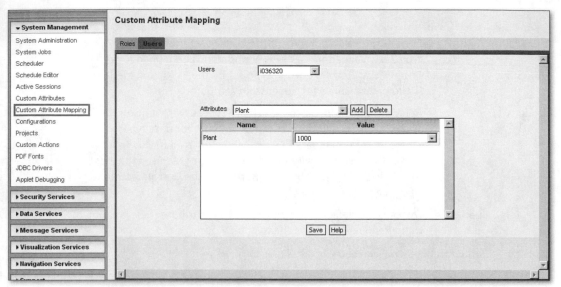

Figure 2.9 Custom Attribute Mapping to Users

Assigning attributes to roles is similar to that of assigning them to users. However, you need to keep in mind the priority that is assigned to the role when assigning a custom attribute to it. The priority is selected from the Priority dropdown list and is set to a default value of 50 for every role. When a user is assigned multiple roles with the same custom attribute but with different values, SAP MII applies the role with the lowest priority (0) last. So, the custom attribute value associated with the role with the lowest priority gets mapped to the user in this case. The value of the custom attribute in the role also overrides the default value of any required custom attributes that might be associated with the user.

To delete a custom attribute that is associated with a user or role, you need to select the row of the custom attribute that you want to delete, click on the Delete button, and then click on Save to make the changes permanent.

2.2.8 Configurations

The Configurations screen, shown in Figure 2.10, provides the option of backing up the system configuration as a ZIP file (xmiibackup.zip) to a user-specified location on the local system and the ability to restore the system configuration from a similar backup archive. This feature is useful when you are transporting the configurations from one SAP MII installation to other (for example, from development to production). You need to assign the ConfigurationManagement security service to a user to enable access to the Configurations screen.

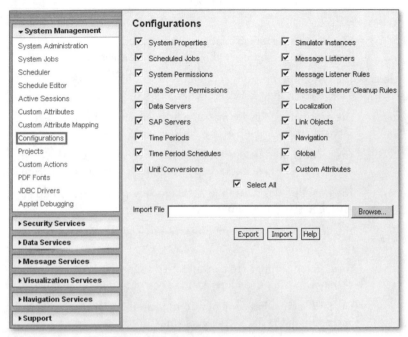

Figure 2.10 Configurations Backup

According to the options that are checked on the screen, the respective configurations are exported to an XML file, and the corresponding file is included in the xmiibackup.zip archive when you click the Export button.

The configuration types explained in Table 2.4 are available for export or import in SAP MII.

Configuration	XML File
System Properties	The system properties are backed up in the file SystemProperties.xml.
Simulator Instances	Each instance is backed up as a separate XML file as <SimulatorServerName>.xml in a folder called Simulator_files in the archive. The default Simulator Instance is backed up as DefaultSimulator.xml.

Table 2.4 System Configuration Backup Properties

Configuration	XML File
Scheduled Jobs	Each scheduled job is backed up as a separate XML file as <ScheduleName>.xml in a folder called Scheduler_Jobs in the archive.
Message Listeners	The Message Listeners configuration created in Message Services are backed up in the file MessageServers.xml.
System Permissions	The system permissions configured in security services are backed up in the file SystemPermissions.xml.
Message Listener Rules	The processing rules for message listeners created in Message Services are backed up in the file MessageProcessRules.xml.
Data Server Permissions	The security permissions for the data servers configured in security services are backed up in the file ServerPermissions.xml.
Message Listener Cleanup Rules	The cleanup rules created in Message Services are backed up in the file MessageCleanupRules.xml.
Data Servers	The data servers configured in Data Services are backed up in the file Servers.xml.
Localization	Localization settings are backed up as a separate XML file, <Language>.xml, in a folder called Localization in the archive.
SAP Servers	The SAP Server alias configurations created in Data Services are backed up in the file SAPServers.xml.
Link Objects	The navigation link objects configured in the visualization services are backed up in the file ContentMap.xml.
Time Periods	The time periods configured in Data Services are backed up in the file TimePeriods.xml.
Navigation	Each role or profile that has navigation profiles associated with it is stored as its corresponding XML file named <Role>.xml or <User>.xml in the corresponding ROLE or USER folder under a common Profiles folder.
Time Period Schedules	The time period schedules configured in Data Services are backed up in the file Schedules.xml.
Global	The global properties defined in the SAP MII installation are backed up in the file Globals.xml.
Unit Conversions	The unit conversion configurations are backed up in the file UnitConversions.xml.
Custom Attributes	The custom attributes configured in system administration are backed up in the file CustomAttributes.xml.

Table 2.4 System Configuration Backup Properties (Cont.)

In the case of an import, you need to browse for the backup archive file containing a previous export of the configuration from the local file system and click on Import to import the configuration archive file into SAP MII.

2.2.9   Projects

The Projects screen, shown in Figure 2.11, allows the SAP MII administrator (and any users with the ProjectManagement System security service assigned) to back up and restore SAP MII projects. This capability is useful when you are transporting the development content from one SAP MII installation to another, such as from development to production.

The Projects screen lists the various projects and their details such as their name, description, whether or not it is system project, when and by whom it was created, and options to delete (❌) and export (🖫) it as a compressed ZIP file.

	Projects					
▾ **System Management**	Name	Description	System Project	Created By	Created	
System Administration	Acceptance Testing 12.1		☐	I040560	5/2/08 4:40:15 PM	🖫 ❌
System Jobs	ASM Manufacturing		☐	I040560	5/2/08 4:18:59 PM	🖫 ❌
Scheduler	BatchHistory		☐	I040644	8/13/08 10:23:23 AM	🖫 ❌
Schedule Editor	Default	Default Project	☑			🖫
Active Sessions	EMO_Mill_Demo		☐	I040560	8/7/08 11:13:02 AM	🖫 ❌
Custom Attributes	I036320		☐	i036320	7/22/08 11:24:20 AM	🖫 ❌
Custom Attribute Mapping	ManufModel		☐	I040560	5/2/08 4:18:05 PM	🖫 ❌
Configurations	MfgAnalytics		☐	I040644	8/14/08 1:33:23 PM	🖫 ❌
Projects	PDC_DB_script		☐	C5109298	6/20/08 4:34:35 PM	🖫 ❌
Custom Actions	PDC_testing		☐	C5109298	6/19/08 6:35:31 PM	🖫 ❌
PDF Fonts	QM_eSOA		☐	I030283	8/21/08 1:28:20 PM	🖫 ❌
JDBC Drivers	Summit_Demo		☐	I040560	6/5/08 11:07:38 AM	🖫 ❌
Applet Debugging	TouchScreenPDC		—	C5109298	8/13/08 3:03:30 PM	🖫 ❌
▸ **Security Services**						
▸ **Data Services**						
▸ **Message Services**						
▸ **Visualization Services**	Import Help					
▸ **Navigation Services**						
▸ **Support**						

Figure 2.11   SAP MII Projects

A project exported from SAP MII contains the project files in the same folder structure that has been defined in the SAP MII Workbench, along with an Export-Manifest.xml file that contains necessary metadata regarding the exported project.

The fields that are present in the ExportManifest.xml file are listed and explained in Table 2.5.

Parameter	Description
Export_User	The user who exported the project.
Hidden_Project	Indicates if the project is a hidden project. Values can be true or false. A hidden project is not visible in the projects list.
Project_Created	The date and time when the project was created.
Project_Created_By	The user who created the project.
Project_Description	Description text of the project.
Project_Name	The name of the project.
System_Project	Indicates if the project is a system project. Values can be true or false. A system project cannot be deleted.
Timestamp	The date and time when the project was exported.
XMII_Version	The SAP MII version on which the project was created and exported.

Table 2.5 SAP MII Project Properties

You do not need to have an ExportManifest.xml to import a project into SAP MII. You can externally create the project structure and import it into SAP MII; however, you should note that if a project with the same project name as an existing project is imported into SAP MII, the existing project is overwritten, regardless of whether it is a system or a hidden project.

2.2.10 Custom Actions

You can use the Custom Action screen, shown in Figure 2.12, for managing custom action blocks used in Business Logic Services. You can refer to Section 9.1 Creating and Deploying a Custom Action Block, to understand how to develop new custom actions to be used in the Business Logic Services Transactions in SAP MII. Custom actions that have already been deployed can be deleted, and those that are new can be deployed using the options available on this screen. You need to assign the CustomActionUpload security service to a user to enable access to the Custom Actions screen.

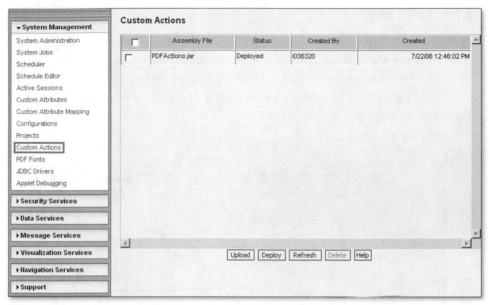

Figure 2.12 Custom Actions Management

To delete an already deployed custom action, choose the custom action by select-ing the check box next to it and clicking on Delete. Deleted actions appear in the Custom Actions list marked as deleted until the server is restarted or another cus-tom action is deployed.

New actions need to be uploaded and then deployed so that they show up in SAP MII Workbench. To upload a custom action Java Archive file into SAP MII, click on Upload to bring up the Custom Action Upload screen.

The Assembly File field should have the custom action assembly jar file location, and any dependency files should subsequently be entered on the dependency files fields. After it is saved, the custom action assembly file along with its dependant jars are uploaded to the SAP MII server. The uploaded actions now appear on the Custom Actions list with the status Not Deployed. To deploy these actions, choose the custom action by selecting the checkbox next to it and click on the Deploy but-ton to deploy it. On deployment of an action, all transactions and queries running at that instance of the server is interrupted; the user sessions are not.

2.2.11 PDF Fonts

The PDF Fonts menu option appears only when the PDF actions have been deployed using the Custom Action upload, as explained in the previous section. The method for deploying these actions is explained in SAP Note 1109054. You use the PDF Fonts screen (Figure 2.13) to upload PDF fonts you can use in the PDF action blocks in the BLS Transactions.

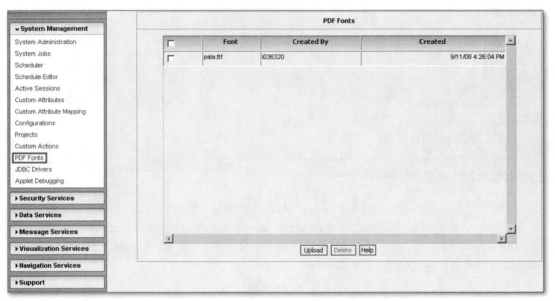

Figure 2.13 PDF Fonts Management

To upload a PDF font into SAP MII, click on Upload to bring up the PDF Font Upload screen. Click on Browse to choose or enter the path of the PDF Font file in the dialog that pops up. After it is saved, the PDF Font appears in the PDF Fonts list. To delete an already uploaded PDF Font, select the checkbox next to it in the PDF Font list and click on Delete. After you have uploaded and deployed the custom action for generating PDF documents, you can use this menu to install custom PDF fonts that you want to use in the PDF documents generated by the BLS Transactions.

2.2.12 JDBC Drivers

You can use the JDBC Drivers menu, seen in Figure 2.14, to deploy Java Database Connectivity (JDBC) drivers for the databases connected by the data servers in SAP

MII. The overview screen displays information about the driver such as the JDBC driver file name, the deployment status, Created By identification, and a Created timestamp.

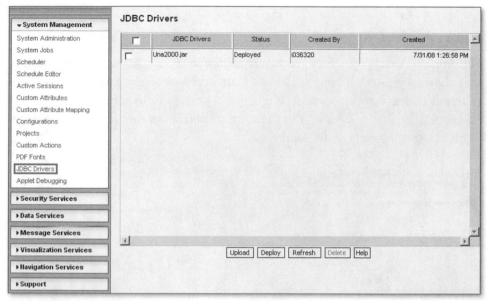

Figure 2.14 JDBC Drivers Management

To delete an already deployed JDBC driver, choose the driver by selecting the checkbox next to it and clicking on Delete. Deleted drivers appear as deleted in the JDBC Driver list until the server is restarted or another driver is deployed.

To upload a new JDBC driver, click on Upload, which brings up the JDBC Driver Upload screen.

Browse to select the JDBC driver you want to upload, and click on Save to upload it to the SAP MII server. The uploaded drivers now appear on the JDBC drivers list with the status Not Deployed. To deploy them, choose the driver by selecting the checkbox next to it and clicking on Deploy. On your deployment of a new driver, all transactions and queries running at any data server instance using the same driver are interrupted; the user sessions are not.

Depending on the database you want to connect to using the data servers (explained in Section 3.1 Data Servers: Connecting to the Manufacturing Plant Floor), and given all the different database vendors in the market today, the standard way to connect to these databases would be to use the JDBC drivers that these vendors have made available. So if you want to connect to proprietary databases like IBM DB2, Microsoft SQL Server, or Oracle databases, a JDBC driver for that particular database is often the only option.

2.2.13 Applet Debugging

The Applet Debugging screen, shown in Figure 2.15, is a troubleshooting utility that allows the SAP MII applets to log debug messages on the Java Runtime Environment Console in the browser, if enabled. These console debug messages help developers in quickly figuring out the source of errors in case an applet does not work as expected and readily fix them.

Figure 2.15 Applet Debugging Configurations

To enable Applet Debugging, check on the Allow Applet Debugging option on the Applet Debugging popup window. The Applet Debugging session is valid only for the current session of the browser, and you need to have the Admin, SystemEditor, SystemSecurityEditor, and System Security roles for your user to debug applets.

You now know about the various configuration options available for administrators of SAP MII. In the next section, you learn about the security services, through which the administrator can control access of users to various services and menus of SAP MII.

2.3 Security Services in SAP MII

Because SAP MII is a development platform, you might need to control the access of the different functionalities and menu options available in SAP MII to different users. For example, you might want to provide the administration menu options such as System Management and Security Services to the administrator users and the configuration and development menus such as Data Services and Message Services to the developers. You can use the security services in SAP MII to control user access on system functionality and data servers. You do this by granting or revoking users' access to the SAP MII services, which form the backbone for the majority of the SAP MII functionality. The security services in SAP MII are of two types: system security and data access security.

2.3.1 System Security

The System Security screen, seen in Figure 2.16, enables the administrator to assign SAP MII services to the SAP MII roles defined in the User Management Engine (UME), which provides access to different functionalities of SAP MII. If the administrator doesn't assign the roles to the services, the users cannot create or change the corresponding configurations, though they might be able to open the menu in read-only mode for some screens.

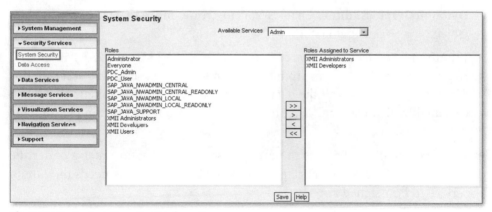

Figure 2.16 System Security Configurations

The SAP MII system security services are as follows:

▶ **Admin:** The most important service in SAP MII. Provides access to all system administration options. Only the Active Sessions and the Applet Debugging screen do not need this security service to be assigned to the user role.

▶ **Configuration:** Not related to any SAP MII screen. Enables the user to migrate configuration data from SAP MII 11.5 to 12.0.

▶ **ConfigurationManagement:** Enables users to import and export SAP MII system configurations using the Configurations menu under System Management.

▶ **ContentEditor:** Controls the ability to edit, import, and export web content using SAP MII Workbench. This service needs the Admin service to be assigned as well.

▶ **ContentList:** Enables users to list all content that they have developed or that have been assigned to them.

▶ **CustomActionUpload:** Enables users to upload custom actions using the Custom Action menu under System Management.

▶ **DataAccessSecurityEditor:** Enables access to the Data Access screen under the Security Services menu in SAP MII. This service needs the Admin service to be assigned as well.

▶ **DataBufferEntry:** Gives access to the Data Buffer Entries screen under the Data Services menu in SAP MII.

▶ **DataBufferJobs:** Enables access to the Data Buffer Jobs screen under the Data Services menu in SAP MII.

▶ **DynamicGraphicsEditor:** Enables you to create and edit Dynamic Graphics Objects via SVG using the SAP MII Workbench.

▶ **IlluminatorService:** The heart of Data Services of SAP MII. All SAP MII queries require it for retrieving data from their intended sources. Denying access to this security service causes all the data queries that use it to stop functioning when executed by that user and also prevents the user from creating and editing the data servers.

▶ **LocalizationEditor:** Enables the user to use the Localization menu under the Visualization Services menu category in SAP MII. This service needs the Admin service to be assigned as well.

▶ **MessageMonitor:** Enables access to the Message Monitor, Failed Messages, and Messages Without Rules menus under the Message Services menu category in SAP MII.

▶ **MessageRuleEditor:** Enables create, view, modify, and delete access to the Message Cleanup Rule Editor menu under the Message Services menu category in SAP MII.

▶ **MessageServerEditor:** Enables users to create, view, modify, and delete access to the Message Listeners menu under the Message Services menu category in SAP MII.

- ▶ **NavigationEditor:** Enables access to the Link Editor and the Navigation menus under the Navigation Services menu category. This service needs the Admin service to be assigned as well.

- ▶ **ProcessingRuleEditor:** Enables users to create, view, modify, and delete access to the Processing Rules Editor menu under the Message Services menu category in SAP MII.

- ▶ **ProjectManagement:** Enables access to the Project menu under the System Management menu category and the ability to import and export projects.

- ▶ **QueryCaching:** Enables users to use the query caching mechanism for query templates and allows access to the cached query results.

- ▶ **ScheduleEditor:** Enables access to the Schedule Editor menu under the System Management menu category, giving the ability to create, modify, and delete scheduled jobs.

- ▶ **Scheduler:** Enables users to start and stop the SAP MII scheduler from the Scheduler menu under the System Management menu category.

- ▶ **ServerEditor:** Enables access to the Data Servers menu under the Data Services menu category and the ability to create, modify, delete, and view Data Servers. This service also requires the Admin service.

- ▶ **SystemEditor:** Enables access to the System Administration, System Jobs, and Applet Debugging menus under the System Management menu category. This service requires the Admin service as well.

- ▶ **SystemInfo:** Mainly a reporting service that lists servers and modes that the servers support.

- ▶ **SystemSecurityEditor:** Enables access to the System Security menu under the Security Services menu category. This service needs the Admin service to be assigned as well.

- ▶ **TemplateEditor:** Controls access to edit any templates (for example, query, display, and so on) created in SAP MII Workbench.

- ▶ **TimeIntervalEditor:** Enables you to view, create, modify, and delete access to Time Periods and Time Period Schedules via their respective menus under the Data Services menu category.

- ▶ **WSMessageListener:** Lets you send HTTP XML messages to SAP MII using the XMIIMessageListener, which listens for HTTP posts. The XMIIMessageListener can be found in the Message Listeners menu under the Message Services menu category.

▸ **XacuteDevelopment:** Controls the ability to view, create, modify, and delete transactions using SAP MII Workbench.

▸ **XacuteRuntime:** Controls the ability to invoke transactions, developed using SAP MII Workbench, through a URL.

To assign an SAP MII service to a role in the System Security menu, select the SAP MII service from the Available Services dropdown list. The roles that are available in UME appear on the list on the left of the screen; the ones that are already assigned to the selected service are in a list on the right. You can select the roles that need to be assigned and then assign them to the selected service by using the (>) or (>>) buttons. Similarly you can un-assign a role from the selected service by selecting the role on the list on the right side and using the (<) or (<<) buttons to bring it to the list on the left. You can select multiple roles on either list by pressing the Shift or Control keys. The (<) and (>) buttons transfer the selected single or multiple rows, whereas the (<<) and the (>>) buttons transfer all entries on one list to the other. When the assignment or un-assignment has been done, click on Save.

2.3.2 Data Access

The Data Access screen, seen in Figure 2.17, enables the administrator to assign SAP MII user roles to the data servers defined using the Data Servers menu (explained in Section 3.1 Data Servers: Connecting to the Manufacturing Plant Floor) under the Data Services menu category. Without the roles assigned to the data server, no data query can be created or executed by the user using that specific data server.

To assign a data server to a role in the Data Access menu, select the data server from the Available Servers dropdown. All the data servers configured in the Data Servers menu appear in the dropdown list. The roles that can be assigned appear on the list on the left of the screen, and the ones that are already assigned appear in a list on the right. You can select the roles that need to be assigned to the required data server and transfer them by the method discussed previously. When the assignment or un-assignment has been done, click on Save.

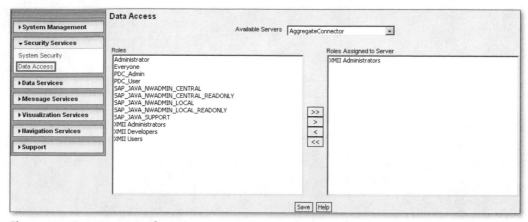

Figure 2.17 Data Access Configurations

2.4   Summary

In this chapter, you have learned how to create users and assign the required roles to them in the J2EE WebAS, how to configure the SAP J2EE logging options, and how to configure the SAP JRA adapter. You have also learned how you can use the System Management and the System Security menu options to configure the system and security options of SAP MII.

In the next chapter, you will learn how to connect to the manufacturing plant floor systems by creating data servers in SAP MII and how to configure the Message Services to receive RFC, IDoc, and HTTP XML messages from the enterprise systems.

This chapter explains the integration aspects of SAP MII, including how to connect to manufacturing plant floor systems using Data Servers, and how to synchronize the plant-floor with other parts of the enterprise using Message Services.

3 Managing Manufacturing Plant Floor Integration with SAP MII

To have a better visibility and control over the manufacturing execution process at the plant floor you need to integrate your plant systems to acquire and update production data from and to those systems and finally generate analytics charts and transactional dashboards with it. In this chapter, you learn about the Data Servers and Message Services in SAP MII and how to configure them to connect to the plant floor systems and receive messages from the enterprise systems.

3.1 Data Servers: Connecting to the Manufacturing Plant Floor

Data Servers in SAP MII are the most important aspect of manufacturing plant floor connectivity because they provide direct and near real-time bi-directional access to the manufacturing data present in different systems and applications on the plant floor. Via standard protocols and application interfaces, the Data Servers provide direct connections to the databases or applications in Levels 2 and 3 of the enterprise. A considerable list of data connectors is provided in SAP MII. You can configure these as Data Servers and, using query templates, retrieve or write data to these systems. In total, 15 connector types are available in SAP MII 12.0; they are as follows:

- Aggregate Connector
- AlarmSuite Connector
- DataSource Connector

- ▶ IDBC Connector
- ▶ IP21 Connector
- ▶ IP21OLEDB Connector
- ▶ InSQL Connector
- ▶ OLAP Connector
- ▶ Open Connector
- ▶ OLEDB Connector
- ▶ Simulator Connector
- ▶ Universal Data Connector
- ▶ Virtual Servers
- ▶ XML Connector
- ▶ Xacute Connector

> **Note**
>
> - ▶ Aggregate Connector was introduced to combine multiple query templates in a single data query. But now this can be achieved more easily and flexibly using Business Logic Services (BLS) Transactions.
> - ▶ AlarmSuite Connector was introduced to connect to Wonderware® AlarmSuite™, which is currently an obsolete application.
> - ▶ IP21 Connector was introduced to connect to AspenTech InfoPlus.21®, which is a real-time information management system for manufacturing processes. It utilizes the Easysoft JDBC/ODBC driver, which you need to deploy to connect to a system Data Source Name (DSN) on the machine where the InfoPlus.21 suite is installed. Now IP21OLEDB Connector is the recommended connector to connect to AspenTech InfoPlus.21, which connects via the Universal Data Server using the OLEDB interface.
> - ▶ XML Connector was introduced to connect to external XML data sources, but now it is easier to achieve the same using BLS Transactions.
>
> These four connectors are now obsolete and we recommend you do not use them anymore.

Each Data Server provides connection to specific applications or systems used on the manufacturing plant floor. Any application or system using one of the previously mentioned connectors can be integrated with SAP MII.

The Data Servers provide different query modes to retrieve different types of data such as current data, historical data, statistical data, and so on. This data varies with the type of Data Servers and is specified when you are configuring the query templates using the Data Servers. Also, each mode might have one or more query methods such as AVG, MIN, MAX, and so on which provide specific data for that specific query mode.

> **Note**
>
> For a sample list of the systems with which SAP MII provides standard connectivity using Data Servers, please see SAP Note 943237.

You can use Data Servers to connect to the plant systems such as Process Historian, Laboratory Information Management System (LIMS), Supervisory Control And Data Acquisition (SCADA), Distributed Control System (DCS), Manufacturing Execution System (MES) and custom or legacy databases to retrieve or update the process data. For example, you can connect to an OSIsoft PI Historian to retrieve the temperature readings as time-series data using Tag Query and plot them in a chart for monitoring or to a legacy SQL database to read the batch details or to update the batch status during production execution.

You need to create a separate Data Server configuration in SAP MII for each plant system you are connecting to. You can create the Data Server configuration from the Data Servers menu under the Data Services menu category.

In the Data Servers configuration screen, as seen in Figure 3.1, the existing Data Servers are shown in the list on the left of the screen. The right of the screen displays currently selected or new Data Server configurations. To create a new Data Server configuration, click on the New button below the configuration screen. A pop-up window appears with the list of available Data Server types. Select the required Data Server type from the dropdown, and click OK. You can copy an existing Data Server configuration by selecting the Data Server configuration from the left list, clicking on the Copy button, and then saving with the Save button. To delete the selected Data Server configuration, use the Delete button. The Summary button displays the configuration summary of the selected Data Server, and the Status button displays the connection status of the selected Data Server configuration. In the pop-up window, the status of the connection, number of used connections, number of available connections, maximum number of used connections, and maximum wait time are displayed. If the No. of Available Connections column displays 0, the connection to the data source is not available. If the connection is successful, the No. of Available Connections column displays 1 or higher.

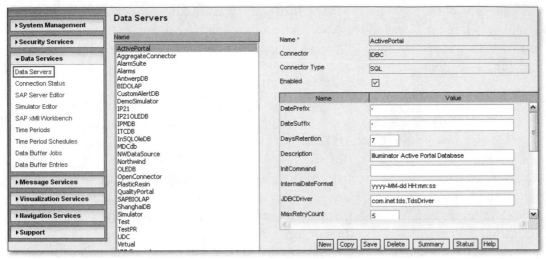

Figure 3.1 Data Server Configuration in SAP MII

Checking the Enabled checkbox in any Data Server configuration makes it enabled and ready for use. You can see the status of all enabled Data Servers configured in SAP MII from the DATA SERVICES • CONNECTION STATUS menu option.

Some properties in the Data Server configuration are the most common, as explained in Table 3.1.

Property	Description
DatePrefix	Prefix for specifying date in the queries created using the Data Server. This is different for different databases. Default value is single quote (') for MS SQL Server. For Oracle it should be TO_DATE('
DateSuffix	Suffix for specifying date in the queries created using the Data Server. Default value is single quote (') for MS SQL Server. For Oracle it is ','MM/DD/YYYY HH24:MI:SS')

Table 3.1 General Data Server Configuration Properties

74

Property	Description
DaysRetention	Number of days the data is buffered for queries using the Data Server, where the buffer option is enabled. Default value is 7.
Description	A single-line description of the Data Server.
InitCommand	Initial command to be executed when a database connection pool is established; can be specified (for example, in Oracle, the Locale can be set using the InitCommand).
InternalDateFormat	Date format to be used in the queries created using the Data Server. Default value is yyyy-MM-dd HH:mm:ss
JDBCDriver	Specifies the Java package that contains the database driver. This is required for all the relational database connectors. You need to specify this for the driver that is uploaded and deployed using the SYSTEM MANAGEMENT • JDBC DRIVERS menu.
MaxRetryCount	The maximum number of retries by the Data Server to establish a connection with the data source.
Password	Specifies the password used to connect to the database. Irrespective of the length of the password, it is always displayed as six asterisks in the configuration.
PoolMax	The maximum number of connections the pool allocates. If a connection is not available at runtime from the pool, then the request waits for a free connection or expires at the timeout. Default value is 100.
PoolSize	Maximum number of connections established in the connection pool. The default value is 1.
RetryInterval	The time for connection retry in milliseconds.
ServerPackage	The SAP MII Java package and class for the specific connector. The value should not be changed.
ServerURL	Driver-specific connection string for the database. Includes the hostname and database port. This is required for all the relational database connectors.

Table 3.1 General Data Server Configuration Properties (Cont.)

Property	Description
TimeOut	Time in minutes after which an unused connection is returned to the connection pool to be used by another request.
UseCount	Number of times a connection is used for data queries before it is closed and all resources are released. This is used by the ODBC data sources to prevent resource leaks while executing large numbers of database queries.
UserName	The user name used for establishing the database connection.
ValidationQuery	The database query executed to validate the connection. Default value is SELECT GETDATE(), but it might differ for different databases. If the database does not support the query, the connection status for the Data Server shows up as an error. For example, the validation query for MaxDB should be changed to "SELECT * FROM DUAL" because "SELECT GETDATE()" will not work in this case.
WaitTime	The time in seconds SAP MII waits for a data source connection before failing.

Table 3.1 General Data Server Configuration Properties (Cont.)

We will now discuss the connector types listed in this section above, barring the ones mentioned as obsolete.

3.1.1 DataSource Connector

The DataSource connector is based on the SAP NetWeaver J2EE engine JDBC DataSource, which is an alias you can create in the Visual Administrator when connecting to a JDBC-compliant data source (for example, Oracle, MS SQL Server, and so on). You can configure the database driver, connection pool, and authentication for the connection in Visual Administrator and manage it with the SAP NetWeaver J2EE engine. Using the DataSource connector, you can create SQL queries in SAP MII. In the DataSource property of the DataSource Data Server configuration, you need to specify the alias of the DataSource you configured in Visual Administrator and the name and optional description of the Data Server configuration, as shown in Figure 3.2. You can use the DataSource connector for connecting to the NetWeaver J2EE engine database, for example, when you have used the NetWeaver J2EE engine database to store custom application–specific data in custom tables.

Name	Value
Connector	DataSource
ConnectorID	
ConnectorType	SQL
Datasource	jdbc/SAPXM1DB
DatePrefix	'
DateSuffix	'
DaysRetention	7
Description	---
Enabled	T
InternalDateFormat	yyyy-MM-dd HH:mm:ss
MaxRetryCount	5
Name	NWDataSource
RetryInterval	60000
ServerPackage	com.sap.xmii.Illuminator.connectors.IDBC

Figure 3.2 DataSource Data Server Configurations

3.1.2 IDBC Connector

The IDBC connector is the most commonly used connector in SAP MII and provides connectivity to legacy databases supporting Java Database Connectivity (JDBC). This connector provides direct connection to any relational database to create a SQL query on its table data. Examples are Microsoft SQL Server, Oracle Database, MaxDB, DB2, and so on. You can also use this connector to connect to any application database, such as an MS SQL Server database of a Manufacturing Execution System. This is useful when you want to retrieve or update data from the composite application to a custom legacy database or any other application database. You can even use an IDBC connector to connect to the NetWeaver WAS database if you create custom application–specific database tables in it. You need to change the following properties for authentication while creating a new IDBC Data Server configuration (Figure 3.3):

- UserName
- Password
- ServerURL

The ServerURL parameter specifies the database connection string that is different for different databases. An example for MS SQL Server 8.0 the ServerURL is as follows:

jdbc:inetdae:<host>:<port>?database=<dbName>&sql7=true

For MS SQL Server 2005 it is:

jdbc:sqlserver://<host>:<port>;databaseName=<dbName>

In addition, you need to upload and deploy a JDBC driver from the SYSTEM MANAGEMENT • JDBC DRIVERS menu, as explained in Chapter 2 Administrating and Configuring SAP MII, for the specific database for which you are configuring the Data Server. You also need to specify the database driver package name in the JDBCDriver property according to the database used (for example, com.inet.tds. TdsDriver for MS Server 8.0 and com.microsoft.sqlserver.jdbc.SQLServerDriver for MS SQL Server 2005).

You can use default values provided with the new configuration for other required properties.

Name	Value
Connector	IDBC
ConnectorID	
ConnectorType	SQL
DatePrefix	'
DateSuffix	'
DaysRetention	7
Description	MSSQL Database
Enabled	T
InitCommand	
InternalDateFormat	yyyy-MM-dd HH:mm:ss
JDBCDriver	com.inet.tds.TdsDriver
MaxRetryCount	5
Name	PlasticResin
PoolMax	100
PoolSize	1
RetryInterval	60000
ServerPackage	com.sap.xmii.Illuminator.connectors.IDBC
ServerURL	jdbc:inetdae:localhost:1433?database=PlasticResin&sql7=true
Timeout	2
UseCount	256
UserName	xmii
ValidationQuery	SELECT GETDATE()
WaitTime	30

Figure 3.3 IDBC Data Server Configurations

3.1.3 IP21OLEDB Connector

The IP21OLEDB connector provides connectivity to AspenTech InfoPlus.21, which is a real-time information management system for manufacturing processes. The IP21OLEDB connector uses the SAP MII OLEDB Universal Data Server (explained in Section 3.1.9 Universal Data Connector) to connect to the AspenTech InfoPlus.21 system.

You can access the data that the InfoPlus.21 suite provides through Tag Queries, which are created using this Data Server in the SAP MII Workbench. Tag data is time-series data for specific process characteristics, represented by a tag, for example, Line1Temperature, Pump1Flowrate, etc. For example, you can retrieve the flow rate of a material or the pressure readings from a production line, which is captured in IP21, in SAP MII by creating Tag Query on this Data Server. You might need this information in various scenarios such as when you are displaying charts for a process characteristic trend, when doing a quality analysis, when aggregating and updating in ERP, and so on. The modes supported by this connector are Current, HistoryEvent, History, and Statistics. It also enables browsing of the IP21 namespace. Because no group hierarchy exists in the IP21 database, the GroupList mode does not return any value.

You need to configure a few properties, listed in Table 3.2, as general properties for this Data Server configuration, and the rest are specific to the mode of query. All properties listed in this table are mandatory.

Property	Description
IP	IP address or hostname of the server where the Universal Data Server (UDS) is installed.
Port	The port of the remote machine where the UDS is listening for requests.
TagListTable	The name of the table that holds a list of all the valid tag names in IP21. Default value is "alltags."
TagListNameColumn	The column name of the TagListTable that holds the tag names. Default value is "record_name."
TagListDescriptionColumn	The column name of the TagListTable that holds the tag description. Default value is "description."
TagInfoTable	The name of the table from which tag info metadata like description, record type, and range information is fetched for a tag. Default value should be left blank, in which case the name of the tag is used as the table name.
TagInfoNameColumn	The column name of the TagInfoTable that holds the tag names. Default value is "name."
TagInfoDescriptionColumn	The column name of the TagInfoTable that holds the tag description. Default value is "name->description."

Table 3.2 General Parameters for IP21OLEDB Data Server Configuration

Property	Description
TagInfoTypeColumn	The column name of the TagInfoTable that specifies the IP21 record number. SAP MII interprets #19 and #1649 as discrete data types and #20 and #1640 as analog data types. The rest are interpreted as analog data types. Default value is "definition."
TagInfoMinRangeColumn	The column name of the TagInfoTable that provides EGU range information used for scaling charts using server provided ranges. This field provides the minimum range value. Default value is "name->graphminimum."
TagInfoMaxRangeColumn	The column name of the TagInfoTable that provides EGU range information used for scaling charts using server provided ranges. This field provides the maximum range value. Default value is "name->graphmaximum."
Writable	Specifies whether or not you can update current values to a tag using the Tag Query.

Table 3.2 General Parameters for IP21OLEDB Data Server Configuration (Cont.)

Apart from the general properties just explained, you need to configure the query mode–specific parameters as explained in the following sections. If a specific query mode is not used for a data server, then that mode-specific parameter need not be configured.

History Mode Parameters

History mode enables you to retrieve historical time-series data in an interpolated manner available in the tag data source. You need to configure the parameters seen in Table 3.3 for History mode. All parameters explained in this table are mandatory for using History mode.

Property	Description
HistoryTable	The name of the table from where time interpolated history data should be retrieved. Default value should be the name of the history table, which is commonly named "HISTORY."
HistoryNameColumn	Specifies the column name in the HistoryTable that represents the tag name. Default value is "NAME."

Table 3.3 HistoryMode Parameters for IP21OLEDB Data Server Configurations

Property	Description
HistoryTimeColumn	Specifies the column name in the HistoryTable that represents the tag value's timestamp. Default value is "TS."
HistoryValueColumn	Specifies the column name in the HistoryTable that represents the tag value at a specific timestamp. Default value is "VALUE."
HistoryQualityColumn	Specifies the column name in the HistoryTable that represents the quality value of the tag data. Default value is "QUALITY."
HistoryPeriodColumn	Specifies the column name in the HistoryTable that sets the data retrieval period. Default value is "PERIOD."

Table 3.3 HistoryMode Parameters for IP21OLEDB Data Server Configurations (Cont.)

HistoryEvent Mode Parameters

The HistoryEvent mode enables you to retrieve historical event data available in the tag data source. The HistoryEvent mode supports two query methods: normal and compressed.

The *normal* method is invoked when the value of the Method field in the query template is blank. The connector then uses the values of the table and column names in the fields of HistoryEventName, HistoryEventTime, HistoryEventValue, and HistoryEventQuality in the connector configuration to retrieve the data. The *compressed* method is not available in the method dropdown and has to be entered manually. This method uses the table and column names in the fields of CompressedHistoryEventName, CompressedHistoryEventTime, CompressedHistoryEventValue, and CompressedHistoryEventQuality to retrieve the data. These two methods are relevant when you need to maintain and access data with different granularity. The compressed data storing method in the Historian does not store all data points but uses different algorithms to reject data that can be interpreted at runtime. You need to configure the parameters in Table 3.4 for HistoryEvent mode.

Property	Description
HistoryEventTable	Specifies the name of the table from where history data should be retrieved. Default value is blank, in which case the name of the tag is used as the table name.

Table 3.4 HistoryEvent Mode Parameters for IP21OLEDB Data Server Configurations

Property	Description
HistoryEventNameColumn	Specifies the column name from the HistoryEventTable that represents the tag name. Default value is "NAME."
HistoryEventTimeColumn	Specifies the column name from the HistoryEventTable that represents the tag value's timestamp. Default value is "IP_TREND_TIME."
HistoryEventValueColumn	Specifies the column name from the HistoryEventTable that represents the tag value. Default value is "IP_TREND_VALUE."
HistoryEventQualityColumn	Specifies the column name in the HistoryEventTable that represents the quality value of the tag data. Default value is "IP_VALUE_QSTATUS."
CompressedHistoryEventTable	Specifies the name of the table from where history data should be retrieved in case the method used in the query is "Compressed." Default value should be left blank, in which case the name of the tag is used as the table name.
CompressedHistoryEventNameColumn	Specifies the column name from the CompressedHistoryEventTable that represents the tag name. Default value is "NAME."
CompressedHistoryEventTimeColumn	Specifies the column name from the CompressedHistoryEventTable that represents the tag value's timestamp. Default value is "IP_TREND_TIME."
CompressedHistoryEventValueColumn	Specifies the column name from the CompressedHistoryEventTable that represents the tag value. Default value is "IP_TREND_VALUE."
CompressedHistoryEventQualityColumn	Specifies the column name in the CompressedHistoryEventTable that represents the quality value of the tag data. Default value is "IP_VALUE_QSTATUS."

Table 3.4 HistoryEvent Mode Parameters for IP21OLEDB Data Server Configurations (Cont.)

Current Mode Parameters

Current mode enables you to retrieve tag values at the current timestamp. You need to configure the parameters in Table 3.5 for the Tag Query using current mode.

Property	Description
CurrentTable	The name of the table from where the current value of the tag data should be retrieved. Default value is blank, in which case the name of the tag is used as the table name.
CurrentNameColumn	Specifies the column name in the CurrentTable that represents the tag name. Default value is "NAME."
CurrentValueColumn	Specifies the column name in the CurrentTable that represents the tag value. Default value is "IP_VALUE."
CurrentTimeColumn	Specifies the column name in the CurrentTable that represents the timestamp of the selected tag. Default value is "IP_VALUE_TIME."
CurrentQualityColumn	Specifies the column name in the CurrentTable that represents the quality value of the tag data. Default value is "IP_VALUE_QUALITY."

Table 3.5   Current Mode Parameters for IP21OLEDB Data Server Configurations

You need to configure an instance for the IP21 system in the Universal Data Server (UDS) of type OLE DB UDS and point it to the server where the AspenTech InfoPlus.21 system is installed. Please refer Section 3.1.9 Universal Data Connector to understand how to configure the UDS instance.

3.1.4   InSQL Connector

The InSQL connector provides the connectivity to Wonderware® IndustrialSQL Server™ (InSQL). Using this Data Server, you can create Tag Queries using the SAP MII Workbench to retrieve process time-series data such as machine readings, temperature, and line speed for a production line as current data or historical data for a time range. The InSQL connector is a special type of IDBC connector because it connects to a JDBC-compliant database provided by InSQL, so most of its configuration parameters are the same as IDBC's parameters. Specify the UseOLEDB property as True for InSQL version 8.x and later, and False for InSQL version 7.x and earlier. You use ServerURL to specify the connection string to the InSQL JDBC-compliant database, and you specify corresponding authentication details in the UserName and Password properties.

3.1.5   OLAP Connector

The OLAP connector provides connectivity to multidimensional data sources such as online analytical processing (OLAP)–based systems supporting the XML for Analysis (XMLA) specification. Examples of OLAP data sources include SAP Business Intelligence (BI) and MS SQL Server Analysis Services. The key elements of an OLAP data source are InfoCubes, which are multidimensional data structures used for faster execution of complex analytical queries. You can use this Data Server to create a Multidimensional Expression (MDX) query over an InfoCube or XMLA data source, the output of which you can use in analysis charts and reports. Some examples might be product yield reports by workcenters and by months. The configuration properties in Table 3.6, which are specific to the OLAP Data Server, are available in the OLAP connector configuration.

Property	Description
Catalog	Specifies the XMLA server or database instance name. For SAP BI, it specifies the InfoCube name.
ColumnNameAttribute	Specifies the string name used by the XMLA server implementation to retrieve the returned column label. For MS SQL Server Analysis Services the default value is "sql:field." For SAP BI, the default value is "name."
DataSourceInfo	Specifies the Microsoft® parameter for connecting to a data store (for example, Provider=MSOLAP; Data Source=local). Not required for SAP BI.
DataTypeAttribute	Specifies the string in XMLA used to return the column data types in the response document. Default value is "type."
DecimalDelimiter	Specifies the character used for decimal notation. It can be either full-stop (.) or comma (,), as configured in the OLAP system.
IP	Specifies the IP address of the server hosting the OLAP services.
Port	Specifies the listening port of the XMLA service on the OLAP server.
ResultInNamespace	Specifies the Boolean indicator for returning Simple Object Access Protocol (SOAP) response from the XMLA server. Specify True for SAP BI.

Table 3.6   OLAP Data Server Configuration Properties

Property	Description
WebService	Specifies the entry point to the XMLA service in the OLAP server. Specify */sap/bw/xml/soap/xmla* for SAP BI, and */xmla/msxisapi.dll* for MS SQL Server Analysis Services. You need to enable the XMLA web interface in SAP BI for using the OLAP Data Server.

Table 3.6 OLAP Data Server Configuration Properties (Cont.)

Note

The OLAP Data Server status does not display any number of available or used connections. This is because OLAP is an on-demand connection, not a persistent connection, meaning that the connection is established not by a connection pool, but only when required to execute a query.

3.1.6   Open Connector

You can use the Open connector to connect to tag-based relational databases to retrieve historical data based on time periods. Using this connector, you can connect SAP MII to Process Historian databases, which store process characteristic data in a time-series fashion and provide the following type of tag-based data:

► Current values

► Historical (time-series) values

► Statistical summaries of historical data

In contrast to the previous query modes, Open connector also supports querying tag groups and tag names from the tag data source using the GroupList and TagList modes. You can create a Tag Query in SAP MII using this Data Server to retrieve current or historical process characteristic information such as temperature readings and flow rates. You can use this Data Server for a custom Process Historian using any relational database such as Oracle, MS SQL Server, or DB2 from which you can query time-series data. It also acts as a tag data source. The TagListQuery, CurrentQuery, HistoryQuery, and HistoryEventQuery parameters should contain the SQL query to select the tag data.

You can use this connector only to query the data from the tag database; you cannot write back. Because Open connector uses JDBC data sources, the connection properties such as JDBCDriver, ServerURL, UserName, and Password are the same as that of the IDBC connector. Apart from these properties, the Open connector has certain specific parameters in the Data Server configuration, as shown in Figure 3.4. However, not all these parameters are mandatory; it depends on which query modes of Open connector the Data Server instance you want to support. The following sections explain the parameters required for different query modes.

Name	Value
Connector	OpenConnector
ConnectorID	
ConnectorType	TAG
CurrentNameColumn	TagName
CurrentQuery	SELECT TOP 1 H.DateTime, H.TagValue, T.TagName FROM HistoryTagValues H,Tags T WHERE T.TagName = '[TagName]' AND (T.ID = H.ID) ORDER BY H.DateTime DESC
CurrentTimeColumn	DateTime
CurrentValueColumn	TagValue
DatePrefix	'
DateSuffix	'
DaysRetention	7
Description	OpenConnector data server for tag data source
Enabled	T
FloatTypeIndicator	6
GroupListNameColumn	Name
GroupListParentColumn	Parent
GroupListQuery	SELECT Name, Parent FROM Groups WHERE Name LIKE '[Mask]%' GROUP BY Parent,Name
HistoryEventNameColumn	TagName
HistoryEventQuery	SELECT H.DateTime,H.TagValue,T.TagName FROM HistoryTagValues H,Tags T WHERE T.TagName = '[TagName]' AND (T.ID = H.ID) AND (H.DateTime >= '[SD]' AND H.DateTime <= '[ED]') ORDER BY H.DateTime
HistoryEventTimeColumn	DateTime
HistoryEventValueColumn	TagValue
HistoryNameColumn	TagName
HistoryQuery	SELECT H.DateTime,H.TagValue,T.TagName FROM HistoryTagValues H,Tags T WHERE T.TagName = '[TagName]' AND (T.ID = H.ID) AND (H.DateTime >= '[SD]' AND H.DateTime <= '[ED]') ORDER BY H.DateTime
HistoryTimeColumn	DateTime
HistoryValueColumn	TagValue
IntegerTypeIndicator	5
InternalDateFormat	yyyy-MM-dd HH:mm:ss
JDBCDriver	com.inet.tds.TdsDriver
MaxRetryCount	5
Name	OpenConnector
PoolMax	15
PoolSize	1
RetryInterval	60000
ServerPackage	com.sap.xmii.Illuminator.connectors.OpenConnector
ServerURL	jdbc:inetdae:localhost:1433?database=LineSpeed&sql7=true
StringTypeIndicator	1
TagInfoDescriptionColumn	TagDesc
TagInfoMaxRangeColumn	MaxEU
TagInfoMinRangeColumn	MinEU
TagInfoNameColumn	TagName
TagInfoQuery	SELECT TagName,TagDesc,MinEU,MaxEU,DataTypeID FROM Tags WHERE TagName='[TagName]'
TagInfoTypeColumn	DataTypeID
TagListDescriptionColumn	TagDesc
TagListNameColumn	TagName
TagListQuery	SELECT Distinct T.TagName, T.TagDesc FROM Tags T, Groups G WHERE (T.TagName LIKE '[Mask]%') AND (G.Name LIKE '[Group]%') AND (T.GroupID = G.ID) ORDER BY T.TagName ASC
Timeout	15
UseCount	256
UserName	xmii
ValidationQuery	SELECT GETDATE()
WaitTime	20

Figure 3.4 Open Connector Data Server Configurations

GroupList Mode Parameters

GroupList mode enables retrieving information about tag groups available in the tag data source. You need to configure the parameters in Table 3.7.

Property	Description
GroupListNameColumn	Specifies the column name that returns the tag group name in the GroupList Query. Default value is "Name."
GroupListParentColumn	Specifies the column name from the GroupList query that returns the Group's parent, if applicable.
GroupListQuery	Specifies the SQL query string that returns the list of tag groups available within the data source. It should include and match the GroupListNameColumn and GroupListParentColumn as specified in the corresponding properties, as required.

Table 3.7 GroupList Mode Parameters for Open Connector Data Server Configuration

TagList Mode Parameters

TagList mode enables you to retrieve tag information and metadata from the tag data source. To use this mode, you need to configure the parameters in Table 3.8.

Property	Description
FloatTypeIndicator	Specifies an integer to indicate the tag datatype. The floating-point data type is specified as 6, which is a default setting and should not be changed.
IntegerTypeIndicator	Specifies an integer to indicate the tag data type. The integer data type is specified as 5, which is a default setting and should not be changed.
StringTypeIndicator	Specifies an integer to indicate the tag data type. The string data type is specified as 12, which is a default setting and should not be changed.
TagInfoNameColumn	Specifies the column from the TagInfoQuery that represents the tag name.
TagInfoDescriptionColumn	Species the column from the TagInfoQuery that represents the tag description.
TagInfoMinRangeColumn	Species the column from the TagInfoQuery that represents the minimum engineering range.

Table 3.8 TagList Mode Parameters for Open Connector Data Server Configurations

Property	Description
TagInfoMaxRangeColumn	Species the column from the TagInfoQuery that represents the maximum engineering range.
TagInfoTypeColumn	Species the column from the TagInfoQuery that represents the tag's data type.
TagInfoQuery	Species the SQL query string that returns the tag information.
TagListNameColumn	Species the column from the TagList query that represents the tag name.
TagListDescriptionColumn	Species the column from the TagList query that represents the tag description.
TagListQuery	Specifies the SQL query string that returns the tag list.

Table 3.8 TagList Mode Parameters for Open Connector Data Server Configurations (Cont.)

History Mode Parameters

History mode enables you to retrieve historical time-series data in an interpolated manner available in the tag data source. You need to configure the parameters in Table 3.9 for the History mode.

Property	Description
HistoryNameColumn	Specifies the column name in the HistoryQuery that represents the tag name.
HistoryTimeColumn	Specifies the column name in the HistoryQuery that represents the tag value's timestamp.
HistoryValueColumn	Specifies the column name in the HistoryQuery that represents the tag value at a specific timestamp.
HistoryQuery	Specifies the SQL query string that returns the historical data from the tag data source.

Table 3.9 History Mode Parameters for Open Connector Data Server Configurations

HistoryEvent Mode Parameters

The HistoryEvent mode enables you to retrieve historical event data available in the tag data source. You need to configure the parameters in Table 3.10 for HistoryEvent mode.

Property	Description
HistoryEventNameColumn	Specifies the column name from the HistoryEventQuery that represents the tag name.
HistoryEventTimeColumn	Specifies the column name from the HistoryEventQuery that represents the tag value's timestamp.
HistoryEventValueColumn	Specifies the column name from the HistoryEventQuery that represents the tag value.
HistoryEventQuery	Specifies the SQL query string that returns historical event data from the tag datasource.

Table 3.10 HistoryEvent Mode Parameters for Open Connector Data Server Configurations

Current Mode Parameters

Current mode enables you to retrieve tag values at the current timestamp. You need to configure the parameters in Table 3.11 for current mode.

Property	Description
CurrentNameColumn	Specifies the column name in the CurrentQuery that represents the tag name.
CurrentValueColumn	Specifies the column name in the CurrentQuery that represents the tag value.
CurrentTimeColumn	Specifies the column name in the CurrentQuery that represents the timestamp of the selected tag.
CurrentQuery	Specifies the SQL query string that returns the current tag values from the data source.

Table 3.11 Current Mode Parameters for Open Connector Data Server Configurations

3.1.7 OLEDB Connector

OLEDB is a Microsoft application programming interface (API) to enable access to data sources using the Microsoft component object model (COM). The SAP MII OLEDB connector provides access to OLEDB-compliant data sources via the Universal Data Server. You can use this Data Server to connect to MS Access, MS Excel files, OSIsoft PI, and GE Fanuc Proficy™ Historian and create SQL query on its data. This capability is useful when you need to retrieve from or write data into a MS Excel file that might be generated by or be sent to another plant system.

The configuration parameters are similar to that of the Universal Data Connector, explained in Section 3.1.9 Universal Data Connector.

3.1.8 Simulator Connector

You can use the Simulator connector to connect to a simulated tag data source available in SAP MII. You can use this for demonstrating, testing, or debugging purposes. The Simulator connector is configured with an XML file that defines groups, tags, and their values. The XML file can be modified using the Simulator Editor screen. It supports the following modes:

- HistoryEvent
- History
- Current

Using this Data Server, you can create Tag Queries based on the simulated XML-based tag data source. You can use default Simulator Data Server available or create new ones as required with different names. In the configuration, you can change only the Description. You can configure the tags available for a Simulator Data Server using the SimulatorInstanceName in the Simulator Editor.

To change the Simulator tags for the default connector or to create the simulator tags for a new simulator Data Server, open the Simulator Editor menu from the menu DATA SERVICES • SIMULATOR EDITOR. In the Simulator Tags tab, select the Simulator Data Server instance name from the Simulator Instance dropdown above. The tags for the default simulator are already available in SAP MII, as shown in Figure 3.5. Select an existing tag or create a tag by clicking the New button. In the Name property, specify a unique name for the tag. In the Type property, the choices are Analog, Discrete, and String. Use Analog for decimal values, such as 192.743; Discrete returns 1 or 0; and String returns alphanumeric values (for example, X25, D38, and so on). The Minimum Value and Maximum Value specify the range of the returned value of the tag. If you mark a tag as Writable, then it enables you to write a new tag value using the Tag Queries. In the Value property, specify a formula to return a tag value. You can use time and mathematical expressions to specify the formula. After creating one or more tags, you need to add those to Simulator Groups from the Simulator Groups tab.

> **Note**
>
> You can use the following characters in the expression for dynamic replacement:
>
> h — Current hour
>
> m — Current minute
>
> s — Current second
>
> r — Current row number in the resultset
>
> n — Total number of rows in the resultset
>
> You can also use the mathematical functions such as rand(), sin(), cos(), log(), and so on in the expressions for mathematical calculations.
>
> Example expressions are as follow:
>
> $((m \times 60 + s) \times (0.0097 + (rand()/100))) + 815$
>
> $250 + 250 \times sin((r \% 60) \times pi / 30)$

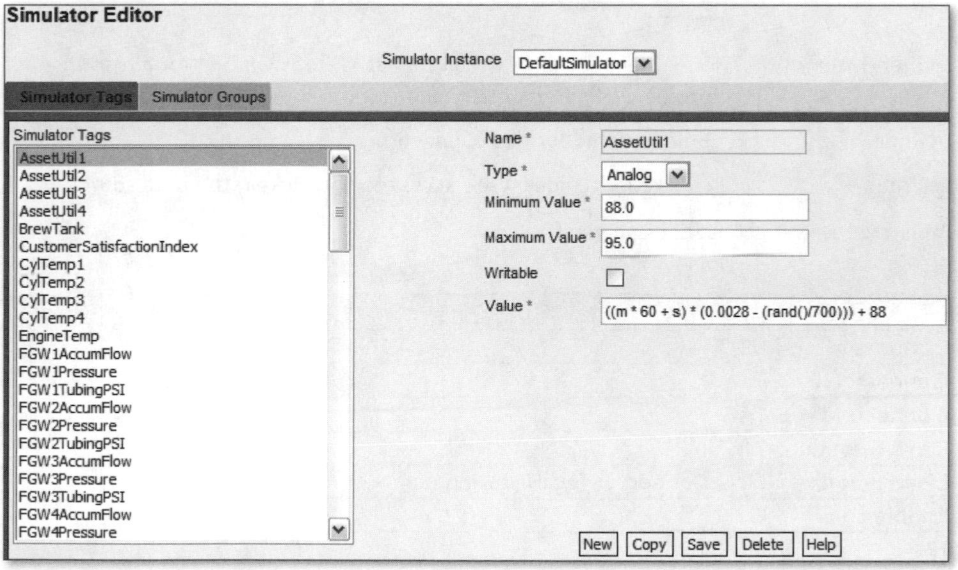

Figure 3.5 Simulator Editor

3.1.9   Universal Data Connector

The Universal Data Connector (UDC) is a connector framework that enables access to the plant systems having Object Linking and Embedding for Process Control (OPC) or OLEDB interfaces via a Universal Data Server (UDS). The UDS can be user-developed and is not restricted to any programming language. The UDC and the UDS talk to each other through TCP/IP sockets, and the UDS in turn talks to the data source using a common protocol understood by both the data source and the UDS. Generally using UDS you can connect to any plant system that provides an OPC or OLEDB interface. You can use this versatile connector to connect to various plant systems such as OSIsoft PI Historian, GE Fanuc Proficy Historian, and so on to retrieve or write the tag data—temperature or pressure reading, motor speed, material flow rate, or any such process information that you might need for the composite application in SAP MII. You need to configure the parameters in the UDC as explained in Table 3.12 and as shown in Figure 3.6.

Property	Description
IP	The hostname or the IP address of the machine where the UDS is running.
Port	The port of the remote machine where the UDS is listening for requests.
QueryTimeout	Time in seconds after which the UDC stops waiting for a response from the UDS after a query and returns.
Name	A unique name for this connection.
Writable	If checked, provides write access to the tags on the data source.

Table 3.12 Universal Data Configurations

Name	Value
Connector	UDC
ConnectorID	
ConnectorType	TAG
DaysRetention	7
Description	UDC Connector for iHistorian
Enabled	F
IP	localhost
MaxRetryCount	5
Name	UDC
Port	8086
QueryTimeout	60
RetryInterval	60000
ServerPackage	com.sap.xmii.Illuminator.connectors.UDC
Writable	false

Figure 3.6 Universal Data Connector Configurations

After a connection to the UDS has been established using the UDC, you can create Tag Queries in the SAP MII Workbench to access data from the data source. The UDS 4.0 provided by SAP supports three types of connection protocol:

▸ **SAP MII OLE DB UDS:** Mircosoft's OLE DB stands for Object Linking and Embedding Database. It is a COM-based API that exposes data from a variety of sources in a uniform manner. You can use SAP MII OLE DB UDS to connect to any data source that supports this Microsoft standard, for example, MS Access or MS Excel data sources.

▸ **SAP MII OPC DA UDS:** OPC stands for Object Linking and Embedding for Process Control. It is a set of industrial standards maintained by the OPC Foundation. This standard aims to unify the way real-time manufacturing plant-floor data is obtained from devices by different manufacturers. OPC DA stands for OPC Data Access. You can use the SAP MII OPC DA UDS to retrieve real-time data from Data Acquisition and Control (DAC) devices like Programmable Logic Controllers (PLCs) and Human Machine Interfaces (HMI) that talk to machines on the shop floor and follow the OPC standard.

▸ **SAP MII OPC HDA UDS:** OPC HDA stands for OPC Historical Data Access. You can use it to retrieve and analyze archived process data from Process Historians and databases. You can connect to devices that support the OPC HDA standard using this UDS.

You need to configure a connection instance in the UDS Admin Console for each plant system or data source you want to connect to. To create a new connection instance in UDS click on the FILE • ADD menu or the Add UDS Instance icon in the toolbar in the UDS Admin Console. Specify a name of the instance, select the type of instance (for example, OLEDB UDS, OPC DA UDS, or OPC HDA UDS) and specify a port number to which the UDS will send data to SAP MII via the UDC. You can specify the port number between 0 - 65535, but check if the specified port is not already in use by other applications in that server. Do not use standard ports like 80 (HTTP Server), 23 (Telnet), 21 (FTP), and so on, and you should choose ports above 1024. After the instance is added, you can specify the OPC server or the connection string for the plant data source. For OPC DA UDS and OPC HDA UDS, click on the Browse (...) button beside the OPC Server property in the configuration window on the right (Figure 3.7). That opens a pop-up window where you can specify the server hostname or IP address and can browse and select the OPC server running on it. For an OLEDB UDS instance, click on the Browse button next to the Connection String property and specify the corresponding data link in the pop-up window. For MS Excel and MS Access data sources, select Microsoft Jet 4.0 OLE DB Provider in the Provider tab in the Data Link properties window. Specify the file location in the Connection tab. For MS Access specify the authentication information if required; for MS Excel the authentication is ignored. You can specify the access permission as Read or ReadWrite in the Advanced tab. For MS Excel you need to specify the following property in the All tab in the Extended Property field: "Excel 8.0;HDR=YES" if the MS Excel file contains header row; otherwise you should specify it as "Excel 8.0;HDR=NO".

Also you need to specify the Threading Model property for the UDS instance as STA for connecting to an MS Excel data source.

You can also connect to AspenTech InfoPlus.21, OSIsoft PI Historian, GE Fanuc Proficy Historian, and so on using the OLEDB interface. For connecting to AspenTech InfoPlus.21, first create a Data Source Name (DSN) in the ODBC Data Source Administrator in the Windows control panel. Add a new System DSN and select AspenTech SQLplus as the data source type. Specify the name of the DSN and the hostname and port of the server where the SQLplus service is running. Also uncheck all the checkboxes in the SQLplus Advanced Setup window by clicking on the Advanced button. Now create a new OLEDB UDS instance in the UDS Admin Console. Click on the Browse button beside the Connection String property and specify the DSN in the Connection tab of the Data Link configuration window.

For connecting to OSIsoft PI and GE Fanuc Proficy Historian, select PI OLEDB Provider and iHistorian OLEDB, respectively, on the Provider tab in the Data Link configuration window for the Connection String property in the UDS instance. In the Connection tab of the Data Link property window you need to provide the location of the data source and the authentication information.

The UDS Admin Console with few sample configurations is shown in Figure 3.7.

You can configure aliases for the tags available in the data source in the UDS instance without any modification in the backend system. This configuration might be useful when you want to group or create new tags for the data query based on the tags available in the plant systems. To configure the tag alias, select the UDS instance in the UDS Admin Console and click on Alias Configuration from the Tools • Configure Aliases menu or the toolbar icon. To view the tags in the backend system, click on the menu UDS • Browse in the Alias Configuration window. In the pop-up selection window you can specify a filter mask and can select the option to generate the alias file. Selecting the option to generate an alias file creates the tag aliases from the data source to the UDS. Then you can view and modify the tag aliases under the Root node. Save the alias configuration after you are finished and specify the UDS instance Mode property as Alias with Dynamic Data under the Cache category in the UDS instance configuration window. You can query the alias tags by creating a Tag Query using the SAP MII Workbench. After the configuration is complete, select the UDS instance and click on the SERVER • START menu option or the Start UDS Instance icon on the toolbar. This action starts the UDS instance acquiring data from the underlying data source. You can execute queries only on a running UDS instance.

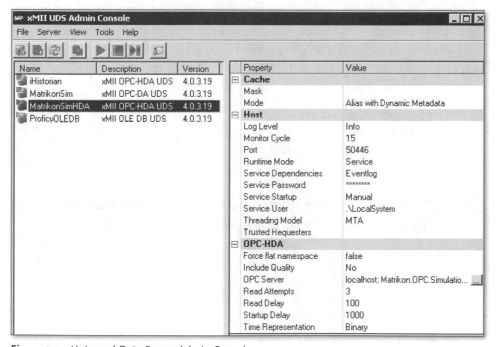

Figure 3.7 Universal Data Server Admin Console

3.1.10 Virtual Connector

You can use Virtual connectors in SAP MII to connect to a Data Server configured in another remote SAP MII installation. SAP MII provides six types of virtual connectors — VirtualAlarm, VirtualIDBC, VirtualOLAP, VirtualTAG, VirtualXML, and VirtualXacute — any of which you can configure as Data Servers. These correspond to the Alarm, IDBC, OLAP, TAG, XML, and Xacute connectors, respectively, and behave in the exact same way. The Virtual connector is described in detail in Section 9.5 Using Virtual Servers for Communication between SAP MII Servers.

3.1.11 Xacute Connector

The Xacute connector is an internal system connector for SAP MII that you can use to execute Business Logic Transactions as data queries (called Xacute queries) created using the Workbench. You always have a default Xacute Data Server configuration named XacuteConnector available along with the standard installation of SAP MII. You can use this default configuration for creating and executing Xacute queries. Only the Description and AutoBind property are modifiable in the Xacute Data Server configuration. If the AutoBind checkbox is checked, then the SAP MII session variables are automatically mapped to the transaction that has transaction properties with the same name. This is explained in detail with examples in Section 9.6 Autobind and Session Variables in SAP MII.

Now that you have learned about the Data Server configuration to retrieve and update plant data, it's time to look at the Message Services configurations, which you can use to receive data from enterprise systems.

3.2 Message Services: Synchronizing the Manufacturing Plant Floor with the Enterprise

Data captured and generated in the enterprise systems (for example, SAP ERP), such as production orders, material inventory data, and work center capacity information, might need to be synchronized with the manufacturing plant floor for detail execution planning and actual execution. You can synchronize this data with the manufacturing plant floor systems in two ways:

▶ **Data Pull:** The manufacturing integration systems pull the data from the enterprise systems on a need basis.

▶ **Data Push:** The data is pushed by the enterprise when required, automatically based on certain events or by user actions.

The pull-based method mostly executes RFC or Enterprise services provided by enterprise systems from SAP MII using the SAP JCo, SAP JRA and WebService action blocks and is explained in details in Chapter 6. The push-based method is often considered necessary because it enables the enterprise system to plan and send data to the plant floor when required. In addition, changes in master data, inventory data, or manufacturing order release can trigger the synchronization of data.

The Message Services module enables users to receive data sent by the enterprise systems. Message Services is one of the modules in SAP MII 12.0 that has been re-engineered and enhanced with many new features for robustness and scalability. The IDoc Listener in SAP MII 11.5 was the predecessor of Message Services in the current release.

Message Services provides the functionality to synchronize enterprise data, such as data from SAP ERP to SAP MII, by asynchronous data transfer. You can use the Message Services to receive IDoc and RFC messages from SAP systems and also XML messages by HTTP Post from any enterprise systems. The messages received in SAP MII are buffered into the system database, and you can either process them automatically according to predefined rules or categorize them for ad-hoc processing. The architecture of Message Services is shown in Figure 3.8.

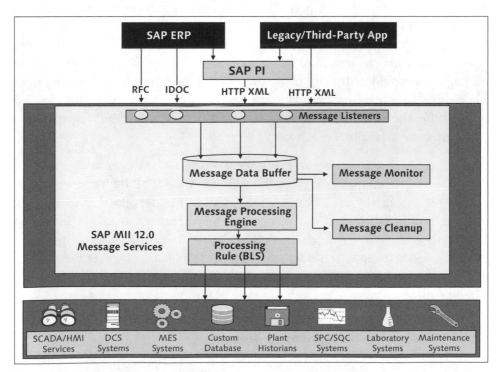

Figure 3.8 Message Services in SAP MII

The main functionalities provided by Message Services in SAP MII are as follows:

- Receive IDoc, RFC, and XML messages by HTTP Post
- Process messages according to processing rule or category
- Monitor buffered messages
- Clean up buffered messages

You can configure message listeners in SAP MII to receive RFC or IDoc messages from enterprise systems asynchronously. The message listeners use SAP Java Connector (SAP JCo), and you need to configure different instances of it for each sender system. The message listener for XML messages by HTTP Post is predefined and preconfigured in SAP MII, and you can use it to receive messages from any system which can send XML messages using HTTP Post.

After configuring the message listeners, you can use the processing rule editor to define rules for messages received from different sender systems. A processing rule can either process the message data automatically or assign the message to a category for ad-hoc processing. Whenever a message is received by the message listener in SAP MII, it is first saved in the database for buffering and then, if a predefined processing rule exists for it, processed automatically. The messages received and buffered in SAP MII can also be deleted automatically by defining message cleanup rules. The message cleanup rules run periodically for conditionally deleting messages from the database. You can monitor the messages received by the different message listeners from the Message Monitor and re-process or delete them individually if required.

You can use Message Services in many scenarios in SAP MII composite applications. One such example is receiving the LOIPRO IDoc for Production Orders or control recipe data (by RFC) from SAP ERP. SAP MII buffers the data as an XML message in the database, and you can use a predefined rule or an ad-hoc processing rule to parse the message data, extract the relevant information, and populate in a custom database table. You can then query this table and populate the production operator dashboard developed in SAP MII, from which the user can view the schedule for a workcenter and subsequently perform order confirmation.

3.2.1 Configuring the Message Listeners

The message listeners in SAP MII are of two types: listeners for RFC and IDoc messages, which you can configure for each sender system, and the HTTP XML message listener, which is a single preconfigured listener for receiving XML messages sent by HTTP Post from any system.

The message listener services are grouped under the menu category Message Services in the SAP MII main menu. Click on this menu to configure the message listeners.

Initially, you find only a single preconfiguration, for the message listener named XMIIMESSAGELISTENER, as shown in Figure 3.9. This is the preconfigured message listener for receiving XML messages by HTTP Post. You cannot delete, disable, or copy this message listener configuration, and it comes along with the standard installation of SAP MII 12.0. You can, however, modify the Description. To send HTTP XML messages to SAP MII, the message needs to be sent to the following URL using HTTP Post as payload XML:

http://<host>:<port>/XMII/Illuminator?service=WSMessageListener&mode=WSMessage ListenerServer&NAME=<UniqueMessageName>&IllumLoginName=<username>&IllumL oginPassword=<password>&Content-Type=text/xml

Replace the *<host>* and *<port>* in the URL by the hostname and HTTP port, respectively, of the MII server. Replace the *<UniqueMessageName>* by the name of the message as specified in the processing rule for the message. If you do not specify a value, the root element name of the XML message is considered the message name, and the processing rule is determined accordingly.

Message Listeners		
Name		
XMIIMESSAGELISTENER	Name *	XMIIMESSAGELISTENER
	Description	xMII Webservice Message Listener
	Enabled	☑
	Status	Running
		New Save Copy Delete Stop Server Summary Help

Figure 3.9 HTTP XML Message Listener Configurations

You can configure as many RFC and IDoc message listeners as required. To do so, click on New in the Message Listeners screen. A new configuration screen appears. Specify the unique Name and optional Description at the general properties section at the top. Deselecting the Enabled checkbox enables the user to define a message listener configuration, but not activate it for use. You can activate or deactivate any message listener configuration as and when required by checking or unchecking the Enabled checkbox, respectively. The Status property displays the current state of the listener. When you configure a new listener, the default status is always Stopped. An existing listener can be started or stopped at any point of time; a stopped message listener cannot receive any messages from the sender systems. The two tabs below the general configuration section in the screen, specify the Server Properties and Client Properties. These are the system details of the sender system required by SAP JCo. The following properties, as seen in Table 3.13, are present in the Server Properties tab.

Property	Description
Gwhost	Hostname for the gateway.
Gwserv	Service name for the gateway.
Progid	Program ID of the server.
Trace	Determines whether the RFC trace is enabled (value of 1) or disabled (value of 0).
Params	Arbitrary parameters for RFC library.
snc_myname	Name of the Secure Network Communication (SNC) interface.
snc_qop	Security level for the SNC interface. Possible values are 1-9.
snc_lib	Path to the SNC library.
Unicode	Determines whether the system connects in Unicode mode (value of 1) or non-Unicode mode (value of 0).
max_startup_delay	Maximum number of seconds that should pass before the server starts.

Table 3.13 Server Properties for Message Listener

Of the server properties listed in Table 3.13, Gwhost, Gwserv, Progid and Unicode are mandatory for the configuration, as shown in Figure 3.10. You can obtain the Gwhost and Gwserv (gateway host and service, respectively) values from the corresponding sender systems, such as SAP ERP, while creating the RFC destinations there. The Progid (Program ID) parameter should be a unique value, which you need to specify in both the message listener configuration in SAP MII and in the sender system's RFC destination configuration. Specify the Unicode property value as 1 if the sender system is Unicode enabled. Leave the other properties blank if they are not required.

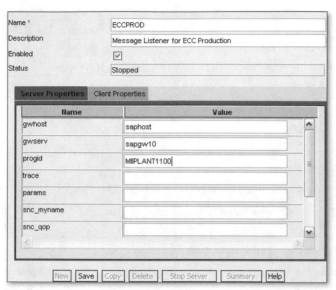

Figure 3.10 Server Properties Configuration for Message Listener

In the Client Properties tab, specify the logon details of the sender system. The properties in Table 3.14 are available as client properties.

Property	Description
Client	Client number of sender system.
User	Username.
alias_user	Alias name for the user.
passwd	Password for the user.
Lang	Language for the user.
Sysnr	SAP system number.
Ashost	SAP application server.
mshost	SAP message server.
gwhost	Gateway host.
gwserv	Gateway service.
r3name	SAP system name.
Group	Group of application servers.
tpname	Program ID of external server program.

Table 3.14 Client Properties for Message Listener

Property	Description
Tphost	Host of external server program.
Type	Type of remote host. Enter 3 for an SAP system and E for an external system.
Trace	Enter 1 to use the RFC trace.
codepage	Initial code page.
abap_debug	Enter 1 to use Advanced Business Application Programming (ABAP) debugging.
use_sapgui	Determines whether you want to use a remote SAP GUI.
Getsso2	Enter 1 to get a Single Sign-On ticket after logging on.
mysapsso2	Determines whether you want to use the specified SAP cookie version 2 as the logon ticket.
x509cert	Determines whether you want to use the specified X509 certificate as the logon ticket.
Lcheck	Enter 1 to enable a logon check.
grt_data	Adds data to the GUI.
use_guihost	Host to which you want to redirect the remote GUI.
use_guiserv	Service to which you want to redirect the remote GUI.
use_guiprogid	Program ID of the server which starts the remote GUI.
snc_mode	Secure Network Communication (SNC) mode.
snc_partnername	Partner name for SNC.
snc_qop	Security level for SNC.
snc_myname	SNC name that overrides the default SNC partner name.
snc_lib	Path to the SNC library.
Dest	SAP ERP Central Component destination.
saplogon_id	String defined for SAPLOGON on a 32-bit Windows system.
extiddata	Data for external authentication.
extidtype	Type of external authentication.
idle_timeout	Amount of time that passes before an idle connection drops.
Dsr	Specify 1 to enable Distributed Statistics Record (DSR) support.

Table 3.14 Client Properties for Message Listener (Cont.)

Of the preceding properties, the following are mandatory (Figure 3.11):

▶ **Client:** SAP ERP/sender system's client number

▶ **User:** Login user for the sender system

▶ **Passwd:** Password of the login user

▶ **Lang:** Language of the login user

▶ **Sysnr:** System number of the SAP ERP/sender system

▶ **Ashost:** Application server hostname of the SAP ERP/sender system if no load balancing is available

▶ **Mshost:** Message server host name of the SAP ERP/sender system if load balancing is available

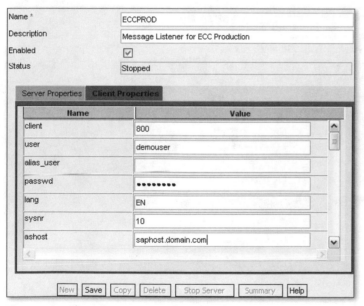

Figure 3.11 Client Properties Configuration for Message Listener

After the details of the listener are specified, save the configuration by clicking the Save button, and a new entry is created in the list at the right of the screen. When saved, a message listener is stopped by default; to start the message listener and to receive RFC and IDoc messages from the sender/SAP ERP system, click on the Start Server button.

The message listener is started successfully if the configuration is correct. Clicking on the Summary button displays the message listener property details. Now, you need a few more configurations to complete the configuration. First, log in to the SAP ERP or the sender system, and open the RFC destination configuration from the following SAP easy access menu: SAP MENU • TOOLS • ADMINISTRATION • ADMINISTRATION • NETWORK • RFC DESTINATION (Transaction code: SM59).

Here a new RFC destination of type TCP/IP needs to be created for the SAP MII message listener. Select TCP/IP and click on New. In the resulting screen, specify an RFC Destination name, the Type as T (TCP/IP), and an optional Description. Select the Registered Server Program option under the Technical Settings tab (seen in Figure 3.12) and specify the same Program ID used in the message listener configuration.

Figure 3.12 New TCP/IP RFC Destination Configuration – General Properties

Also specify the Gateway Host and Gateway Service (Figure 3.13). You can find this information in the Gateway Monitor transaction (Transaction code: SMGW) under the menu option PARAMETERS • DISPLAY.

```
CPI-C Timeout
  ⊙ Default Gateway Value
  ○ Specify Timeout              60    Defined Value in Seconds

Gateway Options
  Gateway Host      saphost                              Delete
  Gateway service   sapgw10
```

Figure 3.13 New TCP/IP RFC Destination Configuration – Gateway Properties

If the system is Unicode enabled, select the Unicode option under the MDMP and Unicode tab.

After you have completed your configuration, save it, and then test it by clicking on the Connection Test button. If the test fails, check the configurations of SAP ERP, SAP MII, and the message listener state.

You can now send RFC data as an asynchronous Transaction RFC (tRFC) call from SAP ERP to SAP MII. However, for sending IDocs, a few more configurations are required. First you need to define a logical system in SAP ERP, and then you need to configure the corresponding Partner Port and Partner Profile, along with the model distribution view. To create a new logical system, open the area menu for IDoc/Application Link Enabling (ALE) configuration (Transaction code: SALE) and click on the Define Logical System option from the menu path BASIC SETTINGS • LOGICAL SYSTEMS • DEFINE LOGICAL SYSTEM.

In the customization table, click on New Entries, specify the new logical system name and description, and save the data (Figure 3.14).

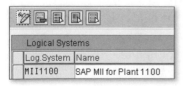

Figure 3.14 New Entry for Logical Systems

Now you need to create a Partner Port. Open the Partner Port Maintenance transaction from the following menu path: SAP MENU • TOOLS • ALE • ALE ADMINISTRATION • RUNTIME SETTINGS • PORT MAINTENANCE (Transaction Code: WE21). You can select the Transaction RFC option from the right menu and create a new Partner Port by clicking the New icon on the toolbar. From there, specify a port name (or use the Generate Port Name option), description, and the RFC destination name created previously (Figure 3.15). Be sure to save the configuration.

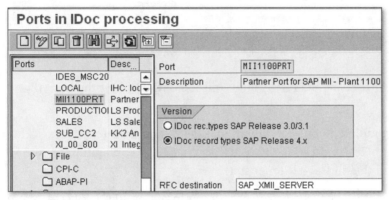

Figure 3.15   Partner Port Configuration

Next you need to create a new Partner Profile using the Partner Port just created. Open the partner profile menu from the following menu path: SAP MENU • TOOLS • ALE • ALE ADMINISTRATION • RUNTIME SETTINGS • PARTNER PROFILES (Transaction Code: WE20). Select Partner Type LS (Logical System) and click on the New icon to create a new configuration. Specify the logical system as the Partner No., and save the data. From there, click on the + icon under the Outbound Parameters option to add a new outbound IDoc message type.

Specify the Partner Type as LS, and the appropriate IDoc message type and Basic Type. In the example shown in Figure 3.16, the LOIPRO IDoc message type has been used. Specify the Partner Port in the Receiver Port field. Also, select the Output Mode as Transfer IDoc Immediately if single IDoc messages need to be sent. Otherwise, select Collect IDocs option and save the configuration.

Partner profiles: Outbound parameters

Partner No.	MII1100	SAP MII for Plant 1100
Partn.Type	LS	Logical system
Partner Role		

Message Type	LOIPRO	Production order
Message code		
Message function		☐ Test

Outbound Options | Message Control | Post Processing: Permitted Agent | Tele... ◄

Receiver port	MII1100PRT 🖉 Transactional RFC	Partner Port for SAP MII - Plant 11
Pack. Size	1	
☐ Queue Processing		

Output Mode
- ◉ Transfer IDoc Immed.   Output Mode   2
- ○ Collect IDocs

IDoc Type

Basic type	LOIPRO01	Master production order
Extension		
View		

☑ Cancel Processing After Syntax Error

| Seg. release in IDoc type | | Segment Appl. Rel. | |

Figure 3.16 Add Message Type to Partner Profile

The final Partner Profile configuration is as shown in Figure 3.17. As with the Partner Profile, you can add as many IDoc messages as required. In Figure 3.17, another IDoc message, LOIROU, has been added.

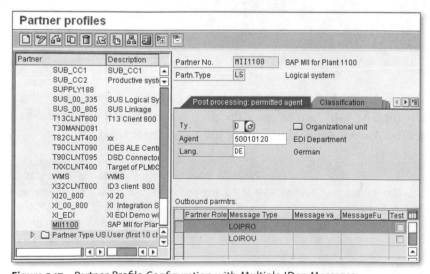

Figure 3.17 Partner Profile Configuration with Multiple IDoc Messages

Next you need to maintain a distribution model and view for sending the IDoc messages. Open the area menu SALE and select the following: IDoc Interface/ALE • Modeling and Implementing Business Processes • Maintain Distribution Model and Distribute Views. Click on the Create Model View icon on the toolbar to create a new distribution model for the IDoc messages.

You can specify short text, a technical name, and the validity date range for the distribution model. Save the distribution model by clicking the Save icon on the toolbar, click on Add Message Type to add new IDoc messages, and select the model view.

Specify the following when you add a new message type:

▶ The logical system as a sender system maintained for the current SAP ERP system

▶ The receiver system as the SAP MII system created as a logical system

▶ The IDoc type as message type

Repeat the preceding steps to add more message types to the distribution model.

The final configuration for the ALE Distribution model is illustrated in Figure 3.18.

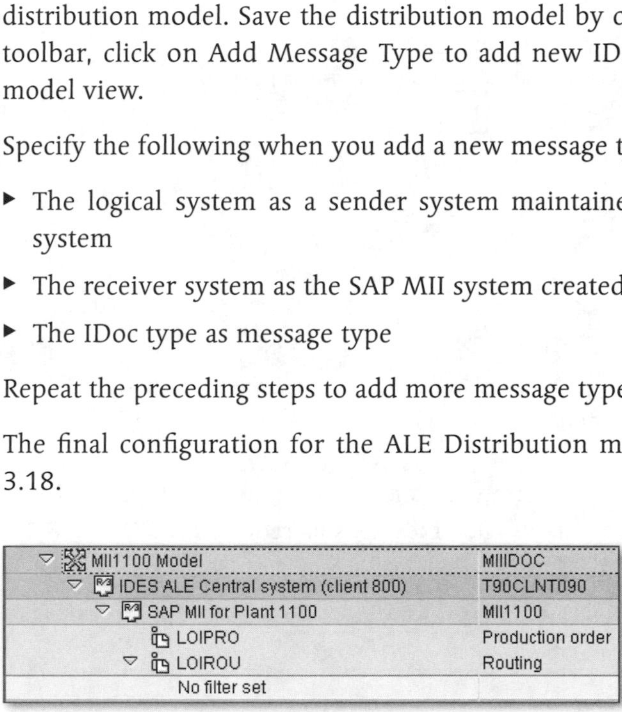

Figure 3.18 ALE Distribution Model Configurations

The message listener and ALE configuration are now complete. Any message (RFC/IDoc) sent by the SAP ERP system using the preceding configuration is received and buffered by SAP MII where the message listener is configured.

> **Note**
>
> You can send IDocs from SAP ERP to SAP MII using standard SAP transactions such as POIT, POIM, and so on or by executing function modules to create IDocs. You can also send RFC data to SAP MII by executing it as tRFC or from standard SAP transactions such as Control Recipe Monitor (CO53). You can execute tRFC by ABAP statements as follows:

```
CALL FUNCTION 'RFC_FUNCTION_MOD_NAME'
          IMPORTING
               PARAM1 = VAL1
               PARAM2 = VAL2
          TABLES
               TABLE1 = TAB1
          DESTINATION 'MII_RFC_DESTINATION'
     IN BACKGROUND TASK.
```

3.2.2 Configuring the Processing Rules for Messages

Processing rules in Message Services are defined to process messages automatically when received from an external sender system. The processing rules are existing Business Logic Transactions that you can use to process the message data received or to send down the message data to manufacturing plant-floor systems. The processing rule is defined for each combination of a message listener and a message name. You can define two types of processing for the messages: rule-based and category-based.

In rule-based processing, you need to specify a Business Logic Transaction as the processing rule. In category-based processing, you need only to assign the message to a category (no automatic processing is done). This means that when a specific message is received by the message listener, it is buffered into the database, and the corresponding processing rule is searched. If a Business Logic Transaction is found as the processing rule, then that transaction is executed, passing the XML message data as an input parameter as specified in the processing rule. If a category is found for the processing rule, then the message is buffered into the database and assigned to a category. You can use the message category to logically group messages for ad-hoc processing. You can use the message data and other details (for example, received timestamp, message listener, message name, and so on) in the Message Services actions in Business Logic Services (BLS), where the messages can be selected for a specific category as well.

For example, you can use rule-based processing when you receive production order details from SAP ERP. SAP MII sends them to the MES for execution, using a BLS as a processing rule. You can use category-based processing where SAP MII doesn't send the messages to any system itself, but exposes a Business Logic Transaction as a Web service. An external system can execute as a Web service and read the messages received and buffered in SAP MII.

To configure the processing rule, open the Processing Rule Editor menu from the Message Services menu category in SAP MII. If no processing rule has been created before, then the left column does not contain any items. Click on New to create a new processing rule. Specify a unique rule name and an optional description of the rule. From the Server Name dropdown, you can select an already-configured message listener. In the Message Name field, select the specific message name (IDoc/RFC name) or an asterisk (*) for any messages. Specifying an asterisk in the Message Name applies the same rule for any IDoc/RFC messages received by the specified message listener. In Message Type, select the All, RFC, or IDoc option if a message listener other than XMIIMESSAGELISTENER is selected as the Server Name. Message Type All signifies that the rule applies to both RFC and IDoc messages. For XMIIMESSAGELISTENER, only the Web service option is enabled, because that listener receives only XML messages sent by HTTP Post. A sample configuration of the processing rule is shown in Figure 3.20.

Processing Type is the most important option in the processing rule and specifies whether the received message is processed by a Business Logic Transaction or simply assigned to a category for ad-hoc processing. If you have selected the Transaction option, then you need to select a Business Logic Transaction (Figure 3.19) that is already available in the server from the corresponding lookup. The selected Business Logic Transaction should ideally have an input parameter of type XML.

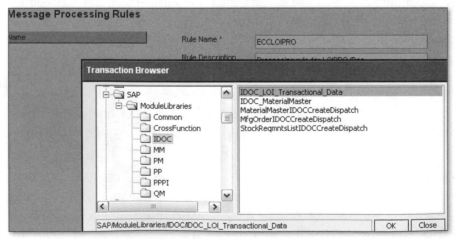

Figure 3.19 Transaction Selection in Processing Rule Editor

After you select the BLS Transaction, all the input parameters of the selected transaction are displayed in the Parameters listbox, and each parameter has a checkbox beside its parameter name. You can check the parameter where the message XML needs to be passed while executing the rule. A text ReceivedMessageXML (Figure 3.20) appears in the Value column. This signifies the XML data of the received message is passed to this input parameter of the transaction while executing it. For the other parameters, you can specify any hard-coded value, if required.

> **Note**
>
> You need to have a predefined BLS Transaction for configuring the transaction-based processing rule. Inside the BLS Transaction you should model the logic to accept the XML message as an input transaction property and process it as required. You do not need to update the status of the message or read the message from the buffer using the Message Service action blocks in BLS transaction because it is passed on as an input parameter to the transaction. After the BLS Transaction is executed, the status of the message gets automatically updated.

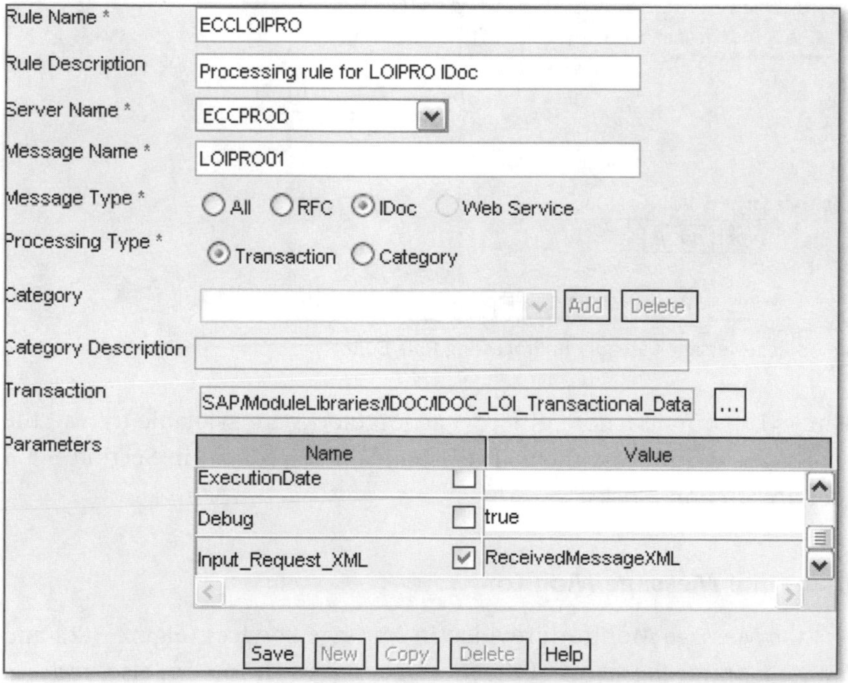

Figure 3.20 Setting Message as Input Parameter of Transaction in Processing Rule Editor

You can save the processing rule by clicking on the Save button to finish editing. A new processing rule is created, and its name appears in the left column of the screen.

To add a category instead of a transaction, you can select the Processing Type as Category and click on the Add button on the Category field (Figure 3.21), or select an existing category from the Category dropdown list. If you create a new category once, it is available in any other processing rule. You can also assign messages received by different message listeners to the same category.

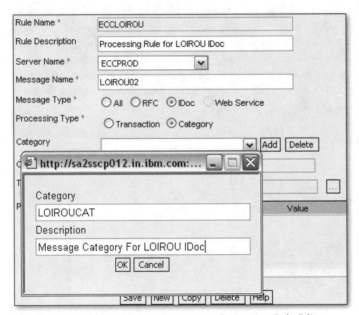

Figure 3.21 Adding Message Category in Processing Rule Editor

In the Business Logic Transaction, different action blocks are available to read the buffered messages and process them. This is explained in detail in Section 6.4.8 Message Services Action Blocks.

3.2.3 Using the Message Monitor

You can use the Message Monitor provided in Message Services (Figure 3.22 and Figure 3.23) to monitor the status of the messages received. You can also perform additional functions, such as reprocessing and deleting messages. The Message Monitor menu provides the monitoring options for all types of messages; also only failed messages and messages without rules are displayed via the two quick-links menus of those names.

The default selection options in the Message Monitor display all messages received by any message listener for the last 24 hours. To filter the message display, you can use the following selection criteria:

- **Server Name:** Select the specific message listener from the dropdown. Selecting an asterisk signifies all message listeners defined in MII.

- **Message Type:** Select specific message types such as IDoc, RFC, and Web service to display only those types of messages.

- **Message Name:** Select specific message names (for example, RFC name, IDoc name, and so on) to display only those types of messages.

- **Message Category:** Select message categories created in the processing rules to display only messages assigned to that category. An asterisk signifies all categories or no categories.

- **From Date:** You can specify the selection start timestamp.

- **To Date:** You can specify the selection end timestamp.

- **Processing Status:** You can select one or more processing statuses for the messages as required. The processing statuses of the messages can be as follows:

  - **Received:** Messages received and buffered by a message listener but not yet processed.

  - **Running:** Processing for the message is running (that is, the BLS specified in the rule is getting executed).

  - **Categorized:** The message has been assigned to a category as specified in the processing rule.

  - **No Rule:** No processing rule has been defined for the message listener and the message name combination.

  - **Failure:** The processing of the message has failed; exception has been logged.

▶ **Success:** The message has been processed successfully according to the processing rule specified.

▶ **Row Count:** Number of messages retrieved by the search in ascending order of date and time.

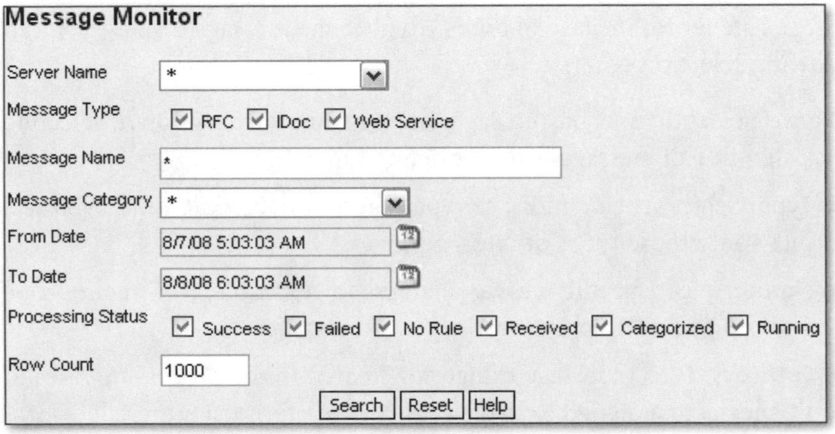

Figure 3.22 Message Monitor Selection Options

The messages displayed in the Message Monitor (Figure 3.23) are displayed with the corresponding details of status, message listener name, message type, message name, message category, received timestamp, and processing timestamp. The statuses of the messages are displayed with a colored icon; when you click the icon, the system displays the status text and a description. The messages successfully processed by transaction-based rules are displayed with a checkered flag icon, categorized messages with a green flag icon, no-rule messages with a white flag icon, and the messages for which the transaction-based rule processing has failed are displayed with a red flag icon. Message category is displayed only if a message category is specified in the corresponding processing rule for the message.

You can select any message displayed in the monitor by checking the checkbox at the header row, and you can perform functions like deleting or reprocessing by selecting one or more messages. Reprocessing can be done for any message, especially for messages with a failure or no rule status. Note that you cannot reprocess a message by transaction-based rule that was originally categorized.

Message Monitor

Number of records found 12

	Status	Server Name	Message Type	Message Name	Message Category	Received Time	Processing Time
☐	🚩	ECCPROD	IDoc	LOIROU02	ROUTINGPLANT1100	2008-08-08 06:29:08.573	
☐	🚩	ECCPROD	IDoc	LOIROU02	ROUTINGPLANT1100	2008-08-08 06:29:10.485	
☐	🚩	ECCPROD	IDoc	LOIPRO01		2008-08-08 06:31:15.8	2008-08-08 06:31:25.78
☐	🚩	ECCPROD	IDoc	LOIPRO01		2008-08-08 06:31:15.945	2008-08-08 06:31:25.932
☐	🚩	ECCPROD	IDoc	LOIPRO01		2008-08-08 06:31:16.03	2008-08-08 06:36:15.769
☐	🚩	ECCPROD	IDoc	LOIPRO01		2008-08-08 06:31:16.15	2008-08-08 06:36:15.891
☐	🚩	ECCPROD	IDoc	LOIPRO01		2008-08-08 06:31:16.247	2008-08-08 06:36:16.021
☐	🚩	ECCPROD	IDoc	LOIPRO01		2008-08-08 06:31:16.783	2008-08-08 06:36:16.147
☐	🚩	ECCPROD	RFC	CONTROL_RECIPE_DOWNLOAD		2008-08-08 06:33:16.582	2008-08-08 06:33:25.51
☐	🚩	ECCPROD	RFC	CONTROL_RECIPE_DOWNLOAD		2008-08-08 06:33:33.098	2008-08-08 06:33:35.507
☐	⇒	ECCPROD	IDoc	LOIPRO01		2008-08-08 06:36:45.702	
☐	⇒	ECCPROD	IDoc	LOIPRO01		2008-08-08 06:36:45.852	

| Delete | Reprocess | Refresh |

Figure 3.23 Message Monitor Display

> **Warning**
>
> Deleting messages permanently deletes them from the SAP MII database. They cannot be retrieved again.

Two quick-links provide for displaying messages with a Failed or No Rule status. In these Message Monitors (Figure 3.24 and Figure 3.25), you can specify only the message listener name and the message type. An asterisk (*) specifies any message listener. You can still perform the usual functions, such as deleting and reprocessing of messages.

Messages Without Rules

Server Name [* ▾]

Message Type ☑ RFC ☑ IDoc ☑ Web Service

[Search]

Number of records found 2

	Status	Server Name	Message Type	Message Name	Message Category	Received Time	Processing Time
☐	🚩	ECCPROD	RFC	CONTROL_RECIPE_DOWNLOAD		2008-08-08 06:33:16.582	2008-08-08 06:33:25.51
☐	🚩	ECCPROD	RFC	CONTROL_RECIPE_DOWNLOAD		2008-08-08 06:33:33.098	2008-08-08 06:33:35.507

| Delete | Reprocess | Refresh |

Figure 3.24 Messages Without Rule Monitor

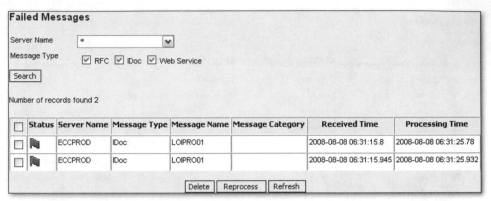

Figure 3.25 Failed Message Monitor

3.2.4 Configuring and Using the Message Cleanup Rules

Received messages are buffered in the MII database by default, regardless of whether or not any processing rule is defined for them. Messages buffered in SAP MII are not deleted automatically, but you can define message cleanup rules. The different parameters for message cleanup rules can be message listener, message type, message name, message age, and processing status. The message cleanup rules run periodically at a specific time interval, which you can specify in the System Administration menu.

To define a new message cleanup rule, open the Editor for Message Cleanup Rule (Figure 3.26) under the Message Services category. You can specify a unique message cleanup Rule Name and an optional Description. Also select the specific message listener from the Server Name dropdown, or select an asterisk for any message listener. Select the Message Type as IDoc, RFC, or Web service, and specify the Message Name as either a specific message name or with an asterisk for any message. In the Message Older Than property, specify the time in hours. Messages buffered in SAP MII longer than this specified time are deleted by the cleanup rule if other criteria are satisfied. You can specify the Processing Status property as either All, which signifies the messages having any of the statuses in the list will be deleted, or any of the usual message processing statuses available, except Running.

Message Cleanup Rule

Name		
DeleteLOIPRO		

Rule Name *   DeleteLOIPRO

Rule Description   Cleanup rule for LOIPRO IDoc

Server Name   ECCPROD

Message Type   ○ All   ○ RFC   ⊙ IDoc   ○ Web Service

Message Name *   LOIPRO01

Messages Older Than *   48   Hours

Processing Status   ○ All   ⊙ Success   ○ Failed   ○ Received   ○ No Rule   ○ Categorized

Enabled   ☑

[Save] [New] [Delete] [Help]

Figure 3.26   Editor for Message Cleanup Rule

You can view the message cleanup rules as a list from the Message Cleanup Rules menu shown in Figure 3.27. In addition, you can enable or disable and execute the cleanup rules from this view. Along with the other attributes of the cleanup rules such as Rule Name, Rule Description, Server Name, and Message Name, the list displays the last rule run status as the Processing Status and the rule activation status itself by a graphic icon in the Status column.

You can enable or disable one or more rules by clicking the Enabled or Disabled buttons. In addition, you can execute the selected rules on an ad-hoc basis by clicking on the Run Rule button. The last message cleanup rule runtime and the next message cleanup rule runtime are also displayed at the bottom of this view.

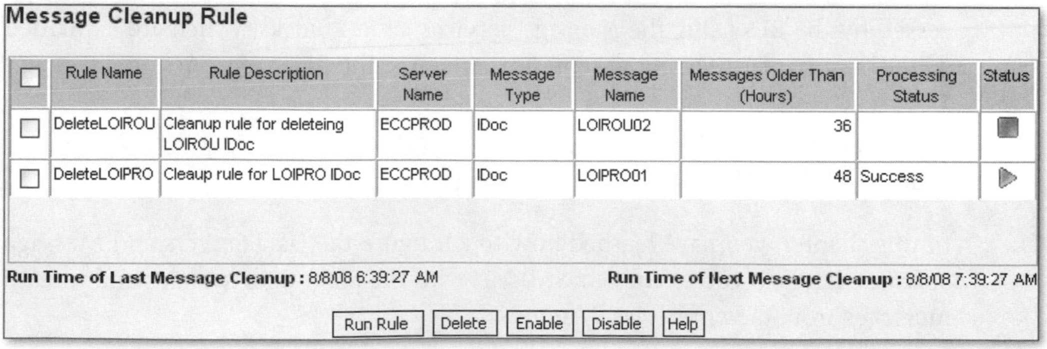

Message Cleanup Rule

	Rule Name	Rule Description	Server Name	Message Type	Message Name	Messages Older Than (Hours)	Processing Status	Status
☐	DeleteLOIROU	Cleanup rule for deleteing LOIROU IDoc	ECCPROD	IDoc	LOIROU02	36		▣
☐	DeleteLOIPRO	Cleaup rule for LOIPRO IDoc	ECCPROD	IDoc	LOIPRO01	48	Success	▷

Run Time of Last Message Cleanup : 8/8/08 6:39:27 AM   **Run Time of Next Message Cleanup :** 8/8/08 7:39:27 AM

[Run Rule] [Delete] [Enable] [Disable] [Help]

Figure 3.27   Message Cleanup Rules List

You can configure the message cleanup run interval from the System Administration menu under the System Management menu category by the RunInterval property. The run interval is the time interval by which all enabled message cleanup rules in the system are executed. By default, the run interval value is one hour (Figure 3.28), which you can change if required.

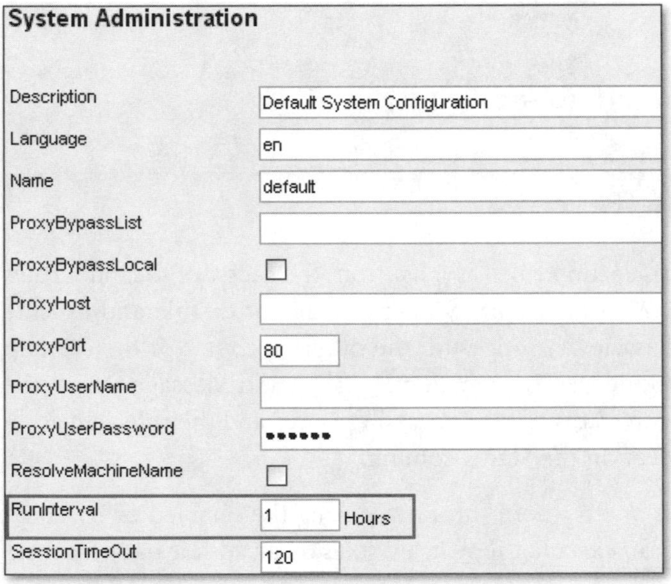

Figure 3.28 Message Cleanup Run Interval Configuration

The messages received by the message listeners can also be retrieved and processed by the BLS using the Message Services action blocks, which are explained further in Chapter 6 Business Logic Transactions: Intelligence in Action.

3.3 Summary

In this chapter, you have learned how to configure the Data Servers and Message Services that help you to connect SAP MII with the plant-floor systems and receive messages from the enterprise systems.

In the next chapter, you will learn about how to work with the SAP MII Workbench and create query templates using the configured Data Servers.

This chapter explains how to use the SAP MII Workbench to develop content and create different types of data queries to manage plant data.

4 Developing Composite Applications in SAP MII: The Basics

SAP MII provides a development and deployment framework that you can use to develop and run composite applications to integrate plant and enterprise systems and provide transactional dashboards and dashboards for monitoring and analytics at the manufacturing plant floor. In this chapter you learn how to use the SAP MII Workbench to create various SAP MII objects. You also learn how to create query templates that use different Data Servers to fetch relevant data from the plant floor.

4.1 Using the SAP MII Workbench

The SAP MII Workbench is an Integrated Development Environment (IDE) for developing and managing SAP MII development objects such as query templates, display templates, Business Logic Transactions, animated objects, and web pages that make use of those elements. It's the development environment for the composite applications you develop on SAP MII.

You can create the following objects using the SAP MII Workbench:

- Business Logic Transactions
- Animated graphics
- Query templates
  - Aggregate query
  - OLAP query
  - SQL query
  - Tag query

- ▶ Xacute query

- ▶ XML query

▶ Display templates

- ▶ iGrid

- ▶ iTicker

- ▶ iChart

- ▶ iSPCChart

- ▶ iBrowser

- ▶ iCommand

▶ Files

Though the other object types are very specific to SAP MII, you can use the File type to create a file with any extension. This is mostly utilized for web pages with .irpt or .html extensions and XML style sheets and image files used in the web pages. The other objects are explained in detail throughout the rest of this book.

The SAP MII Workbench is a Java Swing application that you can invoke using the SAP MII Workbench menu under Data Services. The client system needs Java Runtime Environment 1.4.2_08 or above preinstalled to use the Workbench. The development objects you create using the SAP MII Workbench are saved and executed on the server.

In the following sections you learn about the layout, content organization, security, and other important functionalities of the SAP MII Workbench.

4.1.1 Layout

The Workbench layout consists of a menu bar and a toolbar containing buttons for the most common functions. The lower section of the toolbar is split into two parts, with the one on the left being further divided into the Objects Browser and the Context Sensitive Configuration Options. The right side is the Modeling area, where you can create or edit the various SAP MII development objects (Figure 4.1).

The Object Browser, which also shows when you are saving or opening an object, displays information in a hierarchical fashion about the SAP MII objects that have been created by various users. The Catalog tab of the Object Browser displays contents such as display templates, query templates, Business Logic Transactions, and animated graphics, whereas the Web tab displays all the web contents, such as web pages (.irpt or .html files), image files, XML style sheets, and any other external file types that can be imported or created in the content catalog.

The Context Sensitive Configuration Options pane displays configuration options according to the object you are currently being edited in the Workbench. For query and display templates, it displays two tabs:

► **Template Categories:** Displays the configuration options for the type of display or query template selected.

► **Properties:** Displays basic metadata for the object, such as who created or modified it and when.

The first tab changes if you have an animated object open. In that case, the first tab is called Actions, and it displays the configuration properties for the object. Selecting a Business Logic Transaction displays three tabs: Action, Transaction, and Properties. The Action tab provides a list of action blocks that you can use in the transaction, collected together in logical groups according to the type of functionality they incorporate; for example, actions blocks such as the Tracer, XML Tracer, and the Event Logger are grouped under the Logging category. The Transaction tab gives you access to transaction properties and tasks that can also be performed using the menu bar.

The Modeling area, shown in Figure 4.1, is used for creating or modifying SAP MII development objects. Each object that is being worked on is opened in a new tab on the modeling area, with the name of the object as the name of the tab.

4.1.2 Content Organization and Management

SAP MII mandates that all content is created under a *project*. A project is a collection or logical grouping of development objects that you can organize under one or more folders. We recommend grouping each SAP MII development object type in a separate folder. For example, query templates should be saved in a folder of the same name, and web content should reside under the default web folder in the Web View.

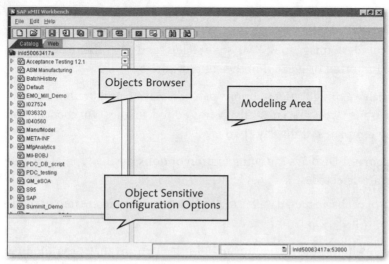

Figure 4.1 SAP MII Workbench

You can create a project manually by right-clicking anywhere on the Catalog or Web View and selecting New Project option from the context menu. The Catalog View is illustrated in Figure 4.2. You can also import project archives directly into the Workbench using the Projects configuration menu option, as explained in Section 2.2.9 Projects.

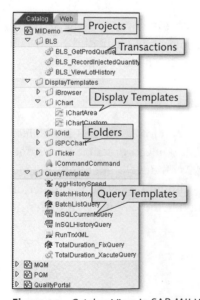

Figure 4.2 Catalog View in SAP MII Workbench

You can export content out of the Workbench by right-clicking on the appropriate content object and selecting the Export menu option. You can import existing external content into a project by right-clicking on the project name and selecting Import, which opens up a window enabling you to select the appropriate file.

> **Note**
>
> Web objects such as HTML/IRPT pages and image files are imported from the Web View of the Content Browser, not from the Catalog View.

To develop a SAP MII composite application start by making a new project and then placing folders under it to create the development objects as explained in the following sections and chapters.

4.1.3 Important Menu Items and Functionality

The SAP MII Workbench provides different menu options for various functionalities required for editing or modeling the development objects.

> **Note**
>
> All SAP MII content objects are stored in the SAP MII database, which is part of the Java Web application server (AS). Web content such as HTML, IRPT, and JSP files are also copied with the full hierarchy of the project, in a folder called CM, which is located in the context root of the SAP MII application deployed in the WebAS and can be accessed by the following URL pattern:
>
> http://<server>:<port>/XMII/CM/<project>/<folder>/<fileName>

Some of the key functionalities provided by the toolbar menu in the SAP MII Workbench are shown in Figure 4.3 and described as follows:

▶ FILE • NEW: Creates a new SAP MII content object. A submenu provides a choice of SAP MII content objects to create.

▶ FILE • NEW PROJECT (Ctrl-P): Creates a new SAP MII project to organize content into.

▶ FILE • SAVE (Ctrl-S): Saves the open object to its current location.

▶ FILE • SAVE AS (Ctrl-A): Saves the open object to a location different than its current location; for example, in a separate folder under the same project or in a folder in a different project.

▶ FILE • SAVE ALL TABS (Ctrl-E): Saves all open content objects in all tabs to their respective locations.

▶ FILE • PUBLISH: Valid for web content only. Copies web content open in the active tab, with its hierarchy, to the CM folder under the application root in the SAP Java Web Application Server (WAS). Use this option if you encounter problems executing your web content.

▶ EDIT • CUT (Ctrl-X) / COPY (Ctrl-C) / PASTE (Ctrl-V): These editing functions can be used to transfer action blocks inside single or multiple Business Logic Services (BLS) Transactions.

▶ EDIT • SETTINGS: These settings help you to customize the look and feel of the SAP MII Workbench. You can change the font size, color, theme, and accessibility features. A restart of the Workbench is required for these settings to take effect.

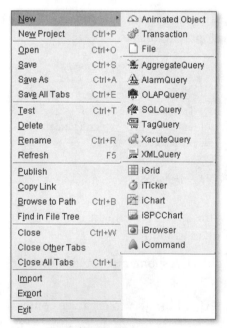

Figure 4.3 File Menu in SAP MII Workbench

4.1.4 SAP MII Content Security

You can assign read or write permissions based on the role of the user to the content that you develop using the SAP MII Workbench. Users who have been granted read access can view and execute development objects such as query templates, display templates, BLS Transactions, and animated objects either from the Workbench or from a web application using SAP MII applets. A user who has write access can modify these objects, in addition to viewing and executing them.

The only exception to this security model is the web content, which cannot be assigned any security roles because it runs on the server and thus is not solely under the purview of SAP MII content security.

The security configuration screen is the same for all SAP MII Workbench content objects and is split into four lists. The lists on the left side display assigned reader and writer roles, and the lists on the right side display available roles (Figure 4.4).

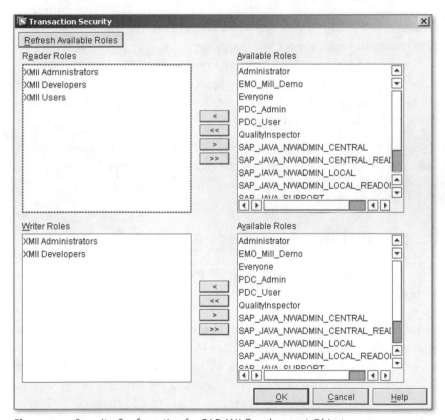

Figure 4.4 Security Configuration for SAP MII Development Objects

You can select the roles that need to be assigned to the required object on the list on the right side, and transfer them to the list on the left side by using the (<) or the (<<) buttons. Similarly, you can un-assign roles from the selected service by selecting the roles on the list on the left side and using the (>) or the (>>) buttons to bring them to the list on the right. It is possible to select multiple roles on either list by pressing the Shift or Control keys. The (<) and (>) buttons transfer the selected single or multiple rows, whereas the (<<) and the (>>) buttons transfer all entries on one list to the other. Don't forget to save the object after assigning or un-assigning roles. You can use the SAP MII standard User Management Engine (UME) roles (XMII Administrators, XMII Developers, XMII Users) or any other roles defined in the UME of the SAP MII Java WebAS.

Now consider a small example to see how this security model works. Production Supervisors Jim and Ram can view production data for shifts in a company, and Plant Managers Bill and Shyam are permitted to create queries. So the users Bill and Shyam are assigned to the XMII Developers role which is assigned to the writer roles in the query templates. The Production Supervisors Jim and Ram are assigned to the XMII Users role, which is assigned only the reader roles to these queries. All other employees who do not have these roles assigned to their users are not permitted to view this information.

Now that you know how to use the SAP MII Workbench and its various menu options, the next section teaches you how to create data queries by configuring the query templates.

4.2   Configuring Query Templates

After you have connected to the plant systems by configuring the Data Servers (explained in Section 3.1 Data Servers: Connecting to the Manufacturing Plant Floor), you need to use query templates in SAP MII to retrieve, change, insert, or delete data from those different data sources. You can use the output of the query templates to plot the charts and run transaction dashboards in SAP MII composite applications. The query templates in SAP MII are configurable templates that enable you to develop SQL and other types of queries by simple configurations. You can even write SQL statements, as required, to query and manage data from different data servers.

SAP MII provides seven types of query templates that need to be configured with the required options to fetch the data you desire. They are as follows:

▶ AggregateQuery

▶ AlarmQuery

▶ OLAPQuery

▶ SQLQuery

▶ TagQuery

▶ XacuteQuery

▶ XMLQuery

> **Note**
>
> As mentioned in Section 3.1 Data Servers: Connecting to the Manufacturing Plant Floor, the Aggregate Connector, AlarmSuite Connector, and XML Connector Data Servers are obsolete now, and thus the corresponding Aggregate, Alarm, and XML queries are also obsolete. Therefore, these are not discussed in this chapter.
>
> The functionality provided by the Aggregate and XML queries can be achieved very easily using BLS Transactions, and we recommend you use BLS Transactions instead of these query templates for achieving the same functionalities.

You can use each of these query templates to query the respective data sources using specific query mode options. Query modes are essentially different "methods" that can be applied to a query template to specify whether to read or write data or to read different types of data such as current data, history data, and metadata information. The query modes differ for different types of query templates, with a few common modes across query templates, and with similar outputs when that mode of query is chosen.

You can create and configure query templates in the Workbench using a configuration environment; the templates are saved in the server as XML files. To create a new query template, go to FILE • NEW in the toolbar menu and select the appropriate query template type. When a query template is opened in the SAP MII Workbench, the configuration parameters for that template are displayed in the Context Sensitive Configuration Options panel in the Template Categories tab. The query templates have six configuration categories that are common to all types of queries available as follows:

- Data Source
- General
- Date Range
- Parameters
- Transformation
- Security

XacuteQuery is the only exception: it does not have the Parameters configuration option as a separate configuration category.

Also depending on the query template type, another specific configuration category is available and explained in later sections of the chapter.

> **Note**
>
> You can construct and invoke all SAP MII queries dynamically, using an HTTP service and passing the relevant parameters for the query template. The URL patterns are as follows:
>
> *http://<servername>:<port>/XMII/Illuminator?Server=<DataServerName>&Mode=<ModeName>&Param.1=<value1>&.....*
>
> You can use the preceding URL to generate a query without having a pre-existing query template.
>
> *http://<servername>:<port>/XMII/Illuminator?QueryTemplate=<template_fullpath>*
>
> You can use the preceding URL to execute a pre-existing query template.
>
> You can also execute a namespace query, such as the TableList mode using the following URL by specifying the Group and Mask parameters.
>
> *http://<servername>:<port>/XMII/Illuminator?server=PlasticResin&Mode=TableList&Group=Table&Content-type=text/xml&Mask=Plastic%*
>
> You can execute any data query from the Workbench using the FILE • TEST menu option or clicking the Execute button in the toolbar.

In the following sections you learn how to configure the six different query template properties listed previously.

4.2.1   Data Source Configuration

The Data Source configuration tab (Figure 4.5) is similar in all types of query templates and is used to specify the Data Server and query mode used. The Available Servers list displays a list of the data servers available for that type of query; thus, a SQL query template displays only the IDBC, OLEDB, and VirtualIDBC data servers available in that system whereas a Tag query template displays IP21, IP21OLEDB, InSQL, OpenConnector, Simulator, UDC, and VirtualTag data servers. Selecting one of the servers from the list populates the Modes dropdown list with the query modes that are supported for that type of query.

Each query mode is actually a different way of querying data from the data source. Based on the query mode, queries can be broadly classified into *namespace queries* and *data queries*. Namespace queries, as their name implies, return name metadata from the data sources, such as the names of tables in a schema or the names of tags in a group. Any query with a mode ending with the word "list" can be classified as a namespace query. A data query, on the other hand, returns actual data from the data sources.

The TagQuery template supports a *method* that is mainly a statistical function that can be optionally applied to the results of a query. The modes and methods are different for different types of query templates and are explained in detail in their respective sections.

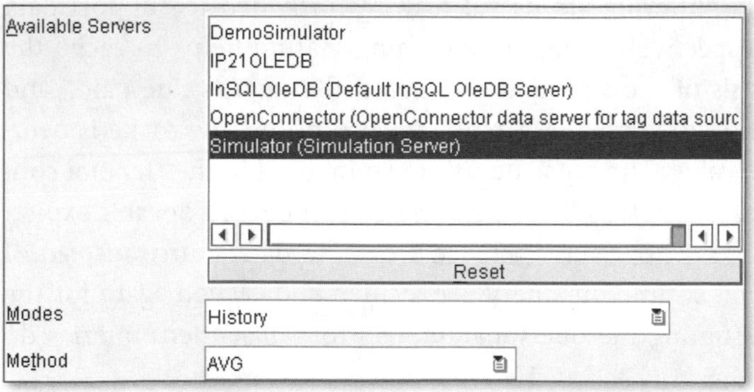

Figure 4.5   Data Source Configuration for TagQuery

4.2.2 General Configuration

The General configuration tab contains the following configuration options:

- ▶ **Row Count:** The maximum number of rows that the query should return, irrespective of the number of rows in the result of the query.

- ▶ **Number Format:** The format in which numeric values in the query are returned.

- ▶ **Use Query Caching:** This should be checked if you want to turn on query caching for that particular query.

- ▶ **Cache Duration:** A numeric value representing the amount of time the query should be cached. This field is enabled only if query caching has been turned on using the Use Query Caching checkbox discussed previously.

- ▶ **Cache Duration Units:** Unit for the cache duration entered previously. Values can be S (seconds), M (minutes), H (hours), and D (days). This field is enabled only if query caching has been turned on using the Use Query Caching checkbox discussed previously.

- ▶ **Comments:** A brief textual comment that shows up on the Data Buffer Entries screen if data buffering has been enabled for the query and the query fails.

- ▶ **Allow Buffering:** Checkbox to indicate whether you want to turn data buffering on for a particular query.

Query caching and data buffering are useful features provided to support data caching and failover, respectively. The query caching feature helps to cache the query results on the basis of the start and end dates, the name-value pairs, and other input parameters. If you pass the parameters at runtime, the cache is overwritten for each unique value. The cache duration, configured in the General configuration screen, denotes how long the data remains cached and doesn't expire. After the configured time is up, data is fetched from the data source instead of from the expired cache next time the query is executed and cached again for the configured duration (assuming the query parameters for subsequent queries do not change).

> **Note**
>
> You can manually clear the query cache by invoking the following URL:
>
> *http://<servername>:<port>/XMII/Illuminator?Service=QueryCaching&Mode=Clear Cache*

With data buffering, data can be queued to be sent to the enterprise from the plant or to other plant systems even when the plant-to-enterprise connectivity is not available. The data is automatically sent when connectivity is re-established. This feature can be used for plants that do not have continuous connectivity to the enterprise and sync once or twice in a day. Apart from supporting some types of queries, the data buffer feature is also provided for asynchronous updates using RFC to SAP systems using SAP JRA action blocks, explained in Section 6.4.3. You should use data buffering only for asynchronous updates to plant systems, for example, updating the production shift information or the material batch information to the plant systems.

The configuration properties relevant to data buffering are DaysRetention, MaxRetryCount, and RetryInterval, which are explained in Section 3.1 Data Servers: Connecting to the Manufacturing Plant Floor. You can view the entries of such queries on the Data Buffer Jobs and the Data Buffer Entries menus (Figure 4.6 and Figure 4.7, respectively), available under Data Services in the main SAP MII menu. The Data Buffer Jobs screen displays an overview of data servers with failed queries that are waiting retries in the Data Buffer.

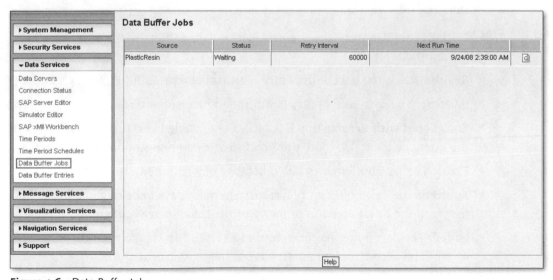

Figure 4.6 Data Buffer Jobs

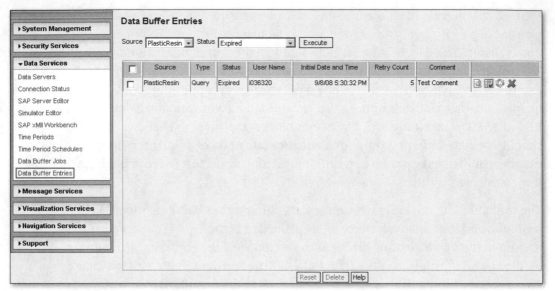

Figure 4.7 Data Buffer Entries

The Data Buffer Entries screen is used to display jobs that are currently in the Data Buffer. The following statuses are available:

- **Initial:** This denotes a new entry in the data buffer that has yet not been resubmitted.

- **Resubmitted:** The data buffer entry has just been resubmitted for execution.

- **Waiting:** The data buffer entry is waiting to be resubmitted.

- **Completed with Errors:** The data buffer entry failed because of some error in the query or the transaction, not because of a communication error.

- **Error:** The data buffer entry failed because of a communications error.

- **Expired:** The data buffer entry has surpassed the days to be retained in the buffer set in the DaysRetention property of the Data Server configuration.

- **Failed:** The data buffer has been retried as set in the MaxRetryCount parameter of the Data Server configuration, but has failed to execute.

You can perform operations on the data buffer entries by using the relevant icons on the data buffer entry list. These operations include viewing data and history and resetting and deleting entries.

> **Note**
>
> XacuteQuery does not support buffering or comments.

4.2.3 Date Range Configuration

The Date Range configuration properties (Figure 4.8) are common to all query templates and provide configuration options for date- and time-sensitive queries. Tag queries are filtered by the datetime configured in their Time columns, whereas SQL queries require you to specify a Date column in the SQL Query Details configuration screen.

The Date Range configuration parameters are as follows:

- **Start Date:** The starting range datetime of the data to be returned.
- **End Date:** The ending range datetime of the data to be returned.
- **Date and Time Format:** The format of the start and end date range values.
- **Duration:** A numeric time duration window for which data in the query should be returned. Relevant only if the Time field (discussed in this list) is filled.
- **Duration Units:** The units of the time duration mentioned previously. Relevant only if the Time field (discussed in this list) is filled.
- **Time:** A time field, entered in the form HH:mm:ss. This field decides the start time. The Duration and Duration Units fields (both discussed previously in this list) decide the length of the period.
- **Time Period:** You can configure a time period in the Time Periods screen under the Data Services menu. The value of the time period as defined in the configuration screen is used to limit data that should be returned and can refer to the StartDate and EndDate as [SD] and [ED], respectively.
- **Schedule:** You can configure a time period schedule in the Time Periods Schedule screen under the Data Services menu. You determine the current and previous shift time periods based on the configuration of the schedule, and you use the relevant time parameters to limit the data in the query.
- **Allow Future Dates:** A checkbox that denotes if future dates should be allowed in the query or if the results should be truncated to the current date.

▶ **Interval Count:** An integer value that denotes into how many regular intervals the time period should be divided.

Because none of the fields are mandatory, the query templates consider the values of the fields in the following order:

▶ Schedule

▶ Time Period

▶ Time

▶ Start Date and End Date

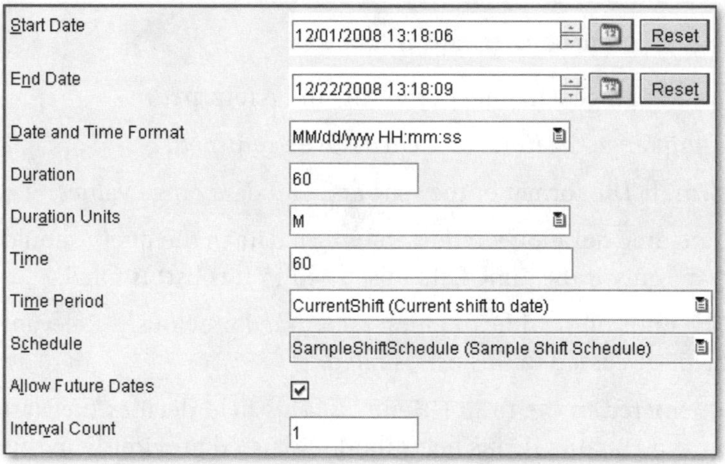

Start Date	12/01/2008 13:18:06 ⇅ 🔲 Reset
End Date	12/22/2008 13:18:09 ⇅ 🔲 Reset
Date and Time Format	MM/dd/yyyy HH:mm:ss ▤
Duration	60
Duration Units	M ▤
Time	60
Time Period	CurrentShift (Current shift to date) ▤
Schedule	SampleShiftSchedule (Sample Shift Schedule) ▤
Allow Future Dates	☑
Interval Count	1

Figure 4.8 Date Range Configuration for Query Templates

The Time Periods screen is shown in Figure 4.9. The following are the configuration parameters for a time period:

▶ **Name:** A unique name for the time period.

▶ **Description:** A brief textual description for the time period.

▶ **Day:** A day of the week for which the time period is valid. Valid values also include Today and Yesterday.

The rest of the configuration options (namely, Time, Duration, Start Date, End Date, and Date and Time Format) have the same functions as those in the Date

Ranges configuration options (discussed previously). SAP provides CurrentMonth, CurrentShift, CurrentYear, PreviousMonth, PreviousShift, and PreviousYear as default schedules. You cannot edit or delete them, and they serve as keywords that you can use when creating a query with time periods and schedules, as explained later in this chapter.

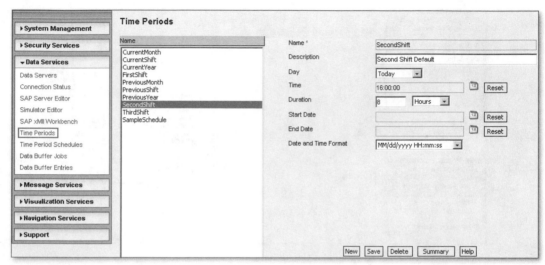

Figure 4.9 Time Periods Configuration

Time Period Schedules are logical groupings of Time Periods that have been created using the Time Periods screen, as explained previously. A schedule should contain one or more Time Periods ordered logically. When this schedule is used in a query, the system determines the appropriate time period to use based on the current date and time.

To create a schedule using the Time Period Schedules menu (Figure 4.10), specify a unique name and an optional description of the schedule. Two list boxes are available: one on the left, which displays the time periods that have been created using the Time Periods menu, and the other on the right, which displays the selected time periods. Both the lists allow multiple selections. You can add time periods to the Selected Time Periods list by selecting them and clicking on the right arrow beside the list. You can delete them from the list by selecting the left arrow. Time periods in the Selected Time Periods list can also be ordered using the up and down arrows beside the list. After configuring the schedule, click on the Save button. To see an overview of all the time periods that have been configured in the server, click on the Time Periods button.

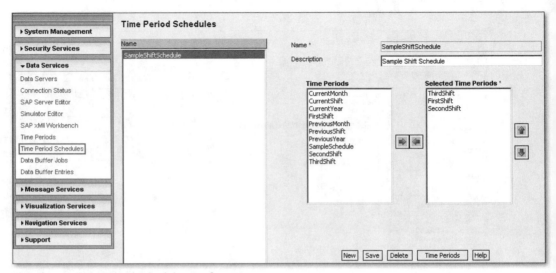

Figure 4.10 Time Period Schedules Configuration

Now take a look at an example where you can use the concepts of Time Periods and Time Period Schedules. The Production Supervisor wants to view the total production of a particular material per month on a year basis. An easy way to achieve this would be to create 12 Time Periods for each month of the year and a Time Period Schedule combining all of these Time Periods, namely "Financial Year." Now if you want to compare the current month's production data to the previous months, all you need to do is to create two queries, one for the current month and one for the previous month. In the Date Range Configuration for the current month query, specify the Schedule as "Financial Year" and the Time Period as the "CurrentMonth" keyword mentioned earlier. For the query for the previous month specify "Financial Year" as the Schedule and the "PreviousMonth" keyword as the Time Period in the Date Range Configuration screen.

While retrieving data, the system dynamically adjusts the queries to return data for the current and previous months according to the current time and the time period keyword. This helps you eliminate the need to write 12 separate current month and previous month queries, one for each month of the year.

In case you just want to know the production data for a particular month, you just need to specify "Financial Year" as the Schedule and the Time Period of that particular month you created as the Time Period.

4.2.4 Parameters Configuration

SAP MII queries support up to 32 parameters, which are variables used as place-holders in a query that can be substituted with dynamic values at runtime and treated as input parameters to the query template. The parameters are in the form of [Param.1] to [Param.32], and you can use them as placeholders for values inside the queries in the Filter conditions. The query fetches results as per the values of these dynamic parameters. The Parameters configuration screen enables you to define default values for these parameters. To specify a default value, type in the value beside the respective parameters (Figure 4.11). You can also accept these input parameters at runtime from the user or other calling applications. In that case the default values, if present, are overwritten with the specified values.

Parameters Table		
Param.		Parameter Value
1	'0001'	
2	'BATCH00002'	
3	'YELLOW'	
4		
5		
6		

Figure 4.11 Parameters Configuration for Query Templates

4.2.5 Transformation Configuration

SAP MII queries support inline XML Style Sheet (XSL) transformations to manipu-late the raw data (for example, by restructuring or aggregating it) for display on web pages. An XSL transformation can be configured for a query template via the Transformations configuration screen; the screen has an Inline Transform field that enables you to select an XSL file from default samples or a style sheet. An XML style sheet might have parameters that format the output of the transformation. See Figure 4.12 for a sample of an XML style sheet.

```xml
<?xml version="1.0" ?>
- <xsl:stylesheet version="1.0" xmlns:xsl="http://www.w3.org/1999/XSL/Transform" xmlns:xalan="http://xml.apache.org/xalan"
    xmlns:lxslt="http://xml.apache.org/xslt" xmlns:calc="http://www.lighthammer.com" extension-element-prefixes="calc" exclude-
    result-prefixes="xalan calc">
    <xsl:output encoding="UTF-8" method="xml" media-type="text/xml" />
    <xsl:param name="C1" />
    <xsl:param name="C2" />
    <xsl:param name="C3" />
    <xsl:param name="C4" />
    <xsl:param name="C5" />
    <xsl:param name="C6" />
    <xsl:param name="C7" />
    <xsl:param name="C8" />
    <xsl:param name="C9" />
    <xsl:param name="C10" />
    <xsl:param name="Expression">NA</xsl:param>
    <xsl:param name="CalcFieldName">CalculatedValue</xsl:param>
    <xsl:param name="CalcFieldDescription">Calculated Value</xsl:param>
    <xsl:param name="CalcFieldMinRange">0</xsl:param>
    <xsl:param name="CalcFieldMaxRange">100</xsl:param>
-   <lxslt:component prefix="calc">
        <lxslt:script lang="javaclass" src="class:com.sap.xmii.Illuminator.ext.ExtFunctions" />
    </lxslt:component>
-   <xsl:template match="/">
-       <xsl:variable name="DivParsedExpression">
            <xsl:value-of select="calc:stringReplace(string($Expression),'/',' div ')" />
        </xsl:variable>
-       <xsl:variable name="ParsedExpression">
            <xsl:value-of select="calc:stringReplace(string($DivParsedExpression),'%',' mod ')" />
        </xsl:variable>
-       <Rowsets DateCreated="{Rowsets/@DateCreated}" Version="{Rowsets/@Version}" StartDate="{Rowsets/@StartDate}"
            EndDate="{Rowsets/@EndDate}">
-       <xsl:for-each select="Rowsets">
            <xsl:copy-of select="FatalError" />
            <xsl:copy-of select="Messages" />
```

Figure 4.12 A Sample XML Style Sheet

You can configure these parameters at design time by specifying the name of the parameter in the Transform Parameter Name and the value of the parameter in the Transform Parameter Value column. These values are dynamically substituted at runtime; if no values are specified, the values defined at design time are treated as default values. You can pass a total of 16 parameters and their values to the query template for the XSL transformation (Figure 4.13).

It is definitely not easy to create an XSL transformation because it requires an advanced knowledge of XML and XPath. We suggest that developers leverage the BLS for reshaping the data to any form they want because it is easy and provides much more flexibility and maintainability of code.

Inline Transform	server://XMII/Stylesheets/IllumCalculator.xsl	Load

Trans. Param.	Transform Parameter Name	Transform Parameter Value
1	Expression	(L1Speed + L2Speed) / $C1
2	CalcFieldName	Average
3	C1	2
4		
5		
6		
7		
8		
9		
10		
11		
12		
13		
14		
15		
16		

Figure 4.13 Transformations Configuration for Query Templates

4.2.6 Security Configuration

The query template security screen is exactly the same as the security screen of all the other objects, and it has been explained in detail in Section 4.1.4 SAP MII Content Security earlier in the chapter.

4.3 Types of Query Templates

Now that you know about the various common configuration options of a data query, it's time to learn how you can configure each of them to fetch exactly the data you need.

4.3.1 OLAPQuery

You can use the OLAPQuery to fetch analytical data from an online analytical processing (OLAP) data source. The OLAP connector is explained in detail in Section 3.1.5 OLAP Connector. The OLAPQuery supports the following modes of data retrieval, in addition to the ModeList and Query modes already discussed:

▶ **CubeList:** Lists all the cubes present in the catalog configured on the Data Servers configuration screen for the OLAP connector.

▶ **DimensionList:** Lists all the dimensions in a given cube.

▶ **MeasureList:** Lists all the measures in a given cube.

▶ **SAPVariableList:** Lists all the SAP Business Information Warehouse (BW) variables in a given cube.

The cube name for the list queries can be passed as a parameter via the Illuminator service, explained later in Section 9.9 SAP MII Services: The Power behind SAP MII, using *Cube=<CubeName>*.

You can use the query mode of the OLAPQuery to create a Multidimensional Expressions (MDX) query and execute it on the OLAP Server.

Other than the common query configuration options, OLAPQuery has two more configuration screens that you need to configure in case the query mode is used. The first is the OLAP Query Details screen, shown in Figure 4.14. This screen has a Cubes dropdown list that displays the cubes available for query and three list boxes titled Dimensions, Measures, and SAP Variables. These boxes display the corresponding data for the selected cube, the "SAP Variables" list being specific to SAP BI. The screen also has a Query text area where you can manually enter an MDX query to fetch the corresponding data. The Paste Dimension, Paste Measure, and Paste SAP Variable buttons paste the selected values from their corresponding lists to this Query text area. The Show Null Values as Zero checkbox replaces null values as zeroes in the result of the query. The Fill Query button, just beside the Cubes dropdown list, fills a default query for the selected cube into the Query text area.

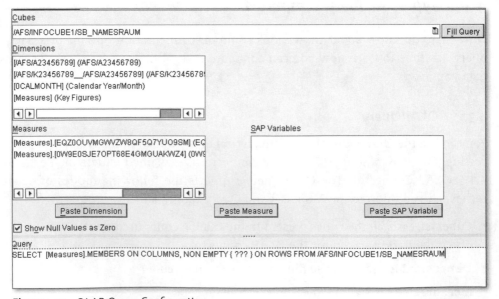

Figure 4.14 OLAP Query Configuration

The second important configuration screen in OLAPQuery is the Alias screen, which you can use to configure aliases or alternative column names for the columns returned by the query. The OLAPQuery supports aliases for up to a maximum of 128 columns.

4.3.2   SQLQuery

You can use the SQL query to retrieve, insert, update, or delete data from databases that have been configured as a Data Server using the IDBC, OLEDB or VirtualIDBC connector. The SQL query supports the following modes, in addition to the ModeList and Query modes:

▶ **ColumnList:** Returns a list of columns for a particular table in the database schema. The Group parameter mentions the table for which you want to retrieve a set of columns, and the Mask parameter can pass a pattern to further filter the results obtained.

▶ **TableList:** Returns a list of all the tables in the connected database schema. The Group parameter mentions the types of tables that you want to retrieve and supports the values System Table, Table, and View. The Mask parameter can pass a pattern to further filter the results obtained.

▶ **Command:** You can use the command mode for SQL statements that do not return any results. This comprises mostly all SQL statements — such as Insert, Update, and Delete — except for the Select statement. If a result is returned by the SQL statement, this mode returns an error. You have to write this query as free SQL statements in the FixedQuery configuration tab.

▶ **FixedQuery:** You should use this mode for formulating complex Select queries that cannot be created in the query mode or for creating database-specific queries that use database-specific keywords. Stored procedures both with and without parameters can also be invoked using this mode. You should write this query as free SQL statements in the FixedQuery configuration tab.

▶ **FixedQueryWithOutput:** This is special mode specific to the Oracle database that you should use only for executing stored procedures or functions that return a Reference Cursor (Ref Cursor) as an output parameter. The Reference Cursor (Ref Cursor) position is marked with a question mark (?) in the query. You should write this query as free SQL statements in the FixedQuery configuration tab.

The SQL query has two specific configuration screens, SQL Query Details and Fixed Query Details. These two are disabled when you select the ColumnList, Model-ist, and TableList modes. The SQL Query Details configuration screen is enabled only for the Query mode, whereas the Fixed Query Details configuration screen is enabled only for the FixedQuery, the FixedQueryWithOutput, and the Command-Query modes. Let's take a look at these two configuration screens in detail to see how the SQL query template can be configured using these screens.

The SQL Query Details screen, shown in Figure 4.15, entails using the query mode. This screen enables you to create a SQL query (Select query) for data retrieval without writing an actual SQL statement. It contains two list boxes: Available Tables, which displays the tables in the database schema, and Available Columns, which displays the columns for the table selected in the Available Tables list. To include the tables you need in the query, add the entries from these lists to the Selected Tables and the Selected Columns lists using the (>) and (>>) buttons. You can also add tables to the lists by typing their values in the corresponding textbox and clicking the Add button. This is useful for specifying a column alias in the selected table.

You can delete entries by clicking on the Delete button and alter their sequence by selecting the Move Up or Move Down buttons. Tables and columns selected in their respective lists are used in the query.

You can specify expressions in the Join Expression, Filter Expression, Sort Expression, and Group Expression text areas or by using the logical operator buttons and the Paste Table and Paste Column buttons provided below each of the text areas. A Join expression retrieves data that is common between two or more tables on the basis of columns that have comparable data between them. A filter expression filters the data on the basis of values in particular columns of a table, similar to using the WHERE keyword in a SQL statement. Here you can specify a condition using input parameters which is passed at runtime. A sort expression arranges the query result data in an ascending or descending fashion on the basis of data in the columns returned. And finally, a Group expression aggregates data of a particular column on the basis of aggregate functions as specified in the expression.

The Date Column at the bottom of the screen enables you to select the date column in the database. This provides the basis for filtering data in case of a time-sensitive query.

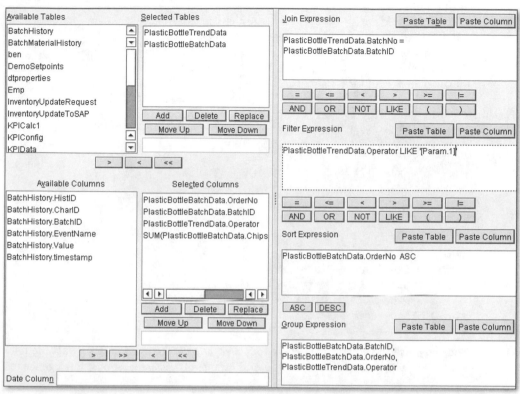

Figure 4.15 SQL Query Configuration

The query shown in Figure 4.15 when executed with input parameter as 'Th%' provides the following output:

OrderNo	BatchID	Operator	TotalChipsPerGram
ORDER00003	BATCH00007	Theodore	657.00
ORDER00003	BATCH00011	Thomas	945.00

The XML output of the same query is as follows:

```
<?xml version="1.0" encoding="UTF-8"?>
<Rowsets DateCreated="2009-03-21T06:52:32" EndDate="2009-03-
21T06:52:32" StartDate="2009-03-21T05:52:32" Version="12.0.4
Build(120)">
<Rowset>
<Columns>
```

```
<Column Description="OrderNo" MaxRange="1" MinRange="0" Name="OrderNo"
SQLDataType="-9" SourceColumn="OrderNo"/>
<Column Description="BatchID" MaxRange="1" MinRange="0" Name="BatchID"
SQLDataType="-9" SourceColumn="BatchID"/>
<Column Description="Operator" MaxRange="1" MinRange="0"
Name="Operator" SQLDataType="-9" SourceColumn="Operator"/>
<Column Description="TotalChipsPerGram" MaxRange="1" MinRange="0"
Name="TotalChipsPerGram" SQLDataType="6" SourceColumn="TotalChipsPerGra
m"/></Columns>
<Row>
<OrderNo>ORDER00003</OrderNo>
<BatchID>BATCH00007</BatchID>
<Operator>Theodore</Operator>
<TotalChipsPerGram>657</TotalChipsPerGram>
</Row>
<Row>
<OrderNo>ORDER00003</OrderNo>
<BatchID>BATCH00011</BatchID>
<Operator>Thomas</Operator>
<TotalChipsPerGram>945</TotalChipsPerGram>
</Row></Rowset></Rowsets>
```

You can parse the preceding query output XML in a BLS Transaction to extract the relevant data, which is explained in Chapter 6 Business Logic Transactions: Intelligence in Action.

The Fixed Query Details screen is shown in Figure 4.16. You can use this configuration screen for Command, FixedQuery, and FixedQueryWithOutput modes to write queries by using SQL statements. This screen contains the same list boxes and the Paste Table, Paste Column, and other buttons that are available on the SQL Query Details configuration screen. The Fixed Query text area enables you to write or create a SQL query using the logical operator buttons. The query parameters significant for stored procedure input can be entered in the Query Parameters text area. The query configuration shown in Figure 4.16 is of mode Command Query and updates the column values in a database based on the input parameters specified as [Param.1], [Param.2], and so on. Note that for parameters of numeric data type you do not need to specify the single quotes around it, whereas for string and date data types you need to do so.

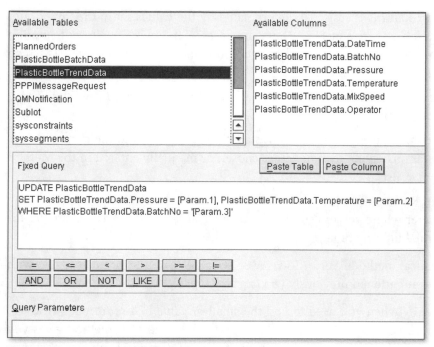

Figure 4.16 Fixed Query Configuration

Consider an example to see when exactly you should use a SQL query. Suppose a company stores its production batch data in a database and you want to retrieve and display the process parameter trend data for different batches to the Production Supervisor in the form of a chart in the production dashboard. The underlying query that retrieves data for that chart should be a SQL query.

4.3.3 TagQuery

You can use TagQuery to query or insert data from all tag-oriented data sources, such as the InSQL, OpenConnector, Simulator, UDC, and IP21 types of data servers. In addition to ModeList, it supports the following modes:

▶ **Current:** Returns the current value of the selected tags.

▶ **CurrentWrite:** Writes data to the value of the tag with the current datetime as a timestamp.

▶ **GroupList:** Returns a list of all the Tag Groups in the data source.

- ▸ **History:** Returns History data interpolated by the values set in the Row Count and Resolution parameters. These are located in the General configuration screen (Section 4.2.2, General Configuration) and the Tag Query Details screen (Figure 4.17), respectively.

- ▸ **HistoryEvent:** Returns real historical values of the tags logged from the history table or database.

- ▸ **Statistics:** Enables you to perform statistical calculations to the current values of the tags using the method either chosen or manually entered in the Method dropdown list.

- ▸ **Taglist:** Returns all tags in the data source or in a tag group. Supports the Group parameter where you can specify the Group Name and the Mask parameter for additional filtering of tags.

The statistical methods MIN, MAX, AVG, TOT, TWA, and SDV are available with MII but as mentioned previously you can also specify your own methods.

You use MIN when you need to find the smallest value in a set of numerical values whereas you use MAX to find the largest value. The AVG method gives you the average value or the arithmetic mean of a set of numerical values. Consider a plant maintenance scenario where you need to monitor the temperature of a shop floor machine at regular intervals because overheating could cause it to fail. The maximum, minimum, and average temperature values of all the recorded values would suffice as a one glance health check of the shop floor machine.

The TOT or the *totalizer* method is generally used when you require the summation of a quantity over a period of time. A good example of its application is to measure the total amount of gas flow in a duct for a process industry.

The TWA method gives you a time weighted average value of a set of numerical values, which can be used, for example, to measure the average concentration of a chemical compound in parts per million (ppm) for samples taken over a period of time for statistical quality control.

The SDV method stands for Standard Deviation, which is used in statistical calculations to determine how closely the data sets are spread around the mean or the average in a set of data. This is useful in Quality Control to determine the correctness of readings recorded over multiple samplings of, say, the concentration of a chemical compound and to maybe flag a suspicious reading.

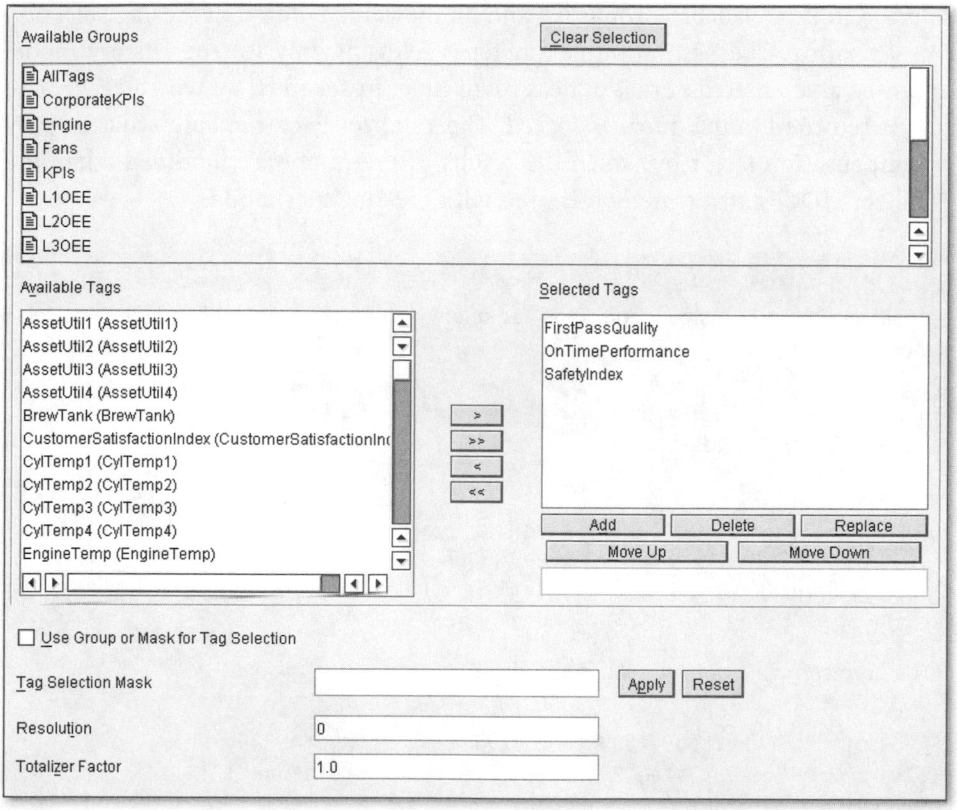

Figure 4.17 TagQuery Configuration

You can configure the Tag query by the Tag Query Details and Values configuration screens. The Tag Query Details screen is shown in Figure 4.17. All the tag groups that are available in the data source or in Universal Data Server (UDS) as alias tags are displayed in the Available Groups list. If no group is selected in the Available Groups list, the Available Tags list displays the first 128 tags that are available in the data source. If a group *is* selected, the Available Tags list displays the tags under that group. You can add or delete the Selected Tags list from the Available Tags list by using the (>), (>>) and (<), (<<) buttons. You can also enter them manually by typing their values in the corresponding textboxes and clicking on the Add button. You can delete entries from the lists by clicking the Delete button, and alter their sequence by clicking the Move Up or Move Down buttons. If you select the Use Group or Mask for Tag Selection checkboxes, the tags in the Selected Tags list are ignored; instead, tags are chosen on the basis of both the group that has been selected in the Available Groups list and on the value entered in the Tag Selection Mask textbox. The Resolution parameter is relevant only for the History mode, and the value entered here is a measure of time, in seconds, by which each value that is returned in the query is spaced. The Totalizer Factor enables you to apply a compensation factor by which the results of the query are modified when the Totalizer (TOT) statistic method is used with the Statistics mode.

Example

When executed in History mode, the Tag query shown in Figure 4.17 provides the following output:

DateTime	FirstPassQuality	OnTimePerformance	SafetyIndex
03/21/2009 06:27:06	29.95	91.36	93.85
03/21/2009 06:47:06	64.36	91.91	92.56
03/21/2009 07:07:06	46.20	93.13	90.50

The corresponding output XML is as follows:

```xml
<?xml version="1.0" encoding="UTF-8" ?>
<Rowsets DateCreated="2009-03-21T07:32:39" EndDate="2009-03-
21T07:32:39" StartDate="2009-03-21T06:32:39" Version="12.0.4
Build(120)">
<Rowset>
<Columns>
<Column Description="DateTime" MaxRange="1" MinRange="0"
Name="DateTime" SQLDataType="93" SourceColumn="DateTime" />
<Column Description="FirstPassQuality" MaxRange="100" MinRange="0"
Name="FirstPassQuality" SQLDataType="8" SourceColumn="FirstPassQuality"
/>
<Column Description="OnTimePerformance" MaxRange="100" MinRange="0"
Name="OnTimePerformance" SQLDataType="8" SourceColumn="OnTimePerforma
nce" /> <Column Description="SafetyIndex" MaxRange="100" MinRange="0"
Name="SafetyIndex" SQLDataType="8" SourceColumn="SafetyIndex" />
</Columns>

<Row>
<DateTime>2009-03-21T06:32:39</DateTime> <FirstPassQual-
ity>48.608067816176</FirstPassQuality> <OnTimePerfor-
mance>96.504166828815</OnTimePerformance>
```

```
<SafetyIndex>91.794365937989</SafetyIndex>
</Row>
<Row>
<DateTime>2009-03-21T06:52:39</DateTime> <FirstPassQual-
ity>40.08375567926</FirstPassQuality>
<OnTimePerformance>92.480000369099</OnTimePerformance>
<SafetyIndex>95.492078980018</SafetyIndex>
</Row>
<Row>
<DateTime>2009-03-21T07:12:39</DateTime>
<FirstPassQuality>79.662037558186</FirstPassQuality>
<OnTimePerformance>96.40473603443</OnTimePerformance>
<SafetyIndex>94.488994936933</SafetyIndex>
</Row></Rowset></Rowsets>
```

The Values configuration screen for Tag query is shown in Figure 4.18, which you need to configure only if the CurrentWrite method is used. In this screen, you can specify default values to be written to specific tags. By default, the Tag Name column is populated by the values that you have selected in the Selected Tags List on the Tag Query Details configuration screen. You can manually enter tag names that you want to write in the Tag Name field and the corresponding value in the Tag Value field. You can pass these values dynamically at runtime, and the values in the Tag Values are overwritten.

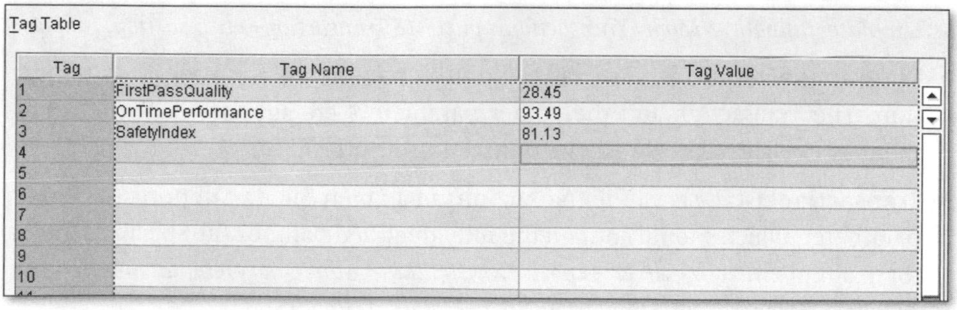

Figure 4.18 Values Configuration for TagQuery

Consider this example to see when exactly you should use a Tag query. You need to create an application that interfaces with a weighing machine on the shop floor in a chemical industry. You could have the weighing machine talk to SAP MII using a UDS, and you could use a Tag query in this case to retrieve the reading of the weighing machine.

4.3.4 XacuteQuery

You can use XacuteQuery to execute Business Logic Transactions from SAP MII applets in web pages. In addition to the query and ModeList modes, the following modes are supported by this query:

▶ **TargetFolderList:** Lists details about all folders under a specified folder, also known as the target folder. You can specify the target folder path using the Folder parameter, which is available as a URL parameter, for example, *http://<server>:<port>/XMII/Illuminator?QueryTemplate=<template_fullpath>& Mode=TargetFolderList&Folder=<folder_fullpath>*. The folders are available as part of the SAP MII projects.

▶ **TransactionFolderList:** Lists details about all folders and subfolders recursively and hierarchically below a folder, specified by the Folder parameter, of the SAP MII Content Browser, for example, *http://<server>:<port>/XMII/Illuminator? QueryTemplate=<template_fullpath>&Mode=TransactionFolderList&Folder=<folder_ fullpath>*.

▶ **TransactionInputList:** Lists all input parameters for a specified transaction. You can specify the transaction path using the Transaction parameter containing the fully qualified path of the transaction. You can also specify an optional Folder parameter containing the fully qualified path of the transaction folder, but if you do, the Transaction parameter can contain only the name of the transaction, for example: *http://<server>:<port>/XMII/Illuminator?QueryTemplate=< template_fullpath>&Mode=TransactionInputList&Transaction=<transaction_fullpath*.

▶ **TransactionOutputList:** Lists all the output parameters for a specified transaction. The Transaction and the Folder parameters are supported. You can pass them as explained previously in TransactionInputList.

▶ **TransactionList:** Lists all the transactions in a given folder. Supports the Folder parameter, which should contain the fully qualified path for the specified folder, for example: *http://<server>:<port>/XMII/Illuminator?QueryTemplate=<template_ fullpath>&Mode=TransactionList&Folder=<folder_fullpath>*.

Other than the query mode mentioned previously, for all other modes the Transaction Details tab is disabled as the other modes are invoked through an URL and do not require this configuration.

> **Note**
>
> SAP MII projects are also treated as folders when representing the hierarchy of the content.

To execute a BLS Transaction you need to use the query mode. The Transaction Details configuration screen, shown in Figure 4.19, is the only screen that you need to configure for an XacuteQuery, apart from the general configurations explained previously. You can manually specify a transaction path in the Selected Transaction textbox, select a transaction from the selection dialog using the Load button, or select a transaction from the Object Browser and click on the Paste from Browser button. The Output Parameter dropdown menu lists the output parameters, and the Input Parameter dropdown list displays the input parameters of the selected transaction. For executing a BLS Transaction you need to select only one output parameter from the dropdown list if it is of type XML; otherwise, you can select * to specify all non-XML type output parameters, if available in that BLS Transaction. The Refresh button refreshes the input and output parameters list in case it has been changed in the BLS Transaction. You can use the Start Date of Mapped Input and End Date of Mapped Input textboxes to give input parameters to which you should map the StartDate and EndDate values. In case of a time-sensitive query, you can enter it either manually or by selecting the required parameter from the Input Parameters list and clicking on the Paste button. Lastly, this screen enables you to map the input parameters of the transaction to the query parameters, from [Param.1] to [Param.32]. This is done by selecting the required parameter from the Input Parameters list and clicking on the Add button. This adds the parameter to the Mapped Param Target column. Then enter the corresponding default parameter value in the Param column, which is overwritten if new values are specified the parameters at runtime. You can delete rows from this table by clicking on the Delete button.

> **Note**
>
> To make input parameters of the BLS Transaction available at runtime while executing the XacuteQuery, you need to add them as Mapped Parameters against the parameter indices as explained previously. Those mapped parameters are then available against their mapped indices while setting their values from the web page, where they can be executed by an applet.

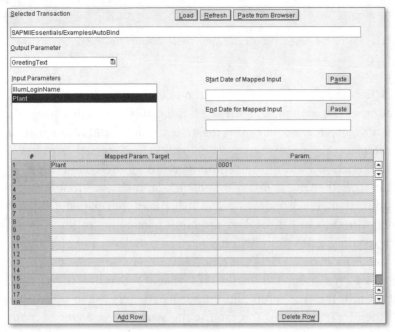

Figure 4.19 Transaction Configuration for Xacute Query

Consider this example to see when exactly you can use an Xacute query. In the example for the SQL query in Section 4.3.2 SQLQuery, suppose the Production Supervisor wants to collate or perform some calculations on the process parameter data that has been returned and combine that with the production order list retrieved from SAP ERP before displaying it on a chart. You would need to model this logic in a BLS Transaction, and also execute the SQL query using the SQL query action block and execute the RFC to get an order list using the SAP JRA action blocks, as explained in Chapter 6 Business Logic Transactions: Intelligence in Action. This transaction can now be wrapped in an XacuteQuery and used as the data source for the chart to be displayed.

4.4   Summary

In this chapter, you learned how to use the SAP MII Workbench to create different SAP MII objects. You also learned how to create different query templates to fetch data from data servers, thus providing real-time plant connectivity.

In the next chapter, you will learn how to create display templates that allow you to graphically represent the data retrieved using query templates.

This chapter explains the techniques of using the SAP MII Workbench to configure various display templates for real-time manufacturing analytics and plant-floor visualizations.

5   Display Templates: Let Your Data Speak

After you have integrated the plant systems and the enterprise systems and configured the query templates to retrieve the relevant data from them, you can use the visualization options in SAP MII to display them as charts or reports to the end-users. In this chapter, you learn how to create and configure engaging visualization applets in web pages using the different display templates available in SAP MII. Display templates are the main visualization components of this application; they are based on data queries and rendered as dynamic Java applets or static images in web pages. These templates provide powerful graphical analytics visualizations such as charts, grids, Statistical Process Control (SPC) charts, and so on, all of which you can use in portal dashboards.

Each display template provides different types and subtypes of graphical components. At runtime, the configured display templates display data streams retrieved by data queries, rendered as Java applets in web pages. Applets are small Java programs that are downloaded from the server at runtime and require a Java runtime in the client machine; they are dynamic and interactive components that support analytics features and auto-refresh, and have certain events, methods, and properties that can be manipulated by JavaScript in the web pages where they are displayed.

You can create a display template in the SAP MII Workbench by selecting a specific display template type and configuring the required properties. The display templates can be integrated into a web page as an applet (explained further in Chapter 8 Web Scripting and Reports: Weaving It All Together) or, if you specify a valid query template in its configuration, can be tested at design time from the Workbench itself by clicking on the Test (⊞) button in the toolbar.

Some common configuration properties in most of the display templates are illustrated in Table 5.1.

Property	Description
Text Color	The color of the text displayed in the applet.
Font Face	The font of the text displayed in the applet.
Font Size	The font size of the text displayed in the applet.
Font Style	The font style (plain, bold, italic) of the text displayed in the applet.
Background Color	Background color of the applet.
Date Format	Date format of the date data types in the applet.
Number Format	Decimal number format of the float, decimal, double data types in the applet.

Table 5.1   Common Configuration Properties of Display Templates

The following are the types of display templates available in SAP MII:

- ▶ iGrid
- ▶ iTicker
- ▶ iChart
- ▶ iSPCChart
- ▶ iBrowser
- ▶ iCommand
- ▶ iCalendar

We now discuss each of these templates in detail.

5.1   iGrid

iGrid is the display template you can use to display data in tabular format. It provides many useful features for data reporting, such as color context-sensitive highlighting and graphical indicator symbols. For example, you can use iGrid to display a material batch status report or a workcenter schedule report in tabular format using different colors for different status. iGrids are read-only display templates where you cannot accept any user input during runtime. You can use data from Tag queries, OLAP queries, or SQL queries to display in the iGrid as reports. In the following sections, we provide information about the iGrid configuration tabs and its specific subtypes.

5.1.1 iGrid Configuration Tabs

To create a new iGrid display template, click on New in the SAP MII Workbench toolbar menu and select the iGrid option from the Display Template category. The configuration properties of the iGrid display template are laid out in different categories — Grid Area, Layout, Header, and so on — in the Template Categories configuration tab, which is located in the bottom-left corner of the Workbench (Figure 5.1).

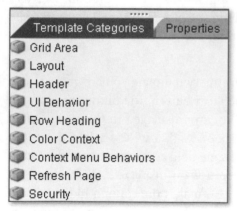

Figure 5.1 Configuration Categories in iGrid

In the Grid Area configuration tab, you can configure general properties of the display template, as shown in Table 5.2.

Property	Description
Grid Type	The subtype of the iGrid display template can be selected from the dropdown. Each of the subtypes of iGrid are explained in a later section of the chapter.

Table 5.2 Grid Area Configuration Properties of iGrid

Property	Description
Grid Color	The foreground color of the grid.
Show Horizontal Grid	Specifies whether or not the horizontal grid lines are displayed in the applet.
Show Vertical Grid	Specifies whether or not the vertical grid lines are displayed in the applet.
Show Scroll Bar	Specifies whether or not the vertical scrollbar is displayed in the applet.
Show Horizontal Scroll Bar	Specifies whether or not the horizontal scrollbar is displayed at the bottom of the applet.
3D Appearance	Specifies whether or not the applet is displayed in 3D appearance.

Table 5.2 Grid Area Configuration Properties of iGrid (Cont.)

You can configure column properties in the Layout configuration category of the iGrid, as shown in Figure 5.2. This is not a mandatory configuration, and you should do this only when one or more columns displayed in the iGrid need to be formatted. (Without the Layout configuration, the columns are displayed using the default formats.)

To configure columns in the iGrid, select the query template you are going to use for the display template by clicking on the Load button; the output columns of the selected query appear. To configure a column displayed in the iGrid, select it from the Column Names list box and click on Add Row. The selected column name in the query appears in the Column Name field as a new row. In the Heading column, specify the heading text that you want displayed. Width specifies the width of the column; a width value of zero makes the column hidden in the iGrid. Format specifies the format for numeric data displayed in the column; you can define format for currency and percentage values and values with different decimal precisions. Alignment specifies the alignment of the data displayed in the column as L (left-aligned), R (right-aligned), or C (center-aligned). The Freeze Column property specifies the first column number from the left, which is a frozen column. The column you freeze by this configuration appears as a fixed column in the applet in the web page, which means that you cannot scroll horizontally.

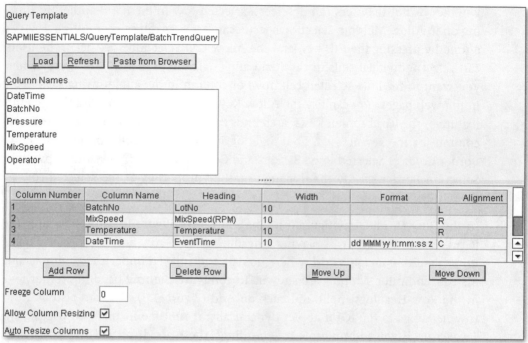

Figure 5.2 Layout Configuration for iGrid

The Allow Column Resizing property indicates whether the user can change the column width at runtime in the applet. The Auto Resize Columns property specifies if the columns are resized automatically at runtime based on the width of the data displayed in it.

In the Header configuration tab, you can configure the properties for the grid header. The checkbox Show Header indicates if the header is displayed for the iGrid. 3D Header specifies if the header is displayed in 3D layout. Header Height specifies the height of the header row; the default value is zero, which means that the header height is auto-sized to fit the text displayed. Font, Font Size, and Font Style specify the font properties of the header text. Text Color and Background Color specify the colors of the header text and background.

In the UI Behavior configuration tab, you can configure properties for user selection in the grid applet. The Allow Selection property specifies whether or not the users can select grid row(s) in the applet, and the Allow Deselection specifies whether or not the users can deselect a selected row in the iGrid applet by click-ing on it. Allow Multiple Selection specifies if the users can select multiple rows at a time by pressing the Ctrl key, and the Allow Cell Selection specifies if the users can select individual cells in the iGrid applet. These properties are useful when you want to read the selected cell, row, or column in the applet using JavaScript in the web pages. You can use the Allow Key Search to enable or disable the Find feature of the iGrid applet. Key search finds the first matching value in the selected column for the key pressed. Font Style of Selected Row, Color of Selected Row, Border Color of Selected Row, Background Color of Selected Row, and Show Row Selection Border specify the dynamic runtime properties of the selected row in the iGrid applet.

In the Row Heading configuration tab, you can configure the row headings for iGrid. This is useful for displaying a heading in each row and is especially help-ful in the ColumnLights grid, where no data is displayed under the columns and, instead, indicator symbols are shown. To configure the row headings, enter text in the Row Headings input and click on Add (Figure 5.3). You can also add the row headings to the iGrid applet dynamically at runtime in the web page using JavaScript. If you add multiple row headings, these are displayed sequentially in the iGrid.

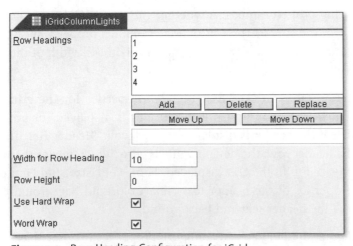

Figure 5.3   Row Heading Configuration for iGrid

In the Color Context configuration tab, you can configure the color context for the displayed rows, columns, and cells based on the data returned by the query (Figure 5.4). In some types of iGrids, the color context is displayed by text color or background color; in other types, such as the Lights grid, the color context is displayed by graphical indicator light icons, such as traffic-light icons. You can use this feature to visually display the status of a machine, the usage decision of an inspection lot in a report, and so on.

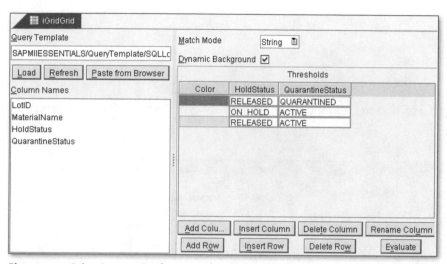

Figure 5.4 Color Context Configuration for iGrid

To configure the color context of iGrid, select the query by clicking on the Load button. The output column names returned by the query appear in the Column Name listbox. The query should have one or more columns on which the value of the color context of the particular row determined at runtime is based. You can define these columns based on the values of other columns in the BLS Transaction by adding the necessary logic, and then use the XacuteQuery here with the additional column. To configure the color context in the grid based on a column value, drag and drop columns from the listbox to the Thresholds on the right. Alternatively, you can add a column by clicking on Add Column or Insert Column, and change the column name by clicking on Rename Column. Click on Add Row or Insert Row to specify the value of the column, which should be matched for color context. Depending on the DataType of the column, select String or Number from the Match Mode dropdown above. The string match matches the exact string specified in the configuration, whereas the number match can take a range. In the Color column in Thresholds, select the color to be displayed in that row of the grid for the specific value of the column. If the data matches the color-context configuration, it is displayed accordingly; otherwise, the default text color specified in the Grid Area configuration is used.

Checking the Dynamic Background checkbox renders the iGrid applet with the row background color configured in the color context (Figure 5.6); otherwise, the text of the data displayed matches the color context (Figure 5.5). The dynamic background in color context is applicable only for the following grid subtypes:

- Grid
- VerticalGrid
- Scoreboard
- VerticalScoreboard

These, in addition to a number of other grid subtypes, are explained later in this section.

Batch	Material	Status	QuarantineStatus
PP_5-1	Polypropylene	RELEASED	ACTIVE
PP_5-2	Polypropylene	RELEASED	QUARANTINED
TPE_8-1	Themoplastic Elastomer	RELEASED	QUARANTINED
PPCO_10-1	Polypropylene Copolymer	RELEASED	ACTIVE
HIPS_9-1	High Impact Polystyrene	RELEASED	ACTIVE
PETE_1-1	Polyethylene Terephthalate	RELEASED	ACTIVE
PETE_1-2	Polyethylene Terephthalate	RELEASED	QUARANTINED
OTHER_7-1	Other	RELEASED	ACTIVE
PVC_3-1	Vinyl/Polyvinyl Chloride	RELEASED	ACTIVE
PVC_3-2	Vinyl/Polyvinyl Chloride	RELEASED	ACTIVE
LDPE_4-1	Low Density Polyethylene	RELEASED	ACTIVE
LDPE_4-2	Low Density Polyethylene	RELEASED	ACTIVE
PS_6-1	Polystyrene	RELEASED	ACTIVE
HDPE_2-2	High Density Polyethylene	RELEASED	ACTIVE
HDPE_2-4	High Density Polyethylene	RELEASED	QUARANTINED

Figure 5.5 iGrid Without Dynamic Background Setting in Color Context

In the Context Menu Behavior configuration tab, you can configure the context menu behavior, which you can access by right-clicking on the grid applet at runtime (Figure 5.7). You find three checkboxes in this tab: the Enable Popup Menu, the Enable Save Data Locally, and the Enable Detail Page Generation. The Enable Popup Menu option specifies if the context menu appears after a right-click by the mouse. The Enable Save Data Locally option specifies if the user can locally save the query data displayed in the grid as a comma-separated value (CSV) file.

Batch	Material	Status	QuarantineStatus
PP_5-1	Polypropylene	RELEASED	ACTIVE
PP_5-2	Polypropylene	RELEASED	QUARANTINED
TPE_8-1	Themoplastic Elastomer	RELEASED	QUARANTINED
PPCO_10-1	Polypropylene Copolymer	RELEASED	ACTIVE
HIPS_9-1	High Impact Polystyrene	RELEASED	ACTIVE
PETE_1-1	Polyethylene Terephthalate	RELEASED	ACTIVE
PETE_1-2	Polyethylene Terephthalate	RELEASED	QUARANTINED
PETE_1-3	Polyethylene Terephthalate	ON_HOLD	ACTIVE
OTHER_7-1	Other	RELEASED	ACTIVE
PVC_3-1	Vinyl/Polyvinyl Chloride	RELEASED	ACTIVE
PVC_3-2	Vinyl/Polyvinyl Chloride	RELEASED	ACTIVE
LDPE_4-1	Low Density Polyethylene	RELEASED	ACTIVE
LDPE_4-2	Low Density Polyethylene	RELEASED	ACTIVE
PS_6-1	Polystyrene	RELEASED	ACTIVE
HDPE_2-2	High Density Polyethylene	RELEASED	ACTIVE
HDPE_2-3	High Density Polyethylene	ON_HOLD	ACTIVE
HDPE_2-4	High Density Polyethylene	RELEASED	QUARANTINED

Figure 5.6   iGrid with Dynamic Background Setting in Color Context

Batch	Material	Status	QuarantineStatus
PP_5-1	Polypropylene	RELEASED	ACTIVE
PP_5-2	Polypropylene	RELEASED	QUARANTINED
TPE_8-1	Themoplastic Elastomer	RELEASED	QUARANTINED
PPCO_10-1	Data ▸ Details	RELEASED	ACTIVE
HIPS_9-1	Print Statistics	RELEASED	ACTIVE
PETE_1-1	Help Current Values	RELEASED	ACTIVE
PETE_1-2	Save as CSV File	RELEASED	QUARANTINED
PETE_1-3	Polyethy	ON_HOLD	ACTIVE
OTHER_7-1	Other	RELEASED	ACTIVE
PVC_3-1	Vinyl/Polyvinyl Chloride	RELEASED	ACTIVE
PVC_3-2	Vinyl/Polyvinyl Chloride	RELEASED	ACTIVE
LDPE_4-1	Low Density Polyethylene	RELEASED	ACTIVE
LDPE_4-2	Low Density Polyethylene	RELEASED	ACTIVE
PS_6-1	Polystyrene	RELEASED	ACTIVE
HDPE_2-2	High Density Polyethylene	RELEASED	ACTIVE
HDPE_2-3	High Density Polyethylene	ON_HOLD	ACTIVE
HDPE_2-4	High Density Polyethylene	RELEASED	QUARANTINED

Figure 5.7   Context Menu in iGrid Applet

The Enable Detail Page Generation option specifies if the user can see the data displayed in the grid as a separate HTML page. The Detail Page Generation option is enabled in the applet at runtime only when the automatic refresh option is not on. The Statistics and Current Values options, which display a detail page with the statistical or current values and bar charts representing the same, are automatically enabled for displaying data from Tag queries.

In the Refresh Page tab, you can configure the automatic refresh behavior of the grid. Automatically Refresh specifies if the grid data is refreshed automatically and periodically at runtime by executing the corresponding data query without any manual intervention. For using this feature you can use a time-sensitive query that has the timestamp as an input parameter. Refresh Rate details the time interval (in seconds) by which the grid data gets refreshed. Initial Update specifies if the grid is updated with the data when it loads for the first time. If the data of the grid depends on some values from user input, you should not check this checkbox, and you need to write the JavaScript in the web page to update the chart at the specific event, for example, a button click. Show Time Refresh Control specifies if the refresh controls (automatic refresh and refresh display) are visible at the bottom of the iGrid applet at runtime.

5.1.2   iGrid Subtypes

iGrid has a few subtypes that mainly differ in the presentation styles and are specified in the Grid Type property in the Grid Area configuration tab. We discuss these in the following sections.

Grid

The most common subtype of iGrid is called simply Grid, and it has optional row-level color-context highlighting. Examples of the Grid subtype were shown in Figure 5.5 and Figure 5.6 (shown previously in the chapter).

ColumnLights Grid

The ColumnLights grid displays color indicators for each column and row instead of for data, as shown in Figure 5.8. The color indicators are displayed according to the color-context configurations.

	LotID	MaterialName	HoldStatus	QuarantineStatus
1	●	●	○	○
2	●	●	○	●
3	●	●	○	●
4	●	●	○	○
5	●	●	○	○
6	●	●	○	○
7	●	●	○	●
8	●	●	○	○
9	●	●	○	○
10	●	●	○	○

Figure 5.8   ColumnLights iGrid

EmbeddedLights Grid

The EmbeddedLights grid displays colored indicators icons with the single character (R, S, Q, and so on) embedded on it based on the color-context configurations (Figure 5.9).

LotID	MaterialName	HoldStatus	QuarantineStatus
PP_5-1	Polypropylene	🔲	🔲
PP_5-2	Polypropylene	🔲	🔲
TPE_8-1	Themoplastic Elastomer	🔲	🔲
PPCO_10-1	Polypropylene Copolymer	🔲	🔲
HIPS_9-1	High Impact Polystyrene	🔲	🔲
PETE_1-1	Polyethylene Terephthalate	🔲	🔲
PETE_1-2	Polyethylene Terephthalate	🔲	🔲
PETE_1-3	Polyethylene Terephthalate	🔲	🔲
OTHER_7-1	Other	🔲	🔲
PVC_3-1	Vinyl/Polyvinyl Chloride	🔲	🔲
PVC_3-2	Vinyl/Polyvinyl Chloride	🔲	🔲
LDPE_4-1	Low Density Polyethylene	🔲	🔲
LDPE_4-2	Low Density Polyethylene	🔲	🔲
PS_6-1	Polystyrene	🔲	🔲
HDPE_2-2	High Density Polyethylene	🔲	🔲
HDPE_2-3	High Density Polyethylene	🔲	🔲
HDPE_2-4	High Density Polyethylene	🔲	🔲

Figure 5.9   EmbeddedLights iGrid

> **Note**
>
> The color-context configuration in the EmbeddedLights grid should be based on a single character value enclosed in < and >. The data query should give the output of the column data to be matched for color context, for example, <R> or <G>, which you can manipulate using the BLS Transaction for each data row. In the color-context configuration, you should specify the same value should within the < and >. The character is displayed inside the colored icon to help the users with color blindness to distinguish between different status icons.

Lights Grid

The Lights grid displays color indicators at the end of each row in an extra column according to the color-context configurations (Figure 5.10).

LotID	MaterialName	HoldStatus	QuarantineStatus		
PP_5-1	Polypropylene	RELEASED	ACTIVE	○	
PP_5-2	Polypropylene	RELEASED	QUARANTINED	○	
TPE_8-1	Themoplastic Elastomer	RELEASED	QUARANTINED	○	
PPCO_10-1	Polypropylene Copolymer	RELEASED	ACTIVE	○	
HIPS_9-1	High Impact Polystyrene	RELEASED	ACTIVE	○	
PETE_1-1	Polyethylene Terephthalate	RELEASED	ACTIVE	○	
PETE_1-2	Polyethylene Terephthalate	RELEASED	QUARANTINED	○	
PETE_1-3	Polyethylene Terephthalate	ON_HOLD	ACTIVE	●	
OTHER_7-1	Other	RELEASED	ACTIVE	○	

Figure 5.10   Lights iGrid

Scoreboard Grid

The Scoreboard grid displays cell-level color-context highlighting instead of row-level (Figure 5.11).

LotID	MaterialName	HoldStatus	QuarantineStatus
PP_5-1	Polypropylene	RELEASED	ACTIVE
PP_5-2	Polypropylene	RELEASED	QUARANTINED
TPE_8-1	Themoplastic Elastomer	RELEASED	QUARANTINED
PPCO_10-1	Polypropylene Copolymer	RELEASED	ACTIVE
HIPS_9-1	High Impact Polystyrene	RELEASED	ACTIVE
PETE_1-1	Polyethylene Terephthalate	RELEASED	ACTIVE
PETE_1-2	Polyethylene Terephthalate	RELEASED	QUARANTINED
PETE_1-3	Polyethylene Terephthalate	ON_HOLD	ACTIVE
OTHER_7-1	Other	RELEASED	ACTIVE
PVC_3-1	Vinyl/Polyvinyl Chloride	RELEASED	ACTIVE
PVC_3-2	Vinyl/Polyvinyl Chloride	RELEASED	ACTIVE
LDPE_4-1	Low Density Polyethylene	RELEASED	ACTIVE
LDPE_4-2	Low Density Polyethylene	RELEASED	ACTIVE
PS_6-1	Polystyrene	RELEASED	ACTIVE
HDPE_2-2	High Density Polyethylene	RELEASED	ACTIVE
HDPE_2-3	High Density Polyethylene	ON_HOLD	ACTIVE
HDPE_2-4	High Density Polyethylene	RELEASED	QUARANTINED

Figure 5.11   Scoreboard iGrid

MultiLights Grid

The MultiLights grid displays multiple colored indicators at the end of each row, highlighting a specific indicator based on color-context configurations (Figure 5.12).

LotID	MaterialName	HoldStatus	QuarantineStatus			
PP_5-1	Polypropylene	RELEASED	ACTIVE	●	●	○
PP_5-2	Polypropylene	RELEASED	QUARANTINED	●	○	●
TPE_8-1	Themoplastic Elastomer	RELEASED	QUARANTINED	●	○	●
PPCO_10-1	Polypropylene Copolymer	RELEASED	ACTIVE	●	●	○
HIPS_9-1	High Impact Polystyrene	RELEASED	ACTIVE	●	●	○
PETE_1-1	Polyethylene Terephthalate	RELEASED	ACTIVE	●	●	○
PETE_1-2	Polyethylene Terephthalate	RELEASED	QUARANTINED	●	○	●
PETE_1-3	Polyethylene Terephthalate	ON_HOLD	ACTIVE	○	●	●
OTHER_7-1	Other	RELEASED	ACTIVE	●	●	○

Figure 5.12   MultiLights iGrid

Vertical Grid

The VerticalGrid displays multiple data row values for each column, horizontally in single rows, and enables color-context highlighting of a whole data row (that is, a column), as shown in Figure 5.13.

LotID	HDPE_2-2	HDPE_2-3	HDPE_2-4
MaterialName	High Density Polyethylene	High Density Polyethylene	High Density Polyethylene
HoldStatus	RELEASED	ON_HOLD	RELEASED
QuarantineStatus	ACTIVE	ACTIVE	QUARANTINED

Figure 5.13   VerticalGrid iGrid

VerticalScoreboard Grid

VerticalScoreboard grid displays multiple data row values for each column, horizontally in single rows. It also enables you to activate color-context highlighting of a specific cell (Figure 5.14).

LotID	HDPE_2-2	HDPE_2-3	HDPE_2-4
MaterialName	High Density Polyethylene	High Density Polyethylene	High Density Polyethylene
HoldStatus	RELEASED	ON_HOLD	RELEASED
QuarantineStatus	ACTIVE	ACTIVE	QUARANTINED

Figure 5.14   VerticalScoreboard iGrid

You can use these different types of iGrid for creating a variety of reports with highlighted data based on certain values. For example, you could use this functionality for reports on batch status or quality inspection usage decisions on inspection lots. By using different types of iGrids, you can highlight the cells or rows based on the status or usage decision values.

Now that you know about the iGrids to create data reports, it's time to explore how you can use the iTicker display template to create self-scrolling applets.

5.2   iTicker

You can use the iTicker display template to display horizontally scrolling dynamic data (such as stock-ticker and alert messages) in Java applets. Color-context configuration is available in iTicker, allowing you to highlight a specific data set in different colors.

To create a new iTicker display template, click on New in the SAP MII Workbench, and select iTicker from the Display Template category. The iTicker configuration has the following category tabs:

▸ Ticker Area

▸ Data Mapping

▸ Color Context

▸ Refresh Page

▸ Security

In addition to the common properties explained in Table 5.1, the Ticker Area configuration tab enables you to configure the properties discussed in Table 5.3.

Property	Description
Include Column Names	Specifies whether or not to display the column names for each value displayed in the iTicker applet.
Color By Column	Specifies if the color-context configuration applies for each column value or the whole data set (row) that matches the configuration.

Table 5.3 Ticker Area Configuration for iTicker

Property	Description
Number of Cell Padding Spaces	Specifies the number of blank spaces inserted between items displayed in the iTicker.
Scroll Delay	Specifies the display text scrolling speed, which varies between 30 and 60. The default value is 30, which is the optimum speed.
Border Color	Specifies the border color of the iTicker applet.
Border Width	Specifies the size of the border of the iTicker applet.

Table 5.3 Ticker Area Configuration for iTicker (Cont.)

In the Data Mapping configuration tab, you can configure the columns of the data query to be displayed in the ticker, as shown in Figure 5.15. Additionally, you can configure the hidden columns in the applet, which can also be accessed by JavaScript at runtime. To configure the data mapping, select the data query by clicking the Load button. The output columns of the selected data query are displayed in the Column Names listbox. Select one or more column names from the Column Names listbox, and drag and drop into the Display Columns listbox (on the right). Alternatively, you can select one or more column names in the Column Names listbox and click on Add to add them in Display Columns. You can also add columns to the iTicker as hidden columns, which are not displayed but available for access by JavaScript at runtime. You can do this by adding such columns to the Hidden Columns listbox in the same way as explained previously.

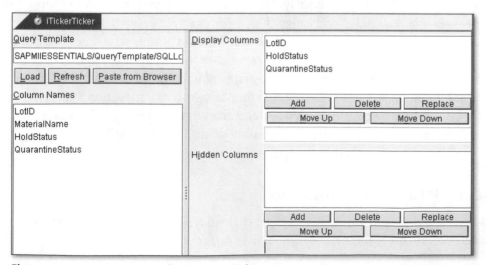

Figure 5.15 Data Mapping Configuration in iTicker

In the Color Context configuration tab, you can configure the color context for iTicker in the same way as you do with iGrid. If the Color by Column option is selected in the Ticker Area configuration tab, then each individual column data matching the color-context configuration is displayed in the configured color (Figure 5.16). Otherwise, the whole data set, such as the row for which the column value(s) matches the color-context configuration, is displayed in the configured color. If the color context is not configured or no match is found, then the data are displayed in the default Text Color or as configured in the iTicker Area configuration.

The Refresh Page configuration is also the same as in iGrid; the only exception is that the Show Time Refresh Control option is not available.

Figure 5.16 iTicker Applet

Now it's time to turn to the configuration of iChart, which is used for creating different types of charts as applets in web pages.

5.3   iChart

iChart provides a variety of configurable charts to display and analyze data visually and is one of the most important and powerful visualization components of SAP MII. You can use iChart to display data returned by data queries in the form of line, area, pie, bar, radar, and gauge charts. For example, temperature or pressure data of different batch samples collected over a period of time would be perfect for iChart. This template can display time-series data for different key values to compare them graphically and enables auto-refreshing for real-time data. You can use the iChart as applets in the Operator Plant Manager's or Production Supervisor's dashboards to provide a real-time view and analytics capability on the production process. In the following sections, we provide an introduction to iChart and go into detail about its subtypes.

5.3.1   iChart Configuration Tabs

To create a new iChart display template, click on New in the SAP MII Workbench, and select iChart from the display template category.

The iChart display template has the following configuration categories:

- ▶ Chart Area
- ▶ Title
- ▶ Data Mapping
- ▶ Legend
- ▶ X-Axis
- ▶ Y-Axis
- ▶ Server Scaling
- ▶ Data Series Details
- ▶ Context Menu Behaviors
- ▶ Refresh Page
- ▶ Security

In the Chart Area configuration tab, you can configure the general properties of iChart, as explained in Table 5.4, by which you can control the display properties of the chart.

Property	Description
Chart Type	Specifies the subtype of the iChart; subtypes are explained later in this section.
Main Border Color	Specifies the border color of the applet.
Main Background Color	Specifies the background color of the applet.
Chart Border Color	Specifies the border color of the chart in the applet.
Chart Background Color	Specifies the background color of the chart in the applet.
Horizontal Grid Color	Specifies the color of the horizontal grid in the chart.
Vertical Grid Color	Specifies the color of the vertical grid in the chart.
Horizontal Grid Line Count	Specifies the number of horizontal grid lines in the chart. For gauge charts, the horizontal grid lines divide the chart into horizontal grid areas.

Table 5.4 Chart Area Configuration Properties in iChart

Property	Description
Number of Vertical Grid Lines	Specifies the number of vertical grid lines in the chart. For gauge charts, the grid lines divide the chart into vertical grid areas.
Gauge Start Angle	Specifies the start angle for the gauge pointer (in degrees). Zero is equal to east. This is applicable only for gauge charts.
Gauge Sweep Angle	Specifies the sweep angle of the gauge pointer clockwise from the start angle (in degrees). Maximum value can be 360. This is applicable only for gauge charts.
Bar Spacing	Specifies the horizontal spacing in pixels between bars. This is applicable only for bar charts.
Bar Group Spacing	Specifies the horizontal spacing in pixels between bar groups. This is applicable only for bar charts.
Bar Margin Spacing	Specifies the horizontal spacing between the chart perimeters and the bars. This is applicable only for bar charts.
Marker Size	Specifies the size of the data point markers in the chart applet. This is applicable only for line charts.
Marker Style	Specifies the data point marker styles. This is applicable only for line charts.
Show Lines	Specifies whether to show markers and not the lines. This is applicable only for line charts.
Interpolate Lines	Specifies whether or not to interpolate lines between the data point readings. This is applicable only for line charts.
Use Screen Resolution	Specifies whether or not to set the rowcount parameter of the data query as the width in pixel for the chart. Should not be used for Alarm queries or queries with HistoryEvent mode.
Allow Item Selection	Specifies if the user can select an item (for example, a marker or a bar) in the chart applet.
3D Display	Specifies whether to show a 3D view of the chart. This is applicable only for bar charts.

Table 5.4 Chart Area Configuration Properties in iChart (Cont.)

Property	Description
Zero-Based Centerline	Specifies whether or not to start the centerline of the chart at zero on the y-axis.
Show Horizontal Grid	Specifies whether or not to show the horizontal grid lines on the chart.
Show Vertical Grid	Specifies whether to show the vertical grid lines on the chart.
Legend Description Label	Specifies the text that precedes the selected tag description below the chart.

Table 5.4   Chart Area Configuration Properties in iChart (Cont.)

Apart from the Chart Type property, which specifies the type of chart to be displayed, you can leave most of the properties as they are, or you can configure them as required for customizing the display.

In the Title configuration tab, you can configure the title and the quick info of the chart applet, as explained in Table 5.5.

Property	Description
Show Title	Specifies whether or not to display the title of the chart.
Title	Specifies the title of the chart to be displayed.
Color	Specifies the color of the title of the chart.
Font	Specifies the font of the title of the chart.
Font Size	Specifies the font size of the title of the chart.
Font Style	Specifies the font style (plain, bold, italics) of the title of the chart.
Display Quick Info Text	Specifies whether or not to display the data values as the mouse pointer is moved over the chart area in the applet.

Table 5.5   Title Configuration Properties in iChart

Property	Description
Display Tag Names as Quick Info Text	Specifies whether or not to display the tag name or the Label column value of the object when the mouse pointer is over that object.
Display X-Axis Values as Quick Info Text	Specifies whether or not to display the x-axis value as quick info when the mouse pointer is over that data point.
Display Y-Axis Values as Quick Info Text	Specifies whether or not to display the y-axis value as quick info when the mouse pointer is over that data point.
Display Datalink Values as Quick Info Text	Specifies whether or not to display the datalink column value. To enable this, at least one datalink column must be specified in the datalink property in Data Mapping configuration.
Display Values as Quick Info Text	Specifies whether or not to display values when the mouse pointer is over an object in the chart.
Display Quick Info Text as Background	Specifies whether or not to display values even when the mouse pointer is not over an object.

Table 5.5 Title Configuration Properties in iChart (Cont.)

In the Data Mapping configuration tab, you can specify the columns of the data queries to be used at runtime, such as legend, description, and value (Figure 5.17). The query specified here provides the data for the chart at runtime. To configure data mapping, select the data query to be used with the iChart by clicking on the Load button. The columns returned by the data query are displayed in the Column Names listbox. You can select the column names and drag and drop them into the listboxes on the right. Value Columns specifies the columns of the data query values that you should use to plot the chart. Label Columns specifies the columns of the data query that you should use for the virtual tag names or the characteristics for which the chart is plotted; these column values are used for plotting the different chart elements (for example, if Batch Number is specified as the Label Column in a line chart, then a line is plotted for each batch number available in the data query output). Description Columns specifies the columns of the data query you should use for the description of the virtual tags or the legends in the chart; the description is also shown at the bottom of the chart when you select a specific legend in the applet. The Label and Description Columns are required for SQL and Alarm queries, but are not required for Tag queries.

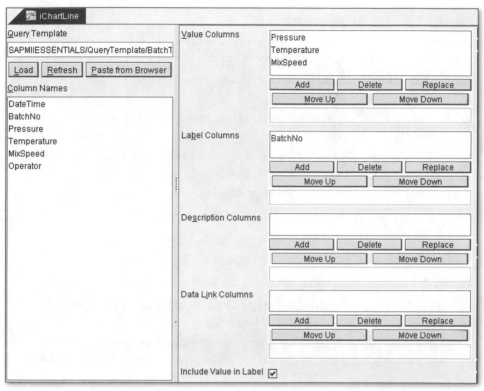

Figure 5.17 Data Mapping Configuration for iChart

In the Data Link Columns, you can specify the columns of the data query used to link each item of the legends. The first mapped Data Link column is also used in the mouse-tracking information texts. Include Value in Label specifies whether or not to include the value column names with the label column names when generating the virtual tag names or legend names in the chart.

In the Legend configuration tab, you can configure the legend properties of the chart. The legends are created in the iChart based on the Label Columns and the Value Columns combination and are shown at the top or right in the chart applet, with different colors for each element (line, bar, and so on) plotted in the chart. You can configure the properties listed in Table 5.6 as Legend properties.

Property	Description
Show Legend	Specifies whether or not to show the legend on the iChart applet.
Show Actual Value Points	Specifies whether or not to display the values beside the legend items.
Delimiter	Specifies the character used to append the label column names and the value column names to create the legend text.
Background Color	Specifies the background color of the legend area in the iChart applet.
Border Color	Specifies the border color of the legend area in the iChart applet.
Border Color of Selected Row	Specifies the border color of the selected row in the legend area in the iChart applet.
Label Color	Specifies the label color of the legend texts.
Font	Specifies the font face of the legend texts.
Font Size	Specifies the font size of the legend texts.
Font Style	Specifies the font style of the legend texts.
Width	Specifies the width allocated to the legend in characters.
Height	Specifies the height allocated to the legend in characters when displayed at the top of the chart.
Show Legend on Top	Specifies whether or not to display the legends at the top of the chart area in the applet. If unchecked, the legends are displayed at the right of the chart area.
Show Tag Names	Specifies whether or not to display the characteristics names (specified by Label Columns in Data Mapping) beside the legends.
Show Tag Descriptions	Specifies whether or not to display the descriptions of the legends (specified by Description Columns in Data Mapping).
Show Values	Specifies whether or not to show the value beside the legends in the iChart applet. This is meaningful only when you have one data value per legend item.
Use Data Series Color	Specifies whether or not to use the data series color as configured in Data Series Detail configuration. If unchecked, then the Label Color is used.

Table 5.6 Legend Properties in iChart Configurations

In the X-Axis configuration tab, you can configure the properties of the x-axis of the chart. Select the query template you want to use using the Load button, as in the Data Mapping configuration. You can then specify the columns from the query in X-Axis Label Columns, X-Axis Value Columns, and Custom Labels properties.

Table 5.7 lists the properties you can configure for the x-axis.

Property	Description
Show X-Axis	Specifies whether or not to display the x-axis in the chart.
Show Tag Descriptions	Specifies whether or not to display the description of the legends as specified by the description columns below the x-axis.
X-Axis Label Columns	Specifies the column names from the query output that should be used to display the labels on the x-axis for each data point in the chart. This is mainly applicable to bar charts.
X-Axis Value Columns	Specifies the column name from the query output that should be used to plot the values of the x-axis.
Label Color	Specifies the color of the x-axis labels.
Label Depth	Specifies the number of rows to display the x-axis labels.
Show Labels	Specifies whether or not to display the label values in the x-axis.
Show 3D Tick Marks	Specifies whether or not to display the tick marks with shadows in the x-axis.
Width	Specifies the width of the x-axis (in characters) for the horizontal bar chart.
Custom Labels	Specifies the custom label names to be displayed below the x-axis. This is applicable to Bar, GroupBar, VariabilityBar, FloatingBar, and StackedBar chart types.
Custom Label Color	Specifies the color of the custom labels.
Show Tick Marks	Specifies whether or not to display the tick-marks on the x-axis.
Tick Color	Specifies the tick colors on the x-axis.
Tick Highlight Color	Specifies the color of the highlighted tick marks on the x-axis.
Number of Major Ticks	Specifies the number of major ticks, that is, the larger tick marks on the x-axis.
Number of Minor Ticks	Specifies the number of minor ticks, that is, the smaller tick marks on the x-axis.
Ticks Per Label	Specifies the number of major tick marks associated with a single label value.

Table 5.7 X-Axis Configuration Properties for iChart

In the Y-Axis configuration tab, you can configure the properties for the y-axis in the iChart, which are almost the same as that of x-axis (Table 5.7).

In the Server Scaling configuration tab, you can configure the global scaling and numeric precisions properties for the iChart, as explained in Table 5.8.

Property	Description
Min. Range Column	Specifies the numeric data column from the query used to create the minimum pen scaling range for the y-axis.
Max. Range Column	Specifies the numeric data column from the query used to create the maximum pen scaling range for the y-axis.
Global Decimals	Specifies the decimal precision used for all numeric data points in the chart.
Global Min. Range	Specifies the fixed minimum value for the pen scaling range of the y-axis. This is applicable only when Use Global Ranges is set to True.
Global Max. Range	Specifies the fixed maximum value for the pen scaling range of the y-axis. This is applicable only when Use Global Ranges is set to True.
Use Global Decimals	Specifies whether or not to use the global decimal precision for each data series on the chart.
Use Global Ranges	Specifies whether or not to use the Global Min. Range and Global Max. Range for each data series on the chart.
Use Global Auto. Scaling	Specifies whether or not to use the automatic scaling for the x-axis and y-axis, calculated based on the query data.
Use Global Server Scaling	Specifies whether or not to use the minimum and maximum ranges returned by the data server used by the data query. Only a few tag connectors provide this feature.
Use Zero-Based Scale	Specifies whether or not to use zero as the minimum range when auto-scaling is enabled.

Table 5.8 Server Scaling Configuration Properties for iChart

In the Data Series configuration tab, you can configure the pen and data series properties of the iChart. The data series configurations are applicable when you plot the chart against multiple key values or in a custom chart, where you can specify the color and style of each pen or legend. The properties outlined in Table 5.9 are available in the Data Series configuration.

Property	Description
Pen ID	Specifies the Data Series ID. A maximum of 32 data series is available.
Color	Specifies the pen color of the selected data series.
Type	Specifies the type of the selected data series in the chart for custom charts.
Marker Style	Specifies the marker style (circle, triangle, diamond, and so on) for the selected data series.
Decimals	Specifies the decimal precision for the selected data series values plotted in the chart.
Minimum Range	Specifies the minimum range of the selected data series plot.
Maximum Range	Specifies the maximum range of the selected data series plot.
Use Server Scaling	Specifies whether or not to use the data series range returned by the tag connector.
Automatically Scale	Specifies whether or not to automatically scale the X- and Y-axis for the data series based on the data values.

Table 5.9   Data Series Configuration Properties of iChart

In the Context Menu Behavior configuration tab, you can configure the iChart context menu behavior properties, as described in Table 5.10.

Property	Description
Allow Popup Menu	Specifies whether or not to display the context menu as a pop-up on mouse right-click on the iChart applet.
Allow Double-Click Refresh	Specifies whether or not to update a time-sensitive chart with the current time on the iChart applet (via double-click).
Allow Legend Item Selection	Specifies whether or not to allow legend item selection by the user on the iChart applet. Selection of a legend item changes the y-axis color to match the selected data series color.
Allow Editing of Query Properties	Specifies whether or not to allow the users to edit the iChart query properties in the applet by, for example, removing a tag name from the chart.

Table 5.10   Context Menu Behavior Configuration Properties for iChart

Property	Description
Allow Editing of Display Properties	Specifies whether or not to allow the user to edit the iChart display properties (such as layout, appearance, and refresh rate) in the applet.
Allow Data to be Saved Locally	Specifies whether or not the user can save the query data displayed in the chart as a comma-separated value (CSV) file locally.
Allow Detail Page Generation	Specifies whether or not the user can see the data displayed in the chart as a separate HTML page. The detail page generation option is enabled in the applet at runtime only when the automatic refresh option is not on.
Show Time Refresh Control	Specifies whether or not to display the time-refresh control navigation bar at the bottom of the iChart applet.

Table 5.10 Context Menu Behavior Configuration Properties for iChart (Cont.)

Using the context menu options in the iChart applet you can also scroll or zoom into the chart, which is helpful when you have a bigger chart over a long axis value.

In the Refresh Page configuration tab, you can configure the automatic refresh properties for the iChart. These are almost the same as that of iGrid, except for an extra property called Allow Automatic Refresh, which specifies whether or not to enable users to use time navigation/refresh controls to refresh the chart automatically and periodically.

5.3.2   iChart Subtypes

iChart has a number of subtypes available that provide different kinds of graphical charts for various types of visualization, as configured in the Chart Area configuration tab.

Line Charts

Line charts are the simplest type of iChart. They display the plotted data as lines and are suitable for time-series data values (Figure 5.18).

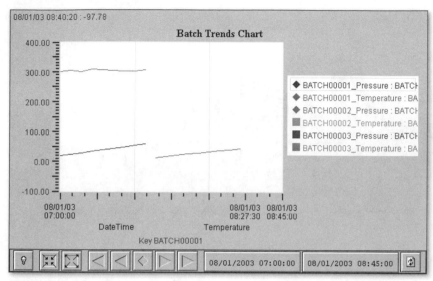

Figure 5.18   Line Chart

Bar Charts

Bar charts display the plotted data as interspersed vertical bars for each key value (Figure 5.19).

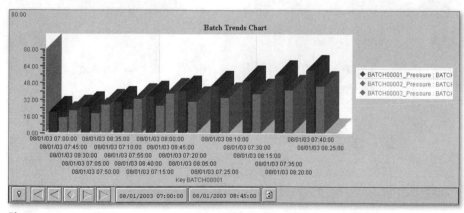

Figure 5.19   Bar Chart

GroupBar Charts

GroupBar charts are a special type of bar chart that display vertical bars in groups ordered by the data set keys according to the observation data (Figure 5.20).

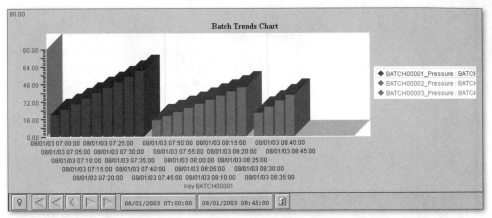

Figure 5.20   GroupBar Chart

Pie Charts

Pie charts display the data values as segments of a circular chart, with the calculated percentage data converted to fractions of 360 degrees (Figure 5.21).

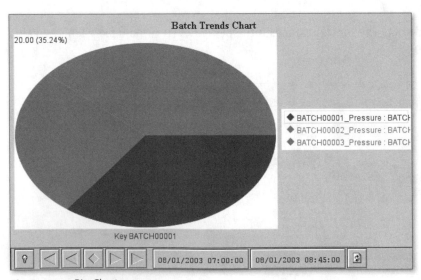

Figure 5.21   Pie Chart

Polar Charts

Polar charts are circular charts; they have an xy plot drawn on a circular grid and show trends in values on the basis of angles (Figure 5.22). Like logarithmic scales, polar charts are useful primarily in mathematical and engineering applications.

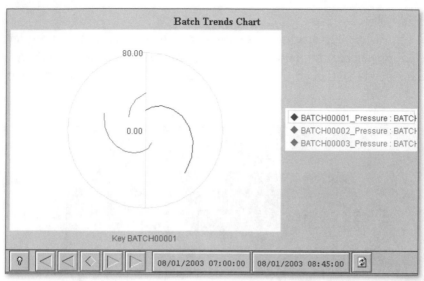

Figure 5.22 Polar Chart

Stacked Bar Charts

Stacked bar charts are bar charts with vertical bars stacked on top of each other displaying the values of different label keys for a specific value column as vertical portions of the bars (Figure 5.23).

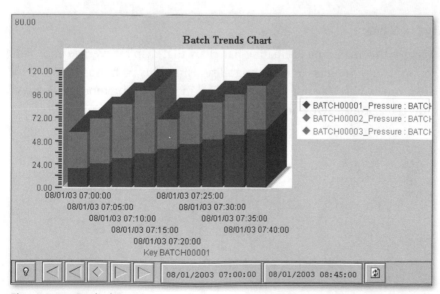

Figure 5.23 Stacked Bar Chart

Floating Bar Charts

Floating bar charts display floating bars with a cross-hair on each bar to display three data points per bar: minimum, maximum, and average (Figure 5.24). You should use a suitable SQL query or Tag query in Statistical mode for floating bar charts.

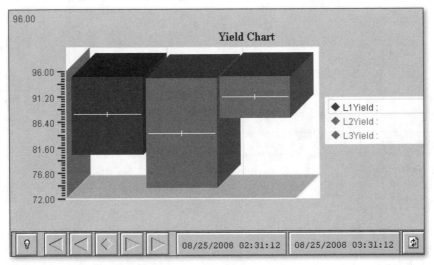

Figure 5.24   Floating Bar Chart

VariabilityBar Charts

VariabilityBar charts are a type of floating bar chart that display average and standard deviation data that plots process variability using plus or minus three sigma (Figure 5.25). You can use Tag queries in Statistical mode with methods AVG, SDV, or TWA. You can also use SQL queries, provided you have a similar data set.

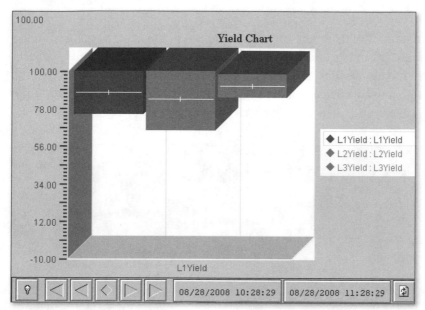

Figure 5.25   VariabilityBar Chart

Gauge Charts

Gauge charts display a rotary gauge with a moving needle within user-specified start and end angles (Figure 5.26). The number of gauges displayed depends on the number of characteristic value columns specified in the Data Mapping configuration, and the sections depend on Horizontal Grid Line Count and Number of Vertical Lines properties specified in the Chart Area configuration.

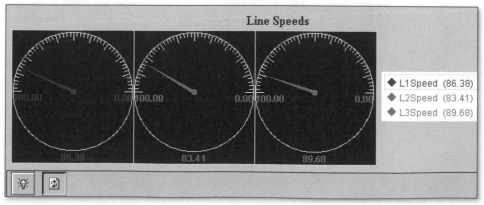

Figure 5.26   Gauge Chart

XY Charts

XY charts are scatter plots where the data is plotted against two variables (Figure 5.27). The first Tag or Data query column specified in the Value Columns property is considered the x-axis value, and the other tags or column names specified in the Value Columns are correlated against that. This chart is useful to determine the variation of other parameters against a specific parameter.

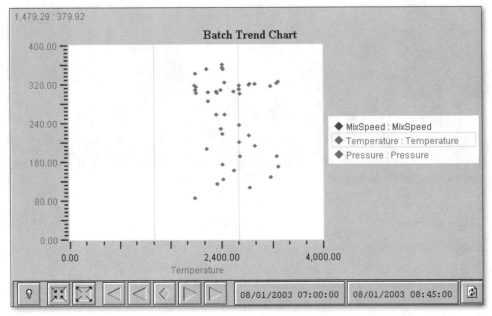

Figure 5.27   XY Chart

XY Regression Charts

XY regression charts are very similar to XY charts, with an additional linear regression line drawn on top of the scattered plot (Figure 5.28). This is useful for linear regression analysis.

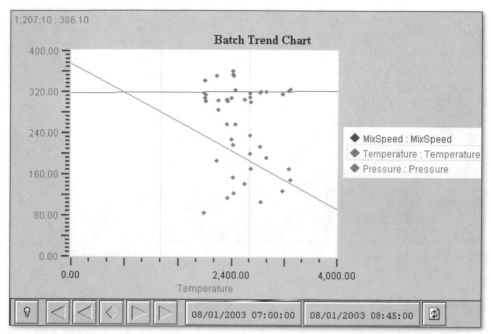

Figure 5.28 XY Regression Chart

Regression Charts

Regression charts are simple linear regression plots, similar to an XY regression chart without the scatter plot.

Strip Charts

Strip charts are dynamic line charts that plot values as a trend graph over time (Figure 5.29). The data query should provide continuous current values. When you refresh the chart, it displays the current trend along with past data points by creating the trend automatically in memory. If the auto-refresh feature is on, the chart updates itself continuously based on the refresh rate and plots the trend dynamically. The RefreshRate parameter in the chart and the RowCount parameter in the query template control the width of the time (x) axis. The duration for the real-time trend is determined by multiplying the RefreshRate by the RowCount. Because Tag queries can provide current values, you can use them for this chart type.

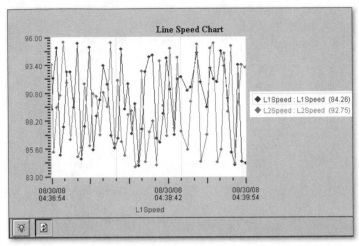

Figure 5.29 Strip Chart

Radar Charts

Radar charts are similar to polar charts, which display values in a circular axis, but without a time dimension (Figure 5.30). Usually this chart is plotted with query data returning key values and their distribution of sample values. The TickColor property in the X-Axis configuration tab controls the color of the spikes from the center of the chart. The TickColor property of the Y-Axis configuration tab controls the color of the concentric polygons that mark each tick mark on the chart. The MajorTickCount property of the Y-Axis configuration tab controls the number of ticks.

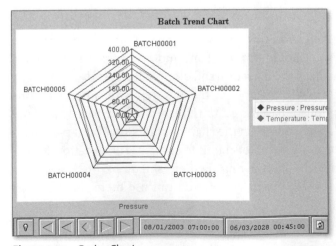

Figure 5.30 Radar Chart

Event Horizon Charts

Event horizon charts display time series–based events as vertical lines (Figure 5.31). The Data query must return a timestamp column for each event ID, which you can specify in the Label Columns property in the Data Mapping configuration tab.

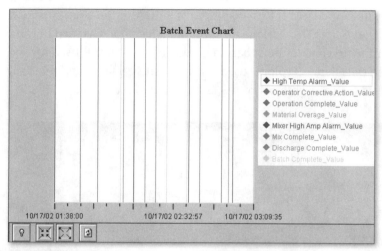

Figure 5.31 Event Horizon Chart

Custom Charts

Custom charts combine different types of charts (such as line, marker, bar, or StackedBar) into a single chart (Figure 5.32). The Value Columns specified in the Data Mapping configuration tab are represented in different forms in the same chart. You can configure the different types of representations of the different data values by the Type property in the Data Series Details configuration tab.

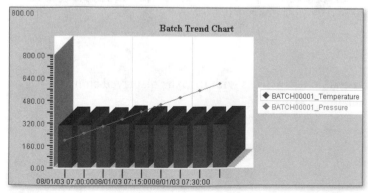

Figure 5.32 Custom Chart

Waterfall Charts

Waterfall charts are a variation of the StackedBar chart. Here each floating bar represents the value for the current x-axis item, but the position of the floating bar along the y-axis represents the cumulative values of the previous bars, with the last bar showing the cumulative values of all the bars as a full vertical bar (Figure 5.33). Negative, positive, first, and last bars are displayed in different Data Series colors, as specified in the Data Series Details configuration tab. The color specified in Data Series 1 is used for the first and leftmost bar, the Data Series 2 color is used for the negative values, the Data Series 3 color is used for the positive values, and the Data Series 4 color is used for the rightmost of the last calculated bar color.

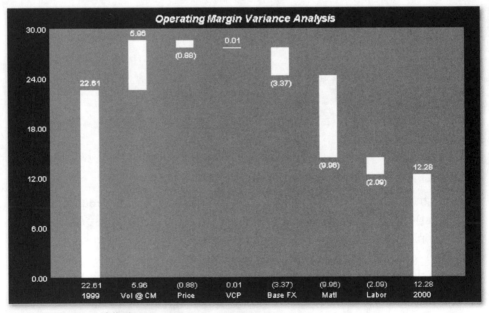

Figure 5.33   Waterfall Chart

Horizontal Bar Charts

Horizontal bar charts are simple bar charts with the bars displayed along the y-axis instead of the x-axis (Figure 5.34).

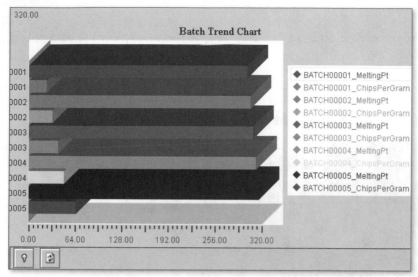

Figure 5.34   Horizontal Bar Chart

Horizontal Group Bar Charts

Horizontal group bar charts are the same as group bar charts, where the bars are grouped in horizontal fashion ordered by the data set keys according to the observation data (Figure 5.35).

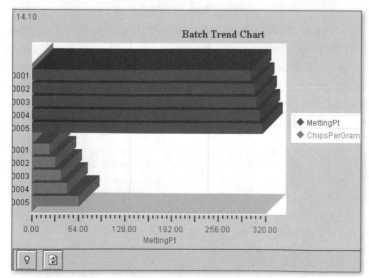

Figure 5.35   Horizontal Group Bar Chart

189

Area Charts

Area charts represent quantitative data by filling up the area below the data points according to the characteristic values (Figure 5.36).

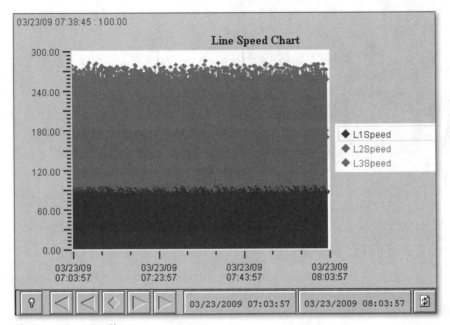

Figure 5.36 Area Chart

You can select the specific types of charts described previously depending on the representation required. You can embed these charts in web pages as applets (as explained in Chapter 8 Web Scripting and Reports: Weaving It All Together) and by dynamically manipulating the parameters using JavaScript, you can provide a real-time visualization of the production process to the Operator, Production Supervisor, or Plant Manager in the SAP MII dashboards.

> **Note**
>
> In addition to adding the chart as an applet in the web page, you can display it as a static image (JPEG/PNG) via the following URL:
>
> *http://<server>:<port>/XMII/ChartServlet?Width=<width pixel>&Height=<height pixel>&QueryTemplate=<querytemplatename>&DisplayTemplate=<displayt emplatename>&Content-Type=image/png&IllumLoginName=<login-name> &IllumLoginPassword=<login-password>&Param.1=<param 1 for query template>*

Apart from the properties specified in the URL, you can add any other properties of iChart and their values in the URL while rendering the image. This is particularly helpful when you want to develop content that can be viewed using mobile devices or from browsers that cannot display Java applets.

You now know how to configure the iChart display template to create different types of charts for visualization of process data. In the next section you learn how to create SPC charts using the iSPCChart display template, which is used for statistical quality analysis.

5.4   iSPCChart

iSPCChart is one of the most powerful display templates or analytics services available in SAP MII. SPC stands for Statistical Process Control, which is used for $3\sigma/6\sigma$ analysis on process control data and quality analysis. iSPCChart in SAP MII has the following general features:

▶ A variety of iSPCChart types such as XBAR, XBAR-MR, XBAR-SDEV, EWMA, MEDIAN, HISTOGRAM, BOX-WHISKER, P, NP, C, U, and so on for different types of process control and statistical quality analysis

▶ Auto-calculated standard statistical and quality indexes

▶ Visual alarms in the chart for SPC rule violation conditions

▶ Comment text addition for each data point

▶ Data point highlighting and suppression capabilities for ad-hoc analysis by user

As specified previously, iSPCChart in SAP MII offers ad-hoc dynamic analysis features to monitor and analyze process trends and process exceptions. It can serve as an important tool for statistical quality analysis.

Usually iSPCChart displays data from SQL or Xacute queries, which provide the data point values along with the Target, Upper Specification Limit (USL), Lower Specification Limit (LSL), Upper Control Limit (UCL), and Lower Control Limit (LCL) values. The data point or the sample values are displayed along with the USL, LSL, UCL, LCL, and Target values, as configured in the SPC chart. Data points violating an SPC rule are displayed with a red mark, per the configured alarm, and comments can be added for any data point displayed on the chart. You can also select any data point in the chart applet and highlight its corresponding attributes, if they are present in any other data points in the chart. This feature might help in doing a root-cause analysis.

You can use the iSPCChart to analyze the quality inspection result by fetching the data from Laboratory Information Management System (LIMS) or SAP Enterprise Resource Planning (ERP) system. Using the control chart you can readily take a decision to reject or accept a particular batch based on the alarms it has generated and understand the maturity and stability of the production process.

5.4.1 iSPCChart Configuration Tabs

iSPCChart has various configuration tabs, such as Parameters, Legend, Upper Chart Area, and much more, as seen in Figure 5.37.

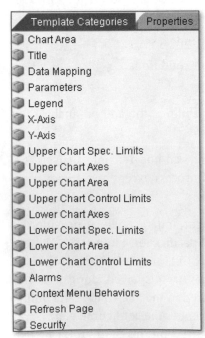

Figure 5.37 Configuration Categories of iSPCChart

In the Chart Area configuration tab, you can control visualizations by configuring the general properties for the SPC chart, as described in Table 5.11.

Property	Description
Chart Name	Specifies the user-defined name of the chart, which you can use as a parameter to retrieve control and specification limits. This is different from the chart title.
Description	Specifies a description of the chart.
Chart Type	Specifies the type of the chart such as XBAR, XBAR-MEAN, HISTOGRAM, and so on. The subtypes of the iSPC charts are explained later in this chapter.
Main Border Color	Specifies the border color of the chart applet.
Main Background Color	Specifies the background color of the chart applet.
Chart Margin	Specifies the distance of the actual chart plot from the margin of the chart in pixel.
Marker Size	Specifies the size of the data point markers in the chart.
Allow Item Selection	Specifies whether or not to allow the user to select the individual data points in the chart applet
Reverse Point Order	Specifies whether or not to display the data in reverse order as returned by the data query. This can be useful for time-series data.
Show Suppressed Points	Specifies whether or not to display the points that are suppressed by the user and not considered for the statistical analysis.
Show Limit Transitions	Specifies whether to display a vertical line wherever the limit changes in the chart. The color of the vertical line is the same as that of the center or target line color of the chart. This is applicable only when the specification limits or control limits values varies with time data.
Show Comment Flags	Specifies whether or not to display a red flag icon beside the data point in the chart that has a user comment associated with it.
Highlighted Attribute Name	Specifies the column name of the data query whose data points should be highlighted in the chart.
Highlighted Attribute Value	Specifies the value of the data points that should be highlighted in the chart.

Table 5.11 Chart Area Configuration Properties for iSPCChart

In the Title configuration tab, you can configure the properties for the chart title. Show Title specifies whether or not to display the title in the chart applet as specified in the Title property. Display Quick Info Text specifies whether or not to display the data values of the column specified in Quick Info Attribute Name as you move the mouse pointer over the chart applet. You can select only the columns specified in the Attribute Columns property of the Data Mapping configuration tab in the Quick Info Attribute Name property dropdown list.

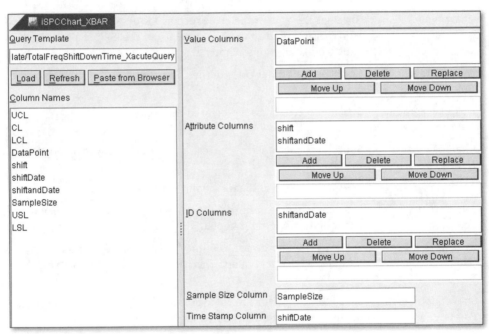

Figure 5.38 Data Mapping Configuration for iSPCChart

In the Data Mapping configuration tab (Figure 5.38), you can specify the data query and corresponding columns that should be plotted in the chart. Select a data query by clicking on the Load button. Add the column whose data values you want to analyze under the Value Columns. Most SPC charts have one value column only. Select the column and click on Add to add it, or simply drag and drop the selected column into the listbox. Add the columns that are additional attributes of the data points in the Attribute Columns listbox. These attribute values might be common for multiple data points, which can be highlighted at runtime in the SPC chart applet for ad-hoc analysis. In the ID Columns listbox, add the column names from the data query that are unique identifiers of the data point, for example, shiftID, orderID, and so on. If the data query returns a sample size column that you want to use instead of static attribute values, specify the column name in the Sample Size Column property. Time Stamp Column specifies the data query column that represents a timestamp for time-series data. You also use it to identify the break points in control limits, if break points are changed and an effective date is set.

In the Parameters configuration tab, you can configure the parameters and constants for different subtypes of control charts, as explained in Table 5.12.

Property	Description
Subgroup Size	Specifies the subgroup size of the analysis sample or the number of raw data points to be included in each chart point. Default value is 1.
Sample Size	Specifies the size of the sample from which the defects are being counted. Default value is 100.
Lambda	Specifies the smoothing parameter used in the EWMA chart type, used to weight the data when computing moving average. The value range is between 0 and 1. An EWMA chart is used in detecting small process shifts. The value of Lambda is related to the size of the shift you are trying to detect, which is considered directly proportional to the size of the shift. Common values of Lambda are 0.05, 0.25, 0.08, 0.10, 0.15.
Lower Limit of Box	Specifies the lower point of the box in BOX-WHISKER SPC chart type, which is typically the first quartile. Default value is 25.
Upper Limit of Box	Specifies the upper point of the box in BOX-WHISKER SPC chart type, which is typically the third quartile. Default value is 75.
Whisker Lower Limit	Specifies the lower whisker point for the BOX-WHISKER SPC chart, which is typically 0%.
Whisker Upper Limit	Specifies the upper whisker point for the BOX-WHISKER SPC chart, which is typically 100%.

Table 5.12 Parameters Configuration Properties for iSPCChart

Property	Description
Histogram Cell Count	Specifies the number of bars or buckets in the HISTOGRAM SPC Chart type.
Tolerance Type	Specifies the tolerance type in the SPC chart. Zero specifies bilateral tolerance, one specifies upper unilateral tolerance (the target being the upper specification limit), and a negative value specifies low unilateral tolerance (the target value being the lower specification limit).

Table 5.12 Parameters Configuration Properties for iSPCChart (Cont.)

In the Legend configuration tab, you can configure the properties for the legends in the iSPC chart applet, which are the same as that in the iChart Legend configuration (explained in Section 5.3 iChart).

In the X-Axis configuration tab (Figure 5.39), you can configure the properties for the x-axis for the SPC chart. Most of the parameters in this configuration tab are the same as that in the X-Axis configuration for iChart (explained in Section 5.3 iChart). X-Axis Label Attribute specifies the data query column to be used as the attribute for the x-axis in the SPC chart. Only the data query columns specified in Attribute Columns in the Data Mapping configuration tab appear in the dropdown list here.

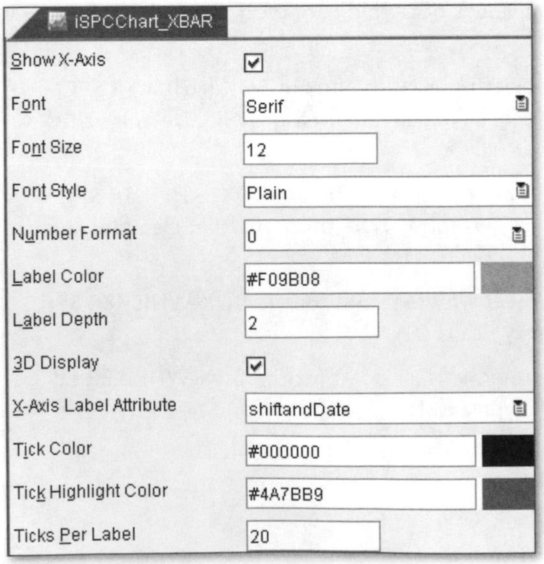

Figure 5.39 X-Axis Configuration for iSPCChart

In the Y-Axis configuration tab, you can configure the properties of the y-axis for the SPC chart. These properties are the same as those in the iChart Y-axis configuration (explained in Section 5.3 iChart).

In the Upper Chart Spec. Limits configuration tab, you can configure the specification limit and other related properties for the upper chart, as explained in Table 5.13.

Property	Description
Upper Spec. Limit Column	Specifies the column from the data query specified in Data Mapping that returns the upper specification limit value.
Target Column	Specifies the column from the data query specified in Data Mapping that returns the target value.
Lower Spec. Limit Column	Specifies the column from the data query specified in Data Mapping that returns the lower specification limit value.
Specification Limit Source	Specifies the data query to use for determining the upper and lower specification limits and the target value. The specification data must be returned in data set format with the columns in the following order: Effectivity Date (datetime data type), LSL (number data type), target (number data type), and USL (number data type). The result set can be multiple rows. The Effectivity Date value of the returned data determines which set of limits to use if multiple limits are returned by the query.
Param [n] for Spec. Limit	Specifies the parameters that can be passed as input when you are executing the Specification Limit Source query. You can pass a maximum of eight parameters. You need to pass the dynamic parameters within brackets, for example, [CHARTNAME], [CHARTTYPE].
Upper Spec. Limit	Specifies the Upper Specification Limit as a constant value, if not specified by the data query.
Target	Specifies the target as a constant value, if not specified by the data query.

Table 5.13 Upper Chart Spec. Limits Configuration Properties for iSPCChart

Property	Description
Lower Spec. Limit	Specifies the Lower Specification Limit as a constant value, if not specified by the data query.
Upper Spec. Limit of Upper Chart User	Specifies the user-defined upper specification limit as a constant value.
Target of Upper Chart User	Specifies the user-defined target as a constant value.
Lower Spec. Limit of Upper Chart User	Specifies the user-defined Lower Specification Limit as a constant value, if not specified by the data query.
Show Upper Specification Limits	Specifies whether or not to show the USL line in the chart applet.
Show Upper User Specification Limit	Specifies whether or not to show the user-defined USL line in the chart applet.
Show Upper User Target	Specifies whether or not to show the user-defined target line in the chart applet.
Spec. Limit Color of Upper Chart	Specifies the color of the specification limit lines for the upper chart.
Color of Upper Chart Target	Specifies the color of the target line for the upper chart.
Spec. Limit Color of Upper Chart User	Specifies the color of the user-defined specification limit lines for the upper chart.
Target Color of Upper Chart User	Specifies the color of the user-defined target line for the upper chart.

Table 5.13 Upper Chart Spec. Limits Configuration Properties for iSPCChart (Cont.)

You can set the specification limits and target by a specific data query, by the same data query used in Data Mapping, or as constant values in the configuration as explained in the previous table. You can also manipulate the specification limits and target at runtime using JavaScript. You can also specify the user-defined limits and target, which are typically manipulated at runtime to do "what-if" analysis.

In the Upper Chart Axes configuration tab, you can configure the x-axis and y-axis general properties and scaling ranges of the upper chart, as explained in Table 5.14.

Property	Description
Show Upper Tick Marks	Specifies whether or not to display the ticks in the upper chart x-axis.
Show Upper Labels	Specifies whether or not to display the x-axis labels for the upper chart.
Min. Range of Upper Chart	Specifies the minimum range of the upper chart y-axis.
Max. Range of Upper Chart	Specifies the maximum range of the upper chart y-axis.
Automatically Scale	Specifies whether or not to automatically scale the y-axis of the upper chart based on the Value Columns and specification and control limits.
Use Zero-Based Scale	Specifies whether or not to always use zero as the minimum range for the y-axis.
Use Server Scaling	Specifies whether or not to use the minmum and maximum ranges if returned by the data server.

Table 5.14 Upper Chart Axes Configuration Properties for iSPCChart

In the Upper Chart Area configuration tab, you can configure the colors and display patterns of the upper chart, as explained in Table 5.15.

Property	Description
Upper Chart Background Color	Specifies the background color of the upper chart.
Upper Chart Border Color	Specifies the border color of the upper chart.
Color of Upper Chart Line	Specifies the color of the line joining the data points in the upper chart.
Color of Upper Centerline	Specifies the color of the upper chart target control limit line.
Upper Bar Color	Specifies the color of the bars in the HISTOGRAM chart type and the box in the BOX-WHISKER chart type.
Color of Upper Chart Marker	Specifies the color of the data points marker in the upper chart.
Selected Marker Color of Upper Chart	Specifies the color of the selected data point marker in the upper chart.
Color of Highlighted Marker on Upper Chart	Specifies the color of the highlighted data points marker in the upper chart.

Table 5.15 Upper Chart Area Configuration Properties

Property	Description
Upper Alarms Color	Specifies the color of the data points marker that violates an alarm condition.
Color of Upper Inner Limit	Specifies the color of the upper inner limit.
Warning Limit Color for Upper Chart	Specifies the warning limit lines color for the upper chart.
Color of Upper Control Limit	Specifies the UCL and LCL lines color of upper chart.
Show Upper Control Limits	Specifies whether or not to show the upper chart control limits.
Show Upper Warning Limits	Specifies whether or not to show the upper chart warning limits.
Show Upper Inner Limits	Specifies whether or not to show the upper chart inner limits.
Show Upper Regions	Specifies whether or not to display the background color of the region among control limits, warning limits, and inner limits using the same color as that of the corresponding line colors.

Table 5.15   Upper Chart Area Configuration Properties (Cont.)

In the Upper Chart Control Limits configuration tab, you can configure the control limits for the upper chart. This configuration is similar to that of the Upper Chart Spec. Limits configuration. You can specify the control limits as column names of the data query used in Data Mapping or from another query specified in Source for Upper Control Limit (Figure 5.40). You can specify the parameters for executing the additional data query in the Param. [n] for Upper Control Limit properties. If you select the checkbox Calculate Control Limits, the control limits can be automatically calculated based on the data point values provided for the upper chart. You can also provide constant values for control limits by specifying the Upper Ctrl Limit of Upper Chart, Upper CL, and Lower Control Limit of Upper Chart properties.

In the Lower Chart Axes configuration tab, you can configure the x-axis and y-axis general properties and scaling ranges of the lower chart. The configurations are very similar to that of the Upper Chart Axes configurations.

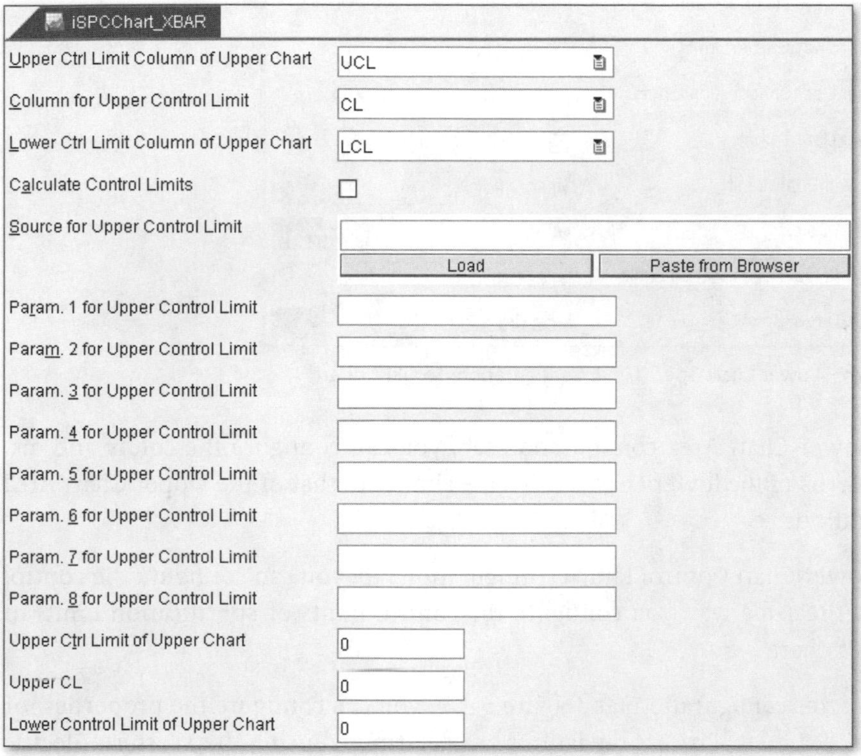

Figure 5.40   Upper Chart Control Limits Configuration for iSPCChart

In the Lower Chart Spec. Limits configuration tab, you can configure the user-defined specification limits (Figure 5.41). The configuration properties are similar to that of the Upper Chart Spec. Limits configuration; however, here you can specify only the user-defined specification limits for the lower chart, because the original specification limit is calculated by the values specified in that of the Upper Chart Spec. Limit configurations.

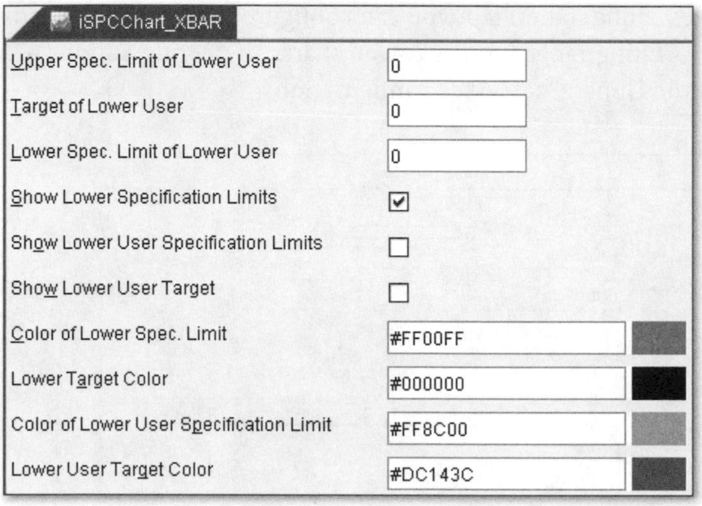

Figure 5.41 Lower Chart Spec. Limit Configurations for iSPCChart

In the Lower Chart Area configuration tab, you can configure the colors and display patterns of the lower chart, which are similar to that of the Upper Chart Area configurations.

In the Lower Chart Control Limits configuration tab, you can configure the control limits in the same way you configure the control limits or specification limits of the upper chart.

In the Alarms configuration tab (Figure 5.42), you can configure the properties for alarm or SPC rules. Process deviations are determined using the Western Electric Company (WECO) rules, and, in iSPCChart, some of the most common WECO rules have been provided as Alarms. The data points satisfying the alarm conditions are displayed in the color specified in Upper Alarms Color or Lower Alarms Color; these are configured in the SPC chart applet, in the Upper Chart Area and Lower Chart Area configurations, respectively. In the Alarms configuration tab, you can use the checkboxes to enable the rule for Upper Limit and Lower Limit. You use Alarm Limit for <Rule Name> to specify the number of data points violating the condition out of the number of data points specified in Alarm Length for <Rule Name>. You can configure the following rules for Alarms in iSPCChart:

1. **Control Limit Alarm:** A condition where data points violate the control limits.

2. **Specification Limit Alarm**: A condition where data points violate the specification limits.

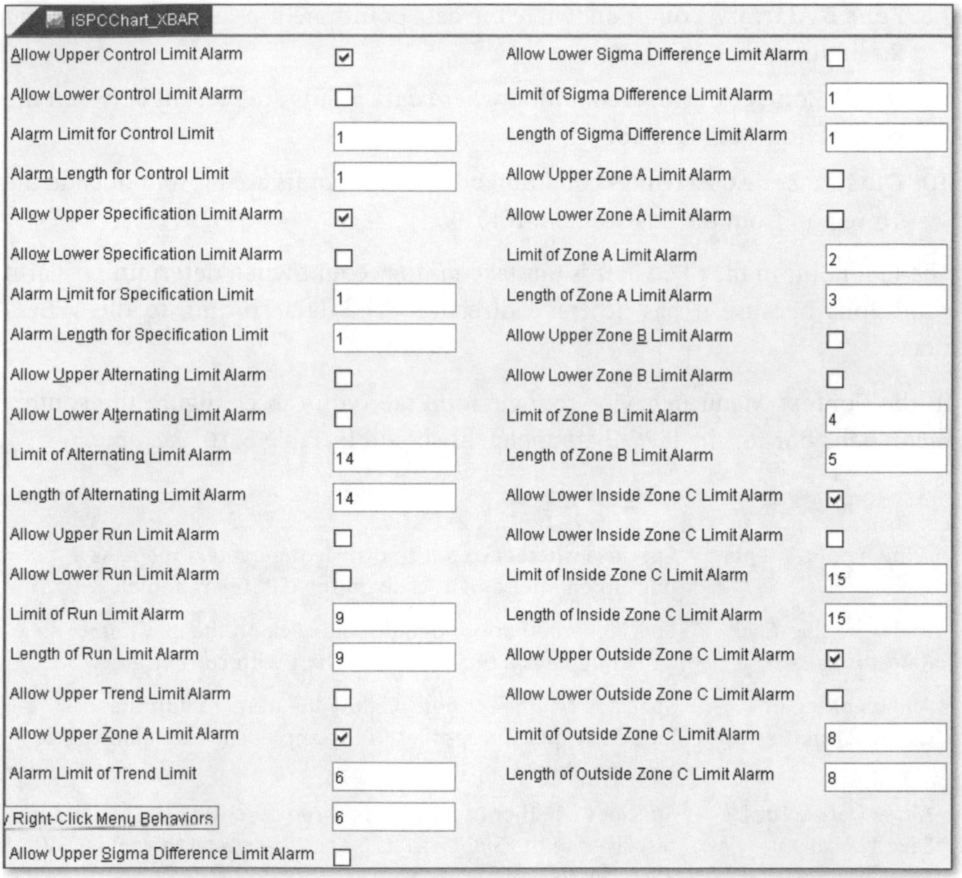

Figure 5.42 Alarms Configuration for iSPCChart

3. **Alternating Limit Alarm**: A condition where data points appear in alternate (up and down) fashion.

4. **Run Limit Alarm**: A condition where data points appear above or below the control line (CL).

5. **Trend Limit Alarm**: A condition where data points show a steadily increasing or decreasing trend.

6. **Sigma Difference Alarm**: This is no longer supported in SAP MII 12.0, though the checkboxes are present in the configuration screen.

7. **Zone A Alarm**: A condition where data points are present between 2σ and 3σ limits in the SPC chart.

8. **Zone B Alarm**: A condition where the data points are present between 1σ and 2σ limits in the SPC chart.

9. **Inside Zone C Alarm**: A condition where data points are present between the control limit (CL) and 1σ.

10. **Outside Zone C Alarm**: A condition where data points are present outside the 1σ region from the control limit (CL).

The first point in the SPC chart is not taken into account when determining alarm conditions because it has no trend direction. This is according to the WECO rules.

In the Context Menu Behavior configuration tab, you can configure the context menu behavior for the iSPCChart applet, as shown in Table 5.16.

Property	Description
Allow Popup Menu	Specifies whether or not to display the context menu as a pop-up on mouse right-click on the iSPCChart applet.
Allow Double-Click Refresh	Specifies whether or not a double-click on the iSPCChart applet updates a time-sensitive chart with current time.
Allow Editing of Query Properties	Specifies whether or not to allow the users to edit the iSPCChart query properties in the applet such as removing a tag name from the chart.
Allow Data to be Saved Locally	Specifies whether or not the user can save the query data displayed in the SPC chart as a comma-separated value (CSV) file locally.
Allow Detail Page Generation	Specifies that, if checked, the user can see the data displayed in the SPC chart as a separate HTML page. The detail page generation option is enabled in the applet at runtime only when the automatic refresh option is not on.
Show Time Refresh Control	Specifies whether or not to display the time-refresh control navigation bar at the bottom of the iSPCChart applet.
Allow Item Selection	Specifies whether or not to allow the user to select data points on the SPC chart.
Allow Comment Editing	Specifies whether or not to allow the user to enter comments on the data points on the SPC chart.
Allow Point Suppression	Specifies whether or not to allow the user to suppress or unsuppress data points on the SPC chart.

Table 5.16 Context Menu Behavior Configuration Properties for iSPCChart

In the Refresh Page configuration tab, you can configure the refresh rate and auto-refresh properties for the iSPCChart, which are the same as those of the iChart.

5.4.2 iSPCChart Subtypes

iSPCChart has a number of subtypes. We discuss these in the following sections.

XBAR Charts

The XBAR chart type plots the mean of the characteristic values in the subgroup (Figure 5.43). The control limits of the XBAR chart are calculated by the following formula, if not specified by the data query or in the control limits configurations:

$$UCL_x = \overline{\overline{X}} + A_2\overline{R}$$

$$LCL_x = \overline{\overline{X}} - A_2\overline{R}$$

where A_2 is a constant value depending on the subgroup size, $\overline{\overline{X}}$ is the overall average of the samples, and $\overline{R}$ is the mean of the ranges.

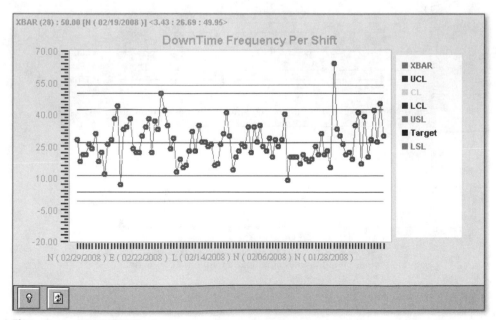

Figure 5.43 XBAR iSPCChart

XBAR-MR Charts

The XBAR-MR chart is an XBAR Moving Range chart that plots two charts (Figure 5.44). The upper chart is an XBAR chart (mean of subgroup data), and the lower chart plots both the range value of this subgroup and the range value of the previous subgroup (where the range is the difference between the largest and smallest values in the subgroup). This chart is usually used with a subgroup size of one, known as the XBAR-Individual Moving Range. The control limits are calculated by the following formula if not specified in the configuration:

$$UCL = \overline{\overline{X}} + 2.659575.\overline{R}$$

$$LCL = \overline{\overline{X}} - 2.659575.\overline{R}$$

For moving range, the control limit formula is as follows:

$$UCL = 3.267287.\overline{R}$$

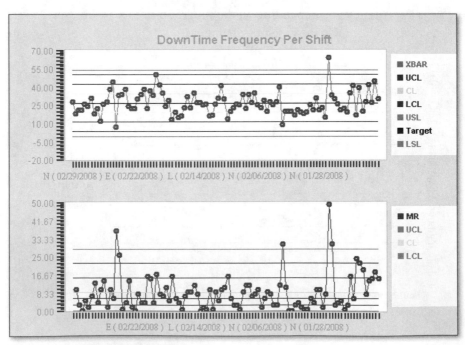

Figure 5.44 XBAR-MR iSPCChart

XBAR-RANGE Charts

The XBAR-RANGE chart type combines an XBAR chart with a range chart to monitor the process when the data is subgrouped (Figure 5.45). As with XBAR-MR, it plots two charts. The upper chart is an XBAR chart (mean of subgroup data), and the lower chart plots the range of the subgroup, where the range is the difference between the largest and smallest values in the subgroup. This chart type is plotted with a subgroup size greater than one. If the control limits are not specified by the data query or in the control limits configuration in the chart, they are calculated by the following formula:

$$UCL_R = D_4\overline{R}$$

$$LCL_R = D_3\overline{R}$$

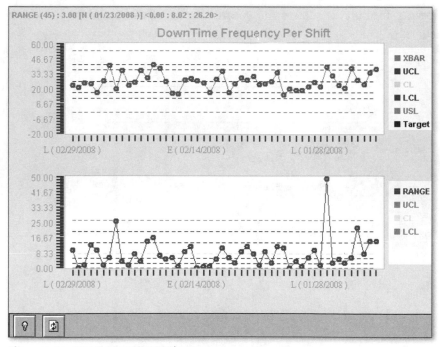

Figure 5.45 XBAR-RANGE iSPCChart

XBAR-SDEV Charts

The XBAR-SDEV chart type is an XBAR chart and a Standard Deviation Chart of ranges (Figure 5.46). The upper chart plots the XBAR (mean of subgroup data), and the lower chart plots the standard deviation of the characteristic values in the subgroup. This chart type is plotted with a subgroup size greater than one. The formula used to automatically calculate the control limits of the range (upper) chart is as follows:

$$UCL = \overline{\overline{X}} + A_3\overline{S}$$

$$LCL = \overline{\overline{X}} - A_3\overline{S}$$

where $\overline{S}$ is the mean of the standard deviation of the subgroups and A_3 is a constant depending on the subgroup size.

The following formula calculates the control limits of the standard deviation (lower) chart:

$$UCL_S = B_4\overline{S}$$

$$LCL_S = B_3\overline{S}$$

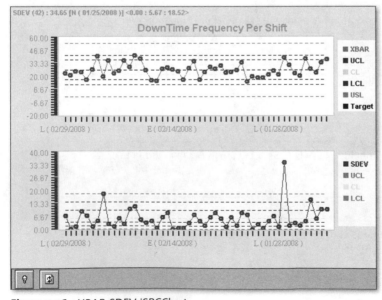

Figure 5.46 XBAR-SDEV iSPCChart

EWMA Charts

The EWMA chart type is an Exponentially Weighted Moving Average control chart that plots the weighted moving average of the characteristic values (Figure 5.47). For the first point in the chart, the following formula is used:

$$EWMA_1 = (1-\lambda)\cdot \overline{\overline{X}} + \lambda\overline{X}$$

where λ (Lambda) is a constant weighting factor that varies from 0 to 1. The variable $\overline{\overline{X}}$ is the overall average, whereas $\overline{X}$ is the actual "observed value."

For the remaining points, the following formula is used:

$$EWMA_{t+1} = (1-\lambda)\cdot EWMA_t + \lambda\overline{X}$$

The automatic control limits calculation is the same as that of the XBAR chart type.

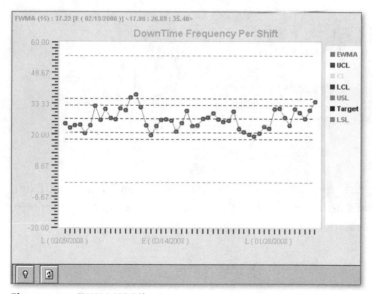

Figure 5.47 EWMA iSPCChart

EWMA-RANGE Charts

The EWMA-RANGE chart type plots two charts; the upper is an EWMA chart, and the lower is a moving range chart (Figure 5.48). The automatic control limits calculation formula for the moving range chart is as follows:

$$\text{UCL}_{\text{EWMA}} = \overline{\overline{X}} + A_2\overline{R}\sqrt{\frac{\lambda}{2-\lambda}}$$

$$\text{LCL}_{\text{EWMA}} = \overline{\overline{X}} - A_2\overline{R}\sqrt{\frac{\lambda}{2-\lambda}}$$

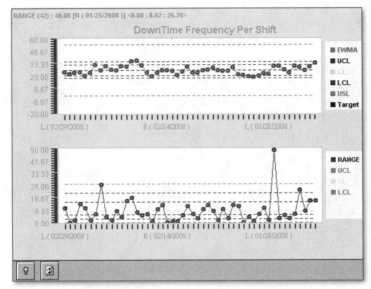

Figure 5.48   EWMA-RANGE iSPCChart

EWMA-SDEV Charts

The EWMA-SDEV chart type plots two charts; the upper is an EWMA chart, and the lower is a standard deviation chart of the characteristic values (Figure 5.49). The control limits calculation formula for the lower chart is as follows:

$$\text{UCL}_{\text{EWMA}} = \overline{\overline{X}} + A_3\overline{R}\sqrt{\frac{\lambda}{2-\lambda}}$$

$$\text{LCL}_{\text{EWMA}} = \overline{\overline{X}} - A_3\overline{R}\sqrt{\frac{\lambda}{2-\lambda}}$$

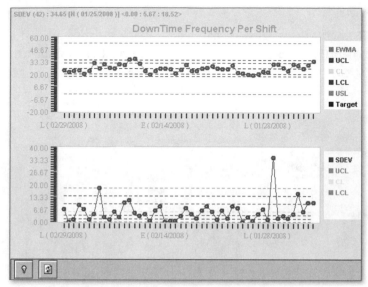

Figure 5.49 EWMA-SDEV iSPCChart

MEDIAN Charts

The MEDIAN chart type plots the median values for the subgroup (Figure 5.50). The control limit calculation is similar to the XBAR chart.

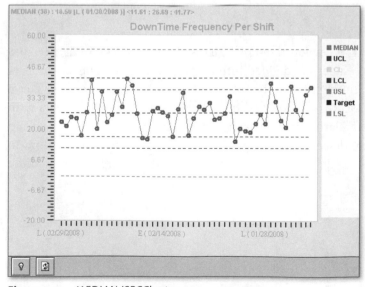

Figure 5.50 MEDIAN iSPCChart

MEDIAN-RANGE Charts

The MEDIAN-RANGE chart type plots two charts, an upper median chart and a lower moving range chart (Figure 5.51). The control limit calculation is similar to the XBAR-RANGE chart.

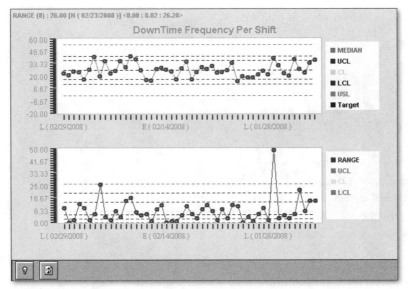

Figure 5.51 MEDIAN-RANGE iSPCChart

HISTOGRAM Charts

The HISTOGRAM chart type plots the statistical distribution of a set of data (Figure 5.52). The data point values are divided into ranges, and the heights of the bars are determined by counting the number of samples within each range. The curve overlaid on the HISTOGRAM shows the theoretical normal for a set of data with the same mean and standard deviation as the actual data. This curve is a visual aid useful for helping you determine if the data came from a normal distribution. In this chart type, you must define the specification limits (USL, Target, LSL) with no control limits.

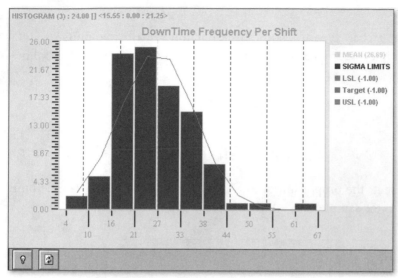

Figure 5.52   HISTOGRAM iSPCChart

BOX-WHISKER CHART

The BOX-WHISKER chart type is ideal for displaying both the center and variability of the process on the same chart (Figure 5.53). It displays a single chart with a spread of data for all visible characteristics, and pictorially describes its pattern of variation using the median set of data, the inter-quartile range, and the extreme values. This chart type is also known as a boxplot.

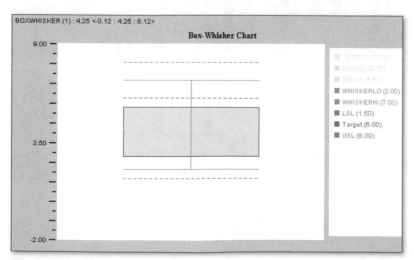

Figure 5.53   BOX-WHISKER iSPCChart

P Charts

You can use the P chart type to measure the fraction of defective units per total units of the sample (Figure 5.54). The control limits are calculated by the following formula:

$$UCL_p = \overline{P} + 3 \cdot \sqrt{\overline{P}(1-\overline{P})}/\sqrt{n}$$

$$LCL_p = \overline{P} - 3 \cdot \sqrt{\overline{P}(1-\overline{P})}/\sqrt{n}$$

where $\overline{P}$ represents the proportion of total defective units in all the sample units and n represents the sample size, which is assumed to be constant.

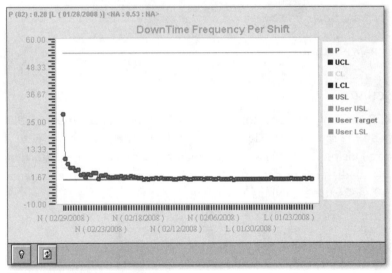

Figure 5.54   P iSPCChart

NP Charts

The NP chart type is similar to the P chart type, with the only difference being that you can use it to measure the actual number of defective units instead of the proportion of defective units (Figure 5.55). The control limits are calculated using the following formula:

$$UCL_{np} = n\overline{p} + 3 \cdot \sqrt{n\overline{p}\left(1 - \frac{n\overline{p}}{n}\right)}$$

$$LCL_{np} = n\overline{p} - 3 \cdot \sqrt{n\overline{p}\left(1 - \frac{n\overline{p}}{n}\right)}$$

$$\text{where } n\overline{p} = \frac{np_1 + np_2 + \cdots + np_k}{k}$$

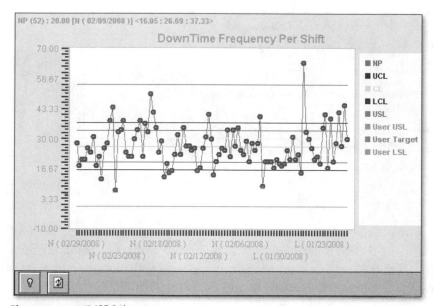

Figure 5.55 NP iSPCChart

C Charts

The C chart type is an attribute control chart that you can use to measure the total number of defects in a sample (Figure 5.56). Unlike P charts, you can use the C chart to measure multiple nonconformities. The control limits are calculated by the following formula:

$$UCL_c = \overline{C} + \sqrt{\overline{C}}$$

$$LCL_c = \overline{C} - \sqrt{\overline{C}}$$

where $\overline{C}$ represents the average number of defects per sample.

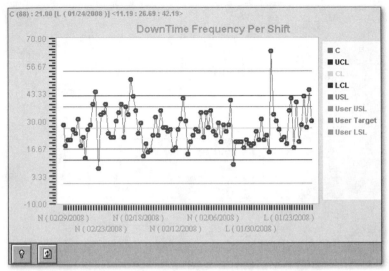

Figure 5.56 C iSPCChart

U Charts

You can use the U chart type to measure the average number of defects per unit (Figure 5.57). The U chart is useful in situations where a product has multiple non-conformities, but the area of opportunity for those non-conformities changes over time. The control limits are calculated by the following formula:

$$UCL_u = \overline{U} + 3\sqrt{\frac{\overline{U}}{a_i}}$$

$$LCL_u = \overline{U} - 3\sqrt{\frac{\overline{U}}{a_i}}$$

where $\overline{U}$ represents the average number of defects per sample of the unit.

You can use these different types of iSPCCharts to create run charts for different types of analysis. They are mainly used to determine the process maturity or defective units for rejection on quality inspection results, batch properties, and shift downtime.

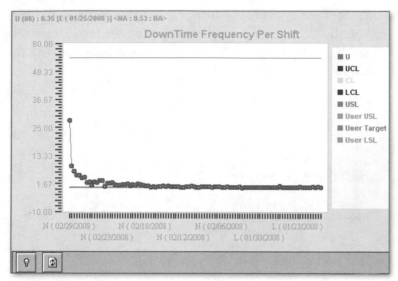

Figure 5.57 U iSPCChart

5.4.3 SPC Analysis Using iSPCChart

iSPCChart in SAP MII offers certain features for analysis by end users. These analyses are possible only while the chart is displayed as an applet in the web page. Using JavaScript, you can execute certain methods of the iSPCChart to set or get the analysis data. The context menu on the applet, which you control with the Context Menu Behavior configurations, provides the menu option for SPC analysis by the user.

The Data Menu category on the context menu of the iSPCChart provides the menu options for displaying and saving the raw data point values, calculated SPC results, and the statistical indexes (Figure 5.58). The Raw Data Details menu option displays the data point values plotted in the chart. The SPC Results menu option displays the calculated SPC and statistical indexes such as Cp, Cpk, Cpm, Cpl, and so on in a new web page, along with the calculated and raw data point values and the alarm details. The Summary Statistics menu option displays only the calculated indexes and limits in a pop-up window. The Data Points of Upper Chart and Lower

Chart Data Points menu options display only the raw data points of the upper and lower charts, along with the limits, in a pop-up window. You can locally save the raw data values or the SPC result values as CSV files by the menu options Save Raw Data as CSV File and Save SPC Results as CSV File.

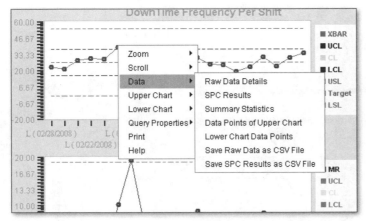

Figure 5.58 Data Context Menu in iSPCChart Applet

The Upper Chart and Lower Chart menu categories contain the menu options relevant for the Upper and Lower charts, respectively (Figure 5.59).

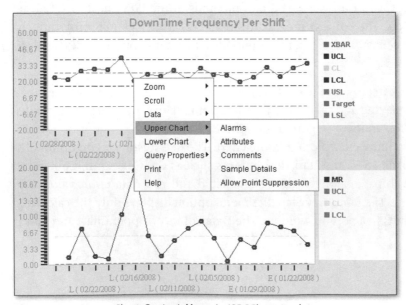

Figure 5.59 Upper Chart Context Menu in iSPCChart Applet

The Alarms menu option, present under the Upper Chart and Lower Chart categories, displays the alarms generated for the SPC chart data in a pop-up window. The data points satisfying the alarm condition are displayed in the Alarm Color in the chart itself. The Attributes menu option opens a pop-up window with the attributes and its corresponding values for the selected data point. You can select an attribute value and click on Highlight to highlight only the data points in the chart having the same attribute value as the selected one (Figure 5.60). This feature is useful for doing a root-cause analysis by determining the relevant attributes responsible for the deviations.

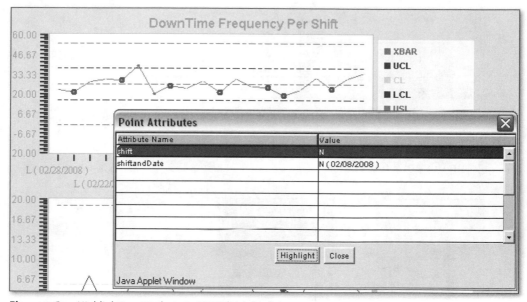

Figure 5.60 Highlighting Attribute in iSPCChart Applet

You can add any comment to any data point in the chart by selecting it and clicking on the Comments menu option. A pop-up window opens where you can view any existing comments or add new comments by clicking on the Add button (Figure 5.61). The data points that already have comments are displayed with a red flag icon in the chart.

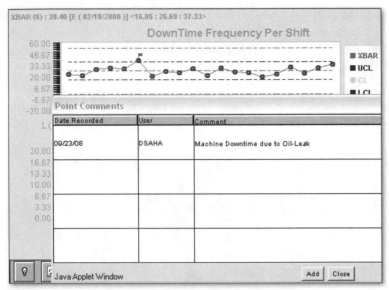

Figure 5.61 Adding Comments to Data Points in iSPCChart

The Sample Details menu option displays the sample values for the selected subgroup (Figure 5.62).

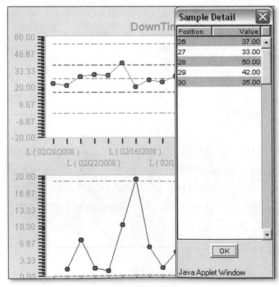

Figure 5.62 Sample Details in iSPCChart Applet

The Allow Point Suppression menu option hides the selected data point from the chart and those are not used for the analysis.

The Lower Chart menu category also has the same menu options of the Upper Chart menu category.

> **Note**
>
> You can display the iSPCChart as a static image (JPEG/PNG) instead of an applet via the following URL:
>
> *http://<server>:<port>/XMII/SPCChartServlet?Width=<width pixel>&Height =<heightpixel>&QueryTemplate=<querytemplatename>&DisplayTemplate=< displaytemplatename>&Content-Type=image/png&IllumLoginName=<login-name>&IllumLoginPassword=<login-password>&Param.1=<param 1 for query template>*
>
> You can also obtain the statistical analysis result by the following HTTP service:
>
> *http://<server>:<port>/XMII/SPCXMLServlet?QueryTemplate=<querytemplatename>& DisplayTemplate=<displaytemplatename>&IllumLoginName= <login name>&IllumLogInPassword=<login-password>&Param.1=<param 1 for query template>*

Now that you know about the different configuration options for iSPCChart, you can create display templates for statistical quality analysis by configuring relevant data queries.

In the next section, you learn how to configure the iBrowser display template to create UI controls as dropdown or tree-view lists.

5.5 iBrowser

You can use the iBrowser display template to display a list of data in a web page as a listbox, tree-view, or dropdown type applet. You can use this applet as a user selection control (for example, dropdown) in the web page for multiple data items, for example, a list of material batches. The configuration of the iBrowser display template is very simple and consists of only three configuration categories:

- General
- Data Mapping
- Security

In the General configuration tab, you can configure the general properties, as explained in Table 5.17 and shown in Figure 5.63.

Property	Description
Text Color of Selected Row	Specifies the text color of the selected row in the applet.
Background Color of Selected Row	Specifies the background color of the selected row only for tree-view display.
Dropdown List Mode	Specifies whether or not the data is displayed in a drop-down list.
Multiple Selection Mode	Specifies whether or not to allow the user to select multiple rows in the list or tree-view modes.
Always Expanded	Specifies whether or not the list of data always appears as expanded in list or tree-view modes.
Data Link Mode	Specifies if the data query returns two columns, where one filters or groups the other (for example, colors for batches or equipment ID for equipment names) for tree view. For listbox or dropdown, the second column is invisible and its values can be accessed by JavaScript methods in the web page.
Initial Value	Specifies the initial value to be selected when the applet loads.
Default Item	Specifies a default value that appears at the top of the list, for example, "Select an Item."
Data Link for Default Item	Specifies the default item used for datalink if the Data Link Mode is selected.

Table 5.17 General Configuration Properties for iBrowser

In the Data Mapping configuration tab (Figure 5.64), you can configure the data query used for the iBrowser display template. Select the query template to use by clicking on the Load button. The columns returned by the data query appear in the Column Names listbox. Select one or more columns and add them to the Display Columns listbox by clicking on the Add button. If you add multiple columns as Display Columns and configure the iBrowser as a dropdown or listbox (we explain how to do this later), then the second column is invisible. For this reason, specify the first column as the display column here. You can determine the value selected in the iBrowser by the user in the web page using the JavaScript methods available for it, as explained in Chapter 8 Web Scripting and Reports: Weaving It All Together.

Figure 5.63 General Configuration for iBrowser

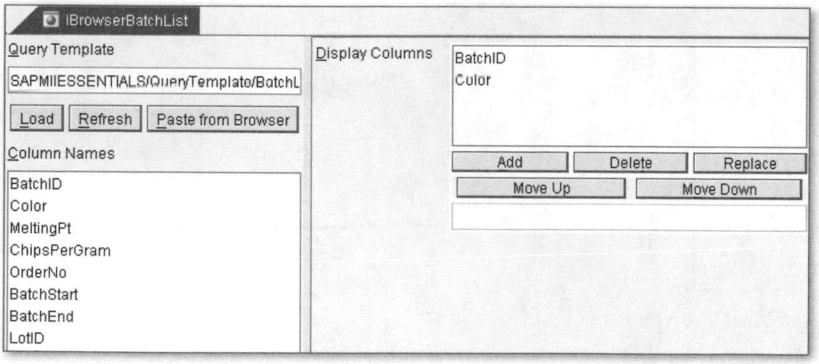

Figure 5.64 Data Mapping Configurations for iBrowser

No automatic refresh or context menu features are available for iBrowser. You can display the iBrowser display template in the dropdown, tree-view, or listbox modes.

If you specify a single column in the Display Columns property in the Data Mapping configuration, and select the Dropdown List Mode option in the General configuration, then the applet is displayed as a dropdown listbox, as shown in Figure 5.65. If you specify two columns as Display Columns, then you need to select the Data Link Mode to display the data as a dropdown listbox.

Figure 5.65   Dropdown iBrowser Applet

If the Data Link Mode option is not selected and you specify multiple columns in Display Columns and in General configuration, then the iBrowser is displayed as tree view (Figure 5.66).

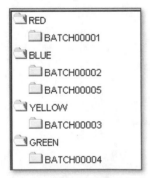

Figure 5.66   Tree-View iBrowser Applet

The iBrowser applet is displayed as a listbox (Figure 5.67) when the following conditions are met: (a) you have not selected the Dropdown List Mode; (b) you have selected the Data Link Mode in General configuration; and (c) you have specified either single column or multiple columns in the Display Columns in Data Mapping configuration.

Figure 5.67 Listbox iBrowser Applet

Now that you know how to configure iBrowser display template for creating drop-down, list, or tree-view applets, in the next section you learn about the iCommand display template and how to configure it to execute SQL queries and BLS Transactions.

5.6 iCommand

The iCommand display template is an invisible display template that you can use to execute, create, update, or delete queries that return no output data from a web page (such as Command queries or Xacute queries). You can also use the iCommand applet to execute data queries that return output; this is required mainly when you don't use a standard display template such as iGrid or iChart, but want to use that data in JavaScript for any client-side presentation logic, or want to display the data using HTML forms or tables. Some of those examples are explained in detail in Chapter 8 Web Scripting and Reports: Weaving It All Together. Authentication and digital signatures are also supported by iCommand to incorporate strict security control and 21 CFR Part 11–compliant solutions, mostly required by the pharmaceutical industry. You can use the same iCommand display template for executing multiple query templates if the security protocol is the same in all cases or if you do not require it at all. You need to add the iCommand applet in the web page with the corresponding query template, which is not shown as a visible applet to the user. You should execute the applet's JavaScript methods by the user events in the Web page — for example, by a button-click — to execute the query or to get the error message. You need to use the iCommand applet, for example, to execute a BLS Transaction as a Xacute query, a SQL query, or a writable Tag query from the web page to update the data in the backend data sources for example, creating order confirmation in SAP ERP, updating batch status in legacy database, and so on.

> **Note**
>
> You do not need to create an iCommand display template to execute queries if authentication is not required. You can simply refer to the iCommand applet in the HTML in the web pages with the corresponding query template without referring to any display template.

The configuration of iCommand consists of only audit and security configurations in the following configuration categories:

▸ General

▸ Security

In the General configuration tab, you can configure the audit mechanism for the iCommand, as explained in Table 5.18.

Property	Description
Audit	Specifies whether or not to enable the audit or authentication features for the user. Enabling this requires the user to provide the authentication information when executing a query using the iCommand from the web page.
Command Audit Role 1	Specifies the User Management Engine (UME) role to which the logged-in user should belong.
Command Audit Role 1 Logon Required	Specifies whether or not the user needs to specify user name and password when executing the query. A pop-up window appears in the web page for the user to specify the logon details.
Confirm Full Name for Audit Role 1	Specifies whether or not the full name of the user as specified in the UME should be confirmed by a pop-up window before executing the query.
Command Audit Role 2	Specifies the second UME role for another user (for example, the supervisor), whose user name and password are prompted before executing the query.
Confirm Full Name for Audit Role 2	Specifies whether or not the full name of the user as specified in the UME should be confirmed by a pop-up window before executing the query.

Table 5.18 General Configuration Properties for iCommand

Property	Description
Category	Specifies the text that can be used to sort or filter log messages.
Command Text	Specifies a descriptive command text.
Return Message	Specifies a text that can be obtained by JavaScript methods in the web page, regardless of whether or not the query is executed.

Table 5.18 General Configuration Properties for iCommand (Cont.)

You can use the auditing feature of iCommand, as explained in Table 5.18, to control authorization and access by executing Xacute or Command queries. You can incorporate digital signature solutions by iCommand, because it provides the parameters required for creating a digital signature. If you use an Xacute query to execute a BLS, then you can access the following environment variables in the BLS Transaction, using the following transaction properties to verify and record the user authentication details:

▶ **CommandGUID:** Unique identifier for the transaction

▶ **CommandUserID1:** Primary user ID

▶ **CommandUserName1:** Primary user full name

▶ **CommandRole1:** Primary role requirement from iCommand template

▶ **CommandMachine:** IP address or machine name of client machine where data was entered

▶ **CommandText:** Text from iCommand template

▶ **CommandDateTime:** Date and time of data entry

▶ **CommandUserID2:** Second user's ID, if necessary

▶ **CommandUserName2:** Second user's full name, if necessary

▶ **CommandRole2:** Second role requirement from iCommand template, if necessary

Add the preceding transaction properties as input parameters of type string in the BLS Transaction and do not assign any value to them and do not map them with the input parameters of the Xacute query either. Inside the BLS Transaction you can use these transaction properties, which have the corresponding values at run-time, to create the digital signature of the user who has executed the iCommand from a web page and can log it as required.

You can execute the iCommand in the web page on user events, such as a button click, by JavaScript method, which is explained in Chapter 8 Web Scripting and Reports: Weaving It All Together.

Now that you know how to configure iCommand to execute queries and specify authentication parameters, in the next section you learn about how to use the iCalendar display template to display a calendar control applet in a web page.

5.7   iCalendar

You can use the iCalendar display template to provide the user a visual way to select a specific date time in a web page (Figure 5.68). You cannot create this display template in the Workbench, and you can only add it to the web page as an applet referring to the standard iCalendar display template. This displays the iCalendar applet in a pop-up window for user selection and does not require any query template reference.

Figure 5.68 iCalendar Applet

5.8   Summary

In this chapter, you have learned how to configure various display templates to create engaging and intelligent visualization applets for analysis and real-time display of manufacturing process data.

In the next chapter, you will learn about the Business Logic Services and how to create Business Logic Transactions using the code-free modeling environment. This will allow you to create business logic for data processing and system integration, embedding intelligence into the manufacturing composites.

This chapter introduces Business Logic Services and explains how to use them to (a) create Web service–enabled transactions for data processing and (b) to develop intelligence in SAP MII–based composite applications.

6 Business Logic Transactions: Intelligence in Action

After you have connected to the plant systems using Data Servers and configured the data queries to retrieve and update the data from and to those systems, you might need to develop custom business logic to aggregate and parse the data and connect to the enterprise systems for retrieving and updating the relevant information, along with generating dynamic dashboard components such as dynamic graphics and charts. In this chapter you learn about Business Logic Services and how to create Business Logic Transactions to model reusable business logic for data processing and system integration.

6.1 Introduction

Business Logic Services (BLS) is the logic execution engine of SAP MII, which you can use to develop executable business logic for data processing, system integration, graphical analytics chart generation, file I/O, alert generation, Key Performance Indicator (KPI) update, and more. The BLS are provided by transactions, which are graphically modeled executable programs developed in the SAP MII Workbench.

BLS Transactions are stored as XML in SAP MII and are interpreted and executed by the BLS engine at runtime. You can execute any BLS Transaction from an applet by using the iCommand display template via the XacuteQuery from a web page. You can also execute it as an XML HTTP service or Web service from an external system. Finally, you can execute the BLS Transactions from the SAP MII Workbench and display the output in a pop-up window there. This last option is mainly used for unit testing and debugging purposes.

You can create a new BLS Transaction from the SAP MII Workbench via FILE • NEW • TRANSACTION. Any BLS Transaction can have multiple input and output parameters, as defined in the BLS Transaction Editor in the SAP MII Workbench. You need to assign each output and input with a data type from the list that is supported by BLS. You can define the input and output parameters of a BLS Transaction by the transaction properties, which you can access via TRANSACTION • TRANSACTION PROPERTIES menu, or in the Transaction configuration tab in the bottom left pane of the Workbench, as shown in Figure 6.1.

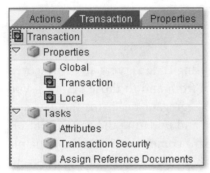

Figure 6.1 BLS Transaction Configuration

Opening the Transaction Properties menu displays the input and output parameters defined for that transaction in a pop-up window (Figure 6.2). You can add a new transaction property by clicking on the Add button, which opens another pop-up window to specify the property name, optional description, and data type, and optional minimum, maximum, and default values. To specify a parameter as an output parameter of the transaction, you need to check the Output Parameter checkbox while defining the property. If the box is not checked, the parameter is considered to be an input parameter for the transaction. The data type of any transaction parameter can be any one of the following:

▶ Boolean

▶ Integer

▶ Double

▶ String

▶ DateTime

▶ XML

Though the other data types are standard W3C data types, an XML data type in an SAP MII BLS Transaction specifies an XML document. You can define the XML structure at design time by specifying the XML in the Value field. Otherwise, you can define the structure of the XML data type parameter by using Reference Documents (explained later in this chapter). The transaction properties already defined are displayed in the main Transaction Property pop-up window with the name, description, input/output flag, and a graphical icon to signify the corresponding data type, as shown in Figure 6.2.

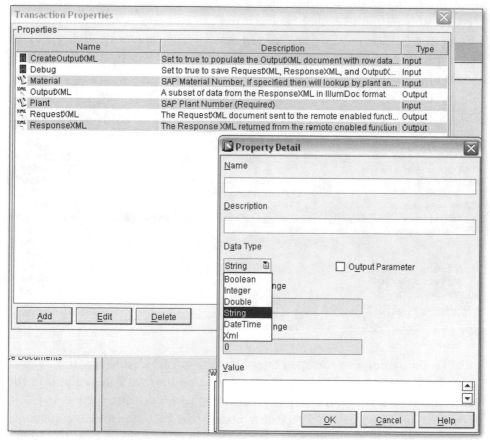

Figure 6.2 Configuring BLS Transaction Properties

You can define and use local properties in the same way as transaction properties (Figure 6.2). The only difference between the two is that local properties can only be used inside the BLS Transaction and are not visible from the calling application. These are analogous to local variables in common programming languages. You can define the local properties in the same Transaction configuration tab (in the bottom left corner of the workbench) or in the toolbar menu via TRANSACTION • LOCAL PROPERTIES.

Also, certain global properties are accessible from any BLS Transaction in the same server. These are properties whose values are valid across the server, such as mail server hostname and ExecutionTimeout. You can edit any global property value for any BLS Transaction. You can also add new global properties and delete existing properties by following the menu path TRANSACTION • GLOBAL PROPERTIES, as shown in Figure 6.3.

Global Properties

Properties

Name	Description	Type
BCLogicalSystemName		Output
BCPassword	SAP BC password for automated transactions	Output
BCServer	Our SAP BC Host Address	Output
BCServerPort	Our SAP BC Port	Output
BCUserName	SAP BC user name for automated transactions	Output
ExecutionTimeout		Output
FTPServer	FTP Server Host	Output
IPMFlag		Input
MailAccount		Output
MailAccountPassword		Output
MailServer		Output
SAPLogicalSystemName		Output

Figure 6.3 Global Properties of BLS Transaction

Any BLS Transaction is made up of one or more sequences, which are the containers or logical groupings of action blocks. An action block is a logical unit in the BLS Transaction that performs a particular action such as creating or parsing XML document, looping through a repeating node of an XML document, assigning a variable value, executing a Remote Function Call (RFC) or Web service, executing a query, and so on. Each BLS Transaction must have at least one sequence created by default that is called the root sequence and that cannot be deleted. The BLS Transactions are modeled graphically in the transaction editor using the action blocks, which you can drag and drop into the main window inside a sequence. You can add sequences below or above one another. You can add any number of sequences below a sequence at the same level, but only a single sequence at the same level above a sequence. You can add a sequence above another sequence by selecting a sequence and selecting the Insert Sequence option from the context menu and below a sequence by selecting the Add Sequence menu option. The sequences you add below one get added from left to right. The order of execution in a BLS Transaction is always from left to right and then top to bottom (Figure 6.4).

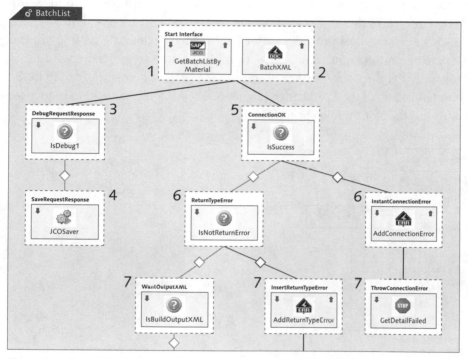

Figure 6.4 Execution Sequence in BLS Transaction

In Figure 6.4, a sample BLS Transaction is shown in design time, where the outer rectangles are the sequences. The action blocks, which are the inner rectangles with a name and an icon on them, are placed inside the sequences. You can add multiple action blocks in a single sequence (with the exception of a few actions blocks, such as Conditional or Repeater). Action blocks that are present in the same sequence get executed from left to right. The numbers are added beside the sequences to explain the sequence of flow in a BLS Transaction. Some sequences are marked with the same numbers, because those sequences are present below a sequence containing a conditional logic action block that decides at runtime to which child sequence the control will flow. Each sequence must have a name; a description is optional. The name is generated by default and can be changed in the sequence properties configuration.

The core building blocks of BLS Transactions are predefined, reusable action blocks that provide built-in functionality for different logic, data processing, connectivity features, and more. They can be used to define a program structure and are provided for a number of functions. These include executing data queries, Remote Function Calls (RFCs), or BAPI from SAP systems; Web services; sending SOAP and HTTP messages to SAP XI; sending and reading emails; statistical quality control (SQC) and statistical process control (SPC) analysis; defining flow logic; and XML parsing and manipulation. The action blocks are categorized according to the functionality they offer and are present in the Actions configuration tab in the bottom-left corner of the Workbench (Figure 6.5), which you can add to sequences via drag and drop or double-clicking.

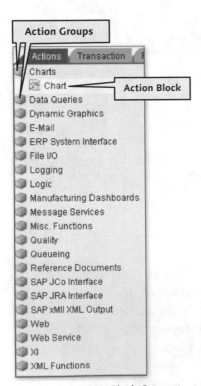

Figure 6.5 Action Block Categories in BLS Transaction

Each action block added in a sequence must have a name (a description is optional), which you can change from the action block configurations. Action blocks have two configuration modes: Object Configuration and Link Configuration. You can invoke these two configuration modes by double-clicking on an action block added to a sequence or by selecting the corresponding menu option from the context menu on that action block.

Each action block has different sets of properties or attributes based on the functionality they provide to which you can assign or read values. Using Object Configuration, you can configure most of the properties of the action blocks with fixed values at design time. Using Link Configuration, you can define the data mapping of the action blocks' attributes. You must perform the Link Configuration in the Link Editor, where you can read or manipulate the values of the attributes of the action blocks. You can also set the configuration properties of the action blocks with dynamic values or variables, which will be replaced by the actual values at runtime, using the Link Configuration.

The Link Editor screen has two tabs: Incoming and Outgoing. The configuration in the Incoming tab is evaluated before the action block is executed, and the configuration in the Outgoing tab is evaluated after the execution of the action block. In other words, the Incoming configuration tab provides the input parameters of the action block whose values can be configured there, whereas the Outgoing configuration tab provides the output parameters of the action block which can be read from other subsequent action blocks. In the Incoming tab, the selected action block appears at the right side of the window as the target; all the action blocks that are present before the selected one appear on the left as the source. In the Outgoing tab, all action blocks present before the selected action block along with that one appear on both sides of the editor, but only the writable or configurable properties appear under their corresponding action blocks on the right. Both read-only and configurable properties appear under their corresponding actions on the left.

Note

The links defined in the Outgoing tab of an action block are skipped in case of the action block execution failure. Therefore, you should not use the Outgoing links section to map properties of action blocks other than the current one.

To map the attributes from a previous action block or transaction and local properties to the attributes of the current action block, you can drag and drop the attribute from the left to the right, or you can select the source action block's attribute (on the left) and double-click the target attribute (on the right) to create a simple mapping or link.

You can also define conditional or complex mapping by using the Expression Editor at the bottom of the Link Editor. Any expression can be written in the Expression Editor, using the functions available in the Functions drop-down list. Complex expressions can involve string operations (for example, concat, substring, and so on) or numeric calculations (for example, addition, subtraction, log, square root, and so on); formatting; date functions; hexadecimal color codes; and so on. Clicking the Evaluate button opens a screen with the result of the expression you defined, or an error if the expression is incorrect.

To add a new mapping, click on the Add button, and to update an existing mapping, click on the Update button. You can delete an existing mapping by clicking on the Delete button. Always select the target action block's property at the right to add, update, or delete its link. You can maintain the runtime sequence of the mapping by moving a selected mapping row in the grid up or down. To add nested expressions (that is, an expression within another expression or variables within an expression), use the Dynamic Link to select a source attribute. This adds that attribute name enclosed within pound (#) signs, which signifies that at runtime the attribute value is a variable name or an XPath expression that has to be evaluated.

Clicking on the Property Value button to select a source attribute adds the current value of the attribute to the Expression Editor. After writing an expression in the Expression Editor, always remember to click on the Add or Update buttons to add the new or changed mapping expression to the target attribute. The Link Editor is shown in Figure 6.6.

Different Link Types are available as radio buttons in the Link Editor. These specify the different types of mappings, as follows:

▶ Assign Value: Simple mapping between non-XML attributes such as string, integer, and so on, where the target attribute gets the same value as the source.

▶ Assign XML: Mapping between two XML-type attributes, where the target attribute gets the source XML document assigned to it, overwriting the current XML (if any).

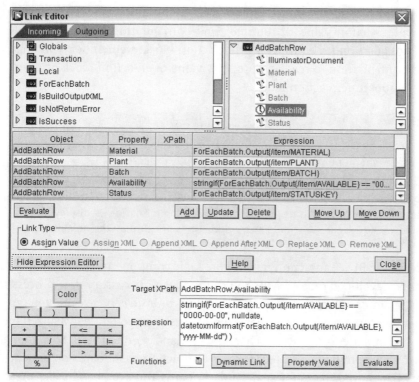

Figure 6.6 Link Editor in BLS Transaction

▶ Append XML: Mapping between two XML-type elements where the target attribute gets the source attribute's XML document assigned to it as a child element under the existing root element of the existing XML.

▶ Append After XML: Mapping between two XML attributes where the source XML documents get added to the target XML document as a sibling. This should be added by selecting a node below the root node of the target XML.

▶ Replace XML: Mapping between two XML attributes where the target XML element and its children get replaced with the source node and its children. This should be added by selecting an element of the target XML.

▶ Remove XML: Mapping to remove the target node and its children. This should be done when an XML attribute value has to be set to null.

For many action blocks, Object Configuration and Link Configuration allow the same properties to be configured. In general, you should use Object Configuration to set the property values of the action block with fixed values at design time. You should use the Link Configuration to map variables to the action blocks' properties that can provide dynamic values at runtime. Link Configuration always overrides the Object Configuration for a property of the action block. Remember, you must use the Link Configuration to read any property value of an action block or transaction from its subsequent action block.

Note

Most of the action blocks have a Boolean output property called Success, which you can use to determine whether or not the action is successfully executed.

You can execute a BLS Transaction for testing purposes from the Workbench via TRANSACTION • EXECUTE (Ctrl-F5) or TRANSACTION • EXECUTE WITHOUT TRACE (Ctrl-F6). When you are executing, the default trace and debug, output information is displayed in a pop-up window. The Execute Without Trace option does not display the default trace.

You need to use the BLS Transactions as the core logic components of the composite applications developed on SAP MII. You can model all necessary data processing logic, system integration by data queries, and RFC or Web service calls; you can read or update buffered messages or files from file systems, generate visualization components as animated graphics or chart images, and so on. The BLS Transactions are executed from the web pages such as transaction dashboards or provide the necessary data to the charts for analysis dashboards and even can be executed as background jobs using schedulers to execute business logic. For example, in a production order confirmation dashboard you need to execute a BLS Transaction in an iGrid applet to populate the order data, which it fetches by executing an RFC or Enterprise service or by parsing the buffered IDoc messages in Messages Services. When confirming the order and when the user specifies the input in the web page, you need to execute another BLS Transaction using iCommand applet to update the data in SAP Enterprise Resource Planning (ERP). Similarly for displaying an SPC chart by retrieving the inspection result data from SAP ERP or from a Laboratory Information Management System (LIMS) you need to model a BLS Transaction that extracts the data, performs the necessary calculation to determine the Upper Control Limit (UCL) and Lower Control Limit (LCL), and finally executes in an iSPCChart applet in the web page. Additionally, using a BLS Transaction you can generate text files or PDF documents with the necessary data and can send mails or write to file systems or send to another remote server using FTP.

Now that we have covered the basics of BLS and how to create a transaction in the SAP MII Workbench, we move on to using the predefined action blocks to model different types of business logic in the BLS transactions.

6.2   Logic, Tracing, and Miscellaneous Functions

The Logic, Tracing and Miscellaneous Functions action blocks provide general programming constructs, tracing and logging, and miscellaneous functions such as calculation, statistical, regression, and unit conversion. These action blocks can be used for the common functionalities you might require when you are developing a Business Logic Transaction.

6.2.1   Logic Action Blocks

The Logic category of action blocks in BLS Transactions consists of the following action blocks:

- Assignment
- Conditional
- For Next Loop
- Repeater
- Switch
- Terminate Transaction
- Transaction Call
- While Loop
- Pause

You use each of the preceding action blocks to control the execution flow in a BLS Transaction. These are the basic programming constructs of BLS Transactions, and at least some of them are required in almost every case.

Assignment Action Block

You can use the Assignment action block to assign the value of one attribute to another. It is the same as "=" (single equal to) in common programming languages. This action has no specific input parameters and no configuration properties. Using this action block you can map only the properties between any action blocks' parameters. You should define the Link Configuration for the Assignment action block in the Outgoing tab only, because it has no Incoming link configuration (Figure 6.7).

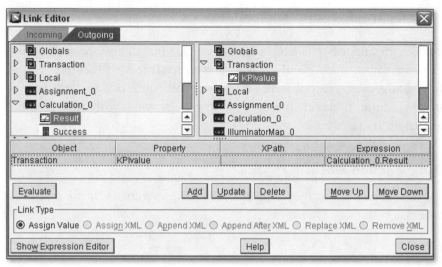

Figure 6.7 Link Configuration for the Assignment Action Block

Conditional Action Block

You can use the Conditional action block to evaluate a logical condition and channel the program flow of a BLS Transaction to a specific path based on the condition. It is similar to if-else keywords in common programming languages. You can provide multiple conditions to evaluate in the Conditional action block; to do this, specify the number of conditions to evaluate in its Object Configuration properties as Number of Inputs, as shown in Figure 6.8. You also need to select a specific Logical Condition such as AND or OR when you want to evaluate multiple condition statements. All given conditions are evaluated using the Logical Condition. You cannot use both AND and OR conditions in a single Conditional action block; to do that, you must use nested Conditional action blocks. Based on the number of inputs specified, the condition placeholders appear in the Link Editor for the action block as Input1, Input2, and so on (Figure 6.9). In each input you need to specify the logical condition, which must evaluate to a Boolean value. It can be any value comparison between two different attributes of action blocks or properties, or it can be a true-or-false evaluation of a Boolean value. You can use the Expression Editor to specify the conditional expression.

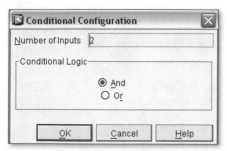

Figure 6.8 Object Configuration for the Conditional Action Block

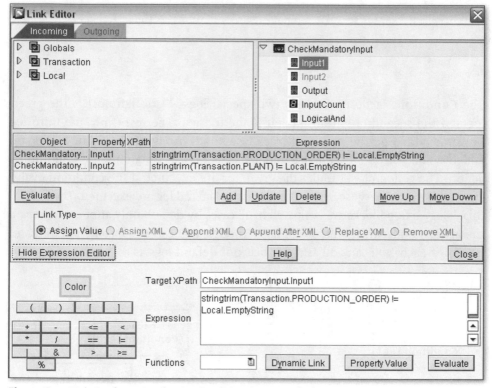

Figure 6.9 Link Configuration for the Conditional Action Block

---

Example

If the Logical Condition used is AND with a multiple number of inputs, the evaluation is as follows:

```
If(<Input1 Expression> AND <Input2 Expression> AND <Input n Expression>)
{ }
Else
{ }
```

If the Logical Condition used is OR with a multiple number of inputs, the evaluation is as follows:

```
If(<Input1 Expression> OR <Input2 Expression> OR <Input n Expression>)
{ }
Else
{ }
```

The Conditional action block has two special legs — the leftmost is the green leg and the second one from the left is the red leg. The rest (from the third leg onwards added on the right) are black, as shown in Figure 6.10. These legs are added when you add a sequence under the sequence containing the Conditional action. The action blocks under the green leg are executed if the condition evaluates to be true; otherwise, the action blocks in the red leg are executed. The default (black leg) action blocks are evaluated in all cases by default only after executing all the actions under the green or red legs. Though you can add exactly one red and green leg each, you can add as many black or default legs as required.

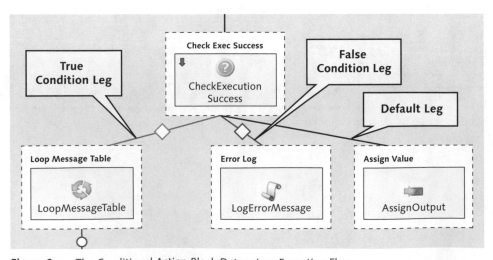

Figure 6.10 The Conditional Action Block Determines Execution Flow

For Next Loop Action Block

You can use the For Next Loop action block to execute a single or a series of action blocks a specified number of times; it is similar to the FOR or LOOP keywords in common programming languages. In the Object Configuration, you can specify fixed values for the From, To, and Step properties, which signify the number of times the loop is executed. You can set the same properties using variables or fixed values in its Link Configuration or Incoming tab (Figure 6.11). The loop begins counting from the integer specified in the From property and does so in increments determined by the values specified in Step property. It stops when it reaches the final value, specified in To property. To terminate the loop before it executes the number of times configured, set the Break property value to True using the Link Editor, for example, after checking a condition using the Conditional action block. The CurrentItem property is a read-only property that specifies the current index of the loop at any point during the loop execution.

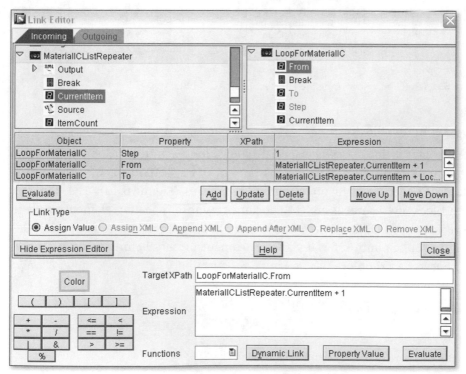

Figure 6.11 Link Configuration for the For Next Loop Action Block

The For Next Loop action has one repeating leg and other default legs, as shown in Figure 6.12. It executes the actions under its repeating leg for the number of times specified in its configuration. The default legs are executed only once in left to right order after all the action blocks under the repeating leg finish execution for the total number of times determined by the loop condition.

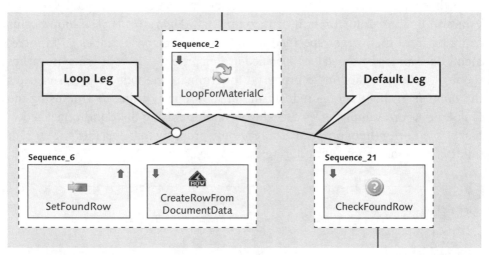

Figure 6.12   Execution Flow Using the For Next Loop Action Block

Repeater Action Block

The Repeater action block is a special type of loop action that loops depending on the number of repeating elements present in an XML document, akin to the FOR...EACH construct in programming languages (Figure 6.13). The Repeater action block always needs an XML document whose repeating element needs to be specified in its Object Configuration as an XPath expression. You can select this using the lookup button for any XML document present before the action block. The Repeater action block has no Link Configuration.

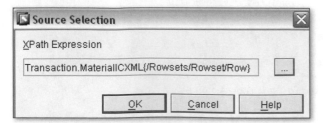

Figure 6.13   Object Configuration for the Repeater Action Block

This action block is useful for parsing output of data query, RFC, Web service, or other XML documents having repeating elements. The Repeater action block has two legs — a blue repeater leg on the left and other default legs (Figure 6.14). The repeater leg is executed, along with all the action blocks present under it, depending on the number of repeating elements present in the source document, which is in the path specified in the XPath expression configuration. The action blocks under the Repeater action get the child elements of the XML document under the current parent repeating element, which are Link properties of the Repeater action. This is useful when creating rows of an XML document based on the data from another document or when parsing an XML document (such as a query or an RFC output). The default legs are executed only once in left to right order after all the action blocks under the repeating leg finish execution for the total number of times determined by the repeating condition.

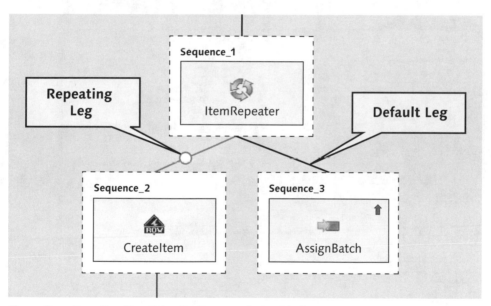

Figure 6.14 Execution Flow Using the Repeater Action Block

> **Note**
>
> You can use XPath expressions in the action blocks for better performance and simpler logic. Refer Section 9.2 Using XPath Expressions in BLS Transactions for more information on how to use XPath in BLS Transactions and an example with the Repeater action block.

Switch Action Block

You can use the Switch action block to control execution flows based on a variable value, which can be either a property of another action block or part of Transaction properties or Local properties. This action block is analogous to the Switch-Case statement in common programming languages. The number of inputs specified in the Object Configuration of the action block determines the number of different possible execution paths required after the Switch action. In the Link Configuration, the MatchValue1, MatchValue2, and so on values need to be evaluated and compared with the InputValue property to determine the execution flow path (Figure 6.15). The numbers of MatchValue properties are based on the number of inputs specified in the Object Configuration. The possible values of the InputValue variable are specified in the MatchValue property.

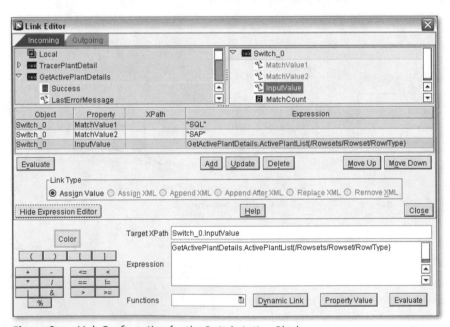

Figure 6.15 Link Configuration for the Switch Action Block

The Switch action's number of switching legs depends on the number of inputs specified (Figure 6.16). If at runtime the input value evaluates to be the same as specified in MatchValue1, then the execution flows to the first switch leg (that is, the leg on the extreme left of the action block). If it is evaluated to be the same as that of MatchValue2, then the execution flows to the second left leg — and so on. A default leg is also available on the right, after the switch legs, and it gets executed if the InputValue matches none of the MatchValues. So, for example, if the number of inputs is defined as 2, then the third leg on the right is the default switch leg, which gets executed if no other switch leg gets executed. Any other leg added after that is the default leg, which gets executed after executing either one of the switch legs or the default switch leg.

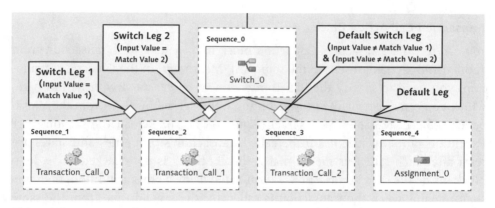

Figure 6.16 Execution Flow Using the Switch Action Block

Terminate Transaction Action Block

You can use the Terminate Transaction Action block to terminate a BLS Transaction execution at any point in the execution flow. You can use this action block under a Conditional action block, which checks an error condition and terminates the transaction if required. In the Object Configuration for this action block, you can specify a Termination Message as a string, which is returned to the calling application on termination if the Show Message During Termination checkbox is selected (Figure 6.17).

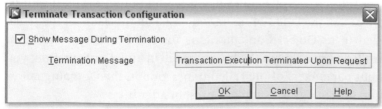

Figure 6.17 Object Configuration for the Terminate Transaction Action Block

In the Link Configuration, you can set these two properties using variables.

Transaction Call Action Block

You can use the Transaction Call action block to execute a BLS Transaction from another transaction present in the same SAP MII server. In the Object Configuration, you need to specify the BLS Transaction to be executed with its full path, which you can select via the Browse button (represented by "...") from the Workbench projects available in the server (Figure 6.18). The Reload Transaction After Execution property specifies if the called transaction's properties and states are reset after each call. This means that if the checkbox is not checked and a loop block inside the called transaction is terminated using a break condition, the same state remains when the transaction is called for the second time from the same transaction. Similarly, the property values of the transaction and its action blocks are also retained for subsequent calls if the property is not set.

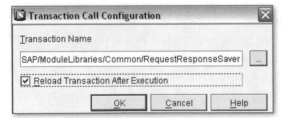

Figure 6.18   Object Configuration for the Transaction Call Action Block

The Transaction Call action block generates its input and output properties to be configured and accessed in the Link Configuration based on the name of the called transaction specified in its Object Configuration. You need to assign the input parameters of the called transaction in the Incoming tab in Link Configuration; you can access the output parameters of the called transaction in the Outgoing tab or in the Link Configuration of any action block present after it.

While Loop Action Block

You can use the While Loop action block to perform a repeating execution for a specific number of times. The MaxIterations value you specify in the Object Configuration determines the number of times the action blocks under the repeating leg of the While Loop action execute. The action blocks under the default leg get executed after the loop terminates. In the Link Configuration you can set the MaxIterations property along with Break (Figure 6.19), which, when set to true, terminates the loop even if the maximum iteration count is not reached. CurrentItem is a read-only property which gives the current iteration value at runtime.

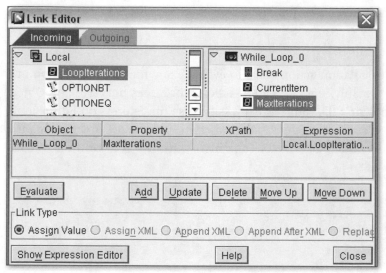

Figure 6.19 Link Configuration for the While Loop Action Block

Pause Action Block

You can use the Pause action block to include a time delay in the transaction execution. This is done in the Delay property of Object Configuration and is a fixed value in milliseconds. It can also be entered in Link Configuration as a fixed or variable value. The transaction execution waits for the time specified in the Pause action block configuration before executing any action block under it.

6.2.2 Miscellaneous Functions Action Blocks

The Miscellaneous Functions action block category consists of action blocks used mainly for mathematical and statistical calculations, such as unit conversions. This category consists of the following action blocks:

- Calculation
- Unit Converter
- Simple Statistics
- Linear Regression
- Minitab Export

Calculation Action Block

You can use the Calculation action block to evaluate any numeric expression in a BLS Transaction. Notably, the Calculation action block does not have any Object Configuration; to define the numeric expression, use the Expression Editor in its Link Configuration and link to the Result property (Figure 6.20). You can link the Result property to another action block's property afterwards to read the calculation result.

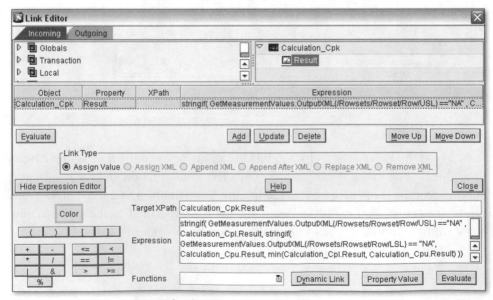

Figure 6.20 Link Configuration for the Calculation Action Block

Unit Converter Action Block

You can use the Unit Converter action block to calculate quantities from one measuring unit to another. Like the Calculation action block, it has no Object Configuration. In the Link Configuration Incoming tab, you need to specify the From, To, and Value as the source unit, target unit, and the value to be converted from source to target, respectively (Figure 6.21). In the Outgoing tab or in any subsequent actions, the output property Result gives the converted value. You need to maintain the unit of measures along with their conversion factor in the toolbar menu GLOBAL • UNIT CONVERSION (Figure 6.22). If the units of measures are not maintained there, you cannot use them for conversion in this action block.

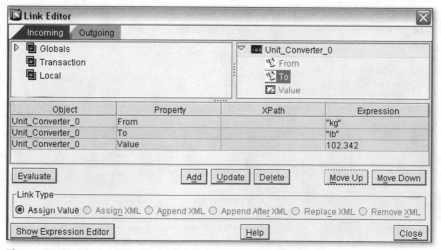

Figure 6.21 Link Configuration for Unit Converter Action Block

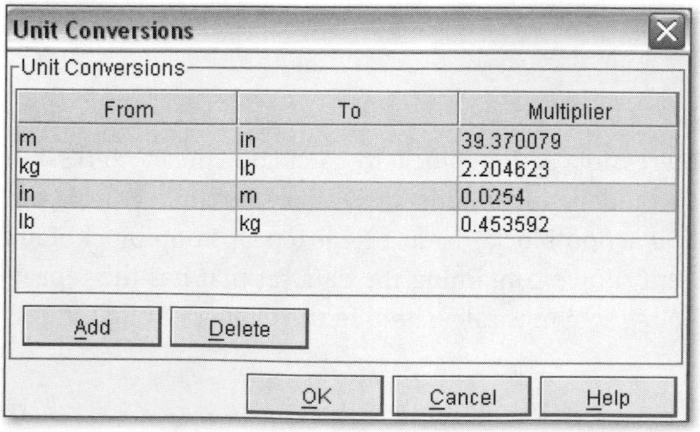

Figure 6.22 Unit Conversion Configuration in Workbench

Simple Statistics Action Block

You can use the Simple Statistics action block to calculate simple statistical indexes such as min, max, average, standard deviation, total, and so forth on a numeric data set. You usually use this action block under a loop or repeater. It has no Object Configuration, and in the Link Configuration you need to link the DataValue property to a numeric value property (Figure 6.23), typically from a repeater or loop action block. Within the loop, the data value gets accumulated, and the Simple Statistics action calculates the statistical indexes that you can access from any action outside the loop (for example, in the default leg of the Repeater action).

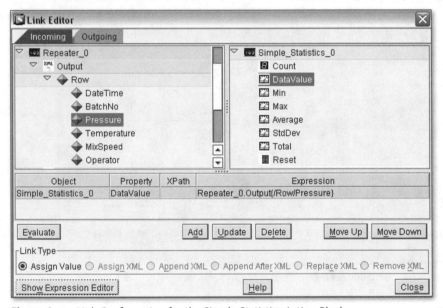

Figure 6.23   Link Configuration for the Simple Statistics Action Block

Linear Regression Action Block

You can use the Linear Regression action block to calculate linear regression between a set of values for an independent and a dependent variable. You should not use the Linear Regression action block inside a Repeater or Loop block. Link directly to the XML document source containing the data set that has the repeating elements over which the regression is calculated. In the Object Configurations of the action block, specify the column names from a data set, such as data query output or an XML document. You need to specify the XML document in the Document Source property by selecting it from another action block's property present before it, or via the Local or Transaction property. You also need to specify the independent variable in the X-Axis Value Column and the dependent variable in the Y-Axis Value Column (Figure 6.24). The column names from the selected documents automatically get populated in the drop-down if the XML document definition is available at design time. Otherwise, you need to specify the column names manually, which should exactly match the column names present in the XML document at runtime.

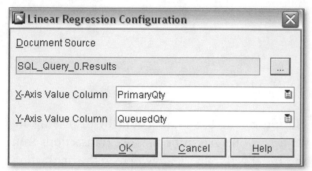

Figure 6.24 Object Configuration for the Linear Regression Action Block

You can specify the same properties in the Incoming tab of the Link Configuration for the action block. The Outgoing tab gives the output properties for the calculated linear regression. The calculated statistical properties are Intercept, Slope, R, and RSquared. The Output XML document contains a Predicted value column for each input data value. Use a Repeater action to loop into the Output XML document to get the predicted value as Repeater_0.Output{/Row/Predicted}.

Minitab Export Action Block

You can use the Minitab Export action block to generate a tab-delimited file from an SAP MII XML document, which can then be imported into Minitab® Statistical Software for multivariant analysis. In the Object Configuration of the action block, specify the source XML document in Document Source by selecting it from the property of a preceding action block. You can also define it using the Local or Transaction Property or Link Configuration.

In the Outgoing tab of Link Configuration or in a subsequent action block's Link Configuration, the Output property gives the tab-delimited data as a string.

6.2.3 Logging Action Blocks

You can use Logging action blocks to display debug messages and add trace and log entries in BLS Transactions. Logging action blocks consist of the following:

▸ Tracer

▸ XML Tracer

▸ Event Logger

Tracer Action Block

You can use the Tracer action block to debug BLS Transactions by displaying any message or value in the trace window while executing the BLS Transactions from the Workbench. You can place the Tracer action block anywhere in the transaction. In the Object Configuration of the action block, you can use the Message property to define a fixed message to be displayed in the tracer window (Figure 6.25). The Level specifies the type of trace message to be displayed. Depending on the value you have specified in Level, the messages are displayed with a [FATAL], [ERROR], [WARN], [INFO], or [DEBUG] prefix. You can specify the same properties in the Link Configuration using fixed values or variables. By default, the trace level is considered to be INFO. The output of the Tracer action helps the developer to debug the transaction during development. It has no effect when the transaction is executed as an applet, a Web service, or an HTTP service.

In Link Configuration, the Message property of the Tracer action enables you to specify complex expressions. You can do this using one or more properties from previous action blocks or any fixed message (Figure 6.26). An example of the output of the Tracer action block is shown in Figure 6.27.

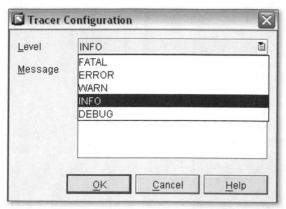

Figure 6.25 Object Configuration for the Tracer Action Block

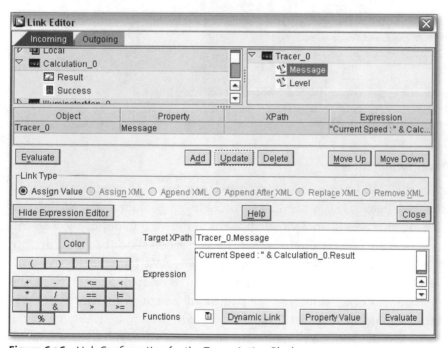

Figure 6.26 Link Configuration for the Tracer Action Block

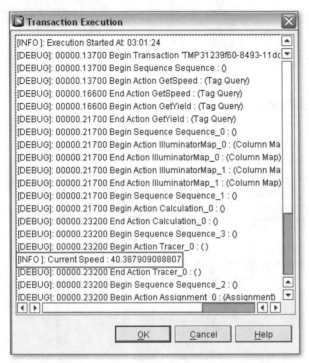

Figure 6.27 Trace Display Using Tracer Action Block

XML Tracer Action Block

You can use the XML Tracer action block to create custom log/trace files to log messages from BLS Transactions, providing a custom logging solution. The XML Tracer writes the log messages in an XML file present in the Web folder of the SAP MII content catalog. The Object Configuration for the action block has the File Path property where you need to specify the location of the XML trace file (Figure 6.28). If the file is not present in that location, a new file is created, and the trace info gets appended to it every time. The file path should begin with *WEB://* or *DB://* and point to a project and folder location in the SAP MII content catalog of the Workbench Web tab. You can configure the same properties with dynamic values using variables in the Link Configuration of the XML Tracer action block.

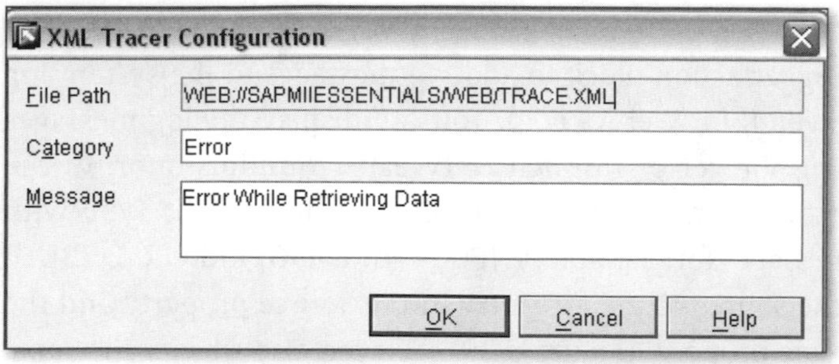

Figure 6.28 Object Configuration for the XML Tracer Action Block

---

Example

The trace file generated by the XML Tracer action is in the form of a SAP MII XML document as demonstrated in the following listing:

```
<?xml version="1.0" encoding="UTF-8"?>
<Rowsets DateCreated="2008-09-17T04:10:14" EndDate="2008-09-
17T04:10:14" StartDate="2008-09-17T04:10:14" Version="12.0.4
Build(120)">
<Rowset>
<Columns>
<Column Description="DateTime" MaxRange="0" MinRange="0"
Name="DateTime" SQLDataType="93" SourceColumn="DateTime"/>
<Column Description="Category" MaxRange="0" MinRange="0"
Name="Category" SQLDataType="1" SourceColumn="Category"/>
<Column Description="DateTime" MaxRange="0" MinRange="0" Name="Message"
SQLDataType="1" SourceColumn="Message"/>
</Columns>
<Row>
<DateTime>2008-09-17T04:10:14</DateTime>
<Category>ERROR</Category>
<Message>Error While Retrieving Data</Message>
</Row>
</Rowset></Rowsets>
```

The XML document contains the Category and Message element values as specified in BLS Transactions, and the system automatically adds a DateTime element for each message. Using the XML query template and iGrid display template, you can display this XML document as a custom log.

Event Logger Action Block

You can use the Event Logger action block to add log messages to the system log (that is, the SAP NetWeaver J2EE WebAS Log). You can display the log messages with the J2EE engine Log Viewer or through NetWeaver Administrator. In the Object Configuration of the Event Logger action block, define Event Type with the severity of the log message (for example, INFO, WARNING, ERROR, DEBUG, and FAILURE). Specify the source of the log entry in the Source property and the log message in the Message property (Figure 6.29). You can also specify the same properties using Link Configuration.

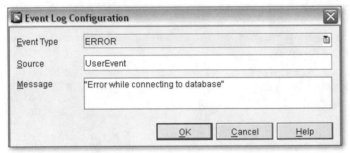

Figure 6.29 Object Configuration for the Event Logger Action Block

Now that you have learned about the logic, miscellaneous functions, and logging action blocks in BLS, we want to turn to the action blocks you can use to work with XML documents in BLS.

6.3   Working with XML

XML parsing and creating XML documents for system integrations and data manipulation are some of the most important and useful functionalities provided by Business Logic Services. You can use the XML Output, XML Functions, and Reference Documents action blocks for manipulating XML documents in BLS transactions.

6.3.1   SAP xMII XML Output Action Blocks

You can use the SAP MII XML Output action blocks to create an XML document in a BLS transaction in the SAP MII XML format. XML used for data transfer in SAP MII follows a specific format.

A sample SAP MII XML format is as follows:

```xml
<?xml version="1.0" encoding="UTF-8" ?>
<Rowsets DateCreated="2008-09-13T11:14:43" EndDate="2006-10-
26T12:37:01" StartDate="2006-10-26T12:37:01" Version="12.0.4
Build(120)">
    <Rowset>
      <Columns>
         <Column Description="Plant" MaxRange="1" MinRange="0"
            Name="Plant" SQLDataType="1" SourceColumn=" Plant" />
         <Column Description="Material" MaxRange="1" MinRange="0"
            Name="Material" SQLDataType="1" SourceColumn=" Material"
/>
      </Columns>
      <Row>
         <Plant>1100</Plant>
         <Material>Y-300</Material>
      </Row>
    </Rowset>
</Rowsets>
```

As in the preceding example, the XML document starts with a `Rowsets` element, which contains the child element `Rowset`, which in turn contains the child `Column` and `Row` elements. The `Column` elements contain the XML elements definition present inside the `Row` elements. `Row` elements contain the actual data within child elements and are repeating in nature. All data query outputs and XML documents created in BLS Transactions follow the same format. This format is referred to in all subsequent action blocks used for XML manipulations in BLS Transaction.

The SAP xMII XML Output action block category consists of the following action blocks:

► Document

► Rowset

► Column

► Row

► Data Item

► Fatal Error

► Message

Document Action Block

You can use the Document action block to define an XML document in the SAP MII XML document format. You need to use the Document action for various scenarios, such as to create an XML document from a different data format or to pass the output of an RFC call or a data query output to the output parameter of the BLS Transaction. To create any new XML document in the BLS Transaction, you need this action block first to define its structure. This is required in the BLS Transaction when output parameters are of type Xml or when you need to create an intermediate XML document in the transaction.

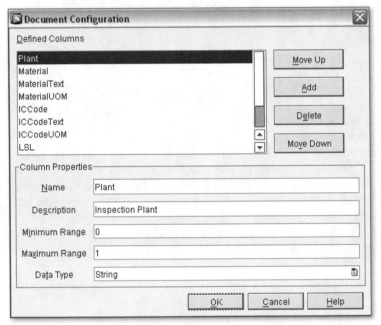

Figure 6.30 Object Configuration for the Document Action Block

You need to specify the XML document definition in the Object Configuration of the action block with properties for each unique element present in the XML document. These properties are Column Names, Description, Minimum Value Range, Maximum Value Range, and Data Type (Figure 6.30). The data type of XML columns can be String, Double, Integer, and DateTime. The XML document you define using this action block has to be a flat structure (with all elements at the same hierarchy); you cannot define hierarchical XML documents using this action block. No Link Configuration is required for this action block, because it consists of the XML document definition only, which you need to define as fixed values at design time. The action block generates the XML elements as defined in Object Configuration as its Link Properties. You should use other action blocks such as Row, Rowset, Column, and so on below this action block to populate the XML document with data.

The Output Link Property of the Document action block takes the structure of the XML document as defined in Object Configuration (Figure 6.31). The Output property also holds the full XML document with data, as created by the subsequent Row action blocks. After you add all rows to the document using the Row action block, you can obtain the full XML document from the Output. This can happen at any point in the BLS Transaction after the Document action. Under the Document action, you can typically add the rows to the document by using the Repeater and Row actions in its repeating leg. In the default or non-repeating leg of the Repeater action you can use an Assignment action to assign the output XML document of the Document action to a Transaction or Local Property. You can also assign it to any other action block's properties using the Link Configuration options.

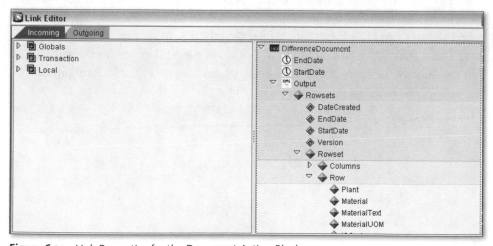

Figure 6.31 Link Properties for the Document Action Block

Rowset Action Block

You can use the Rowset action block to add a `<Rowset>` element in an XML document defined by the Document action block. This is useful because it can be done dynamically while you are defining the XML structure instead of at design time. Rowset is a subdocument inside the main XML document. You can use different Rowset elements to group multiple XML documents, whose individual structures are specified by the Row elements, in a single XML document. The Rowset action block should be used after any action or property which provides an XML document. Specify the Document Object (that is, the XML document defined by the Document action) in the Object Configuration of the Rowset action block using the lookup button. Link Configuration for the Rowset action block is not required, but if you haven't already done so in Object Configuration, you can use Link Configuration to specify the XML document object in IlluminatorDocument. As a result, the XML document you define by the Document action gets a new Rowset element.

Column Action Block

In an XML document defined by the Document action, you can use the Column action block to add a new column definition. This is also useful when defining the XML structure dynamically or extending an existing document structure. If you want to add a new column, you must specify the appropriate XML output in the Document Object property in Object Configuration. Select the output of the XML document (the top-level node if the XML document contains only a single Rowset; otherwise, the specific Rowset). You also need to specify the following column properties in Object Configuration: Name, Description, Minimum Range, Maximum Range, and Data Type. This adds a new column to the XML document (Figure 6.32). You can specify the same property values dynamically in the Link Configurations.

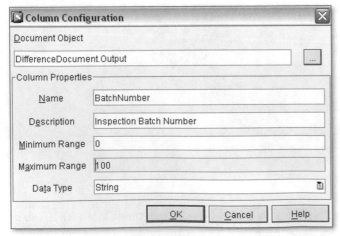

Figure 6.32 Object Configuration for the Column Action Block

Row Action Block

You can use the Row action block to add data rows as ⟨Row⟩ elements, and their child elements, in an XML document defined by the Document action block. This action block actually fills up the XML document with data in a BLS Transaction and is placed under a Repeater or Loop action block to add multiple data rows. The Object Configuration of the Row action block is the same as that of the Rowset action block, where you need to specify the XML document defined by the Document action block. Select the Output of the XML document (the top-level node if the XML document contains only a single Rowset; otherwise the specific Rowset). After you specify the XML document in the Document Object property in Object Configuration, the Link properties are automatically generated based on the columns defined in the XML document. You can set these properties with values in the Link Configuration (Figure 6.33). You must specify the data values in the Row using the Link Configuration of the same action block, because the row properties are not accessible from any other subsequent action block.

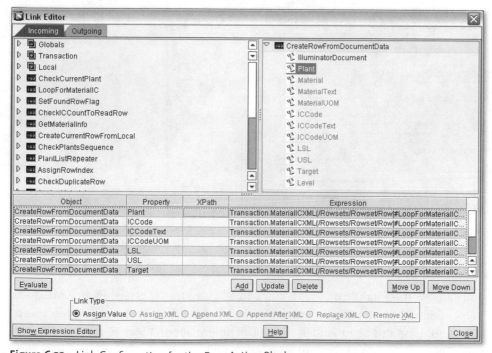

Figure 6.33 Link Configuration for the Row Action Block

Data Item Action Block

When not specified in the Link Configuration of the Row action block, you can use the Data Item action block to add a data item under a `<Row>` element. Using this action block, you can add the data items of the rows separately (unlike the Row action block where all the row data items need to be specified together in its Link Configuration). You should add the Data Item action block under a Document and its corresponding Row action block in the BLS Transaction. In the Object Configuration of the Data Item action block, specify the XML document defined by the Document action block in the Document Object property (Figure 6.34). Select the Output of the XML document (the top-level node if the XML document contains only a single Rowset; otherwise, the specific Rowset). You must specify the column name in the Name property, which should match an existing column name in the XML document. You can specify the data of the column in the Value property, either in the Object Configuration as a fixed value or in the Link Configuration as a dynamic value.

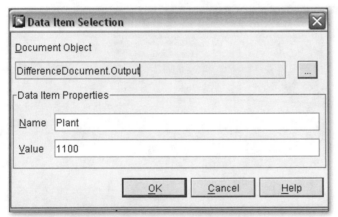

Figure 6.34 Object Configuration for the Data Item Action Block

Fatal Error Action Block

You can use the Fatal Error action block to add an error message in an XML document, defined by the Document action block, with the `<FatalError>` elements. You should use this action block after a Document action block in the BLS Transaction. The error message element is added directly under the `<Rowsets>` element in the output XML document. In the Object Configuration of the Fatal Error action block, you need to specify the target document, which can be a document defined by the Document action block, in the Document Object property. You can specify the error message as a fixed value here (Figure 6.35) or as a dynamic value in Link Configuration. All rows, if added previously, get removed when the Fatal Error is added to an XML document. You can read the data present under the `<FatalError>` element in an SAP MII XML document by the JavaScript methods of the iCommand applet in a web page.

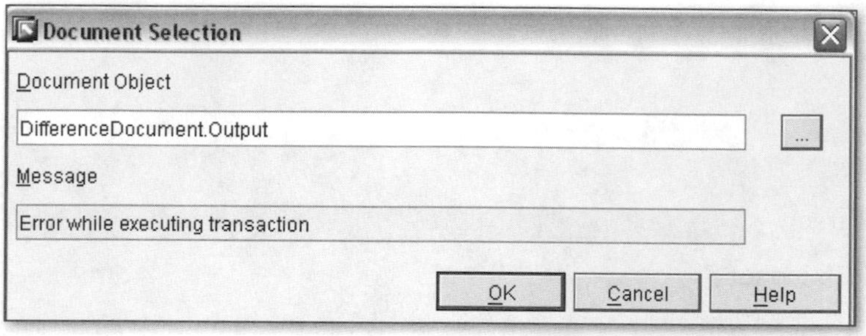

Figure 6.35 Object Configuration for the Fatal Error Action Block

Message Action Block

You can use the Message action block to add an information message under the `<Messages>` element in an XML document defined by the Document action block. The message gets added under the `<Rowsets>` element and after the data item rows, if present. Object Configuration and Link Configuration are the same as that of the Fatal Error action block, where you need to specify the XML document defined by the Document action along with the information message text.

6.3.2 XML Functions Action Blocks

The XML Functions action block category consists of the action blocks that you can use for XML parsing and various functions in SAP MII XML documents (such as column aliasing, calculated columns, join, sort and filter, and so on). You might need to use these action blocks when you are aggregating multiple XML documents or manipulating a XML document output. It consists of the following action blocks:

▶ Aggregate Statistics

▶ Calculated Columns

▶ Column Aliasing

- ▶ Column Stripper
- ▶ Crosstab
- ▶ Distinct Value Extractor
- ▶ Generic Sort Filter
- ▶ Joiner
- ▶ Normalize
- ▶ Union
- ▶ Totalizer
- ▶ Time Interpolator
- ▶ String to XML Parser
- ▶ String List to XML Parser
- ▶ XSL Transformation

Aggregate Statistics Action Block

You can use the Aggregate Statistics action block to get calculated statistical indexes on a repetitive data element present in an XML document. In the Object Configuration of the action block, you need to specify the XPath expression of this repetitive element (Figure 6.36). The XML document can be the output of a data query, an XML file read by the XMLLoader action, an XML document defined by the Document action, or an XML document passed as an input of the transaction. You can also specify the XPath expression via Link Configuration in the ValueSource property.

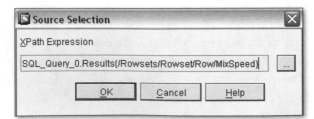

Figure 6.36   Object Configuration for the Aggregate Statistics Action Block

In the Outgoing tab of Link Configuration, or in the subsequent action blocks, you can read the output properties of the Aggregate Statistics action block. The output properties available are Min, Max, Average, StdDev, Total, and Count, which are calculated based on the values of the repeating element of the XML document specified in the ValueSource as a XPath expression.

Calculated Columns Action Block

You can use the Calculated Columns action block to add calculated columns to an XML document, which can be a data query output, input parameter, XML defined by Document action, and so on. The value is calculated based on the values of other columns in the XML document. The new calculated column is added under the <Row> element for each data row. In the Object Configuration of the action block, you can add one or more calculated column definitions, as shown in Figure 6.37. Select the XML document present as an output property of a preceding action block, or in the Transaction or Local properties of the BLS Transaction in the Document Source property using the lookup. Specify the calculated column name, its data type, and the calculated expression for its value.

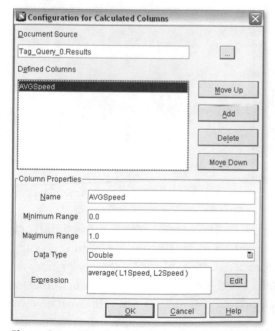

Figure 6.37 Object Configuration for the Calculated Column Action Block

By clicking on the Edit button, you can specify the expression for the column value using the Expression Editor (Figure 6.38). The columns available in the specified XML document are displayed in the Columns property of the Expression Editor. Selecting those and the built-in functions from the Functions dropdown list, you can specify an expression. Click on OK to accept the expression specified.

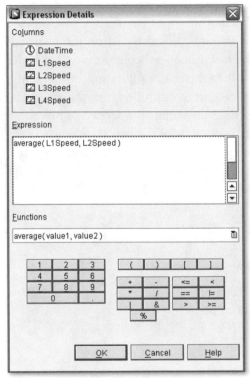

Figure 6.38 Expression Editor in Object Configuration for the Calculated Column Action Block

No Link Configuration is required for this action block because the action block automatically generates the XML document on its Link properties. You can assign that XML document to any other subsequent action block's property or transaction output property in its Outgoing Link Configuration, or any subsequent block's Link Configuration. At runtime, the calculated column has the value specified by the expression.

Column Aliasing Action Block

You can use the Column Aliasing action block to create an alias for an element in an SAP MII XML document, that is, in the output XML document the column name specified in the alias appears for the specific column instead of its original name. In the Object Configuration, specify the XML document in the Document Source property (Figure 6.39). The element names present in the XML document under the `<Row>` element automatically get populated in the dropdown list for the Column to Alias property. Select the element or column name from the dropdown list and specify the Alias Name. You can specify a maximum of eight elements for aliasing.

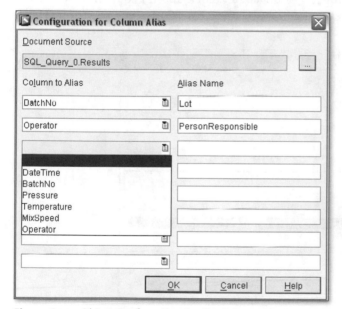

Figure 6.39   Object Configuration for the Column Aliasing Action Block

You can configure the same properties using Link Configuration. After it's configured by Object Configuration, the output property of the action block automatically takes up the same XML document structure as specified in its Document Source property with the alias names as well for the elements specified. You can assign this XML property to another subsequent action block's property or transaction output parameter from the Link Configuration of any subsequent actions.

Column Stripper Action Block

You can use the Column Stripper action block to remove a column or element present under the <Row> element from an SAP MII XML document. In the Object Configuration of the action block, specify the source XML document in the Document Source property. The XML document can be present as a property of any preceding action block or as a transaction property. The elements present under the <Row> element automatically get populated in the Column to Remove dropdowns. Select the element name from the dropdown so that it doesn't appear in the output XML document, as shown in Figure 6.40. You can specify a maximum of eight elements. The same properties can be specified in the Link Configuration. In this case, the Output property of the action block doesn't contain the elements or columns specified in its configuration.

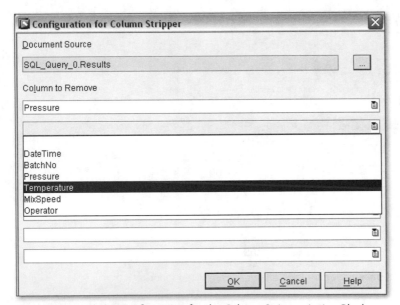

Figure 6.40 Object Configuration for the Column Stripper Action Block

Crosstab Action Block

You can use the Crosstab action block to calculate subtotals of the data columns present under the <Row> element, based on a maximum of four category columns. In the Object Configuration of the action block, select the XML document (Figure

6.41). The element or column names under `<Row>` get automatically populated in the Column dropdown. Select the category column names by which the subtotals for the data columns have to be calculated. You can configure the same properties using the Link Configuration.

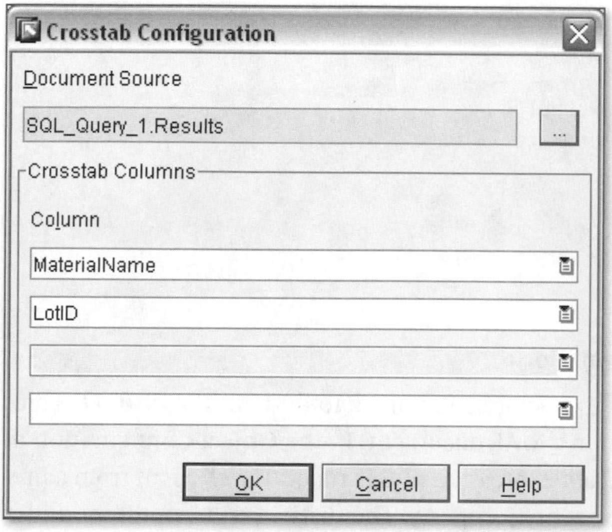

Figure 6.41 Object Configuration for the Crosstab Action Block

The Output XML property of the action block gets the structure of the specified XML document and calculates the subtotals.

Example

In the following example, the `MaterialName` and `LotID` are specified as the crosstab columns. In the output XML, the extra `<Row>` element has been added with the sub-totals of the numeric column values. The third row added gives the total of the specific material across all its `LotID`. As a result, the value in the LotID column is returned as "- - -".

```
<Row>
<DrilldownDepth>2</DrilldownDepth>
<MaterialName>Polypropylene</MaterialName>
<LotID>PP_5-1</LotID>
<PrimaryQty>25000</PrimaryQty>
<SecondaryQty>0</SecondaryQty>
</Row>
```

```
<Row>
<DrilldownDepth>2</DrilldownDepth>
<MaterialName>Polypropylene</MaterialName>
<LotID>PP_5-2</LotID>
<PrimaryQty>35000</PrimaryQty>
<SecondaryQty>0</SecondaryQty>
</Row>

<Row>
<DrilldownDepth>1</DrilldownDepth>
<MaterialName>Polypropylene</MaterialName>
<LotID>---</LotID>
<PrimaryQty>60000</PrimaryQty>
<SecondaryQty>0</SecondaryQty>
</Row>
```

Distinct Value Extractor Action Block

You can use the Distinct Value Extractor action block to find out the distinct values present in a repetitive element in a XML document. In the Object Configuration of the action block, specify the XPath expression of this repetitive element from a previous action's property or transaction property. The distinct values present under that column are available in the output of this action block. You can configure the same property in Link Configuration.

In the Outgoing Link Configuration of this action block, or in the subsequent action block's Link Configuration, you can access the Output XML property of the action block. This contains only a single column or element as <Item>, with the distinct value under the <Row> element (Figure 6.42). The number of <Row> elements present in the XML depends on the number of distinct values available in the source XML. The total number of distinct values or the number of <Row> elements in the output XML is also available in the Count property.

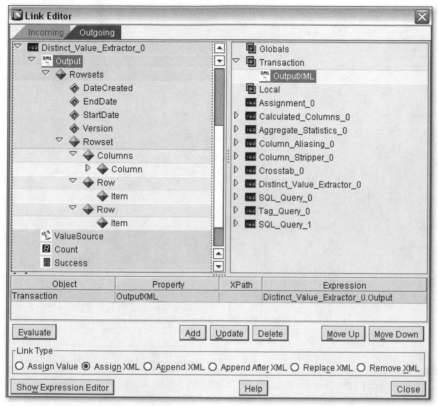

Figure 6.42 Link Properties for the Distinct Value Extractor Action Block

Generic Sort Filter Action Block

You can use the Generic Sort Filter action block to sort and filter the columns or elements present under the <Row> element in an XML document. In the Object Configuration of the action block, specify the XML document (Figure 6.43). The columns present in the document get populated automatically in the Sort and Filter Column dropdowns. Select the column names by which the XML document is to be sorted, along with the corresponding sorting order and type. Similarly, in the Filter criteria, select the column names and the corresponding condition, filter value, and type. You can specify a maximum of four columns in the sort and filter criteria. You can configure the same properties in Link Configuration. The Output XML property of the action block gives the XML document with the sorted and filtered data, which you can access in its Link Configuration Outgoing tab or any subsequent action block's Link Configuration.

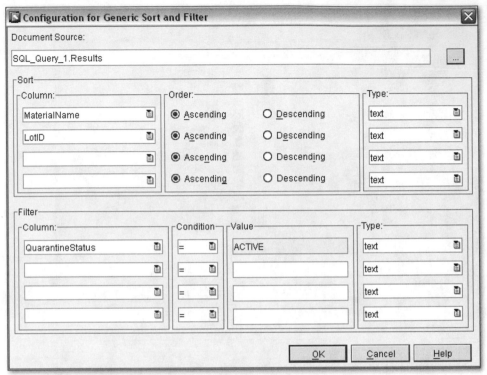

Figure 6.43 Object Configuration for the Generic Sort Filter Action Block

Joiner Action Block

You can use the Joiner action block to create a single XML document from two different XML documents. This is done by joining a maximum of four columns that are common across the two documents. This is similar to the ANSI SQL join condition between two database tables. In the Object Configuration of the action block, specify the two XML documents in Source of Parent Document and Child Document Source (Figure 6.44). Select the join type as Inner, Outer, or Full Outer, which means the same as database join conditions. You can specify the column names in the dropdown. You can also specify the same properties using Link Configuration. In Outgoing Link Configuration, or any subsequent action's Link Configuration, you can access the Output XML document, which gives the XML document created by using the join conditions.

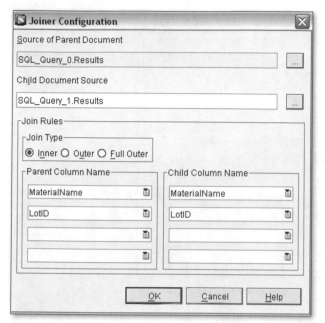

Figure 6.44 Object Configuration for the Joiner Action Block

Normalize Action Block

You can use the Normalize action block to change a multi-rowset XML document (for example, an XML document created by the output of an Aggregate Query) into a single Rowset document. Multi-rowset XML documents consist of multiple `<Rowset>` elements, each Rowset having certain `<Columns>` within the `<Row>` elements. To use the Normalize action, all the `<Rowset>` elements must have one common `<Column>`. Using this value, the multiple Rowsets are joined together into a single Rowset.

In the Object Configuration of the action block, specify the XML document (Figure 6.45). You can also specify the same property using Link Configuration. The Output property of the action block gives the XML document with a single `<Rowset>`, which you can access from any subsequent action block using Link Configuration.

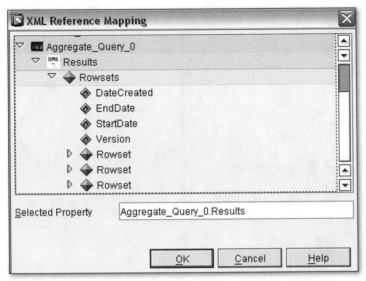

Figure 6.45 Object Configuration for the Normalize Action Block

---

Example

The following is an example of a multi-rowset XML document:

```
<?xml version="1.0" encoding="UTF-8"?>
<Rowsets DateCreated="2008-09-21T00:46:09" EndDate="2008-09-
21T00:46:08" StartDate="2008-09-20T23:46:08" Version="12.0.4
Build(120)">
<Rowset>
<Columns>
<Column Description="DateTime" MaxRange="1" MinRange="0"
Name="DateTime" SQLDataType="93" SourceColumn="DateTime"/>
<Column Description="L1Speed" MaxRange="100" MinRange="0"
Name="L1Speed" SQLDataType="8" SourceColumn="L1Speed"/>
</Columns>
<Row>
<DateTime>2008-09-21T00:46:08</DateTime>
<L1Speed>95.903343328737</L1Speed>
</Row>
</Rowset>
<Rowset>
<Columns>
<Column Description="DateTime" MaxRange="1" MinRange="0"
Name="DateTime" SQLDataType="93" SourceColumn="DateTime"/>
<Column Description="L2Speed" MaxRange="100" MinRange="0"
Name="L2Speed" SQLDataType="8" SourceColumn="L2Speed"/>
```

```
</Columns>
<Row>
<DateTime>2008-09-21T00:46:08</DateTime>
<L2Speed>90.089207265474</L2Speed>
</Row>
</Rowset>
<Rowset>
<Columns>
<Column Description="DateTime" MaxRange="1" MinRange="0"
Name="DateTime" SQLDataType="93" SourceColumn="DateTime"/>
<Column Description="L3Speed" MaxRange="100" MinRange="0"
Name="L3Speed" SQLDataType="8" SourceColumn="L3Speed"/>
</Columns>
<Row><DateTime>2008-09-21T00:46:09</DateTime>
<L3Speed>95.786009656963</L3Speed>
</Row>
</Rowset>
</Rowsets>
```

After using the Normalize action, the preceding XML document will be as follows:

```
<?xml version="1.0" encoding="UTF-8"?>
<Rowsets DateCreated="2008-09-21T00:46:09" EndDate="2008-09-
21T00:46:08" StartDate="2008-09-20T23:46:08" Version="12.0.4
Build(120)">
<Rowset>
<Columns>
<Column Description="DateTime" MaxRange="1" MinRange="0"
Name="DateTime" SQLDataType="93" SourceColumn="DateTime"/>
<Column Description="L1Speed" MaxRange="100" MinRange="0"
Name="L1Speed" SQLDataType="8" SourceColumn="L1Speed"/>
<Column Description="L2Speed" MaxRange="100" MinRange="0"
Name="L2Speed" SQLDataType="8" SourceColumn="L2Speed"/>
<Column Description="L3Speed" MaxRange="100" MinRange="0"
Name="L3Speed" SQLDataType="8" SourceColumn="L3Speed"/>
</Columns>
<Row>
<DateTime>2008-09-21T00:46:08</DateTime>

<L1Speed>95.903343328737</L1Speed>
<L2Speed>90.089207265474</L2Speed>
<L3Speed>95.786009656963</L3Speed>
</Row>
</Rowset>
</Rowsets>
```

In this example, the DateTime element value is used to join the multiple Rowsets.

Union Action Block

You can use the Union action block to combine two XML documents in a single XML document as two data sets with different `<Rowset>` elements. In the Object Configuration, specify the XML documents in Source Document 1 and Source Document 2. You can specify the same properties using the Link Configuration. The Output XML property of the action block gives the XML document with two `<Rowset>` elements combining the two source XML documents.

Totalizer Action Block

You can use the Totalizer action block to calculate totals or accumulated results for a specific column value in an XML document. Using this action block, you can add new columns to an XML document with any of the following modes:

▶ **Accumulator:** This is relevant for a numeric column. If the current column value is less than the previous column, then the accumulator column value is calculated as follows:

(Scaling Factor) × [Current Value + (Max Range - Last Value)].

If the current column is greater than the previous values, the accumulator value is calculated as

(Scaling Factor) × (Current Value - Last Value).

▶ **Counter:** This is relevant for a numeric column. If the current column value is less than the previous value, the counter value is calculated as

Scaling Factor × (Current Value).

If the current column value is greater than the previous values, the counter value is calculated as

Scaling Factor × (Current Value - Last Value).

▶ **Integral:** This is relevant for a numeric column. The integral value is calculated as follows:

Scaling Factor × [Time Span since previous Record in seconds × (Current Value - First Value)].

▶ **Transitions:** This is relevant for both numeric and non-numeric columns. If the current value is equal to the previous value, or if the value is null, then the result is zero. Otherwise, the result is one.

▶ **Time:** This is relevant for a numeric column. If the column value is not zero, the identified time stamp column interval is calculated using the following algorithm:

Scaling Factor × (Current Date - Last Date) in seconds.

In the Object Configuration of the action block, specify the XML document (Figure 6.46). The columns present in the XML document get automatically populated in the Name dropdown. Specify the Scaling Factor and Maximum Range, and select the Totalizer Mode to use (as explained previously). Click on the Add button to add the totalizer column to the XML document. This column gets added as a new column in the XML document as *<ColumnName>.<ModeName>*. Click on Delete to delete an existing totalizer column. No Link Configuration is required for this action block. The totalizer columns defined by the Object Configuration get added in the Output XML property of the action block, which you can access in the Outgoing Link Configuration or any subsequent action block's Link Configuration.

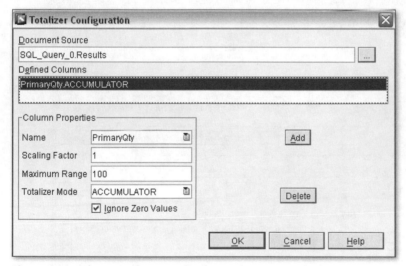

Figure 6.46 Object Configuration for the Totalizer Action Block

Time Interpolator Action Block

You can use the Time Interpolator action block to combine multiple `<Rowset>` elements. For example, consider data sets that have values with different time intervals; this makes it difficult to relate the data or to create a single data set that can be used for a group-bar chart. The Time Interpolator action block creates a single data set combining the columns present in the different data sets. If a specific time point yields data sets that don't have values, and other data sets that do, the Time Interpolator action block substitutes "NA" values for the former cases with the latter. In the Object Configuration of the action block, specify the XML document in the Document Source property, which contains multiple data sets with `<Rowset>` elements. Each has a timestamp column.

String To XML Parser Action Block

You can use the String To XML Parser action block to convert a string having a valid XML value into an XML document. The action block has no Object Configuration. In the Link Configuration, specify the XML string by mapping any transaction property, a previous action block's property, or a fixed value (Figure 6.47). The Output XML property of the action block gives the XML document.

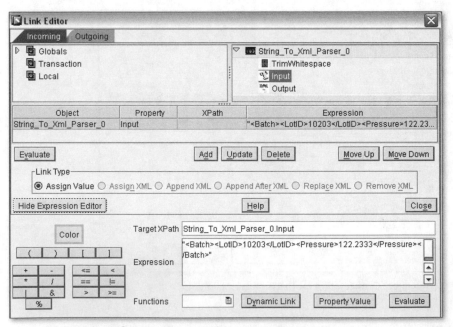

Figure 6.47   Link Configuration for the String To XML Parser Action Block

String List To XML Parser Action Block

You can use the String List To XML Parser action block to convert a string list with values separated by a delimiter into an XML document.

Example

A string input of Alarm Description, 2008-07-01T17:47:18, 2245 gets converted into the following XML:

```
<Rowsets DateCreated="2008-07-07T14:19:39" StartDate="2008-07-
07T14:19:39" EndDate="2008-07-08T14:19:39" Version="9.5">
<Rowset>
<Columns>
<Column Name="Item" SourceColumn="Item" Description="Item"
SQLDataType="1"MinRange="0" MaxRange="0" />
</Columns>
<Row>
<Item>Alarm Description</Item>
</Row>
<Row>
<Item>2008-07-01T17:47:18</Item>
</Row>
<Row>
<Item>2245</Item>
</Row>
</Rowset>
</Rowsets>
```

The action block has no Object Configuration. In the Link Configuration, specify the string in the Input parameter as a delimiter-separated list of data from either a transaction property or from any previous action block's property. You can specify the delimiter in the Delimiter property; comma (,) is used by default. Setting TrimWhitespace to True trims the space between the data values in the string, if present. Setting StripQuotes to True removes double quotes in the data value. The Output XML property gives the XML document created using the data values in the input string. All the data values are added under the `<Item>` element, which is present under the `<Row>` element.

XSL Transformation Action Block

You can use the XSL Transformation action block to apply an XML style sheet (XSL) to an XML document in a BLS Transaction. You can specify the XSL to be applied as a URL by using the Transform URL property in Object Configuration.

You can also do this in the Link Configuration, as a URL in the Transform property, or as the whole XSL document itself in the InputXSL property. Input specifies the input XML document to be transformed by the XSL. In the Outgoing tab or in any subsequent action block's Link Configuration, the Output property gives the transformed XML document, and the TextOutput property gives the same XML as a string.

6.3.3 Reference Documents Action Blocks

Reference Documents in SAP MII are pre-existing XML schemas or documents that enable you to create XML documents in BLS Transaction. You find this useful when you are creating mappings to industry standard messages such as B2MML, OAG, and so on for which standard XML schema documents for the messages are readily available from the respective standard governing bodies. You can assign any action block's properties and local or transaction properties of a transaction of the type Xml to a Reference Document. When you do this, the XML property takes up the XML structure specified by the Reference Document, which is a predefined XML document or schema. The Reference Document category in BLS Transaction consists of the following action blocks:

▶ Reference Document Loader

▶ Reference Schema Loader

Reference Document Loader Action Block

You can use the Reference Document Loader action block to load an existing XML file into a BLS Transaction and assign it to a transaction, local, or action property to define the structure of the XML document. In the Object Configuration of the action block, you can specify the XML document to be loaded from any project content present in the SAP MII server (Figure 6.48).

To assign the Reference Document to a property of type Xml, click on Assign Reference Document in the Transaction configuration tab or use the Workbench menu path TRANSACTION • ASSIGN REFERENCE DOCUMENT. Select the transaction, local, or action block's property in the upper part of the window. Using the XMLContent property, specify the *<Reference Document>*.XmlContent in the Link to Other Object (Figure 6.49). Click on Assign Reference Document to assign the Reference Document to the selected property. You can delete an existing assignment by selecting the property and clicking on Remove Reference Document button.

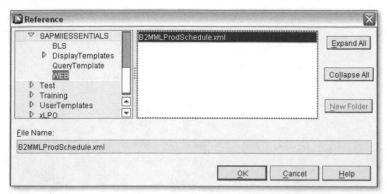

Figure 6.48 Object Configuration for the Reference Document Loader Action Block

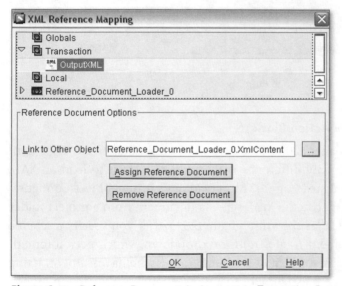

Figure 6.49 Reference Document Assignment to Transaction Property

In Link Configuration, the assigned property gets the same structure of the XML document that has been assigned as its Reference Document (Figure 6.50). This helps to create the XML document and assign values to its elements.

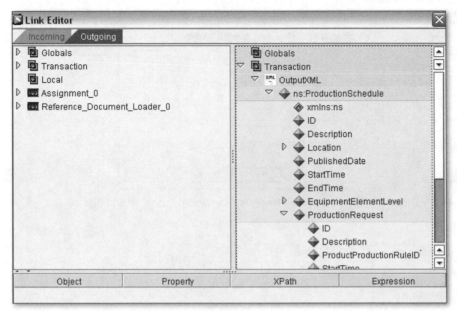

Figure 6.50 Reference Document Assigned Property

Reference Schema Loader Action Block

The Reference Schema Loader action block is similar to the Reference Document Loader action block. The only difference is that you can use it to load an XML schema (.xsd) document instead of an XML document. In the Object Configuration of the action block, specify the XML schema document from a project folder available in the Workbench, as shown in Figure 6.51. After you specify a schema document, select the Element Name from the dropdown, which gets automatically populated with the schema elements present in the schema document. Using this, the Reference Document assignment to a transaction, local, or action block's property is exactly the same as that of the Reference Document Loader action block. The assigned property takes the same XML structure as defined in the XML schema document.

Now that we have reviewed the different action blocks relating to XML documents in BLS Transactions, we can discuss the integration of SAP MII with the enterprise system.

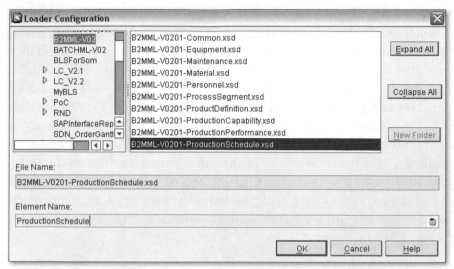

Figure 6.51 Object Configuration for the Reference Schema Loader Action Block

6.4   Connecting to the Enterprise Systems

SAP MII BLS offers a few action blocks that enable a connection between the enterprise business system and the plant floor. Typically, this integration is provided by SAP Java Connector (JCo) or Java Resource Adapter (JRA) actions to execute RFC or BAPI from Advanced Business Application Programming (ABAP)–based systems and Web service and SAP XI actions to connect to SAP and non-SAP systems. The application also provides action blocks to manipulate IDoc, RFC, or XML messages received by SAP MII using the Message Services and manufacturing dashboard actions to update Key Performance Indicators (KPIs) or create alerts in the SAP ECC system.

6.4.1   Creating an SAP Server Alias

To execute RFC or BAPI using the SAP JCo, you can create SAP-server aliases for the ERP systems, which you can use in the action block configurations for the SAP server connection information. The SAP server aliases are configured with the physical server and login information, which you can change at any point of time without changing the BLS Transactions, which uses them for executing RFC by

SAP JCo action blocks. To configure an SAP server alias, open the alias editor via Data Services • SAP Server Editor (Figure 6.52). The existing SAP server aliases are displayed in the listbox on the left of the screen, and the selected configuration appears on the right. Click on the New button to create a new alias. Select JCo, BC, or WAS from the dropdown appearing on the pop-up window. JCo configuration is required for using the SAP JCo Interface action blocks; BC for the SAP Business Connector action blocks; and WAS for the SAP NetWeaver AS Interface action blocks. Specify a unique name, an optional description, and the server hostname or IP address. In the table, specify the connector-specific properties for the server for which the configuration is created. Click on the Save button to save the configuration. You can copy an existing configuration using the Copy button and delete by the Delete button. Clicking on the Summary button displays the configuration summary in a pop-up window.

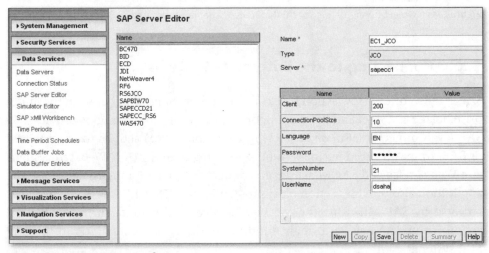

Figure 6.52 SAP Server Configuration

> **Note**
>
> Though you can execute RFC/BAPI without using an SAP Server alias, it is not recommended because a change in the connection information means changing all BLS Transactions where it is used. Using the SAP Server Alias, you would need only to change the configuration in the SAP Server Editor, and not in the BLS Transactions.

6.4.2 SAP JCo Interface Action Blocks

Using the SAP JCo Interface action blocks, you can execute any RFC or BAPI from an SAP system with transaction or session handling. You can use these action blocks when you want to retrieve data from SAP systems or need to update from the plant floor. For example, when you are retrieving the production order details and creating production order confirmation from the transaction dashboards created in SAP MII to SAP ERP, you can use these action blocks. This category of action blocks consists of the following:

- SAP JCo Start Session
- SAP JCo Function
- SAP JCo Commit
- SAP JCo Rollback
- SAP JCo End Session

SAP JCo Start Session Action Block

You can use the SAP JCo Start Session action block to initialize a JCo session for executing one or more RFC or BAPI with transaction handling. Typically, you should use this for executing RFC or BAPI that changes the data in the SAP server and doesn't have an internal commit inside the function module. This action block simply starts the JCo session and has no configuration for the specific RFC or BAPI to execute. It is required only if the SAP JCo Function action block is used in the BLS transaction. In Object Configuration of the action block, specify the SAP RFC server details by using the SAP server alias, as shown in Figure 6.53. All SAP server aliases existing in the SAP MII installation appear in the dropdown. On selecting a specific alias, the corresponding configurations for server connections and login are populated in the input fields. Pool Connections specifies a connection pool used for connecting to the SAP system (instead of an ad-hoc connection). Though you can specify the individual properties here as well, we recommend that you use an SAP server alias (for the reasons mentioned in the previous section). You can specify the same properties using the Link Configuration.

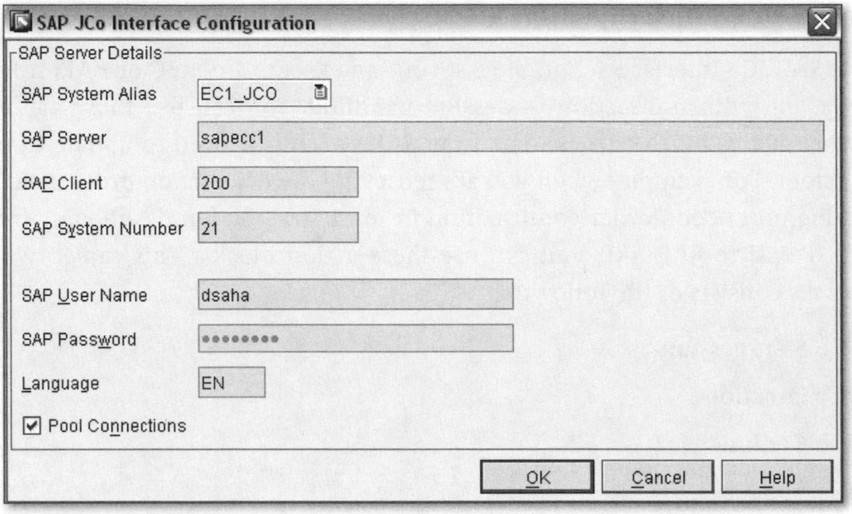

Figure 6.53 Object Configuration of the JCo Start Session Action Block

SAP JCo Function Action Block

You can use the SAP JCo Function action block to execute an RFC or BAPI from an SAP system. You must always use it with the SAP JCo Start Session action block. In Object Configuration of the action block, specify the SAP JCo Start Session action block, which must be present before this action in the BLS Transaction. This action block takes the server connection and logon information from the SAP JCo Start Session action block only. Specify a search pattern (using wildcard characters) for the RFC name in the Search Pattern textbox, and click on Get List (Figure 6.54). The matching RFC names from the SAP server are displayed in the list. Select the RFC to be executed, and it appears in the RFC Name textbox. Click on OK. A pop-up window asks, "Do you want to generate request/response documents?" If you click on the Yes button, then it gets the RFC metadata XML from the SAP server and generates request and response properties for the action block. You can then use these generated properties in Link Configuration. Checking the Execute Function checkbox specifies whether or not the RFC will be executed while executing the action block. If not checked, the RFC will not be executed, though the input mapping will be generated as specified.

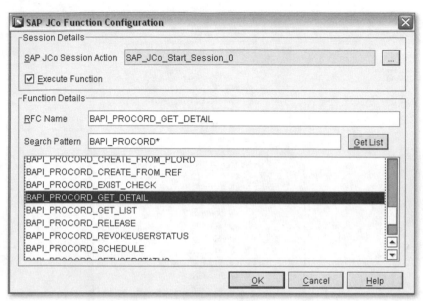

Figure 6.54 Object Configuration for the SAP JCo Function Action Block

In the Link Configuration of the action block, use the Link Editor to specify or link the input parameters of the RFC present under the Request XML property (Figure 6.55). The output parameters from the RFC are available under the Response XML property of the action block, which you should access in the Outgoing tab of the action block's Link Configuration or in subsequent action blocks' Link Configurations. You also have a parameter available in the Outgoing tab or subsequent Link Configurations for the action block called LastErrorMessage, which gives the system error message, if any, while executing the RFC.

You can add multiple SAP JCo Function action blocks in sequence to be executed in a JCo session.

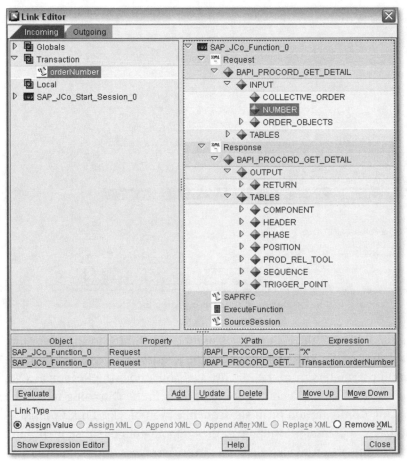

Figure 6.55 Link Configuration for the SAP JCo Function Action Block

SAP JCo Commit Action Block

You can use the SAP JCo Commit action block to commit a transaction within a JCo session. To check the success conditions and commit the transaction, add the action block after the SAP JCo Function actions and the subsequent Conditional action block. In the Object Configuration of the action block, specify only the SAP JCo Start Session action block's reference from the BLS Transaction present before it. In the Outgoing Link Configuration, the LastErrorMessage property gives the error message, if any, while committing the transaction.

SAP JCo Rollback Action Block

You can use the SAP JCo Rollback action block to rollback a JCo session in a BLS Transaction. This is the exact opposite of the SAP JCo Commit action block. The configurations for the SAP JCo Rollback action are exactly the same as that of the SAP JCo Commit action and are explained in the previous section.

SAP JCo End Session Action Block

You can use the SAP JCo End Session action block to terminate a JCo session that was started by the SAP JCo Start Session action. The Object Configuration and Link Configuration for this action block are the same as that of the SAP JCo Commit action, where you need to specify the SAP JCo Start Session action only. You must use this action block to terminate the connection if the JCo Start Session action block is used before to open the connection.

> **Note**
>
> Together with the JCo Commit and Rollback actions, the SAP JCo Start Session, Function, and End Session action blocks help to implement transaction handling in SAP MII when you are executing a series of RFCs to update data in an SAP system. If you want to execute multiple RFCs in a sequence, and the failure of one RFC call in the chain should cause the entire series of RFC calls to be aborted, such transactional control is advised.
>
> This applies to the corresponding SAP JRA action blocks as well, which are discussed in the following sections.

6.4.3 SAP JRA Interface Action Blocks

The SAP JRA Interface action blocks are very similar to the SAP JCo Interface action blocks. The only difference is that the former uses the SAP Java Resource Adapter (SAP JRA) for executing RFC and BAPI instead of SAP JCo. Also the connection parameters to the SAP system used in SAP JRA are maintained in Visual Administrator and not in SAP MII (SAP Server Editor) in contrast to SAP JCo. SAP JRA is more stable and robust than SAP JCo, and we recommend it for executing RFC or BAPI. To use the SAP JRA Interface action blocks, you must install and configure SAP JRA in the SAP NetWeaver Java WebAS (as explained in Chapter 2 Administrating and Configuring SAP MII).

SAP JRA Start Session Action Block

You can use the SAP JRA Start Session action block to establish a connection session with an SAP system for executing any BAPI or RFC using the SAP JRA Function Call action block. In the Object Configuration of the action block, select the SAP JRA connection factory as configured using the Visual Administrator in SAP NetWeaver. The connection and logon information for the SAP system is automatically taken from the connection factory selected, but, if required, you can specify the logon information here as well. This information includes the SAP Client, SAP User Name, SAP Password, and Language, all of which is used if the Use Local Settings checkbox is checked (Figure 6.56). You can specify the same properties using the Link Configuration.

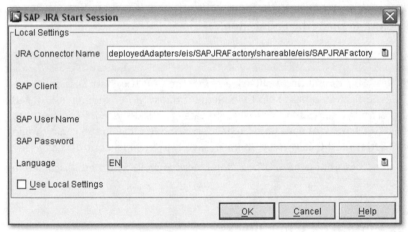

Figure 6.56 Object Configuration for the SAP JRA Start Session Action Block

SAP JRA Function Call Action Block

You can use SAP JRA Function Call action block to execute RFC or BAPI, and you must use it after an SAP JRA Start Session action block. In the Object Configuration, specify the JRA Start Session action block (Figure 6.57). It takes the connection and logon details from that action block only. To enable data buffering (that is, the retry mechanism because of connection failure), check the checkbox Use Data Buffering. (Data buffering is explained in detail in Chapter 4 Developing Composite Applications in SAP MII: The Basics.) Also specify the Retention Time in Days, Max. Retry Count, and Retry Interval for Data Buffering. To specify the RFC or BAPI, type the function module name (with a wildcard pattern, if required) in the Search Pattern and click on the Get List button. The matching RFCs and BAPIs from the SAP system are then displayed. Select the appropriate RFC from the list, and it appears in the RFC Name textbox. To enable autocommit for the single RFC call, check the checkbox Automatically Commit. After you click OK, the action block gets the metadata for the specified RFC from the SAP system and assigns the structure to its Request and Response XML properties (available in Link Configuration).

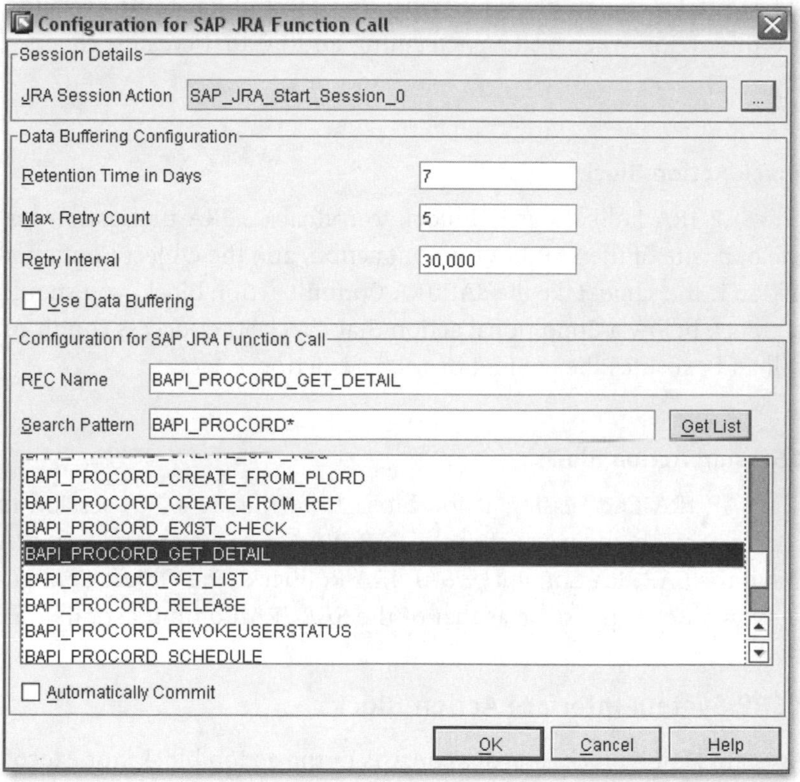

Figure 6.57 Object Configuration for the SAP JRA Function Call Action Block

In Link Configuration, assign the input parameter values of the RFC using the Link Editor. In the Outgoing or subsequent action block's Link Configuration, you can access the Response XML, which consists of the output parameters of the RFC. These are the same as the properties of the SAP JCo Function action.

SAP JRA Commit Action Block

You can use the SAP JRA Commit action block to commit a JRA transaction session for one or more RFC calls. You must add this action block after the SAP JRA Start Session and SAP JRA Function Call actions. In the Object Configuration, specify the SAP JRA Start Session action block for which the commit has to be executed. You should use this action when you are executing an RFC that creates, changes, or deletes data.

SAP JRA Rollback Action Block

You can use the SAP JRA Rollback action block to rollback a JRA transaction session. This is the opposite of the SAP JRA Commit action, and the Object Configuration for this action is the same. Like the SAP JRA Commit action block, you should add this action block below a Conditional action that checks the success condition for the RFC call and executes the commit or rollback action.

SAP JRA End Session Action Block

You can use the SAP JRA End Session action block to terminate a JRA session in the BLS transaction. You should use it after the SAP JRA Start Session and SAP JRA Function Call and the SAP JRA Commit or SAP JRA Rollback. The Object Configuration of the action block is the same as that of the SAP JRA Commit action.

6.4.4 SAP ERP System Interface Action Blocks

The SAP ERP system action block category consists of the action blocks for executing RFC or BAPI using older technologies, such as SAP Business Connector, SAP JCo (without session management), and RFC SOAP interface. These action blocks are the predecessors of the SAP JCo Interface and SAP JRA Interface action blocks and were introduced in older releases of SAP MII when those others were not available. Currently, these action blocks are deprecated and not recommended. This category consists of the following action blocks:

► SAP Interface Repository

► SAP Business Connector

► SAP BC Start Session

► SAP BC Commit

► SAP BC Rollback

► SAP NetWeaver AS Interface

► SAP JCo Interface

> **Note**
>
> The action blocks in this category that are obsolete now are not explained here.

SAP JCo Interface Action Block

You can use the SAP JCo Interface action block to execute a single BAPI or RFC without session management from SAP systems using SAP JCo. This action block is exactly the same as the SAP JCo Function action block explained in Section 6.4.2 SAP JCo Interface Action Blocks, except that the same session cannot be maintained between multiple RFC calls. In the Object Configuration of the action block, specify the connection and logon information to the SAP system by selecting the SAP server alias from the SAP System Alias dropdown (Figure 6.58). Specify a search pattern for the RFC name in the Search Pattern field, and click on Get List to get the matching RFC names from the SAP system. Select the appropriate RFC name, which then appears in the RFC Name field. Checking the Automatically Commit Transaction checkbox executes a commit call after the specified RFC execution. This is relevant only if the RFC manipulates the data in the SAP system. Execute Function specifies whether the RFC will be executed or not. After you click OK, the metadata XML for the specified RFC is fetched from the SAP system. You can configure this metadata XML using Link Configuration in the same way as in the SAP JCo Function action block.

Figure 6.58 Object Configuration for the SAP JCo Interface Action Block

6.4.5 Using SSO in JCo Action Blocks

In the SAP JCo action block, you might need to use Single Sign-On (SSO) to pass the user credentials for executing the RFC in the SAP backend system. The SAP JCo Interface action and SAP JCo Start Session action blocks provide link parameters for passing the SSO2 logon ticket from the Java WebAS to the ABAP WebAS. This enables the user credentials used in the SAP MII Web page (irpt) to be passed to the JCo action blocks for executing the RFC when you are executing the BLS Transaction via XacuteQuery and the iCommand applet. Note that if you want to use this feature, the login user name must be the same for the Java (SAP MII) and the ABAP WebAS (SAP ERP). To enable this feature, specify the SAPUserName property value to $MYSAPSSO2$ in the Link Configuration. Then define a transaction property named MYSAPSSO2 and link that to the SAPSSO2Ticket, as shown in Figure 6.59. Setting the SAPUserName property to $MYSAPSSO2$ means that you need to use the SSO2 logon ticket. It is then automatically passed from the user credentials to invoke the web page that uses XacuteQuery to call the BLS Transaction. Also, make sure to check the Autobind property in the Data Server's XacuteConnector configuration, because the MYSAPSSO2 transaction property actually refers to an environmental variable of SAP MII, which sends the SSO2 logon ticket. Finally, you must configure the certificate for logon ticket in both the sender (Java WebAS) and receiver (ABAP WebAS).

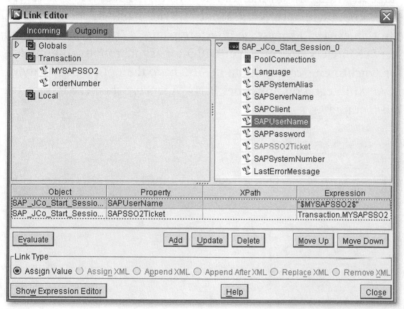

Figure 6.59 Link Configuration in the JCo Start Session Action Block for SSO Configuration

6.4.6 SAP XI Action Blocks

You can use the SAP XI action blocks to send messages to SAP Exchange Infrastructure (XI/PI) outbound interfaces using the sender HTTP or SOAP adapters. To use these action blocks, you must configure the Configuration Scenario in the Integration Directory of SAP XI. You can use these action blocks to send messages to SAP ERP via SAP PI without directly executing an RFC or Enterprise Service from SAP MII. This category consists of the following action blocks:

▶ HTTP XI

▶ Web Service XI

HTTP XI Action Block

You can use the HTTP XI action block to send messages with an outbound message/service interface in SAP XI using the sender HTTP adapter. In Object Configuration of the action block, use the Server Name property to specify the SAP XI system hostname or IP address, and the Port property to specify the HTTP port (Figure 6.60). Specify the logon information for the SAP XI user in the SAP User Name, SAP Password, and Language properties. Depending on the sender HTTP adapter configuration in the SAP XI Integration Directory, select HTTP or HTTPS from the Protocol dropdown. Specify the sender service name in Service Name, its namespace in Namespace, its message interface name in Interface Name, and the quality of service in QOS. Specify EO or EOIO for asynchronous communication, and BE for synchronous communication. You have the option of specifying the additional SAP XI integration properties Party, Agency, Scheme, Message ID, and Queue ID, if required.

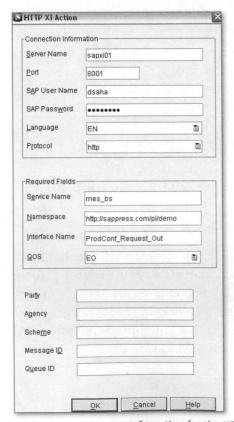

Figure 6.60 Object Configuration for the HTTP XI Action Block

You can specify the same properties using the Link Configuration screen. Also in Link Configuration, you must link the XML document being sent to the SAP XI interface to the InputDocument property (Figure 6.61). Note that the XML document must be of the same format as defined by the message interface in XI. You can access the output XML property Results in the Outgoing Link Configuration or in the Link Configuration of any subsequent action block that gives the response message from SAP XI in case of synchronous communications.

Figure 6.61 Link Configuration for the HTTP XI Action Block

Web Service XI Action Block

You can use the Web Service XI action block to send XML messages to outbound message/service interfaces using the sender SOAP adapter. This action block uses the WSDL URL generated from a message/service interface in SAP XI to send the

SOAP message. Its configuration is exactly same as that of the Web Service action block explained in the next section.

6.4.7 Web Service

The Web Service action block is the single action block under this category.

Web Service Action Block

The Web Service action block executes a Web service from any system or SAP Enterprise Services using its WSDL URL to send and receive SOAP messages. In the Object Configuration for the action block, specify the WSDL URL of the Web Service in the URL property and an optional User Name and Password, if required (Figure 6.62). Click on the Next button. The WSDL received from the specified URL is parsed, and the corresponding Web service port and operation are displayed. From there, you need to select the relevant operations and port . After you click OK, the WSDL request and response document XML metadata is fetched by the action block and assigned to its Link Properties.

Figure 6.62 Object Configuration for the Web Service Action Block

In Link Configuration of the action block, you can specify any input parameter by linking the input properties of the request XML document with fixed values or with the transaction or local properties or other action block's properties (Figure 6.63). The Outgoing Link Configuration, or any subsequent action block's Link Configuration, provides access to the response XML document for the Web service.

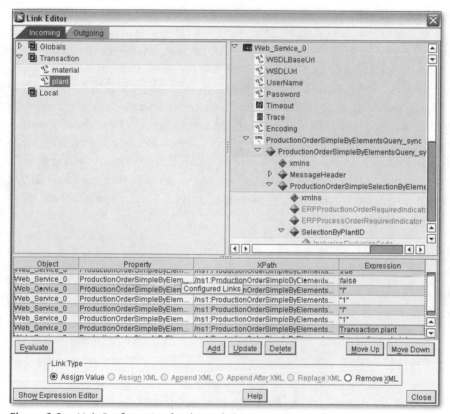

Figure 6.63 Link Configuration for the Web Service Action Block

6.4.8 Message Services Action Blocks

You can use the Message Services action blocks to read and manipulate the messages received from external systems such as RFC, IDoc, and HTTP XML. As explained in Section 3.2 Message Services: Synchronizing the Manufacturing Plant Floor with the Enterprise, the messages received are buffered in the SAP MII

WebAS database. You can then use these action blocks for ad-hoc (category-based) processing. You need not use these action blocks in the transactions specified as processing rule in the Message Services, because in that case the message is passed to the transaction as XML in a transaction input property and the message processing status is automatically updated after the transaction gets executed. These action blocks are useful when you want to know the message ID of the messages buffered and process them by the message ID. You can use these action blocks in transactions where you want to process the messages and extract the relevant information including the message ID or in transactions that are called by external systems to get the message data. For example, say you have sent the production order IDocs from SAP ERP to SAP MII. They are received and buffered using the Message Services and assigned to a category as processing rule. Then you can use a BLS Transaction that runs in the SAP MII scheduler and periodically reads the messages from the buffer using these action blocks, extracts the relevant header information (for example, order number, plant, and so on) along with the message ID, and inserts them into a custom database table. Later you can read the basic information from this database table and by the corresponding message ID get the detail information by reading the message content. This action block category consists of the following action blocks:

- Query Messages
- Read Message
- Update Message
- Delete Message

Query Messages Action Block

You can use the Query Messages action block to find a list of buffered messages in SAP MII with Message Services by a set of selection criteria. In the Object Configuration of the action block, specify the message listener name in Server Name; the XML or RFC or IDoc message name in Message Name and the category defined in the processing rule in Message Category (Figure 6.64). Select the Message Type and Message Status from the list of options. Specify the date range for message selection in Start Date and End Date. The Row Count property specifies the maximum number of messages to be retrieved by the query.

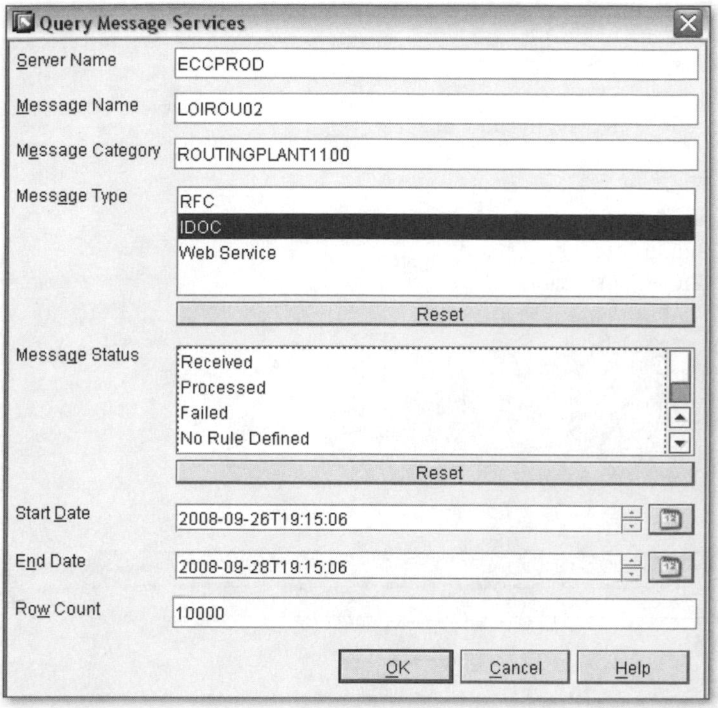

Figure 6.64 Object Configuration for the Query Messages Action Block

You can configure the same properties in Link Configuration. In the Outgoing Link Configuration, or in any subsequent action block's Link Configuration, you can access the BufferListDoc XML property, which gives the list of messages. This list includes information about each message, which appears under the JCOMessage element (Figure 6.65). You can use a Repeater action block to loop into the JCOMessageList element to process each message's information, or assign the whole XML document to another action block or transaction property.

Example

The following is an example of a JCOMessageList XML document returned by the action block:

```
<?xml version="1.0" encoding="UTF-8"?>
<JCOMessageList>
<JCOMessage>
<MessageId>45</MessageId>
<JcoServerName>ECCPROD</JcoServerName>
<MessageName>LOIROU02</MessageName>
```

```
<Category>ROUTINGPLANT1100</Category>
<MessageType>2</MessageType>
<Status>6</Status>
<DocNumber>_0000000000758809</DocNumber>
</JCOMessage>
<JCOMessage>
<MessageId>46</MessageId>
<JcoServerName>ECCPROD</JcoServerName>
<MessageName>LOIROU02</MessageName>
<Category>ROUTINGPLANT1100</Category>
<MessageType>2</MessageType>
<Status>6</Status>
<DocNumber>_0000000000758810</DocNumber>
</JCOMessage>
</JCOMessageList>
```

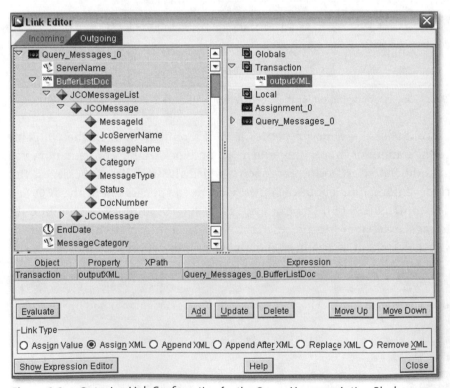

Figure 6.65 Outgoing Link Configuration for the Query Messages Action Block

Read Message Action Block

You can use the Read Message action block to read the XML message content of the messages received and buffered by Message Services. Each message buffered by Message Services has a unique message ID, which is returned by the Query Messages action block's output. In the Read Message action block, assign the MessageId from a Repeater action block used to loop into the Query Messages action block's <JCOMessage> element (Figure 6.66). The Outgoing Link Configuration of the Read Message action block has two XML output properties: JCOMessage and MessageDocumentXML. JCOMessage XML returns the metadata information for the message, and MessageDocumentXML returns the actual message XML content.

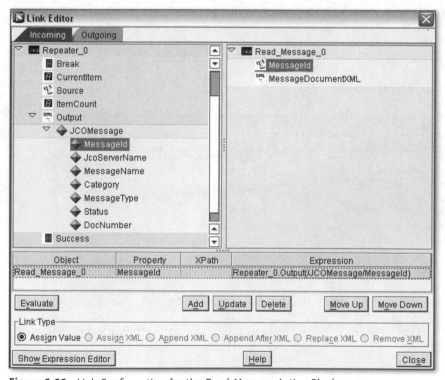

Figure 6.66 Link Configuration for the Read Message Action Block

Update Message Action Block

You can use the Update Message action block to update the status and status text for a buffered message. This would be appropriate, for example, after ad-hoc processing by a BLS Transaction. In Link Configuration, specify the MessageId, Status, and MessageStatusText (Figure 6.67), which you can also specify in the Object Configuration with fixed values. The MessageId property is the unique ID for each message, which can be obtained from the Query Messages action block's output XML. In the Status property, specify a numeric value for the message processing status (1-6) from the following list:

- ▸ RECEIVED = 1
- ▸ PROCESSSED = 2
- ▸ FAILED = 3
- ▸ NORULEDEFINED = 4
- ▸ RUNNING = 5
- ▸ CATEGORIZED = 6

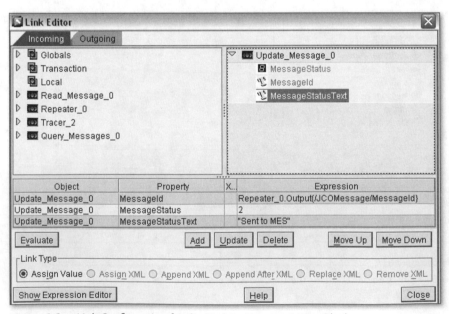

Figure 6.67 Link Configuration for the Update Message Action Block

In the MessageStatusText, specify text as a comment to the message processing status, which is displayed as a tooltip under the Status column in the Message Monitor screen, which is located under the Message Services menu.

Delete Message Action Block

You can use the Delete Message action block to delete a buffered message from the SAP MII database. You need to specify the MessageId of the message to be deleted in its Object or Link configuration. The message specified by the MessageId is deleted permanently from the SAP MII database.

6.4.9   Manufacturing Dashboards Action Blocks

You can use the Manufacturing Dashboards action blocks to update KPI values or create alerts in the SAP ERP system. These action blocks are useful when you want to update the different KPIs in SAP ERP or want to create an alert from the plant systems via SAP MII. For example, you can configure a KPI called Line1OEE that SAP MII can calculate in the BLS Transaction by retrieving the relevant data from various plant systems and update the KPI value in SAP ERP. You can then view this KPI in the Plant Manager dashboard available in the Portal content for the Plant Manager role in SAP Enterprise Portal. Similarly, you can create an alert for the Maintenance Supervisor in SAP ERP in case of a machine breakdown, which is sensed by a Supervisory Control And Data Acquisition (SCADA) or Distributed Control System (DCS) and reported to SAP MII as a Tag query output. This category consists of the following action blocks:

▶ SAP KPI Update

▶ SAP Alert

SAP KPI Update Action Block

You can use the SAP KPI Update action block to update a KPI value in an SAP ECC system by internally executing the RFC EPM_KPI_DATA_INSERT. Configure the KPI definitions in an SAP ECC 5.0 or 6.0 system using customization for Plant Manager 1.0 or 2.0, respectively. In the Object Configuration, specify the SAP system information using the SAP Server Alias and the KPI Name and KPI Value to be updated (Figure 6.68). The KPI Name that is specified here must match the

Key Figure definitions created in the SAP ERP customization. To pass dynamic values, you can also specify all of these properties, including Single Sign-On (SSO) by logon ticket, in Link Configuration. In Link Configuration you can also specify an additional property called KPISource.

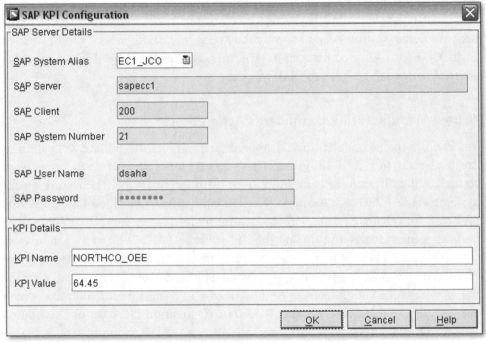

Figure 6.68 Object Configuration for the SAP KPI Update Action Block

SAP Alert Action Block

You can use the SAP Alert action block to create an alert in an SAP ABAP system by internally executing the RFC SALERT_CREATE, which is displayed in the SAP Alert Inbox. To use this action block, you must use the SAP transaction ALRTCAT-DEF to preconfigure an alert category by the name XMII in the target SAP system. When you are configuring the alert category, specify the recipient users or roles. In the Object Configuration of the action block, specify the SAP system using the SAP System Alias, Alert Header Text, Alert Short Text, and Alert Long Text, all of which appears in the alert displayed to the recipient users (Figure 6.69). You can specify the same properties using the Link Configuration.

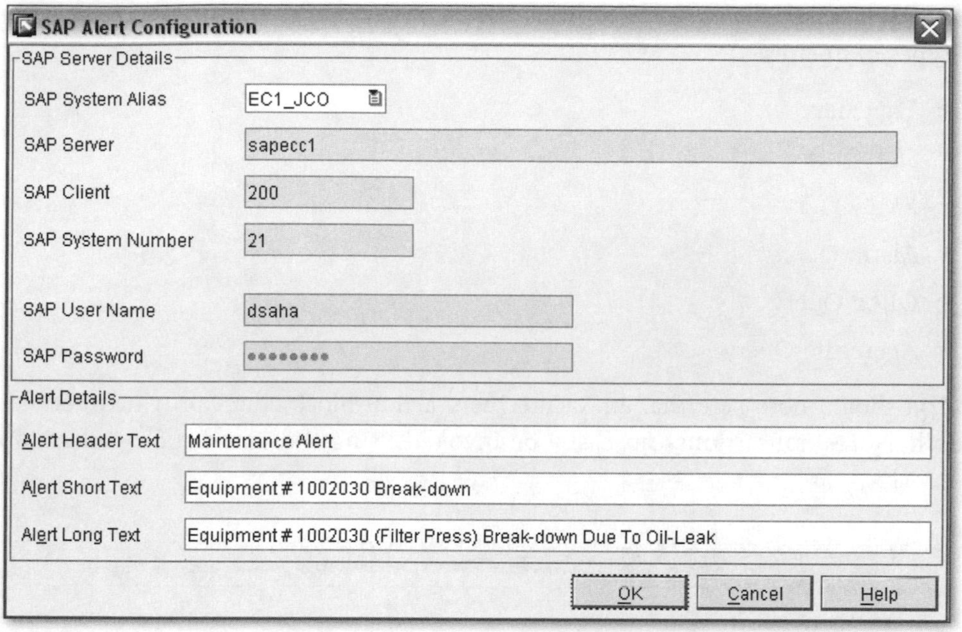

Figure 6.69 Object Configuration for the SAP Alert Action Block

You know now about the RFC, Web services, Message Services, KPI, and Alert action blocks available in BLS Transactions for enterprise system connectivity. In the next section, we look into the different action blocks available for connecting to plant-floor systems and managing plant data.

6.5 Managing the Plant Data

You can use BLS Transactions to execute the data queries you have created as query templates. This, in turn, enables you to connect to the manufacturing plant-floor systems and build business logic to parse and process data.

6.5.1 Data Queries Action Blocks

The Data Queries action block category contains six types of data query action blocks, one each for each type of data query. You can use these action blocks to execute the query templates and manipulate their outputs in the Business Logic Transactions. You can also assign input parameters to the underlying query templates via these action blocks, as defined in the corresponding query templates.

The following Data Query action blocks are available for executing the different types of queries:

- ▸ Tag Query
- ▸ SQL Query
- ▸ XML Query
- ▸ Alarm Query
- ▸ OLAP Query
- ▸ Aggregate Query

You should note here that an XacuteQuery action block is not provided because other BLS Transactions can easily be invoked using the Transaction Call action block.

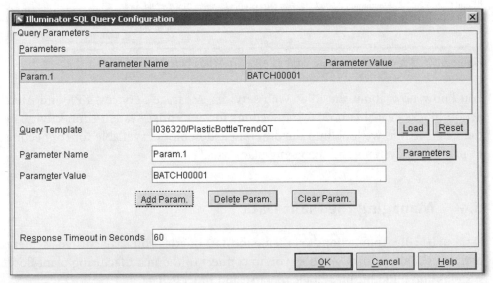

Figure 6.70 Object Configuration for the Data Query Action Block

The configuration screens of these query action blocks are exactly the same. Use the Query Template property to specify the required query template (Figure 6.70), and use the Parameter Name and Parameter Value properties to specify fixed Parameter values for the query template. Alternatively, you can dynamically assign these values using Link Configuration. Select the parameter name by clicking the

Parameters button, and add the parameters by clicking on the Add Param. button. You can delete an existing parameter by clicking the Delete Param. button, and you can remove its value by clicking on the Clear Param. button.

The Link Configuration screens for the Data Query action blocks contain all the parameters that are available in the respective query templates; these have been explained in detail in Section 4.2 Configuring Query Templates. The parameters that are common to all the Query action blocks and as such are of specific interest, are the parameters Param.1 to Param.32, which enable you to pass input parameter values to the underlying query parameters by explicitly setting their values in the transaction. If you use an XSL transformation for the query result, you can pass the parameter names used in the XSLT transformation as XParamName.1 to XParam-Name.16, and their corresponding values as XParamValue.1 to XParamValue.16.

Other than the parameters that are available as configurable options on the Query Template configuration screen, you can configure two other parameters — Debug and Trace — only from the Link Configuration screen. They both accept Boolean values and have a default value of False. Both can be turned on by explicitly setting a value of True. Whereas the Trace option enables logging of trace messages in the SAP NetWeaver WebAS log, the Debug option enables debug-level logging of messages to the Java Virtual Machine console.

> **Note**
>
> You can modify the Debug and Trace parameters using JavaScript from an HTML or an IRPT page by invoking the *setDebug(BOOLEAN)* and *setTrace(BOOLEAN)* methods on the query object of the iCommand applet. Also you can use *isDebug()* and *isTrace()* methods to get the Debug and Trace status, respectively.

Column Map Action Block

This category also contains the Column Map action block, which simplifies the path hierarchy in the returned data in XML format by reducing it to only column names. This helps you create complex calculated columns or other complex expressions in the Business Logic Editor without sacrificing the legibility of the written expression. The output of the Column Map action is shown in Figure 6.71; it has just the column name properties instead of the complex XML structure (XPath) to which it refers.

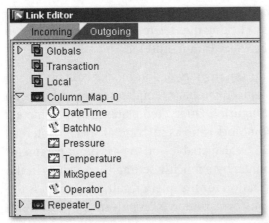

Figure 6.71 Output of a Sample Column Map Action

If your query returns multiple rows, you can use the Column Map action in conjunction with the Repeater action block and configure the Row Source property of the Column Map to accept the Row from the Repeater output. This is done in Object Configuration (Figure 6.72). If a single row is expected as the result of the query, the Repeater can be done away with, and the output of the Results parameter of the Query action block can be specified only in the Source of Query Results parameter.

Figure 6.72 Object Configuration of the Column Map Action Block

6.5.2 Queuing Action Blocks

The Queuing action blocks in SAP MII enable you to create simple data queue implementation. A queue is a data structure that can be used to store data as they arrive, and in the sequence they arrive. Though ideally a queue enables you to insert values at the rear end and query for data at the front end, the SAP MII Queue is more like an associative array that stores XML messages with user defined IDs as the key. Therefore, any message to be retrieved just needs to be looked up by its unique ID. You can use the Queue action blocks to insert the message in the Queue from one BLS transaction and then retrieve it from another one.

The following action blocks are present in this category:

- Queue Get
- Queue Put
- Queue List
- Queue Delete

Queue Get Action Block

You can use the Queue Get action block to retrieve an XML message with a specified ID. The Object Configuration Screen of this action block has the Queue Name and the ID parameter, as shown in Figure 6.73, just as in the Link Configuration screen. A Queue is created when you use the Queue Put action block to put messages to a queue. Specify the Queue Name as the name of the queue from where the message should be retrieved. The ID is the unique identifier associated with the message. This action block returns the XML message in the output parameter Message.

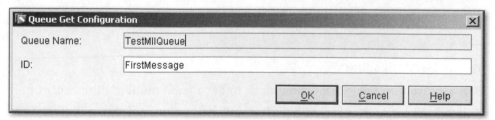

Figure 6.73 Object Configuration for the Queue Get Action Block

Queue Put Action Block

You can use the Queue Put action block to put an XML message into a queue. In the Object Configuration of this action block (Figure 6.74), you need to specify the

Queue Name and ID parameters, along with the Message parameter. This parameter accepts an XML structure and stores it in the queue specified by the Queue Name and with the message ID, which you can specify using a property of type XML by the Link Configuration. A new queue is created if one is not already present by the Name specified. You can specify the same parameters in Link Configuration with dynamic values.

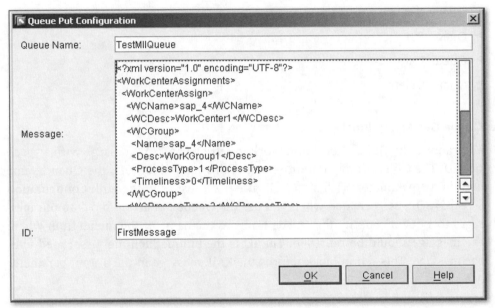

Figure 6.74 Object Configuration for the Queue Put Action Block

Queue List Action Block

You can use the Queue List action block to list a fixed number of messages from a queue. In the Object Configuration of the action block, specify the number of items to be listed in the Maximum Number of Queue Entries parameter and the name of the queue to query from in the Queue Name parameter (Figure 6.75). This returns the IDs of the specified number of messages in the MessageList XML output parameter in the Rowsets/Rowset/Row format.

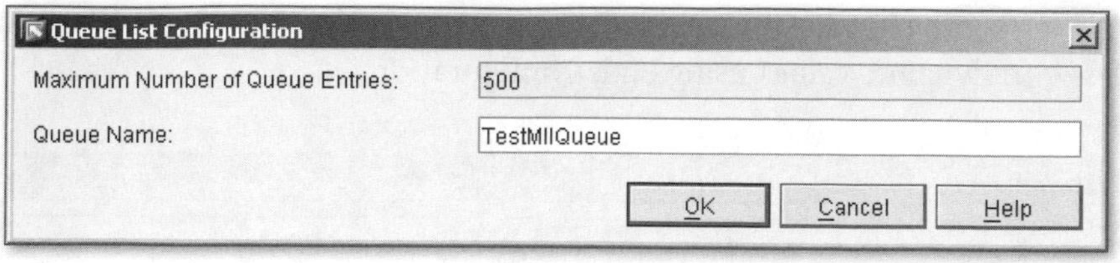

Figure 6.75 Object Configuration for the Queue Put Action Block

Queue Delete Action Block

The Queue Delete action block deletes a particular message from a specified queue. The configuration screen is exactly the same as the Queue Get action block and accepts the same parameters.

You now know about the different action blocks available for connecting to plant-floor systems and managing plant data. In the next section, we explore how to use that data in conjunction with action blocks that generate chart images, animated objects, and statistical quality control (SQC) analysis.

6.6   Charts, Animated Objects, and SQC Analysis

Chart and SQC action blocks provide the ability to generate analysis charts and animated graphics as images from a display template. You can use these graphics in dashboards and web pages or send them by mail. These action blocks are also required for performing statistical quality analysis on the process data.

6.6.1   Charts Action Blocks

The Chart action block category consists of a single action block: Chart. You can use this action block to dynamically generate an encoded image of an iChart display template at runtime, which can then be sent by mail or displayed as a static image in a web page. Specify the query template and the display template for the iChart in the Object Configuration of the action block and the parameter name and value (Figure 6.76). Select the parameter name by clicking the Parameters button, and add the parameters that will be used during runtime by clicking on the Add Param. button. You can delete an added parameter by clicking on the Delete Param. button and clear its value by clicking on the Clear Param. button. You can set all these properties with dynamic values using Link Configuration.

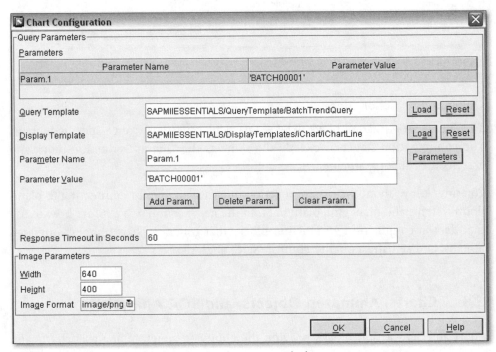

Figure 6.76 Object Configuration for the Chart Action Block

The Chart action block has an output/read-only property called EncodedImage in Link Configuration; it gives the image content to be saved by an Image Saver action block. The EncodedImage property is available in the Outgoing Link Configuration or in subsequent action block's Link Configurations. You can use the Image Saver action block after the Chart action block and link the EncodedImage property to it to save the generated chart image in the SAP MII content catalog (Figure 6.77).

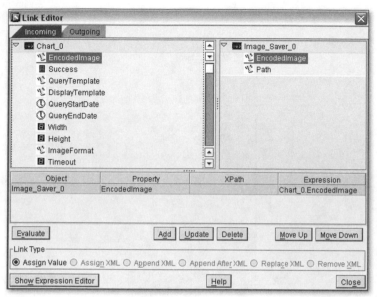

Figure 6.77   Link Configuration for Saving Generated Chart Image

6.6.2   Quality Action Blocks

You can use the Quality action blocks to generate static images of SPC charts from the iSPCChart display template and to get the SQC analysis results from an SPC chart.

The Quality action block category consists of two action blocks:

▸ SPC/SQC Chart

▸ SPC/SQC Analysis

SPC/SQC Chart Action Block

The SPC/SQC Chart action is very similar to that of the Chart action block, and you can use it to generate the static encoded image for an iSPCChart display template. The Object Configuration and Link Configuration for the SPC/SQC Chart action block are very similar to that of the Chart action block. The only difference in the configurations of the SPC/SQC Chart action block and the Chart action block is that you must specify the iSPCChart display template and its corresponding properties in the former. You can save the EncodedImage generated by the SPC/SQC Chart action block by using the ImageSaver action, just as you can with the Chart action block.

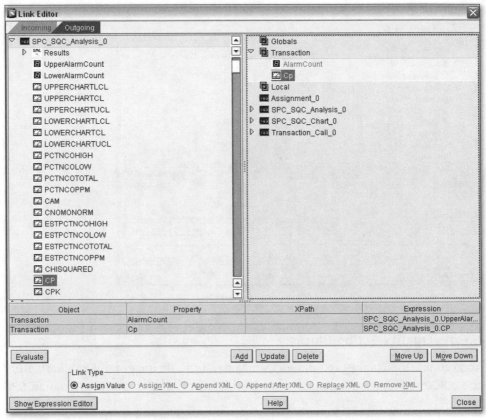

Figure 6.78 Outgoing Link Configuration for the SPC/SQC Analysis Action Block

SPC/SQC Analysis Action Block

You can use the SPC/SQC Analysis action block to access the output data and quality indices of an SPC chart created using the iSPCChart display template without actually generating the chart image. The Object Configuration of the SPC/SQC Analysis action block is the same as that of the SPC/SQC Chart action block and the Chart action block: you must specify the query template and display template along with input parameters (if any). Similarly, the Link Configuration for the SPC/SQC Chart action block is the same as that of the SPC/SQC Chart action block, where you can configure all the input properties with dynamic values in the Incoming tab. In the Outgoing Link Configuration or in other actions after the SPC/SQC Analysis action block, the complete set of SPC/SQC data is available. You can link these to other action block or transaction properties, as shown in Figure 6.78. The UpperAlarm-

Count and LowerAlarmCount properties give the number of alarms or rule violations according to the configured alarms in the display template. The complete set of statistical or SQC indexes such as Cp, Cpk, Control Limits, Specification Limits, and so on are also available as separate output parameters, along with the raw and calculated data points used to plot the SPC chart in the Results XML document. You can use these data to create a report or for further analysis.

Example

An example of SQC analysis XML provided as the output of the SQC analysis is as follows:

```
<?xml version="1.0" encoding="UTF-8"?><Rowsets DateCreated="2009-
03-29T15:33:37" EndDate="2009-03-29T15:33:37" StartDate="2009-03-
29T15:33:37" Version="12.0.4 Build(120)">
<Rowset><Columns>
<Column Description="Statistic Name" MaxRange="0" MinRange="0"
Name="NAME" SQLDataType="1" SourceColumn="NAME"/>
<Column Description="Statistic Value" MaxRange="0" MinRange="0"
Name="VALUE" SQLDataType="8" SourceColumn="VALUE"/>
</Columns>
<Row>
<NAME>CP</NAME><VALUE>1.149980713219</VALUE></Row>
<Row><NAME>CPFIX</NAME><VALUE>NA</VALUE></Row>
<Row><NAME>CPK</NAME><VALUE>1.149980713219</VALUE></Row>
<Row><NAME>CPKFIX</NAME><VALUE>NA</VALUE></Row>
<Row><NAME>CPL</NAME><VALUE>1.149980713219</VALUE></Row>
<Row><NAME>CPM</NAME><VALUE>1.155774103604</VALUE></Row>
<Row><NAME>CPU</NAME><VALUE>1.149980713219</VALUE></Row>
<Row><NAME>CR</NAME><VALUE>0.869579801213</VALUE></Row>
<Row><NAME>EFFECTIVE_LSL</NAME><VALUE>-0.675190230723</VALUE>
</Row>
<Row><NAME>EFFECTIVE_TARGET</NAME><VALUE>26.69</VALUE></Row>
<Row><NAME>EFFECTIVE_USL</NAME><VALUE>54.055190230723</VALUE></Row>
<Row><NAME>ESTPCTNCOHIGH</NAME><VALUE>0.134981268617</VALUE></Row>
<Row><NAME>ESTPCTNCOLOW</NAME><VALUE>0.134981268617</VALUE></Row>
<Row><NAME>ESTPCTNCOPPM</NAME><VALUE>2699.625372346082</VALUE></Row>
<Row><NAME>ESTPCTNCOTOTAL</NAME><VALUE>0.269962537235</VALUE>
</Row>
...
```

The preceding XML is just a part of the generated XML document that actually contains more quality indices that are calculated by the SQC analysis along with the sampler raw data.

6.6.3 Dynamic Graphics Action Blocks

Dynamic graphics action blocks work with SVG documents, which are discussed in detail in Chapter 7 Animated Objects: Making Dynamic Visualizations. These action blocks help you render SVG documents in standard image formats like JPEG and PNG and also create, scale, and combine the generated images. You can use these animated objects for real-time monitoring dashboards such as displaying the status of a machine or the temperature or pressure reading of a flow line. The following action blocks are available in this category:

▶ SVG Renderer

▶ Animation Renderer

▶ Image Combiner

▶ Image Creator

▶ Image Scaler

SVG Renderer Action Block

You can use the SVG Renderer action block to generate an encoded image from an SVG document. In Link Configuration, specify the SVG document, which is of type XML, in the parameter Input. It then returns an image in the EncodedImage string property. The format of this image is specified in the ImageFormat parameter, which is located in both Link Configuration and Object Configuration.

Animation Renderer Action Block

The Animation Renderer action block works in tandem with any standard SVG object, whether it comes with SAP MII or is separately created. In the Object Configuration, browse and select the SVG object from the content catalog that you would like to render (Figure 6.79). This action block generates SVG XML output in the Output parameter. If you have checked the Render Image checkbox, this action block can also generate an image in the format specified in the Image Format property. You can scale the generated image to the height and width you desire using the Scaled Width and Scaled Height parameters. The generated image is available in the EncodedImage property. Other than these, the public properties of the loaded SVG object are also available in the Link Configuration, to which you can assign desired values to configure the action block. You can also assign the EncodedImage property to a transaction output property of type string and display that in a web page as an image by executing the BLS Transaction using the Runner service and dynamically refreshing using JavaScript.

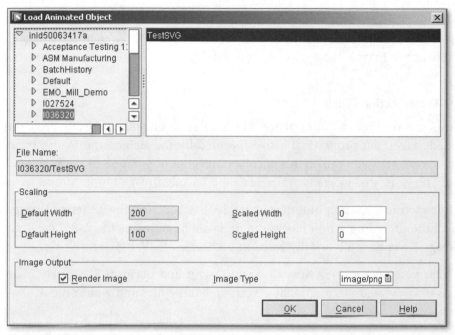

Figure 6.79 Object Configuration for the Animation Renderer Action Block

Image Combiner Action Block

The Image Combiner action block combines two images or imprints one image on top of another image. In Link Configuration, specify the background image in the EncodedImageInput1 parameter and the image that should be imprinted on the background image in the EncodedImageInput2 parameter. Specify the encoded images by linking the output properties of the SVG Renderer, Animation Renderer, or Image Loader action block. Specify the coordinates at which the second image will be superimposed on the background image by using the parameters X and Y. The generated image is available as the EncodedImage output property.

Image Creator Action Block

You can use the Image Creator action block to create basic images with a user-defined background color. Specify the background color in the BackgroundColor property and the size in the Height and Width input properties. You can perform this specification in either Object Configuration or Link Configuration. You should ideally use this generated image as a background over which you can use the Image Combiner action block to imprint other images. The generated image is available as the EncodedImage output property.

Image Scaler Action Block

You can use the Image Scaler action block to scale an image specified by the EncodedImageInput property at a size specified by the Height and Width input parameters. Again, you can do this in either Object Configuration or Link Configuration. The generated image is available as the EncodedImage output property.

The EncodedImage string output parameter that contains the generated image from all the preceding action blocks can be saved as an image file. You save it via the Image Saver action block discussed in Section 6.7.1 Web Action Blocks.

Now that you have learned how to create images and perform SQC analysis on process data, we want to discuss how you can handle files and web content.

6.7   Web, Email, and File Handling

You can manipulate files and web content from BLS Transactions. For example, you can read or save HTML, text, XML, and image files; you can transfer files using FTP and HTTP; you can create and change PDF documents; and you can send and read emails. The following sections discuss how to perform these functions using action blocks.

6.7.1   Web Action Blocks

The Web action blocks enable you to manipulate web content and load and save HTML, XML, text, and image data from a specific location. The following action blocks are part of this category:

▸ HTML Loader

▸ HTML Saver

- XML Loader

- XML Saver

- Text Loader

- Text Saver

- Image Loader

- Image Saver

- HTTP Post

- Scrape HTML Page

HTML, XML, Text, and Image Loader Action Blocks

The HTML, XML, Text, and Image Loader action blocks, and their corresponding Saver action blocks, are all similar to each other. The Loader action blocks essentially load data in the format they are supposed to handle from a URL or from a location in the file system. In the Object Configuration of the action block, specify the URL of the web resource (Figure 6.80). You can also specify a location in the SAP MII server content catalogue via the following URLs: *web://<ProjectName>/WEB/<FolderName>/<FileName>/* or *db://<ProjectName>/WEB/<FolderName>/<FileName>/*. These action blocks support basic HTTP authentication. If the web resource you are trying to load needs authentication, you can specify that authentication in the LoginName and LoginPassword parameters. You can also specify a value in seconds after which the request times out in the TimeOut parameter. You can configure the same parameters using Link Configuration. The loaded content is available in the StringContent output parameter for the HTML and Text Loader action blocks; in the XMLContent output parameter for the XML Loader action block; and in the EncodedImage output parameter for the Image Loader action block.

> **Note**
>
> If you use *web://<ProjectName>/WEB/<FolderName>/<FileName>/* syntax when you are creating a new object in the web folder visible in the Web view, then the object is created in the specified location and also gets published to the web folder in the SAP MII server. This is different from *db://*, which creates the object only in the SAP MII content catalog and does not publish it explicitly in the corresponding web folder.

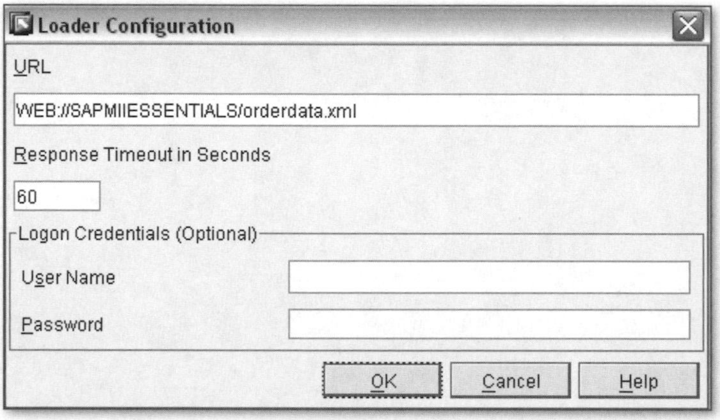

Figure 6.80 Object Configuration for the HTML Loader Action Block

HTML, XML, Text, and Image Saver Action Blocks

The Saver action blocks enable you to save any web content to the SAP MII content catalog in the form of HTML, XML, text, and images. In Object Configuration or Link Configuration, assign the Path parameter to the location where the file should be stored. Then link the parameters StringContent, XMLContent, or EncodedImage with the corresponding data sources for the HTML, Text, XML, and Image Saver action blocks, respectively. You should note here that these Saver action blocks can save data from any SAP MII action block that might return data in the format they accept and are not limited only to the data that the Loader action blocks return.

HTTP Post Action Block

The HTTP Post action block enables you to send a document to a URL using the HTTP POST method. In Object Configuration, specify the URL to post to, the user name and password for the authenticated user, and the encoding type (Figure 6.81). Using Link Configuration, assign the document that needs to be posted in the action block's PostData property and the content type that specifies the type of content that is being posted in the ContentType property. The default value of the ContentType is *application/x-www-form-urlencoded*, which signifies that the data has been posted from an HTML form. If you want the HTTP service to return data in the form of XML, you should check the ReturnAsXML parameter; if you want string output, select the ReturnAsString parameter (both in Link Configuration). Upon executing the POST request, this action block returns the HTTP status code and text of the request in the StatusCode and StatusText parameters. You can access these via the Outgoing Link Configuration or in any subsequent action block's Link Configuration.

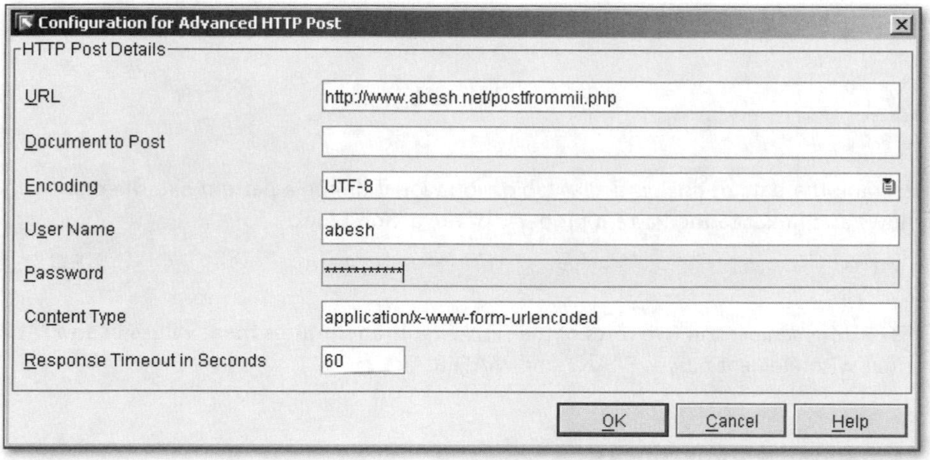

Figure 6.81 Object Configuration for the HTTP Post Action Block

Scrape HTML Page Action Block

The Scrape HTML Page action block enables you to glean data from an HTML page and create a XML document out of it. You do this by specifying a search pattern; then, anything that matches the pattern in the linked HTML document is returned in the standard SAP MII /Rowsets/Rowset/Row XML format. Specify the search pattern in the Pattern parameter and the HTML source in the Source parameter in Link Configuration. A common practice is to load the HTML document using the HTML Loader action block preceding it and link its StringContent property to the Source property of this action block. In the search pattern, enclose the element whose value needs to be scraped in curly braces: {}. If the element to be looked up spans multiple lines, use the special character {WS}, which indicates that all white spaces and line breaks should be ignored. The scraped content is returned in XML format in the Output property.

> **Example**
>
> The following is an example of how you can utilize the Scrape HTML page action block. A sample HTML block is as follows:
>
> ```
> <TABLE BORDER="1">
> <TR><TD align="center"><B>Plant</B></TD>
> <TD align="center"><B>Material Name</B></TD></TR>
> <TR><TD align="left">0001</TD>
> <TD align="right">Y-300</TD></TR>
> <TR><TD align="left">0001</TD>
> <TD align="right">Y-301</TD></TR>
> </TABLE>
> ```
>
> To scrape the data of this particular table, you would define a pattern like the one that follows and link it to the Pattern property of the action block:
>
> ```
> <TR>{WS}<TD align="left">{PLANT}</TD>{WS}<TD align="right">{MATERIAL}</
> TD>{WS}</TR>
> ```
>
> This pattern scrapes the two rows of the HTML table and returns these values in an XML format with element names PLANT and MATERIAL.

6.7.2 Email Action Blocks

The Email action blocks enable you to send and receive emails from BLS Transactions. You find two action blocks in this category:

- ▶ Send Mail
- ▶ Read Mail

Send Mail Action Block

The Send Mail action block enables you to send email messages using a mail server. The Configuration screen is split into two sections, Mail Server Details and E-mail Message Details, as shown in Figure 6.82. In the Mail Server Details screen, fill in the Mail Server parameter, which specifies the SMTP server or Exchange server; Port, which specifies the port on which the mail server runs; and Connection Timeout and Send Timeout, which store the timeout values in seconds for connect and send requests to the server. Specify the MailAccount and the MailAccountPassword properties with the authentication information for the mail server. Next, in the E-mail Message Details screen, specify details about the message you want to send, along with any attachments that it might have.

Figure 6.82 Object Configuration for the Send Mail Action Block

Specify the sender and receiver email addresses in the FromAddress and ToAddress properties, the subject of the email in Subject, and the actual email message in Message. The MessageMimeType property indicates the type of email to be sent. You would need to set it to Text/HTML to send HTML messages and Text/Plain to send plain text messages.

The AttachmentMimeType indicates the type of attachment that has been attached to the email. For example, it should be Text/XML for an XML document and Application/ZIP for a zipped archive. Both the MessageMimeType and AttachmentMimeType fields are available on the Object Configuration screen, as Content Type and Attachment Content Type fields, and in addition to the values that appear in the dropdown lists, you can also assign their user-defined mime types manually. You should configure the Attachment parameter to the path of the file on the server that you would need to attach to the email message. This property can be over-ridden by the AttachmentContent parameter, which, when configured, accepts the content of the attachment in a string parameter. The AttachmentContent is especially useful when you want to insert a chart or an image that has been generated by the SPC/SQC/Chart/SVG action blocks. In such a case, you can map the EncodedImage property to the AttachmentContent property. A suitable value for AttachmentMimeType should be chosen, depending on the output image format.

Read Mail Action Block

The Read Email action block, which enables you to read the content of mail from a mail server, has the same configuration options as the Send Email action block. Additionally, specify the Protocol parameter which denotes the protocol used to read messages from the mail server. POP and IMAP4 are the supported protocols, as shown in Figure 6.83. The Read Timeout parameter specifies the timeout value in seconds for a read request sent to the server, and the Attachment Folder parameter specifies the folder on the mail server from where the mail attachments should be picked. When checked, the Leave Messages on Server checkbox (Read Only parameter in Link Configuration) ensures that the messages on the server are not deleted when they are downloaded by the action block. The downloaded email messages are returned in the output parameter Messages in the standard SAP MII Rowsets/Rowset/Row XML format.

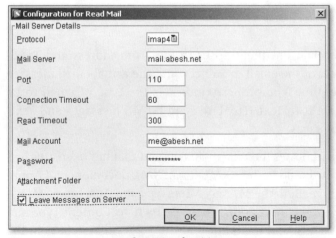

Figure 6.83 Object Configuration for the Read Mail Action Block

6.7.3 PDF Action Blocks

The PDF action blocks enable you to create a document in the Adobe PDF format from a BLS Transaction. This is helpful for generating reports in a common document format.

Note

The PDF action blocks require the iText third-party library. You can find instructions on how to download and configure the PDF action block in SAP Note 1109054.

The following action blocks are available under the PDF action block category:

- PDF Document
- PDF Table
- PDF Image
- PDF Bar Code
- PDF Horizontal Line
- PDF Text
- PDF Page

PDF Document Action Block

The PDF Document action block is the starting point for creating a PDF document. The Object Configuration of this action block is divided into various groups, as shown in Figure 6.84. You can specify the metadata specific to the document such as Title, Author, Subject, Keywords, and Creator in their respective fields. The Document Properties group of configuration options enables you to configure the Page Size, Width, Height, and Orientation (Portrait or Landscape) and enables visibility of page numbers on pages. The Margins group of properties enables you to configure a Top, Bottom, Left, and Right margin of the document. The Watermark Properties enable you to insert an image as a watermark in the background of the document. You can load the watermark image using an Image Loader action block and link to the WatermarkEncodedImage property using the Link Configuration. The Header and Footer groups of configuration properties enable you to specify text that should appear on the header and footer of every page, along with options to change font, color, size, background color, and alignment. You can save the resulting PDF document using the Image Saver action block, by linking the Output parameter of this action block to the EncodedImage property of the Image Saver action block. Also you can stream the PDF document in a web page by executing the BLS Transaction using the Runner service and linking the PDF document action block's Output property to a transaction output parameter of type string.

This can then be displayed or streamed dynamically at runtime using this URL:

http://<server>:<port>/XMII/Runner?Transaction=SAPMIIESSENTIALS/Examples/Samp lePDF&OutputParameter=PDFOutput&Content-type=application/pdf&isBinary=true

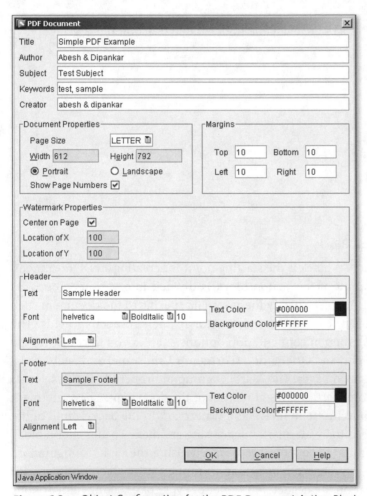

Figure 6.84 Object Configuration for the PDF Document Action Block

PDF Page Action Block

The PDF Page action block is the simplest of all the action blocks in this category and simply adds a page to the PDF document you specify in the PDF Document property.

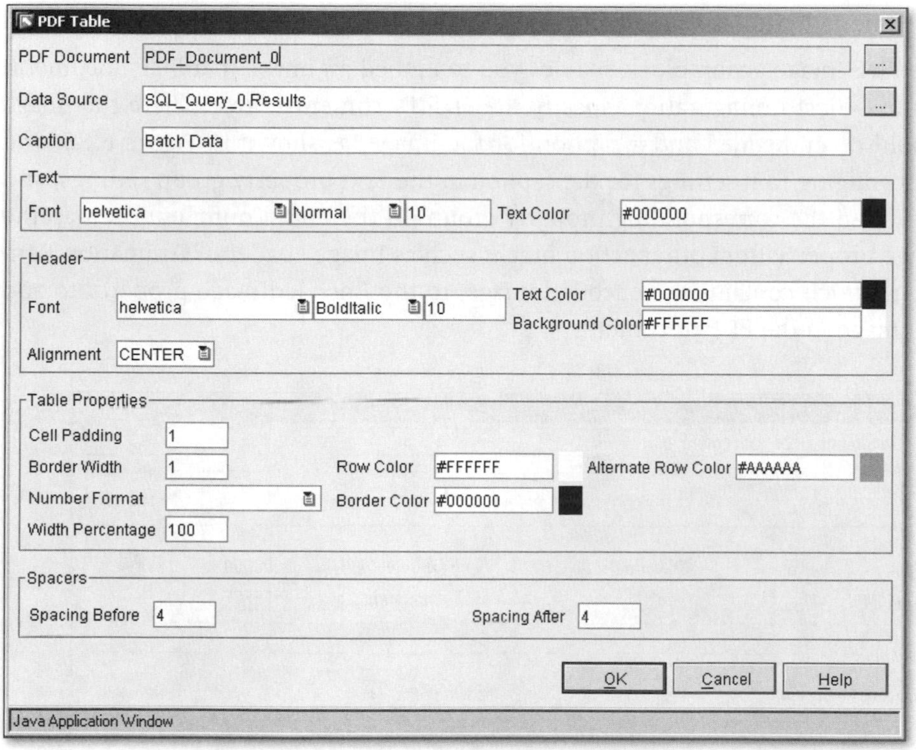

Figure 6.85 Object Configuration for the PDF Table Action Block

PDF Table Action Block

The PDF Table action block enables you to insert a table in a PDF document. The configuration screen of this action block is also divided into configuration property groups. In Object Configuration, specify the PDF Document this table should be part of and an Illuminator Data Source, which ideally is the results of an SAP MII query or a XML document created out of an RFC response. This should form the data of the table, as shown in Figure 6.85. Specify the caption for the table in the appropriate field. Configure the font, alignment, color, and background color for the caption in the Header property group parameters, and the font settings for the table text in the Text property group parameters. You can configure common table properties such as cell padding, cell border, row, and alternate row color in the Table Properties group of parameters. You can add Spacers before and after the table, and can configure them in the corresponding group.

PDF Image Action Block

The PDF Image action block enables you to embed an image in a PDF document. In the Object Configuration, specify the PDF Document source where the image should be embedded and a caption for the image, as shown in Figure 6.86. You can configure font settings for the caption in the Text property group settings, and spacers in the corresponding property group. In the Link Configuration map the image property from other action blocks such as Image Loader or Animation Renderer, which contains the encoded image, to the EncodedImage property to add the image in the PDF document.

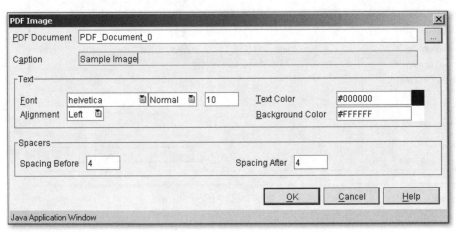

Figure 6.86   Object Configuration for the PDF Image Action Block

PDF Barcode Action Block

The PDF Barcode action block enables you to insert a barcode in a PDF document. Bar codes are a method of representing data as horizontal bars of varying width that can be optically read by certain machines. In the Object Configuration of the action block, select the PDF Document in which the barcode should be inserted and the Bar Code Text that needs to be encoded as a barcode (Figure 6.87). Configure the barcode generation options such as the barcode representation type, alignment, and size via the properties in the Bar Code Properties group. Configure spacers options in their corresponding property group.

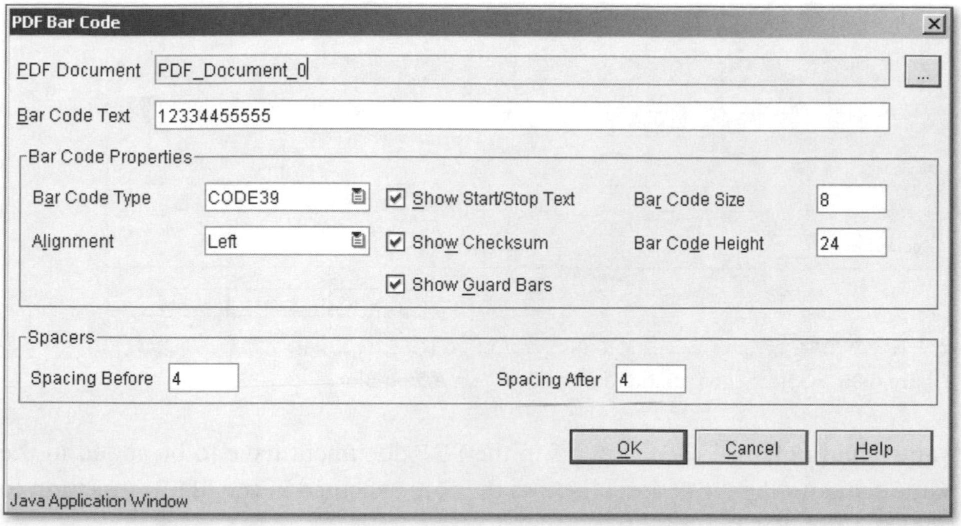

Figure 6.87 Object Configuration for the PDF Barcode Action Block

PDF Horizontal Line Action Block

The PDF Horizontal Line action block is one of the simplest of the PDF actions; all it does is insert a horizontal line in the PDF Document specified in the Object Configuration. Specify the width and color of this line in the Line Properties group.

PDF Text Action Block

You should use the PDF Text action block when you want to insert text or document content specified by the Text parameter into a PDF document specified by the PDF Document parameter. This is done in the Object Configuration of the action block. You can configure the font properties and alignment of the text in the Text group of properties and spacer options in its corresponding group, as shown in Figure 6.88.

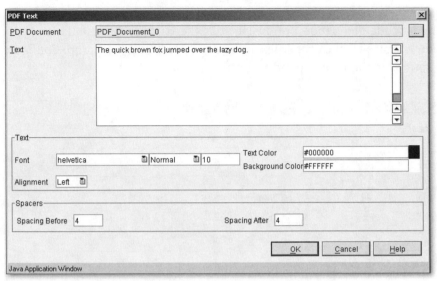

Figure 6.88 Object Configuration for the PDF Text Action Block

You should note that the elements in the PDF document have to be added in the same sequence by the action blocks as they are executed in the BLS Transaction to generate the PDF document.

6.7.4   File I/O Action Blocks

The File I/O category of action blocks enables you to list, create, change, delete, and perform other maintenance actions on local files and remote files through FTP. The following action blocks fall under this category:

- ▶ Write File
- ▶ Get File List
- ▶ Delete File
- ▶ Create Directory
- ▶ Flat File Parser
- ▶ FTP Input
- ▶ FTP Output
- ▶ FTP Get File List
- ▶ FTP Delete File

- ▸ FTP Create Directory
- ▸ Create Zip Archive

Write File Action Block

The Write File action block enables you either to create a new file or append content to an existing file. In Object Configuration, specify the appropriate file name and path. Then choose either CREATE or APPEND, as shown in Figure 6.89. You should link the Text to be written to the file in its Link Configuration.

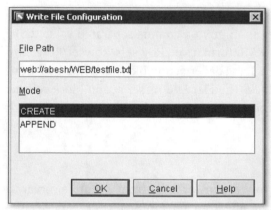

Figure 6.89 Object Configuration for the Write File Action Block

---

Note

We recommend you specify the file path using the *web://<projectname>/WEB/ <foldername>/<filename>* syntax so that the generated file is stored as content in the server and can be accessed centrally. You can also specify the fully qualified path of a file on the server, though doing so is uncommon other than for development debugging purposes.

Get File List Action Block

The Get File List action block enables you to retrieve a list of files under a particular folder. Specify the location of the folder, the content you want to list, and a filter Mask, which might contain wildcard characters, to filter the files you want to list. The Output from this action block is an XML document in the /Rowsets/ Rowset/Row format, and returns the Name, Date, LastWriteDate, Size, ReadOnly, and FullPath details of each file.

Delete File Action Block

The Delete File action block simply takes in the fully qualified path to a file in the file-system or content catalog that you want to delete and then deletes it.

Create Directory Action Block

The Create Directory action block is also simple; it takes in the fully qualified path to a folder in the file-system or content catalog you want to create and then creates it.

Flat File Parser Action Block

The Flat File Parser action block takes as an input a comma-separated value (CSV) file and converts it to the SAP MII XML format of /Rowsets/Rowset/Row. You should ideally load the CSV file using a Text Loader action block and link its output to the Text property of this action block. The Flat File Parser action block returns the data from the CSV file in XML format through which you can loop through and parse as required.

FTP Input Action Block

The FTP Input action block enables you to transfer a file from a remote server to the SAP MII content catalog using the File Transfer Protocol (FTP). Specify the details pertaining to the remote FTP server, such as the FTP Server address, the FTP Port, and authentication information, in the Object or Link Configuration of the action block (Figure 6.90). Also specify the Remote Folder path where the file resides, its name as Remote File, the fully qualified path of the local folder, and the Local File name with which it should be stored.

Figure 6.90 Object Configuration for the FTP Input Action Block

FTP Output Action Block

The FTP Output action block does the exact opposite of the FTP Input action block; it copies a local file to a remote server using FTP. The configuration for this action block is exactly the same as the FTP Input action block.

FTP Get File List Action Block

The FTP Get File List action works the same way as the Get File List action block explained earlier in this section, with the only difference being that it retrieves the file list of a remote folder using FTP. In addition to the FTP server and the user authentication configuration settings, it requires the name of the Remote Folder and a Mask by which the file list will be filtered.

FTP Delete File Action Block

The FTP Delete File action block deletes a file in a specified directory on a remote server using the FTP protocol. You need to specify the Remote Folder and the Remote File to be deleted, along with the FTP server and authentication settings.

FTP Create Directory Action Block

The FTP Create Directory action block creates a folder in a specified directory on a remote server using the FTP protocol. You need to specify the Remote Parent Folder and the New Directory parameters, along with the FTP server and authentication settings.

Create Zip Archive Action Block

The Create Zip Archive action block creates a compressed zipped archive of single or multiple files that you can specify as a configuration parameter for the Source File Name field. You can specify the name of the zipped output file using the Zip File Name configuration field. Although Object Configuration enables you to specify a single file to be zipped, you can zip multiple files together by using a Repeater action block. For example, the output from a Get File List action block can be linked to a Repeater, output of which can in turn be linked to the Source-FileName property of the Create Zip Archive action block.

6.8   Executing BLS Transactions

You can execute a BLS Transaction from a web page applet via an Xacute query, as we mentioned before. In addition, you can execute it as SOAP or simple HTTP Web service from external systems or Web service clients or from web pages using AJAX calls. Each BLS Transaction, when saved, automatically becomes a Web service, which has a WSDL document URL. The WSDL URL for a BLS Transaction is as follows:

http://<server>:<port>/XMII/WSDLGen/<project>/<folder>/<BLSTransactionName>

However, you face certain limitations in using WSDLGen (SAP MII 12.0 SP4) when you are generating the WSDL for a BLS Transaction, which you should be aware of. If the BLS Transaction has input parameters of type XML, then the WSDLGen generates the WSDL referring to the input parameter data types as XML only (Figure 6.91), which cannot be interpreted by any external standard Web service clients because no XML data type called Xml exists. Therefore, we recommend that you should not use the input parameters of type XML when you want to execute the BLS Transaction as a Web service. If an XML document needs to be passed as the input parameter, one workaround is to pass it as a string data type and then use the String to XML Parser action block to convert it into a XML inside the BLS Transaction.

For example, if the Input structure is:

```
<Input>
    <Plant/>
    <WorkCenter/>
</Input>
```

It should be encoded as follows:

```
&lt;Input&gt; &lt;Plant/&gt; &lt;WorkCenter/&gt; &lt;/Input&gt;
```

Alternatively, you can also use the xmldecode(STRING) Workbench function in the Link Editor to parse it back to XML.

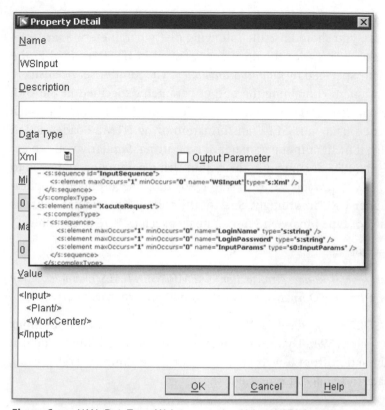

Figure 6.91 XML DataType Misinterpretation Using WSDLGen

Also if you have multiple output parameters for the BLS Transaction of type XML, then those are interpreted as string data type in the WSDL and the XML structures are not specified in WSDL, though you might have provided it using the default value while defining them.

You can also execute a BLS Transaction as an HTTP call via the following URL:

http://<server>:<port>/XMII/Runner?Transaction=<folder>/<Transactionname>&<Inpu ParamName1>=<value1>&<InpuParamName n>=<value n>&OutputParameter=<outpu tParamName>&Content-Type=<content-type>&isBinary=<true|false>XacuteLoginName= <username>&XacuteLoginPassword=<password>

Basic authentication and SSO by SAP logon ticket are also supported authentication modes for which you do not have to pass the XacuteLoginName and Xacute-LoginPassword parameters.

If you want to send a document in one of the input parameters of the BLS Transaction using HTTP Post, you should use the following query parameter: *InputParameter=<inputparamname>*. This adds the document present in HTTP payload in the input parameter value specified by *<inputparamname>*. The Runner service usually returns an XML document containing the output parameter specified in the URL with its value. You can also get HTML content in the output by generating the same in the BLS Transaction using an XSLT Transformation or by HTML Loader action blocks and returning it in an output parameter of type string. Similarly you can get an encoded image or a PDF document in the output string parameter. You need to specify the Content Type property as text/xml, text/html, image/png, or application/pdf in the runner URL accordingly. Specify the isBinary parameter value as true if the content is of type binary and not an image; such as PDF document.

An example URL would be:

http://<server>:<port>/XMII/Runner?Transaction=SAPMIIESSENTIALS/Examples/SamplePDF&OutputParameter=PDFOutput&Content-type=application/pdf&isBinary=true

You can use the WSDLGen to execute a BLS Transaction from external applications or user interfaces such as Web Dynpro or Visual Composer. In addition, you can execute a BLS Transaction from a web page by calling the Runner service using AJAX to stream data and images from SAP MII.

6.9   Summary

In this chapter, you have learned about Business Logic Services and how to create BLS Transactions in SAP MII using various predefined action blocks. This enables you to model reusable business logic for system integration, data parsing, and analysis, thereby delivering intelligence to composite applications.

In the next chapter, you will learn how to work with animated objects to create dynamic visualizations and how to use them in monitoring dashboards.

This chapter explains how to configure and use animated objects for creating monitoring dashboards with dynamic visualization.

7 Animated Objects: Making Dynamic Visualizations

After you have integrated the plant and enterprise systems and developed the custom logic to retrieve, aggregate, and update data to various systems you might need monitoring dashboards where you can have a real-time visualization of the manufacturing process and get visual warnings on process exceptions. In this chapter, you learn how to create and use animated objects to provide dynamic visualizations for real-time monitoring in manufacturing dashboards.

SAP MII provides various visualization options in the form of visualization applets such as iGrid, iCharts, and iSPCCharts. With the numerous options available in the display templates, these applets enable you to visualize the data the way you want it. The various options available for these display templates are explained in detail in Chapter 5 Display Templates: Let Your Data Speak. However, at times you might want a more varied and unique user interface, mostly for real-time monitoring or visual alerting, than what can be achieved by using the standard display templates. For example you might want to monitor the current temperature in a tank from the dashboard that can be provided by a Thermometer animated object or the status of a production line using the SVG Alerter or SVG Light. In the following sections, we discuss the options available for configuring dynamic graphics to achieve the same results.

7.1 Introduction

SAP MII supports dynamic graphics in the form of Scalable Vector Graphics (SVG), which is an open standard based on XML and developed by the World Wide Web Consortium (W3C). This standard enables creating dynamic vector graphics using standard XML allowing the display of real-time process information (such as temperature, pressure, tank level, machine status, and Key Performance Indicators (KPI) trends) in the monitoring dashboards. Through the SVG Renderer and the Animation Renderer action blocks (described in detail in Section 6.6.3 Dynamic Graphics Action Blocks), this capability is closely integrated with SAP MII Business Logic Transactions. The Animation Renderer takes an animated object and generates an output in the form of an image, whereas the SVG Renderer takes in an XML SVG document and then generates an image as output. You can then save these images using the ImageSaver action block or pass the encoded image content in the output parameter of the transaction property, enabling them to be used in web pages and reports.

Figure 7.1 shows how a sample SVG graphic looks before it has been configured. You can define various properties of the animated object that can be manipulated externally at runtime by a BLS Transaction and can be used to set the visual parameters of the animated object such as the temperature gauge of a thermometer, needle position of a gauge dial, color of the status indicator icon, and so on. Based on the process parameters, a BLS Transaction can generate these animated graphics accordingly, which can be refreshed in the web pages periodically to provide an animated effect.

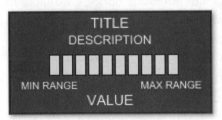

Figure 7.1 Horizontal LED Meter Animated Object

7.2   Configuring an Animated Object using the SAP MII Workbench

To generate an animated image using the Animation Renderer action in a BLS Transaction you first need to create and configure an animated object. You can then use that animated object to generate an animated image using the BLS Transaction. You can create an animated object using the FILE • NEW • ANIMATED OBJECT menu option in the SAP MII Workbench. After an animated object has been created, the various options for configuring it become available in the bottom left pane of the screen.

The following configuration categories are available for animated objects:

▶ Select SVG Document

▶ Properties

▶ Calculated Properties

▶ View SVG Document

▶ Links

▶ Preview

▶ Description

In the following sections, you learn about the different configuration categories of the animated object, and how to configure them to create an animated graphic.

7.2.1   Select SVG Document

Clicking the Select SVG Document link brings up a selection dialog that enables you to browse and select an SVG document from available SAP MII Workbench projects, as shown in Figure 7.2.

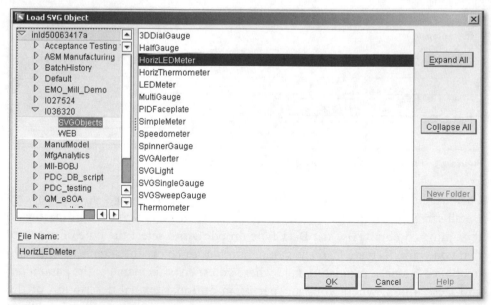

Figure 7.2   SVG Object Selection Configuration

7.2.2 Properties

You can use the Properties configuration screen to define an animated object's public properties that can be accessed and manipulated from a BLS Transaction (Figure 7.3). The screen looks very similar to the Transaction Properties or Local Properties screen for a BLS Transaction (described in Section 6.1 Introduction). You can link these properties to the different visual parameters of the animated object, such as needle position, thermometer gauge, color, and so on, to manipulate them dynamically.

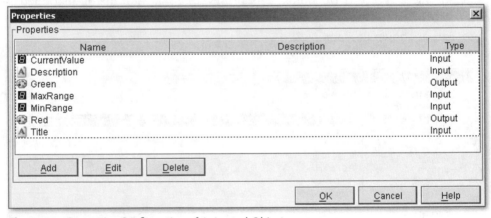

Figure 7.3 Properties Configuration of Animated Object

Clicking the Add or Edit button after selecting a property brings up the Property Detail screen, seen in Figure 7.4, where you can add three types of properties to the animated object. Use the Data Type dropdown to select the type of property that you want to create, namely, string, number, or color. The screen also has two textboxes: Name, a mandatory field where you specify the name of the parameter, and Description, where you can specify an optional textual description of the property. In case you want to create a constant property whose value should not be changed externally, you can check the Locked checkbox. This checkbox renders the particular variable nonmodifiable, designating it as an Output parameter.

The Value Field changes with the selection of the Data Type and enables you to set a default value for the property. This field is a text area for a string data type, a numerical field for a number data type, and a color field for a color data type. For color data types, you can specify a color value in hexadecimal and verify the color preview in the preview field right next to it.

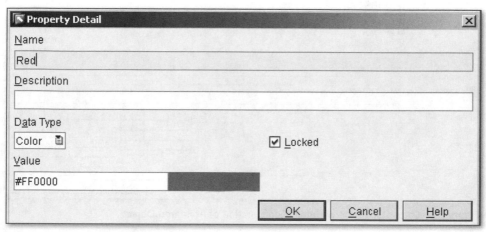

Figure 7.4 Property Detail Configurations of Animated Object

7.2.3 Calculated Properties

Calculated properties are similar to the local properties of an object. They are not accessible outside the animated object and are derived after performing arithmetic and logical operations on object properties and other calculated properties. The Calculated Properties overview screen is the same as that for Properties, described previously.

Clicking the Add or Edit button after selecting a property brings up the Calculated Property Detail screen, seen in Figure 7.5, where you can add or modify calculated properties. The Name, Description, and Data Type fields on this screen are the same as those seen in the Properties configuration. You also find a Defined Properties list, which displays all object properties defined in the Properties configuration screen (described in the previous section).

The Expression Editor area features an Expressions text area where you can specify logical and mathematical expressions for a given calculated property. This is done by using the mathematical and logical operator buttons and functions supported by SAP MII, available in the Functions dropdown box on this screen.

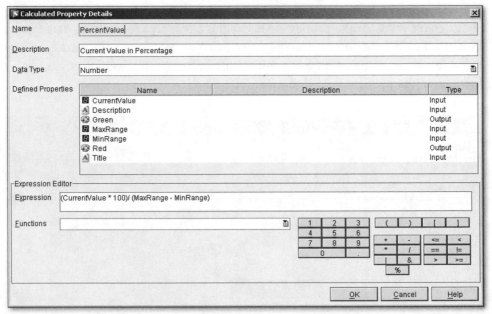

Figure 7.5 Calculated Property Details Configuration of Animated Object

7.2.4 View SVG Document

You can use the View SVG Document screen to view the source of the SVG document that has been loaded. It is the simplest screen of all. It is a read-only screen; you cannot modify the properties of the document here.

7.2.5 Links

You can use the Links configuration screen to assign public properties, calculated properties, and mathematical and logical expressions to the various configurable elements of the SVG document. This enables you to modify the display and other attributes of the SVG documents dynamically at runtime in the BLS Transaction where they are being used. For example, you can configure the needle position of the gauge dial or the thermometer reading of the animated object by defining the value or specifying a logical expression. The Links configuration screen, seen in Figure 7.6, has two display boxes: Properties at the left, which lists all the public and calculated properties of the animated object, and SVG Elements at the right, which lists all the SVG elements to which you can assign a value. If it's a one-to-one assignment between the animated object properties and the SVG elements, you can create the mapping by dragging and dropping the source property on the Properties list to the target property in the SVG Elements list. To map an expression to an SVG element, use the buttons below for logical and mathematical elements and the Functions dropdown to build the expression in the Expression text area. Select the element on the right to which this expression needs to be mapped from the SVG Elements list and click on the Assign Link button to assign the link. The Remove Link button deletes the link that has been assigned to the selected SVG element; and the Get Value from SVG button retrieves the value of the element that is originally present in the SVG document. This value can serve as a reference value in case you are unsure as to what type of value needs to be mapped to which element.

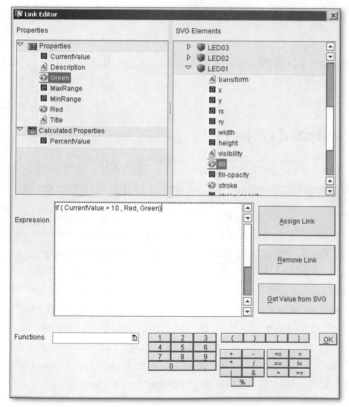

Figure 7.6 Link Configuration of Animated Object

7.2.6   Preview

The Preview screen, seen in Figure 7.7, is also simple. It provides a preview of the animated object when the various properties are defined and mapped.

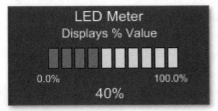

Figure 7.7   Preview of an Animated Object

7.2.7   Description

You can use the Description configuration screen to optionally add a textual description to the animated object.

7.3   Displaying Animated Objects

Now we can show you how to use dynamic graphics in lieu of the standard SAP MII visualization applets. Generally, you can use dynamic graphics in two distinct ways:

▸ In the simplest case, you can create a BLS Transaction in which the output of an AnimatedObject Renderer action block, which has been configured to use the required animated object, is passed on to the input of an Image Saver action block, which saves the rendered image to a location on the server. To reflect dynamic data, you would need to execute the BLS Transaction periodically using the SAP MII scheduler, so that the existing image is overwritten by an image representing the new data values. The image can now either be included in a SAP MII Report or be attached to emails that have been programmatically generated by BLS Transactions as reports to the Production Supervisor, for example, alert mails.

▸ An advanced scenario involves streaming the animated graphics as an image via the SAP MII Runner service and embedding it on a web page. In this case the SAP MII Runner service (explained in Chapter 6 Business Logic Transactions:

Intelligence in Action) executes a BLS Transaction that provides the encoded image for the animated object in its output property, which is displayed in a web page and periodically refreshed. An example, with sample code as to how you can achieve this scenario, is provided in Chapter 8 Web Scripting and Reports: Weaving It All Together.

As mentioned earlier in this chapter, animated objects would be an ideal candidate for use in real-time monitoring dashboards. For example, the Production Supervisor in a plant wants to compare the current production throughput on different machines on the shop floor with the shift target. He also needs to keep an eye on key production KPIs like Lost Time incidents and so on. Figure 7.8 displays a Production Comparison Dashboard that has been created solely using animated objects. The relevant data for the KPIs and production rate data are retrieved and parsed in BLS Transactions. Based on that data the animated objects are generated as images, which are then refreshed periodically in the web page.

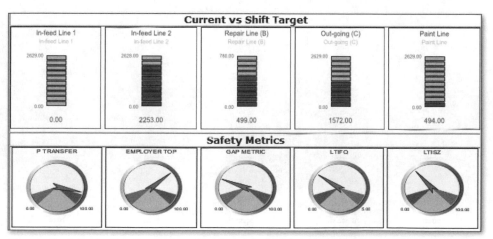

Figure 7.8 A Production Comparison Dashboard Built with Animated Objects

You now know how to create and configure animated graphics to spruce up the data visualization capabilities of your SAP MII application. In the next chapter we will discuss how you can use reports and web scripting to form a coherent web application by weaving together query and display templates, animated objects, and Business Logic Transactions.

This chapter explains how to use HTML and JavaScript to integrate templates and transactions in web pages and how to integrate these web pages in both the SAP MII portal and the SAP Enterprise Portal.

8   Web Scripting and Reports: Weaving It All Together

After you have integrated the plant and enterprise systems to retrieve and update relevant data, addressed the solution gaps by developing custom logic, and configured the visualization templates to display transactional data, reports, or charts, you need to finally put them together in a user interface through which the end users can interact with them as an end-to-end application.

The user interfaces of SAP MII composite applications are typically web pages accessed through the portal as transactional and analysis dashboards for manufacturing plant-floor operations. In this chapter, we explore the basics of web scripting and reports in SAP MII, explaining how you can use the display and query templates on a web page for presenting content to the end users of the SAP MII composite applications. We also focus on some special use case scenarios and solutions. You also learn how this content can be accessed by the plant personnel through the SAP MII portal and the SAP Enterprise Portal.

8.1   Web Scripting

As explained in the previous chapters, data retrieval and update transactions and visualization in SAP MII are achieved by query and display templates, respectively. You can integrate these templates via web-based user interfaces such as Java applets, which are small applications that run on a Java-enabled Web browser. You can integrate these applets to the HTML pages to present them to the end users via the SAP Enterprise Portal or SAP MII portal.

You can also customize output for web browsers that do not support Java. You accomplish this by having charts rendered at the server side and displayed as images in browsers. Also, you can generate HTML tables, explained later in this chapter, as an alternative to iGrid applets for non-Java enabled web browsers.

SAP MII applets act mainly as containers, with a display object and a query object as their primary components. Four simple lines of HTML can embed an applet into a web page, as shown in the following example.

Example

```
<APPLET NAME="BatchTrendChart" CODEBASE="/XMII/Classes" CODE="iChart"
ARCHIVE="illum8.zip" WIDTH="400" HEIGHT="200" MAYSCRIPT>
<PARAM NAME="QueryTemplate" VALUE="SAPMIIESSENTIALS/Examples/Batch/
BatchTrendQuery">
<PARAM NAME="DisplayTemplate" VALUE="SAPMIIESSENTIALS/Examples/Batch/
BatchTrendChart">
</APPLET>
```

Take a look at this code to see exactly what it tries to achieve. The code begins with the <APPLET> tag. The NAME attribute assigns a unique name to the applet, which you use to reference the applet when you are scripting using JavaScript. The CODEBASE attribute points to the path from where the code for the applet should be loaded. The ARCHIVE attribute specifies the file from where the code of the applet should be loaded. The CODE attribute specifies the object type of the display template. (SAP MII has the codes of all applets in a zipped archive, *illum8.zip*, which greatly reduces the file size — and therefore the loading time — of the SAP MII applets.) The HEIGHT and WIDTH attributes specify the height and width of the embedded applet, and the MAYSCRIPT attribute enables scripting with the applet. You need to specify the required query and display objects as the QueryTemplate and the DisplayTemplate parameters by providing the fully qualified path to their respective templates as *<projectname>/<foldername>/<templatename>*.

The applet displayed on the web page reflects the configuration of the display template. However, you can modify the default or configured parameters of the referenced templates by specifying them as parameters to the applet. This is accomplished via the PARAM tag, as shown in the following example.

> **Example**
>
> ```
> <APPLET NAME="BatchTrendChart" CODEBASE="/XMII/Classes" CODE="iChart"
> ARCHIVE="illum8.zip" WIDTH="400" HEIGHT="200" MAYSCRIPT>
> <PARAM NAME="QueryTemplate" VALUE="SAPMIIESSENTIALS/Examples/Batch/
> BatchTrendQuery">
> <PARAM NAME="DisplayTemplate" VALUE="SAPMIIESSENTIALS/Examples/Batch/
> BatchTrendChart">
> <PARAM NAME="ShowTagDescription" VALUE="true">
> </APPLET>
> ```

As in any object-oriented, architecture-based language, the query and display objects have their own events, properties, and methods. In some cases, the properties can also be objects in their own rights and have their own events, properties, and methods.

You can use these applets to display data reports as iGrids, charts as iCharts or iSP-CCharts, and drop-downs or tree views as iBrowser objects. You can also update data in backend systems by executing SQL Command queries or BLS Transactions as Xacute queries via iCommand.

8.1.1 Common Applet Methods

SAP MII applet methods enable users to use JavaScript to perform particular actions on applet objects. These actions include, but are not limited to the following: changing their query or display templates, setting input parameter values to the query or reading a selected cell value from an iGrid or a selected data point in a chart, and changing display properties. We should mention here that all access to SAP MII applets, including access to their properties, is implemented through getter and setter methods, which you can use to read or write a property value, respectively. The most important and often used methods are those that return a reference to the display and query objects. The getQueryObject() method returns a reference to the underlying query object of the applet; the getGridObject(), getTickerObject(), and getBrowserObject() methods return references to the iGrid, iTicker, and iBrowser objects, respectively; and the getChartObject() returns a reference to the iChart and iSPCChart object for iChart and iSPCChart display templates, respectively. By getting a reference to the query or display object, you can invoke methods on these objects to either set their properties or perform some functionality.

Some of the commonly used applet methods are listed in Table 8.1.

Method	Description
getDisplayTemplate()	Returns the name of the display template used, along with its fully qualified path.
getQueryTemplate()	Returns the name of the query template used, along with its fully qualified path.
getPropertyValue(PROPERTYNAME)	Returns the value of a session property passed as PROPERTYNAME. Session properties are used for passing data between different SAP MII pages.
refresh()	Refreshes the display object by reloading the data after executing the query in the referenced query template.
setDisplayTemplate(TEMPLATENAME)	Sets the display template of the applet with the passed TEMPLATENAME value. The TEMPLATENAME property should contain the name of the display template name with its fully qualified path.
setQueryTemplate(TEMPLATENAME)	Sets the query template of the applet with the passed TEMPLATENAME value. The TEMPLATENAME property should contain the name of the query template name with its fully qualified path.
setPropertyValue(PROPERTYNAME, VALUE)	Sets the value of a session property with the name PROPERTYNAME with the value specified in VALUE.

Table 8.1 Common Applet Methods

The iCommand applet, which is an invisible applet used to execute update queries (SQL Command queries, Tag queries in CurrentWrite mode, and Business Logic Services (BLS) as Xacute queries) has several methods worth mentioning, listed in Table 8.2. These methods are specific to this applet, and provide you with more flexibility to handle data.

Method	Description
executeCommand()	Executes the query template with the parameters set.
getColumnCount()	Returns the count of the number of columns returned by the query.
getColumnName(COLUMN)	Returns the name of the column as specified by the COLUMN parameter, which is the index for which the column name should be returned.
getLastError()	Returns the error message of the last error, if any. The executeCommand() method returns a Boolean value of "true" if the execution succeeds and a value of "false" if it does not. This value can be checked, and in case the execution fails, the error message returned can be printed.
getRowCount()	Returns the count of the rows returned by the query.
getValue(COLNUM, ROWNUM)	Gets the data returned by the query in the particular column and row index specified by COLNUM and ROWNUM parameters.
getValueByName(COLNAME, ROWNUM)	Gets the data returned by the query in the particular column name and row index specified by COLNAME and ROWNUM parameters.

Table 8.2 iCommand Applet Methods

Other than the object methods listed in Table 8.1 and Table 8.2, you have some utility methods available to all display and query objects that help perform utility functions. Some of them are dateFromXMLFormat(XMLDATE, DATEFORMAT), which converts an XML format date to the date format specified by the DATE-FORMAT variable; xmlEncode(STRING), which converts XML special characters, for e.g., >, < to their corresponding string equivalent such as > and < whereas xmlDecode(STRING), does just the opposite.

> **Note**
>
> The updateChart(RELOADDATAFLAG) and updateGrid(RELOADDATAFLAG) methods are two important methods relevant to iCharts, iSPCCharts, and iGrids. These methods update their respective display objects with new data by executing the underlying query, depending on the value of the RELOADDATA flag.

If set, this updates the chart and reloads the data of the chart after executing the query. For a time-based query, updateChart()/updateGrid() uses the dates mentioned in the StartDate and EndDate parameters in the query templates. This is different from refresh(), which uses the current date and calculates the start and end dates by adjusting the set Duration and Duration Units values.

8.1.2 Common Applet Properties

You can use the SAP MII applet properties to configure both the visual and functional behavior of the applets. SAP MII does not allow direct access to the properties of these applets, but instead follows design patterns to allow access through getter and setter methods. Therefore, you can get the value of a property PROPERTYNAME by just invoking the getPROPERTYNAME() method. Similarly, it's possible to set the value of the required property by the setPROPERTYNAME(value) method of the object whose properties need to be set. You should note here that these properties are relevant to the query and display objects returned by the getQueryObject() and getDisplayObject() methods, respectively.

Numerous methods are available for each display object, and, though some properties are common to all, each display object type also has specific properties. (The details of the methods for each of these display object types can be found in the SAP MII help documentation.) The most important of these methods are getParam(INDEX) and setParam(INDEX, VALUE), which are relevant for the query object and are used to get and set query template parameter values that are denoted by Param.1 to Param.32 in the query templates. The INDEX denotes the index of the parameter and can take values from 1 to 32; VALUE denotes the value that needs to be passed on to the underlying query parameter.

8.1.3 Common Applet Events

Applet events are triggered when something specific to the applet, as specified by the event, occurs. This can be the act of clicking on a single row of the iGrid, or the completion of an applet loading. Table 8.3 lists common applet events and details about when they are triggered.

Event	Trigger
CreationEvent	Triggered when the applet finishes loading on the web page.
FirstUpdateEvent	Triggered when the applet uses the query templates to query data from the data source and then loads it for the first time after its creation.
SelectionEvent	Triggered when an item is selected on the applet, for example, a row on the iGrid.
UpdateEvent	Similar to the FirstUpdateEvent, but triggered every time the data is updated by querying the data source via the query template.
DoubleClickEvent	Triggered when an item on the applet is double-clicked.

Table 8.3 Common Applet Events

Again, each applet has more events specific to their implementation; information on these events is available in the SAP MII help documentation. All applet events accept a string data type specifying the name of the JavaScript function to be invoked on that event.

The applet events are a handy way of responding to user interaction and other triggers that might not be possible with regular JavaScript events. Take into consideration the following two cases where the applet events can be put to good use.

The first use case, for example, requires the updating of one or more charts to display data for a particular material batch number that has been passed on as a variable from the previous page. This should be done when the page loads. To achieve this, use the CreationEvent of the chart applet to execute a JavaScript function to set the batch number from the session variable and update the chart. We recommend not using the onLoad event of HTML tag BODY, which is triggered when the Web page finishes loading, because though the page might have finished loading, the applet might not have, and any reference to it via JavaScript returns a null value. The only way to avoid this is to use the CreationEvent of the respective applets. The example that follows explains this scenario.

Example

```
<APPLET Name="BatchTrendChart" CODEBASE="/XMII/Classes" CODE="iChart"
ARCHIVE="illum8.zip" WIDTH="400" HEIGHT="200" MAYSCRIPT>
<PARAM NAME="QueryTemplate" VALUE="/SAPMIIESSENTIALS/Examples/Batch/
PlasticBottleTrendQT">
<PARAM NAME="DisplayTemplate" VALUE="/SAPMIIESSENTIALS/Examples/Batch/
PlasticBottleTrendDT">
<PARAM NAME="CreationEvent" VALUE="BatchTrendChartCreated">

</APPLET>
<SCRIPT LANGUAGE="JavaScript">
function BatchTrendChartCreated () {
//Get the value of Batch Number passed from the referring page
var BatchNo = document.BatchTrendChart.getPropertyValue("Batch");

//Set the BatchNo as a parameter to the Applet's Query Template
document.BatchTrendChart.getQueryObject().setParam(1,BatchNo);

//Update the chart with the retrieved data
document.BatchTrendChart.updateChart(true);
}
</SCRIPT>
```

In this example, the `CreationEvent` applet event is passed as a parameter to the applet, with the parameter value specifying the name of the JavaScript function that should be called when that event triggers. The code required to update the chart is then coded into the function.

A second use case is a combination of an iGrid and iChart/iSPCChart, where the grid displays a list of items and the chart displays a trend for the item that has been selected. This can be achieved by an interaction in which the user selects the row on the grid and then clicks on a button to display the chart of the corresponding selected item. However, from a usability standpoint, the button click is unnecessary and the whole process can be brought down from a two-step process (selecting a row and clicking a button) to a single step (selecting a row). This is easy to achieve, but can only be done by utilizing the SelectionEvent event of the iGrid. The example that follows explains this scenario.

Example

```
<APPLET Name="BatchListGrid" CODEBASE="/XMII/Classes" CODE="iGrid"
ARCHIVE="illum8.zip" WIDTH="400" HEIGHT="200" MAYSCRIPT>
<PARAM NAME="QueryTemplate" VALUE="/SAPMIIESSENTIALS/Examples/Batch/
PlasticBottleBatchQT">
<PARAM NAME="DisplayTemplate" VALUE="/SAPMIIESSENTIALS/Examples/Batch/
PlasticBottleBatchDT">
<PARAM NAME="SelectionEvent" VALUE="UpdateBatchTrendChart">
</APPLET>

<SCRIPT LANGUAGE="JavaScript">
function UpdateBatchTrendChart() {

//Get the value of Batch Number from the selected row in the iGrid
var BatchNo = document.BatchListGrid.getGridObject().getSelectedCell-
Value(1);

//Set the BatchNo as a parameter to the Applet's Query Template
document.BatchTrendChart.getQueryObject().setParam(1,BatchNo);

//Update the chart with the retrieved data
document.BatchTrendChart.updateChart(true);
}
</SCRIPT>
```

In this case, use of the `SelectionEvent` enables seamless event handling of the iGrid click event without the use of an intermediate button.

Note

Using the HTML code mentioned in the beginning of Section 8.1, you can integrate applets in an .html or .irpt page created using the SAP MII Workbench menu NEW • FILE, or via an external Web page development editor such as Microsoft FrontPage™ or Adobe Dreamweaver™.

In this section, you have learned how to create a coherent web application by weaving together different SAP MII objects as Java applets using JavaScript. In the next section, you learn some basic information about SAP MII reports, including how they are different from normal HTML pages and when you should use them.

8.2   SAP MII Reports

The reporting subsystem of SAP MII enables the generation of data reports from the data queries configured as query templates by generating HTML dynamically and eliminating the need of complex scripting and Java applets.

You should note that the reporting subsystem is very basic and does not replace the use of applets in SAP MII. We do not recommend using applets for SAP MII reports because the sole aim of the reporting subsystem is the creation of printable reports. Thus, when you need a highly interactive page with complex communication between the various applets, SAP MII applets with scripting are recommended. However, web pages with applets are not suitable for printing as is. On the other hand, when a printable representation of data is required in the form of a static report with no possible user interactions, then you can use SAP MII reports.

SAP MII reports must have the .irpt extension. All files with this extension are processed by the ReportServlet in the server that is the heart of the reporting subsystem and provides the reporting functionality of SAP MII.

SAP MII reports make use of the <SERVLET> tags instead of <APPLET> tags. <SERVLET> tags can invoke the Illuminator service (explained in Section 9.9 SAP MII Services: The Power behind SAP MII) to execute data queries. This is accomplished by querying a data source and then using the HTML tables to display data and ChartServlet and SPCChartServlet services to generate static images of the iChart and iSPCChart applets. You can modify both the data and the display of this data by using XML Style Sheet (XSL) style sheets.

You can pass dynamic data to a report either through the setProperty Value(PROPERTYNAME, VALUE) method on an applet in the previous page or through query parameters in the URL, such as *Batchreport.irpt?BatchNo=BATCH00 001&Plant=Chicago*. You can also pass these values through an HTTP POST request, which is particularly useful when the data is being submitted from an HTML form. If the form has the elements with the names BatchNo and Plant, or if they are passed as URL parameters, the same can be accessed from a subsequent report by encapsulating the variable names in curly braces such as {BatchNo} and {Plant}. You can also use the same approach on the parameter values of the SERVLET tag.

The following example code provide examples of how the SERVLET tag can be put to use in an SAP MII report accessing session variables as explained previously.

Example

```
<!-- display query output data by XSL transformation -->
<SERVLET NAME="Illuminator">
<PARAM NAME="QueryTemplate" VALUE="SAPMIIESSENTIALS/Examples/Batch/
BatchTrendQuery">
<PARAM NAME="Param.1" VALUE="{BatchNo}">
<PARAM NAME="Content-Type" VALUE="text/xml">
<PARAM NAME="StyleSheet" VALUE=" /SAPMIIESSENTIALS/Examples/Batch/Il-
lumRowsetTable.xsl">
</SERVLET>

<!--display iChart as a static image -->
<SERVLET NAME="ChartServlet">
<PARAM NAME="QueryTemplate"
VALUE=" SAPMIIESSENTIALS/Examples/Batch/BatchTrendQuery">
<PARAM NAME="DisplayTemplate" VALUE="SAPMIIESSENTIALS/Examples/Batch/
BatchTrendChart">
<PARAM NAME="Param.1" VALUE="{BatchNo}">
<PARAM NAME="Title" VALUE="Trend for Batch: {BatchNo}">
<PARAM NAME="Width" VALUE="300">
<PARAM NAME="Height" VALUE="200">
</SERVLET>
```

As you can see from this example, using the SERVLET tag is quite easy. Among the Illuminator, ChartServlet, and SPCChartServlet services, the service you want to use is passed as the NAME attribute of the SERVLET tag. You can pass various parameters such as the query and display templates, the height and width, query parameters, and the title of the chart as parameters. With the Illuminator service, the Content-Type is set to XML, which returns the data from the data source in a XML format. This is done to make way for the XSL transformation of the returned data using the XML style sheet mentioned in the StyleSheet parameter. You can omit the Content-Type and the XML style sheet altogether; in this case, the returned data is displayed in tabular form in an HTML table, using a default style sheet provided by SAP MII. An XML style sheet is required to format the data using an XSL document, in which case the Content-Type should be changed to text/xml, and the appropriate StyleSheet parameter should be specified. The SERVLET tag is quite similar to the APPLET tag, and can accept almost all of the parameters that can be specified for the APPLET tag.

8.3   Customizing Content for Mobile Devices

Features of mobile devices are generally limited when it comes to displaying rich interactive data on a web page; generally a standard SAP MII content page with Java applets fails to render on such a device. However, you can fix this problem by using SAP MII reports and XSL transformations to convert the dynamic content into static content using the <SERVLET> tag as explained in the previous section.

Other than the methods mentioned previously, you can also use the ChartServlet and iSPCChartservlet for the inline generation of images based on supplied URL parameters. The following is an example of how you can achieve this.

> **Example**
> ```
> <IMG SRC="/XMII/ChartServlet?Width=300&Height=200&QueryTemplate=SAPMIIE
> SSENTIALS/Examples/Batch/BatchTrendQuery&DisplayTemplate=SAPMIIESSENTIA
> LS/Examples/Batch/BatchTrendChart&Content-Type=image/jpg">
> ```

As demonstrated in this example, a call to the ChartServlet or the SPCChartServlet can be directly issued as a URL from the SRC attribute of an HTML image. Combining this with dynamic parameters, as explained in the SAP MII reports section, gives you the ability to generate truly dynamic images based on dynamic parameters.

8.4   SAP MII Scripting: Common Use Case Scenarios

Now it's time to have a look at how applets can be made to represent a use case or business scenario by using JavaScript in an HTML page.

8.4.1   Displaying Data

The display of a query template's output data is ideally determined by the cardinality of the data. If it is a single cardinality data, such as process order header information, HTML form fields are generally the method of choice. However, if the data contains multiple data items, such as order operations, you should use a tabular format, either using the iGrid or using HTML tables. You can also display a single row of data, using an iGrid with the Grid Type set to VerticalGrid mode other than using an HTML form. You need to configure the use of the iGrid in the

VerticalGrid mode in the Grid Area tab of the iGrid configuration. The VerticalGrid mode enables you to display a grid with its header displayed vertically instead of horizontally and, with a little bit of configuration, can be made to look just like an HTML form with fields and labels.

An alternate approach of using the iGrid applets would be using dynamic scripting, which works well both for single and multiple rows of data. If the data returned is in a single row, you can display it in a form field or in an HTML table. The trick is to execute a query template that returns the required data, using an iCommand applet, and then, if multiple rows are returned, use the getRowCount(), getColumnCount(), and the getValue() methods to create an HTML table. If a single row is returned, fill in the required HTML form fields using the getValue() method.

The following example explains the how to generate HTML input field or HTML table using JavaScript in the web page to display single-row or tabular data.

Example

```
<APPLET NAME="iCommand" WIDTH="1" HEIGHT="1" CODE="iCommand" CODE-
BASE="/XMII/Classes" ARCHIVE="illum8.zip" MAYSCRIPT>
<PARAM NAME="QueryTemplate" VALUE="SAPMIIESSENTIALS/Examples/Batch/
PlasticBottleBatchDataQT">
<PARAM NAME="DisplayTemplate" VALUE="SAPMIIESSENTIALS/Examples/Batch/
iCommandDT">
</APPLET>
<SCRIPT LANGUAGE="JavaScript">
function DislayBatchData() {
//execute the iCommand
document.iCommand.executeCommand();
//get the row count
var rowcount = document.iCommand.getRowCount();
//get the column count
var colcount = document.iCommand.getColumnCount();
//if a single row is returned display in form fields
if (rowcount == 1){
        for(i=1; i<= colcount; i++){
                document.write("<input type='text' value='" + document.
iCommand.getValue(i,1) + "'><br/>");
    }
```

```
}else{
//if multiple rows returned, draw a HTML table
document.write("<table border='1'>");
        for(i=1; i<= rowcount; i++){
                document.write("<tr>");
                  for(j=1; j<= colcount; j++){
                        document.write("<td>");
                        document.write( document.iCommand.
getValue(j,i));
                        document.write("</td>");
                    }
        document.write("</tr>");
        }
document.write("</table>");
}
</SCRIPT>
```

8.4.2 Creating/Changing Data

Creating or updating backend data using SAP MII scripting is a bit different compared to the technique used for displaying data. The iGrid does not inherently support updating of data by directly editing the data fields; therefore, data cannot be directly updated from the iGrid interface. If you need to update cells of an iGrid one at a time, you can use a simple pop-up or the JavaScript prompt() function to create a pop-up dialog upon the click of a cell. You can then pass the value to the query template via an iCommand applet, and the data source updated with the value. The iGrid then needs to be updated or refreshed to reflect the changed value. The following example explains this scenario with the relevant code.

Example

```
<!-- iGrid applet for data display -->
<APPLET NAME="iGrid" WIDTH="640" HEIGHT="400" CODE="iGrid" CODEBASE="/
XMII/Classes" ARCHIVE="illum8.zip" MAYSCRIPT>
<PARAM NAME="QueryTemplate" VALUE="SAPMIIESSENTIALS/Examples/Batch/
PlasticBottleBatchDataQT">
<PARAM NAME="DisplayTemplate" VALUE="SAPMIIESSENTIALS/Examples/Batch/
PlasticBottleGrid">
```

```
<!-- Use the DoubleClickEvent to get the Cell Value -->
<PARAM NAME="DoubleClickEvent" VALUE="editCellValue">
</APPLET>
<!-- iCommand applet for data update -->
<APPLET NAME="iCommand" WIDTH="1" HEIGHT="1" CODE="iCommand" CODE-
BASE="/XMII/Classes" ARCHIVE="illum8.zip" MAYSCRIPT>
<PARAM NAME="QueryTemplate" VALUE="SAPMIIESSENTIALS/Examples/Batch/
PlasticBottleUpdateQT">
<PARAM NAME="DisplayTemplate" VALUE="SAPMIIESSENTIALS/Examples/Batch/
iCommandDT">
</APPLET>


<SCRIPT LANGUAGE="JavaScript">
//JavaScript function for iGrid applet's double-click event
function editCellValue(){
//get the selected cell row
selColumn = document.iGrid.getGridObject().getSelectedCellRow();
//get the selected cell column
selRow = document.iGrid.getGridObject().getSelectedCellColumn();
//get the primary key: BATCHID displayed in the first column of the
selected cell
batchID = document.iGrid.getGridObject().getCellValue(selRow, 1);
//get the value of the selected cell
selCellValue = document.iGrid.getGridObject().getSelectedCellValue(sel
Column);
//prompt the user to enter a new value
updatedValue = prompt("Enter a new value : " , selCellValue);
//if a new value was supplied update the values to the query template
params and execute the query
if (updatedValue != null){
document.iCommand.getQueryObject().setParam(1,updatedValue);
document.iCommand.getQueryObject().setParam(2,batchID);

if (document.iCommand.executeCommand()){
//if update was successful update the iGrid
document.iGrid.updateGrid(true);
```

```
}else{
//else print the error message
alert(document.iCommand.getLastError());
}
}
}
</SCRIPT>
```

If you need to update multiple cells of a row, the best approach is to display the contents of the cell in HTML form fields upon the click of a row. You can then modify the values and click on a button to update the data to the backend by executing an XacuteQuery (for BLS Transaction) or SQLQuery, via the iCommand applet. Again, the iGrid needs to be updated or refreshed to reflect the changes. The following example explains this scenario with the relevant code.

Example

```
<!-- iGrid applet for data display -->
<APPLET NAME="iGrid" WIDTH="640" HEIGHT="400" CODE="iGrid" CODEBASE="/
XMII/Classes" ARCHIVE="illum8.zip" MAYSCRIPT>
<PARAM NAME="QueryTemplate" VALUE="SAPMIIESSENTIALS/Examples/Batch/
PlasticBottleBatchDataQT">
<PARAM NAME="DisplayTemplate" VALUE="SAPMIIESSENTIALS/Examples/Batch/
PlasticBottleGrid">
<!-- Use the SelectionEvent to get the Cell Value -->
<PARAM NAME="SelectionEvent" VALUE="fillRowValue">
</APPLET>
<!-- iCommand applet for data update -->
<APPLET NAME="iCommand" WIDTH="1" HEIGHT="1" CODE="iCommand" CODE-
BASE="/XMII/Classes" ARCHIVE="illum8.zip" MAYSCRIPT>
<PARAM NAME="QueryTemplate" VALUE="SAPMIIESSENTIALS/Examples/Batch/
PlasticBottleUpdateQT">
<PARAM NAME="DisplayTemplate" VALUE="SAPMIIESSENTIALS/Examples/Batch/
iCommandDT">
</APPLET>
<SCRIPT LANGUAGE="JavaScript">
//JavaScript function for iGrid applet's row selection event
```

```
function fillRowValue(){
//get the selected row
selRow=document.iGrid.getGridObject().getSelectedRow();

//get the row values of the selected cell one by one and fill up the
form fields
batchColor = document.iGrid.getGridObject().getCellValue(selRow,1);

//fill the Batch Color
document.all.colorBatch.value = batchColor;

methingPoint = document.iGrid.getGridObject().CellValue(selRow,2);

// fill the batch Melting Point
document.all.meltingPoint.value = meltingPoint;

//populate the other form fields
//...............................................

}

//Update the data to the backend on the click of a button

function updateRow(){

//Set the parameters in the Query template

document.iCommand.getQueryObject().setParam(1,updatedValue);

document.iCommand.getQueryObject().setParam(2,batchID);

//set other query template input parameters

//...............................................................

if (document.iCommand.executeCommand()){

//if execution was successful update the grid
document.iGrid.updateGrid(true);

}else{

//else display the error message
alert(document.iCommand.getLastError());

}

}

</SCRIPT>
```

8.4.3 Displaying Charts

Data speaks more for itself when it is represented visually in the form of charts. Displaying static charts is relatively simple and straightforward; you can embed them in a web page with only a few lines of code (as explained in the "Web Scripting" section). To create a dynamic chart that changes with the change in data — for example, when the data source in the backend is updated — call the refresh() method of the chart applet.

If you want to change the type of chart or use different chart visualizations without inserting multiple types of chart in a single page, you can easily do so with a few lines of scripting, as explained in the following example.

Example

```
<APPLET NAME="iChart" WIDTH="640" HEIGHT="400" CODE="iChart" CODE-
BASE="/XMII/Classes" ARCHIVE="illum8.zip" MAYSCRIPT>

<PARAM NAME="QueryTemplate" VALUE="SAPMIIESSENTIALS/Examples/Batch/
PlasticBottleTrendQT">

<PARAM NAME="DisplayTemplate" VALUE="SAPMIIESSENTIALS/Examples/Batch/
PlasticBottleTrendDT">

</APPLET>

<SCRIPT LANGUAGE="JavaScript">

//This function switches between Line and Bar chart types.

function switchChartType(){

//get the current Chart Type
chartType = document.iChart.getChartObject().getChartType();

//if the chart type is 'Line'
if (chartType == "Line"){

//change chart type to 'Bar'
document.iChart.getChartObject().setChartType("Bar");

//refresh the chart
document.iChart.refresh();

//if chart type is 'Bar'
}else{

//change chart type to 'Line'
document.iChart.getChartObject().setChartType("Line");

//refresh the chart
document.iChart.refresh();

}

}

</SCRIPT>
```

A scenario in which the displayed iChart changes with the data selected on a corresponding iGrid was already explained in the "Common Applet Events" section earlier in this chapter.

8.4.4 Using the iBrowser

You can use the iBrowser display template to display a list of data in using dropdown or tree-view controls, as explained in Chapter 5 Display Templates: Let Your Data Speak. Consider a simple example using the PlasticResin database data. In this example the iBrowser is used in Data Link Mode to display the Batch Number in the dropdown, with Color as the Data Link column. When the user selects a batch in the iBrowser dropdown, details of all batches with the same color are displayed in an iGrid.

When an item in the iBrowser is selected, the SELECTIONEVENT gets triggered. In the event handler of the SELECTIONEVENT you can read either the selected value or the corresponding hidden (data link) value of the iBrowser. The following example explains this scenario with the relevant code.

Example

```javascript
<script language="javascript">
function UpdateBatchGrid(){
//get the index of the batch selected in the iBrowser dropdown.
var selectedBatchIndex = document.selectBatch.getSelectedIndex();
//get the color of the batch by retrieving the data link value at the
selected index.
var selectedBatchColor = document.selectBatch.getDatalinkValueAt(select
edBatchIndex);
//set parameter for the iGrid Query Template to filter batches by the
selected batch's color.
document.gridBatchDetails.getQueryObject().setParam(1, selectedBatch-
Color);
//refresh the iGrid
document.gridBatchDetails.refresh();
}
</script>
```

```
<!-- iBrowser applet to display a dropdown list of batches -->
<APPLET NAME="selectBatch" WIDTH="200" HEIGHT="20" CODE="iBrowser"
CODEBASE="/XMII/Classes" ARCHIVE="illum8.zip" MAYSCRIPT>
<PARAM NAME="QueryTemplate" VALUE="SAPMIIESSENTIALS/Examples/Batch/
PlasticBottleBatchData">
<PARAM NAME="DisplayTemplate" VALUE="SAPMIIESSENTIALS/Examples/Batch/
BatchColorBrowser">
<PARAM NAME="SelectionEvent" VALUE="UpdateBatchGrid">
</APPLET>
<!-- iGrid applet to display details of batches with the same color as
the selected batch -->
<APPLET NAME="gridBatchDetails" WIDTH="640" HEIGHT="400" CODE="iGrid"
CODEBASE="/XMII/Classes" ARCHIVE="illum8.zip" MAYSCRIPT>
<PARAM NAME="QueryTemplate" VALUE="SAPMIIESSENTIALS/Examples/Batch/
PlasticBottleFilterbyColor">
<PARAM NAME="DisplayTemplate" VALUE="SAPMIIESSENTIALS/Examples/Batch/
PlasticBottleBatchDetails">
</APPLET>
```

8.4.5 Displaying Animated Objects

To stream an animated object to a web page you need the help of the SAP MII Runner service. But before that you need to create a BLS Transaction that would generate the image from an animated object and stream it. In a new BLS Transaction, add an Animated Object Renderer action and configure it to use the required animated object. In the Animated Object Renderer configuration screen, in the Image Output configuration settings, check the Render Image checkbox to generate an image that can be accessed via the EncodedImage output property of this action block. You would also need to choose the Image Type, .jpg or .png, the format to which it should render. Create an output transaction property called Output of the type String. In the Outgoing links configuration section of the Animated Object Renderer action block map the EncodedImage output property of this action block with the Output Transaction property. Now you need to invoke this transaction via the Runner service and set the Content-Type with respect to the Image Type settings that you had configured for the Animated Object Renderer action block. It should be image/jpg for a JPEG image and image/png for PNG. An example URL with the parameters would be the following:

*http://<server>:<port>/XMII/Runner?Transaction=SAPMIIESSENTIALS/Examples/FanS
peedSVG&Outputparameter=OutputImage&Content-type=image/png*

Example

```
<!-- animated image streamed by Runner -->
<!-- HTML code to display the image and corresponding buttons -->
<img src="http://<server>:<port>/XMII/Runner?Transaction=SAPMIIESSENTIA
LS/Examples/FanSpeedSVG&Outputparameter=OutputImage&Content-type=image/
png" name="fanSpeed"><p>
<button onclick="javascript:animateImage()">Autorefresh Image</button>
<button onclick="javascript:clearAnimation()">Stop Autore-fresh</but-
ton>
<!--JavaScript functions to manipulate the image -->
<script language="JavaScript">
//declare a public variable 'Time' which will hold the return value of
the 'setTimeout' method and will be used to clear the timeout later.
var Time;


function animateImage(){
//Declare a new variable imagename and assign the value of the streamed
image as an URL to it.
var imagename;
imagename = "http://<server>:<port>/XMII/Runner?Transaction=SAPMII
SSENTIALS/Examples/FanSpeedSVG&Outputparameter=OutputImage&Content-
type=image/png";


//Assign the value of the variable declared earlier to the source of
the HTML image tag.
document.images["fanSpeed"].src = imagename;


//recursively call the same function at 10 seconds intervals
Time = setTimeout("animateImage()", 10000);
}
function clearAnimation(){
clearTimeout(Time);
}
</script>
```

Though in the preceding example the animateImage() function is provided on a button click event you can also add it in the body onLoad event.

Many other complex scenarios make use of the powerful scripting capabilities of SAP MII. The preceding examples provide you with the approach that should be applied to a problem, given the vast capabilities — and limitations — of the applets and scripting world.

Note

SAP MII Productivity Wizards are a set of standalone programs that ease the content development, publishing, and scripting aspects of SAP MII content. They are down-loadable from the SAP Developer Network (SDN) (*http://sdn.sap.com*) via the following navigation path:

SDN • DOWNLOADS • MANUFACTURING TOOLS • XMII 12.0 SAMPLE PROJECTS AND TOOLS • CLICK HERE FOR DOWNLOAD • XMII PRODUCTIVITY WIZARDS.

Three wizards are available to you upon successful installation, and all of them require logging onto the SAP MII system using their own individual login dialogs.

▶ **Content Generation:** The Content Generation Wizard lists all query and display templates in separate panes and enables you to generate HTML code for embedding these objects in a web page. Options for specifying parameters for these objects are available as well. The generated HTML code is copied to the clipboard and can be pasted directly to the required web page source file.

▶ **Publish Assistant:** The Publish Assistant enables you to download and upload web content (such as HTML and IRPT pages) from and to the SAP MII server. The web pages can then be modified locally and published back to the SAP MII server.

▶ **Script Assistant:** The Script Assistant lists all the applet types, applet methods, and object methods for the SAP MII applets. This is especially useful because it serves as a one-stop-shop for all the web scripting methods. This wizard also provides a text area where code can be manually inserted and then copied and pasted, with minor changes, to the web page.

8.5   Localizing the Web Content

Sometimes, you need the same HTML content developed in SAP MII deployed across multilingual locations and in such cases translation of the text in the content is required. It is not only cumbersome to maintain different language versions of the same content but also difficult development-wise.

SAP MII provides the facility to localize strings that you can use in the HTML content using the Localization menu available under Visualization Services • Localization (Figure 8.1). You would need to define keys that would be dynamically substituted at runtime with the localization values that you have defined for that particular user in her profile. To create a new localization key, click on New and enter a value for the field Name. This value would serve as the localization key that you should use in your HTML content that would be substituted at runtime and is mandatory. The default language is English, and you also need to define a value for this key in the English language. The other languages available are German, Spanish, French, Japanese, Portuguese, Russian, and Chinese. If a user has any language assigned to her profile other than those just mentioned, the default language (English) is used. After you have defined your localization strings for the key, click on Save to save the settings.

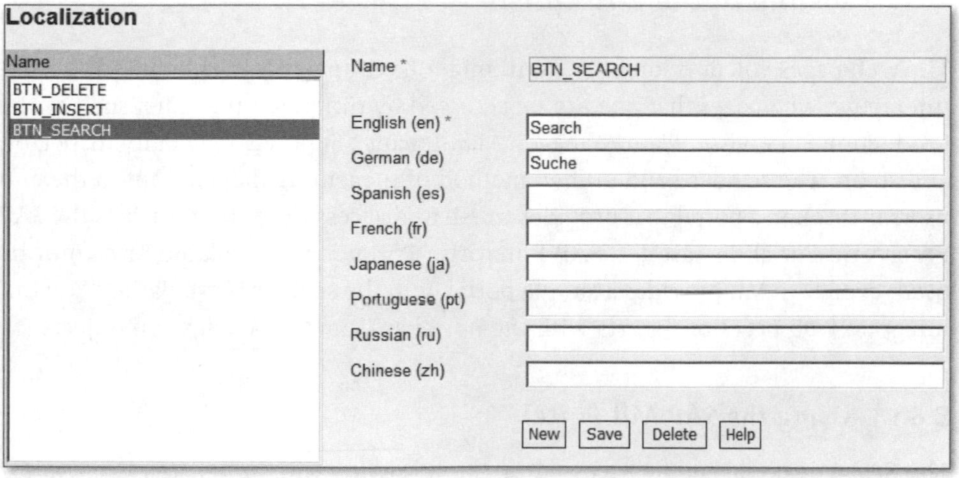

Figure 8.1 The Localization screen of SAP MII

To use the localization settings in your HTML content, the first and foremost thing that you need to keep in mind is that you would need use an IRPT page, that is, use the extension of the web page file as .irpt instead of .htm/.html. Localization keys need to be processed and substituted by the ReportServlet mentioned in Section 8.2 SAP MII Reports before they are rendered as HTML in the browser. Now to use the localization settings in your HTML content you would need to insert it as {##KEY_NAME} in the required places. As shown in Figure 8.1, if you want to localize the search text in your application, you would need to create a localization key with the name, for example, BTN_SEARCH and strings "Search" for English and "Suche" for German. Now to integrate this localization in your HTML application, for example, as a button, you would need to specify it as `<button>{##BTN_SEARCH}</button>` in your HTML code. This code would now pick up the localization strings at runtime according to the language settings of the user's system and replace them with the corresponding strings at runtime.

In this section you have learned about SAP MII reports and scripting, including some typical use case scenarios. In the following section, you learn how you can configure the SAP MII portal or SAP Enterprise Portal to deliver this content for role-based access to the end users.

8.6 Enterprise Portal Integration: Make the Shop Floor Visible to the Enterprise

The web pages you develop in SAP MII might have analytics dashboards and user-interactive web pages that need to be accessed by different end users, such as the Production Supervisor, Plant Manager, Maintenance Supervisor, Quality Inspector, and so on. The standard and unified method of presenting that content to the end users is through a portal that provides role-based access to content, such as the SAP Enterprise Portal. In case the SAP Enterprise Portal is not available or cannot be used, even SAP MII provides a simple portal with the standard installation. You can integrate web pages or reports with the portal as iViews or navigation objects.

8.6.1 Using the SAP MII Portal

The SAP MII portal can be accessed by the following URL: *http://<server>:<port>/XMII*.

You can configure the portal using the Navigation Services menu available in the SAP MII menu. To configure the navigation objects, open the Navigation screen (Figure 8.2). Select the roles or users defined in the User Management Engine (UME) from the Select Role or User dropdown. The navigation items you configure here are available for the specified user or role only when logged in to the SAP MII portal. To add navigation menus or page links select the NavigationItems node, and select ADD • ADD CHILD to add a new navigation item.

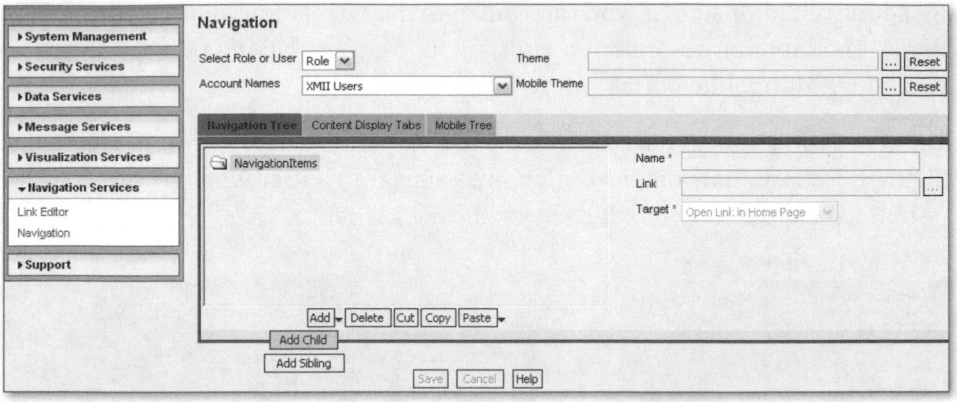

Figure 8.2 Navigation Configuration

In the Navigation – Record Detail screen, seen in Figure 8.3, the navigation item added can be a group node having no page link or an actual page link menu. Specify the name of the node or navigation item in the Name property on the right. Specify the web page link in the Link property, using the Browse button. The page should be present in the SAP MII content catalog if you use the lookup button to select the page link. Use the Target property from the dropdown to specify how the page specified in the link opens in the portal. The Open Link in Home Page option specifies that the page opens in the main display window on the right of the screen, whereas the Open Link On Top option specifies that the page opens in the same window in place of the portal. The Open Link in New Window option specifies that the page opens in a new window.

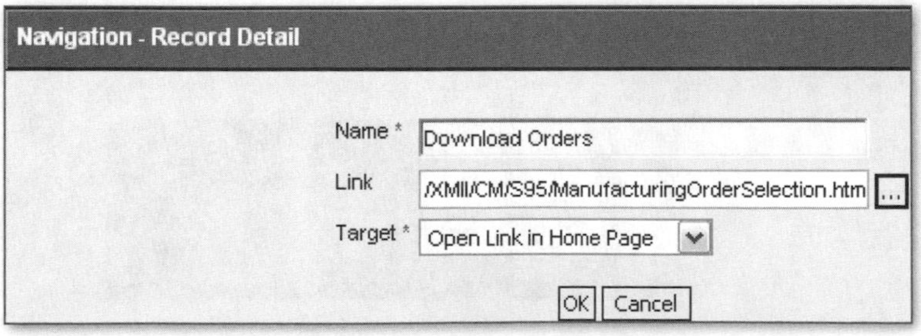

Figure 8.3 Configuring Page for Navigation Menu

You can also create links or navigation menu items using the Link Editor menu, available under Navigation Services menu category; or you can use the links or standalone navigation items created there by selecting them from the Links tab.

By adding child or sibling, you can configure the navigation items as hierarchical items. The same menu options are visible to the users having that specified role when logged in to the portal.

The Navigation Configuration screen for the SAP MII Portal is shown in Figure 8.4. Figure 8.5 shows how the navigation links appear to a user when he logs into the portal, having the roles to which he or she is assigned.

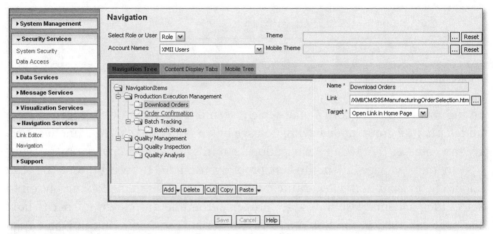

Figure 8.4 Navigation Configuration for Portal

Figure 8.5 SAP MII Portal Menu

Security and other features, such as session management and environment variables access, are the same in the SAP MII portal as they are in SAP MII.

Now that we've covered configuring the SAP MII portal with role-based navigation links, we turn to how this can be achieved using the SAP Enterprise Portal.

8.6.2   Using the SAP Enterprise Portal

You can integrate the HTML and IRPT web pages into the SAP Enterprise Portal as URL iViews. To create a new iView, log in to the SAP Enterprise Portal (*http://<server>:<port>/irj/portal*) with a user having a Content Administration role. Open CONTENT ADMINISTRATION • PORTAL CONTENT from the roles and workset menu at the portal's top navigation area. Select a specific portal content folder and role, and add a new URL iView from the iView Templates. Specify the iView name and ID and the URL of the SAP MII web page. You can copy the URL of the web page from the page in the SAP MII Workbench web catalog by selecting the page and clicking on the Copy Link context menu option. The URL of the SAP MII web page typically adheres to the following URL pattern:

http://<server>:<port>/XMII/CM/<project>/<folder>/<pagename>

Using Single Sign-On with the SAP Enterprise Portal

The SAP MII web pages used in the SAP Enterprise Portal as URL iViews, require authentication with a user available in SAP MII UME. The users using the SAP Enterprise Portal are actually getting authenticated while logging in to the portal. This means that the users need to log in twice to access the iViews configured with SAP MII content. As a result, in most cases, you need to provide Single Sign-On (SSO) between the SAP Enterprise Portal and SAP MII. Using SSO, the authentication used in the portal can be re-used for SAP MII; but in this case, the same users must present with the same user ID in both systems. The SSO configuration using the logon ticket is the same as that configuration between any two SAP NetWeaver J2EE systems, as described in the SAP Note 1083421.

To configure the SSO between the SAP Enterprise Portal and SAP MII, first download the SSO2 logon ticket certificate from the SAP Enterprise Portal. Navigate to SYSTEM ADMINISTRATION • SYSTEM CONFIGURATION from the top navigation, and then select KEYSTORE ADMINISTRATION from DETAILED NAVIGATION (Figure 8.6). In the Content tab, select SAPLogonTicketKeypair-cert from the dropdown, and click on the Download verify.der File button. Save the certificate file in the local file system.

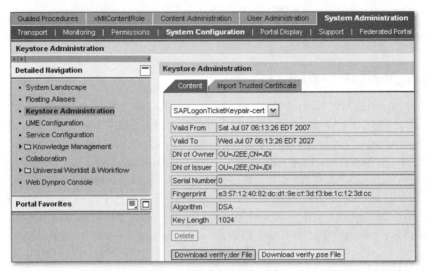

Figure 8.6 SSO2 Logon Ticket Certificate Download from SAP Enterprise Portal

Now open the SSO2 wizard in the SAP MII WebAS by using the URL *http://<server>:<port>/sso2* and logging on as an administrator. Click on Add Trusted System and choose the By Uploading Certificate Manually option (Figure 8.7).

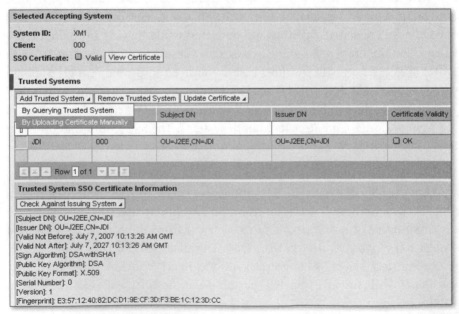

Figure 8.7 Uploading the SSO2 Logon Ticket Certificate in the SAP MII WebAS SSO Wizard

In the screen that appears, specify the System ID of the SAP Enterprise Portal system and the Client as 000. Add the certificate path from the local file system using the Browse button. Click on Finish in the next screen to complete the certificate upload process. If it is maintained as a Technical System in the System Landscape Directory (SLD), you can also automatically add the certificate by querying the SAP Enterprise Portal system. To use the SSO between the SAP Enterprise Portal and SAP MII, ensure that both the systems' date and time are the same and that they have the same time zone configured.

In this section you have learned how to configure the URL iViews for SAP MII pages in the SAP Enterprise Portal and how to set up the SSO configurations for uniform access to content.

8.7   Summary

In this chapter you have learned about web scripting to create web pages and reports using SAP MII applets and delivering the user interfaces to the end users through the SAP MII portal and the SAP Enterprise Portal.

In the next chapter, you will learn about some of the advanced features and tips and tricks of SAP MII composite application development.

This chapter explains the advanced techniques used in SAP MII composite application development. These techniques include creating custom action blocks and dynamic data queries and using XPath expressions in BLS Transactions, table inputs for JCo action blocks, session variables, virtual servers, and SAP MII services.

9 Advanced Techniques for SAP MII Composite Application Development

Because SAP MII is a flexible development platform for manufacturing composite applications, you can tweak it to achieve different scenarios and optimize application development and performance of the application. In this chapter you learn some of the advanced tips and tricks of SAP MII composite application development, which you can use when you are developing manufacturing composites.

9.1 Creating and Deploying a Custom Action Block

Though most of the standard functionalities required when you are developing composite applications are available as predefined action blocks in SAP MII, in some cases you might need to implement specific requirements that can be reused across different installations and are complex to implement. You can implement such custom functionalities using custom action blocks for Business Logic Services (BLS) Transactions. In this section, you learn how to create custom action blocks to use custom processing logic. These custom action blocks can be integrated with BLS Transactions and used like any standard action block and can be developed for any features that you can reuse in multiple BLS Transactions. This process requires development in Java using some SAP-delivered libraries, which are available for free download from the SAP Community Network. The library is available as a JAR file called XMII.JAR from the following link and menu path:

https://www.sdn.sap.com/irj/sdn/manufacturing-tools

SAP MII SAMPLE PROJECTS AND TOOLS • CUSTOM ACTION DEVELOPER KIT

The custom action block is a Java class that extends a super class called `Action-ReflectionBase`, which is defined in the SAP MII library. This class implements certain interfaces methods required by any action block. To create a new custom action, create a Java project using SAP NetWeaver Developer Studio 7.0 (or any other Java integrated development environment (IDE)). Add the XMII.JAR library in the Java Build Path of the project as an external library and then define a package and a new class extending the `ActionReflectionBase` super class:

```
public class <className> extends ActionReflectionBase {

}
```

You also need to add the corresponding import statement to the package, as follows:

```
import com.sap.xmii.xacute.actions.ActionReflectionBase;
```

Define the class attributes with private scope, which include the input and output properties of the action block. You also need to define the corresponding getter and setter methods inside the class for those class attributes. The general rule is this: For a class attribute, if a setter method is present, it is treated as an input property for the action block (visible in the Incoming tab in Link Editor); if a getter method is present, it is treated as an output property (visible in the Outgoing tab in Link Editor); and if both are present, then they are treated as both input and output properties for the action block. The data types in Java that you should use to declare the input and output properties of the action block are as follows:

- Java.lang.String (String)
- int (Integer)
- boolean (Boolean)
- java.util.Calendar (DateTime)
- double (Double)
- com.sap.lhcommon.xml.XMLDataType (Xml)

The data types within parentheses, except for the Java data types listed, specify the corresponding data type in SAP MII BLS Transactions.

Certain methods defined in the super class need to be implemented for various functionalities in the custom action class. These are as follows:

1. Method `GetIconPath`

```
/* (non-Javadoc)
 * @see com.sap.xmii.xacute.core.ActionReflectionTemplate#GetIconPat
h()
 */
public String GetIconPath() {
    return "/com/sappress/mii/customaction/excel2xml.png";
}
```

This method returns the file path of the icon to be displayed in the SAP MII Workbench for the custom action block in the BLS Transaction editor. The icon file can be present anywhere inside the project folders path, which should be specified with the `return` keyword, with the project folder as the root.

1. Method `isConfigurable`

```
/* (non-Javadoc)
 * @see com.sap.xmii.xacute.core.IConfigurable#isConfigurable()
 */
public boolean isConfigurable() {
    return true;
}
```

This method returns a value of true if the custom action has object configurations. A value of false means that the action block has no object configurations in the BLS Transaction. If this method is not implemented, the default value is true.

1. Method `ShowConfigurationDialog`

```
/* (non-Javadoc)
 * @see com.sap.xmii.xacute.core.IConfigurable#ShowConfigurationDial
og(java.awt.Window, com.sap.xmii.xacute.core.Transaction, com.sap.xmii.
xacute.core.Step)
 */
public int ShowConfigurationDialog(Window parentWindow,  Transaction
transaction, Step step) {

    AbstractActionDialog dialog = AbstractActionHelper.
getInstance(parentWindow, this, <DialogClassName>.class, transaction,
step);
    int result = dialog.ShowDialog();
    return result;
}
```

This method specifies the Object Configuration dialog for the custom action block in the BLS Transaction. We recommend you create a separate custom class extending the `AbstractActionDialog` super class (defined in the *com.sap.xmii.xacute. actions.shared* package in the XMII.JAR library) to define the Object Configuration dialog, which is a Java Swing–based dialog. The dialog class is explained later in this section. This method is executed when Object Configuration is executed at design time

1. Method `Invoke`

```
/* (non-Javadoc)
   * @see com.sap.xmii.xacute.core.IInvoke#Invoke(com.sap.xmii.xacute.
core.Transaction, com.sap.xmii.xacute.core.ILog)
   */
  public void Invoke(Transaction transaction, ILog log) throws
Exception {
try
  {
/* action business logic */
    _success = true;
  }
  catch( Exception e )
  {
   log.error(e.getMessage());
   _success = false;
  }
 }
```

This is the most important method, and it is invoked when the action block is called as part of the transaction execution. In this method, write the code to execute the business logic that the action block provides. Read the input properties (private class attributes with the setter method) and assign values to the output properties (private class attributes with the getter methods). You can access any properties for the transaction from the transaction variable object, available as the input parameter of the method. The super class `AbstractXacuteAction` has a class attribute `_success` of type Boolean; you should set this to true upon successful execution of the action and to false in the catch block. You can use the log variable object of type ILog to add trace messages to the SAP NetWeaver log.

You can use the `com.sap.lhcommon.xml.XMLHandler` and `com.sap.xmii.common. IllumXmlUtilities` classes to create and manipulate SAP MII XML documents used in the action block.

You can develop the Object Configuration dialog invoked in the ShowConfigurationDialog() method as a separate Java class by extending the super class `AbstractActionDialog`, defined in the *com.sap.xmii.xacute.actions.shared* package in the XMII.JAR library.

```
public class <DialogClassName> extends AbstractActionDialog {
}
```

The corresponding import statements are as follows:

```
import com.sap.xmii.xacute.actions.shared.AbstractActionDialog;
import com.sap.xmii.xacute.actions.shared.ActionUtilities;
import com.sap.xmii.xacute.core.Step;
import com.sap.xmii.xacute.core.Transaction;
```

Declare the input fields to be displayed in the configuration dialog as the class attributes. You can use the Java Swing controls, such as JTextField, JComboBox, JRadioButton, and so on, as the types of those variables.

Implement the following two constructor methods for the class. Calls to the corresponding super constructors should be inside them.

```
    public <className>(JFrame parentFrame, Object
actionObject,Transaction transaction, Step step) {
       super(parentFrame, actionObject, transaction, step);
       }
```

```
    public < className>(JDialog parentFrame, Object actionObject,
Transaction transaction, Step selectedAction) {
       super(parentFrame, actionObject, transaction, selectedAction);
    }
```

You need to implement the following super class methods as well:

1. Method `prepareDialog`

```
    /* (non-Javadoc)
     * @see com.sap.xmii.xacute.actions.shared.AbstractActionDialog#prep
areDialog()
    */
   protected void prepareDialog() {

     setSize(350, 150);
     setTitle("... Configurations");
   }
```

In this method, set the size and title of the Object Configuration dialog window.

1. Method `createLayoutObjects`

```
/* (non-Javadoc)
 * @see com.sap.xmii.xacute.actions.shared.AbstractActionDialog#crea
teLayoutObjects()
 */
protected void createLayoutObjects() {
    <textfieldName> = new JTextField(10);
}
```

In this method, initialize the input field objects (that is, class attributes) displayed in the configuration dialog.

1. Method `layoutMainPanel`

```
/* (non-Javadoc)
 * @see com.sap.xmii.xacute.actions.shared.AbstractActionDialog#layo
utMainPanel()
 */
protected void layoutMainPanel() {
    JPanel mainPanel = new JPanel(new GridBagLayout());
    GridBagConstraints c = new GridBagConstraints();
    c.gridy = 0;
    c.insets = ActionUtilities.standardSquareInsets;
    c.weightx = 1.0;
    c.anchor = GridBagConstraints.WEST;
    c.fill= GridBagConstraints.NONE;
    mainPanel.add(new JLabel("Label Name"), c);
    c.gridy = c.gridy + 1;
    c.weightx = 1.0;
    c.anchor = GridBagConstraints.CENTER;
    c.fill = GridBagConstraints.HORIZONTAL;
    mainPanel.add(excelFilePathField, c);
    getContentPane().setLayout(new GridBagLayout());
    GridBagConstraints e = new GridBagConstraints();
    e.insets = ActionUtilities.standardSquareInsets;
    e.gridy = 0;
    e.weightx = 1.0;
    e.weighty = 1.0;
    e.fill = GridBagConstraints.BOTH;
    getContentPane().add(mainPanel, e);
    e.gridy = e.gridy + 1;
    e.weightx = 1.0;
```

```
      e.weighty = 0.0;
      e.fill = GridBagConstraints.NONE;
      e.anchor = GridBagConstraints.EAST;
      getContentPane().add(okPanel, e);
   }
```

In this method, define the layout of the Object Configuration dialog using the Java Swing classes.

1. Method `setAction`

```
   /* (non-Javadoc)
    * @see com.sap.xmii.xacute.actions.shared.AbstractActionDialog#setA
ction(java.lang.Object)
    */
   protected void setAction(Object obj) {
      Object actionObject = super.getAction();
      //set the input field value from the action
}
```

In this method, the input field values in the configuration dialog are set from the pre-existing values of the action configuration. You can access the current action object from the super class method `getAction()`, which should be typecast to the custom action class type. Get the class attribute values from the action object using the getter methods, and assign them to the input field class attributes of the dialog class.

1. Method `performOK`

```
   /* (non-Javadoc)
    * @see com.sap.xmii.xacute.actions.shared.AbstractActionDialog#perf
ormOK()
    */
   protected boolean performOK() throws Exception {
      Object actionObject = super.getAction();
      //set the action attribute values from the input field value
      return true;
   }
```

This method is executed when the OK button is clicked on the configuration dialog. Inside this method, pass the values of the input fields to the action object. You can get the action object by the super class method `getAction()`, and you should typecast to the custom action class type.

Finally, after developing and building the classes, create an XML file where you need to specify the class name, assembly file name, dependency, and so on. In this XML file, you can also specify multiple action block classes to be uploaded and deployed together. Create the new XML file name as catalog.xml. A sample XML file is as follows.

> **Example**
>
> The following is an example of a sample catalog.xml:
>
> ```
> <ComponentCatalog>
> <Category Name="ExcelFileUtils" Description="Utilities for Excel File
> Handling">
> <Component Type="Action" Name="Excel2XML" Description=""
> Label="Excel to XML" ClassName="com.sappress.mii.customaction.
> Excel2XML" AssemblyName="FileUtils.jar" Dependencies="A.jar"
> HelpFileName="http://www.mysite.com/miicustomaction/actionname"/>
> </Category>
> </ComponentCatalog>
> ```

The XML starts with the `ComponentCatalog` element as its root element. Under that, in the `Category` element, specify the category of the action block in the BLS Transaction. Each action block in the BLS editor is displayed in the Actions configuration pane, grouped under specific action block categories (specified by the category name in the XML). The `Component` element specifies the details of the action blocks deployed. Add the `Component` element as a child of the `Category` element, and specify `Action` in the `Type` attribute. Specify the name and description of the action block in the `Name` and `Description` attributes, and the text to be displayed on the action block in the `Label` attribute. Specify the Java class created for the action block, with its full package name, in the `ClassName` attribute. The `AssemblyName` attribute specifies the Java Archive (JAR) filename for the action block class files, and `Dependencies` specifies the JAR filename of the Java libraries used in the action block class implementation. You should not specify XMII.JAR in Dependencies, because it is always available as part of the SAP MII runtime when the action block is deployed in the WebAS. Specify the help file URL, if any, in the `HelpFileName` attribute. For each action block deployed, different Component elements must be added in the catalog.xml file.

After the catalog.xml file is ready, you need to create the assembly file as specified in the `AssemblyName`. The assembly file should be a JAR file containing the action block Java classes, any images, and the catalog.xml file. Place the catalog.xml file at the root of the Java project folder of the action block, and create the JAR file using the following command line:

```
jar -cf <assemblyname>.jar catalog.xml <classname>
```

You should specify the class name with the full package path, if any, for example, *./com/sappress/mii/customaction/*.** or *./com/sappress/mii/customaction/myactionclass.java*. If resource files are also present in the class folder, use the previous class name pattern, which includes all files present inside the class folder in the JAR file.

After the assembly file is created, you must upload and deploy it in SAP MII. Close all SAP MII Workbench sessions and temporarily stop all running transactions before uploading the custom actions. Navigate to SYSTEM MANAGEMENT • CUSTOM ACTIONS in the SAP MII main menu, and click on Upload. Specify the assembly JAR filename in the Assembly File, and the dependent JAR files in Dependency Files. Click Save. After you have saved, check the checkbox beside the line entry and click on Deploy. This deploys the custom actions and their dependencies in the WebAS. The custom actions are now available under the specified action category in any BLS Transaction editor. If they are not visible in the Workbench, clearing the Java cache usually solves the issue.

In this section you have learned how to create and deploy custom action blocks, which you can develop to incorporate any custom logic in BLS Transactions. In the next section, you learn how to optimize transactions for better performance by using XPath expressions in BLS Transactions.

9.2 Using XPath Expressions in BLS Transactions

In this section you learn how to optimize BLS Transactions using XPath expressions for XML parsing. XPath is an abbreviation for XML Path Language, and it enables you to easily select nodes in an XML document using a path-like notation. XPath also has various functions that enable you to manipulate the document nodes and their data.

Because XML is used heavily in BLS Transactions in many action blocks as input or output parameters, all expressions that you define using them, either in Object Configuration or in Link Configuration, are essentially XPath expressions. Technically, you do not need to know much about XPath expressions because they can be easily configured and managed using the Object Configuration and Link Configuration. However, a working knowledge of them gives you the edge in creating optimized BLS Transactions that perform more efficiently. For example, XPath expressions are especially useful when you need to access specific values from a large amount of data.

The following simple example shows how you can simplify a transaction using XPath expressions. In this example, we query the PlasticBottleBatchData table in the PlasticResin database, and filter out the batches that produce red-colored bottles. The color of a batch is stored in a column of the same name, and the filtration can easily be done in the SQL query itself by defining a filter expression of COLOR = RED. However, for the sake of this example, pretend this is not an option (which might actually be the case if the data is coming from a non-SQL data source where filtering at the query level is not possible). The only other option left is to use a Repeater action block at the query results, followed by a Conditional action block that checks for the same filter criteria just mentioned. The transaction details are shown in Figure 9.1.

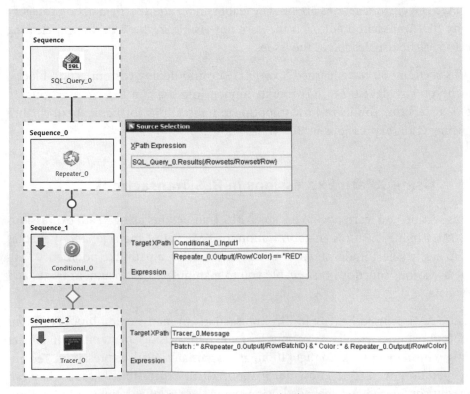

Figure 9.1 BLS Transaction Configuration without XPath Filtering Expression

The output of this transaction would give you just what you want, that is, batches that produce red-colored bottles, as shown in Figure 9.2.

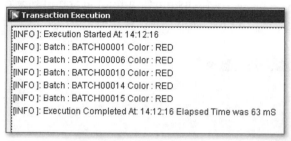

Figure 9.2 Output of the BLS Transaction without XPath Filter Expression

However, here is a caveat. The Repeater in the preceding case would have to loop through all the rows returned by the SQL query before the Conditional block filters them out. Therefore, if the query returns, for example, one thousand rows, the repeater would have to iterate through them all. And if the number of rows returned by the SQL query is large, the Repeater action block would be a significant performance hit.

But what if you could filter out the results at the Repeater action block to loop only on the Rows that satisfied the filter criteria for the color of the bottles? XPath enables you do just that. Now take a look at the XPath expression at the configuration screen of the Repeater: `SQL_Query_0.Results{/Rowsets/Rowset/Row}`. This expression tells the Repeater to loop on each of the `Row` nodes under `Rowsets` and `Rowset`. If you want to tell the Repeater to loop only on those Rows that have a value of RED, you need to rewrite the XPath expression as follows: `SQL_Query_0.Results{/Rowsets/Rowset/Row[Color='RED']}`. This is shown in Figure 9.3.

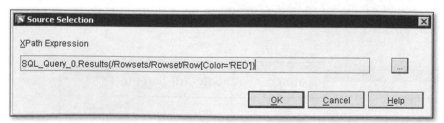

Figure 9.3 XPath Expression with Filter in Repeater Action Block Configuration

This expression would also eliminate the need for the Conditional action block below the Repeater.

Now, upon executing the modified Transaction sans the Conditional action block, you see the same output shown earlier in the chapter (Figure 9.4).

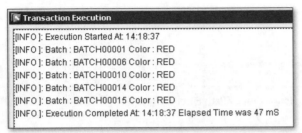

Figure 9.4 Output of the Modified BLS Transaction with XPath Filter Expression

Notice the difference in the execution times in the two transactions. Though the database table had only 18 rows while executing, there was a significant decrease in the execution time, from 63 milliseconds to 47 milliseconds.

Now consider the same scenario, but this time you want to pass the color of the batch as a variable of the transaction through a transaction property. To enable this, you create a transaction property of the type Input called BatchColor, in which you can specify the color of the batch you want to select. How do you ensure that you are using the XPath expression you defined for the Repeater block? The answer is simple: use Dynamic Substitution, where the value of the color by which the data is filtered gets substituted at runtime.

Dynamic Substitution, though it can be done manually, becomes much easier to do when you use the built-in XPath Selection screen. This is opened by clicking the button with the ellipsis (...) in the Object Configuration of the Repeater action, as shown in Figure 9.5.

Figure 9.5 Launch XPath Selector Screen

In the XPath Selection Screen, delete the hard-coded value RED, select the transaction variable BatchColor, and click on the Insert Dynamic Link button (Figure 9.6). If you want to specify the value of the property instead, click on the Insert Property Value button. The final Link Configuration should look like `SQL_Query_0.Results{/Rowsets/Rowset/Row[Color='#Transaction.BatchColor#']}`, as in Figure 9.6.

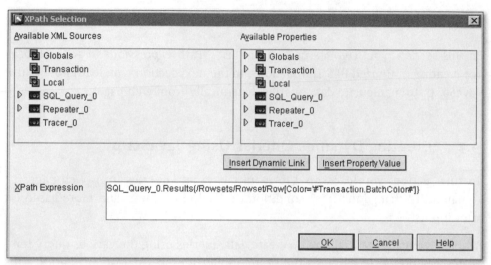

Figure 9.6 XPath Selection Configuration

Now you define a value of YELLOW for the transaction property BatchColor and then execute the transaction. The `#Transaction.BatchColor#` placeholder in the preceding XPath expression is replaced dynamically at runtime with the value passed, and only the batches that produced yellow-colored bottles are returned.

Though we took the general example of a Repeater action block because this is where user defined XPath expressions are most used, bear in mind that you can use them for virtually all SAP MII action block configuration and links.

> **Note**
>
> XPath also provides the best way of counting the number of occurrences of a particular XML node in an XML document. For example, if you want to count the number of rows returned by a SQL query, the XPath function `count()` can be used to determine this without the use of any complicated logic or the Repeater action block.
>
> `SQL_Query_0.Results{count(/Rowsets/Rowset/Row)}` returns the number of row nodes in the result of the SQL query, and thus the row count of the returned data.

In this section, you have learned how to use XPath expressions in action blocks for creating optimized BLS Transactions. In the next section, you learn how to use JavaScript to manipulate data queries dynamically from web pages.

9.3   Creating Dynamic Queries Using JavaScript

In this section, you learn how to manipulate data queries from web pages to dynamically change the filter conditions, selection columns, and more based on user inputs.

You have already learned how to create data queries using the various query templates (Chapter 4 Developing Composite Applications in SAP MII: The Basics). This section is an advanced look at data queries, where we manipulate the queries at runtime using JavaScript.

All data queries have corresponding getter and setter methods in JavaScript. These methods enable you to set virtually all the parameters of the query that can be manually configured in the query template. For example, in the case of a SQL query, you can configure the columns the query returns, the filter expression to filter the data, and a Sort and Group expression.

Now we take a small example to show you how a simple SQL query can be modified to filter the data returned. The scenarios that we take a look at involve:

▶ Returning only a fixed count of rows of data

▶ Displaying only the columns that we want

▶ Sorting the data according to any field we specify

We use the PlasticResinBatchData query template for this example, which queries a database table to get the batch information.

First, you create an HTML page to display the batch list data in an iGrid. The required HTML code to do so is as follows.

Example

```
<html>
<head>
<title>Dynamic Query</title>
</head>
<body>
<APPLET NAME="batchList" WIDTH="600" HEIGHT="400" CODE="iGrid" CODE-
BASE="/XMII/Classes" ARCHIVE="illum8.zip" MAYSCRIPT>
<PARAM NAME="QueryTemplate" VALUE=" SAPMIIESSENTIALS/Examples/Batch/
PlasticBottleBatchDataQT">
</APPLET>
</body>
</html>
```

This displays a list of all the batches in the iGrid applet that are there in the database table.

9.3.1 Dynamically Specifying Selection Columns

Now suppose that you need only to display the OrderNo, BatchID, and Color columns at runtime. Simple JavaScript enables you to achieve this end. Specify the columns for selection in the input of the `setColumns(ColumnsList)` method of the `QueryObject`, as a command-delimitated string. Refer to the code in the example that, which you can add in a JavaScript function and is executed on CREATION-EVENT of the applet or on any other user event, such as button click:

```
document.batchList.getQueryObject().setColumns("BatchID, OrderNo,
Color");
document.batchList.refresh();
```

9.3.2 Limiting Number of Rows of Data Returned

If you want to limit the rows of data returned by a query, you can achieve that using JavaScript by invoking the `setRowcount(NumberofRows)` method, where you can specify the number of rows to be selected by the query. Sample code follows:

```
document.batchList.getQueryObject().setRowcount(5);
document.batchList.refresh();
```

9.3.3 Filtering Data

What if you want to see only data filtered by the values of a particular column, such as batches that produce green-colored bottles? JavaScript enables you to set a filter expression to the query at runtime. Ideally, the filter expression is the part of the SQL statement after the where clause. The following piece of JavaScript should do the trick:

```
document.batchList.getQueryObject().setFilterExpr("Color = 'GREEN'");
document.batchList.refresh();
```

You can join multiple filter expressions together, just as in the case of a SQL statement, using the AND or OR operator; for example, `Color = GREEN AND OrderNo = ORDER00003`.

9.3.4 Sorting Data

Sorting data in single or multiple columns enables you to do a comparative study of the data. You can sort the data at the data source using JavaScript by using the `setSortExpr()` method. For example, if you want to sort the batch list in descending order on the basis of their `MeltingPt` column, the JavaScript code looks as follows:

```
document.batchList.getQueryObject().setSortExpr("MeltingPt DESC");
document.batchList.refresh();
```

As with the filter expression, you can define multiple columns, for example, "`MeltingPt, ChipsPerGram ASC`". The keywords `ASC` and `DESC` refer to the way the data is sorted, namely, in ascending or descending order, respectively.

In this section you have learned about JavaScript dynamic query manipulation techniques, which enable you to manipulate output as required by the user. In the next section, you learn how to use table input parameters when you are executing a BAPI/RFC.

9.4 Executing a BAPI/RFC with a Table as an Input Parameter

Business APIs (BAPIs) or Remote Function Call–enabled function modules (RFCs) are two of the most common ways of retrieving or updating data from and to SAP backend systems. These are remote procedure call–enabled methods that you can invoke using SAP Java Connector (JCo) Interface or SAP Java Resource Adapter (JRA) Function action blocks to pass the input and table parameters in XML format. This procedure is fairly easy when remote function call–enabled function modules have simple input parameters, such as single parameters or structures, but things get trickier when they have tables as input.

We want to take an example and walk you through the process of invoking a BAPI — BAPI_PRODORDCONF_CREATE_TT — which we use to create Time Ticket Production Order Confirmations. This BAPI is often used in SAP Enterprise Resource Planning (ERP) and has a TIMETICKETS parameter as input, an ideal case for the current scenario.

9.4.1 Solution Overview

The approach involves creating two local parameters in the Business Logic Transaction; call them BAPITABLEROW and BAPIINPUTSTRUCTURE. The parameter BAPITABLEROW stores a single row and, when it has been populated, appends the row to BAPIINPUTSTRUCTURE, which ideally should consist of the whole table input structure of the BAPI, the table TIMETICKETS, but without any rows. After you build the table structure, the only step that remains is to assign the whole modified BAPIINPUTSTRUCTURE to the input structure of BAPI_PRODOR-DCONF_CREATE_TT in the SAP JCo Interface action block.

9.4.2 Solution Walkthrough

First create a local property in the Business Logic Transaction: BAPITimeTickets of data type XML. This should correspond to a single row of the TIMETICKETS table. The item node must be present below the root node to represent an RFC table row in BLS and should look like the one shown in Figure 9.7.

> **Note**
>
> To define the XML structure of the local or transaction properties you can specify the default value with the XML when you are defining them or can use a Reference Document Loader action to specify the structure using sample XML.

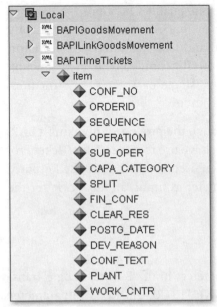

Figure 9.7 Structure of the BAPITimeTickets Local Property

The next local property that you need to create should have the Input and Tables parameters of the BAPI, but with no rows beneath TIMETICKETS, which is the only Tables parameter that you need to populate. Call this parameter BAPIRequest-InputXML, as shown in Figure 9.8. This property should be of the type Xml.

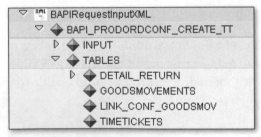

Figure 9.8 Structure of the BAPIRequestInputXML Local Property

The next logical step is to create rows of the TIMETICKETS table. If you are using a Repeater to loop on rows of a structure, assign the value of each parameter from the output of the Repeater to the corresponding parameter in the BAPITimeTickets property structure. Then, append the structure to the TIMETICKETS table parameter in the BAPIRequestInputXML property. Refer to Figure 9.9 and Figure 9.10 to see how this should be done.

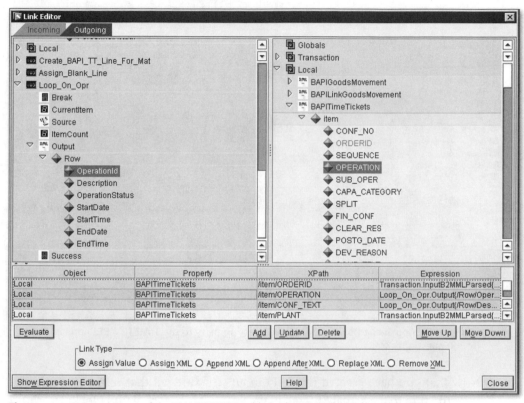

Figure 9.9 Creating Rows of the TIMETICKETS table in the BAPITimeTickets Local Property

Inside the Repeater loop, add another assignment action block to append the item rows to the TIMETICKETS table node in BAPIRequestInputXML. In the Link Editor, select the item node of the BAPITimeTickets property on the left, and the TIMETICKETS node of the BAPIRequestInputXML on the right (Figure 9.10). To append the items, use the Append XML Link Type and click on Add.

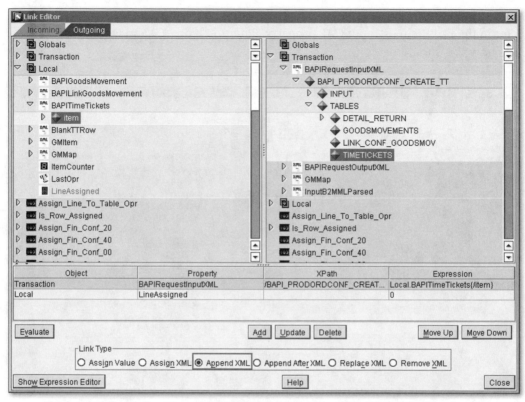

Figure 9.10 Appending Rows of BAPITimeTickets property to the TIMETICKETS node of the BAPIRequestInputXML

Now that you have created the BAPI input structure, all that remains is to assign this structure to the actual RFC call in the SAP JCo Interface action block. To achieve this, select Assign XML to assign the local property BAPIRequestInputXML to the input structure BAPI_PRODORDCONF_CREATE_TT, outside the upper repeater loop (Figure 9.11).

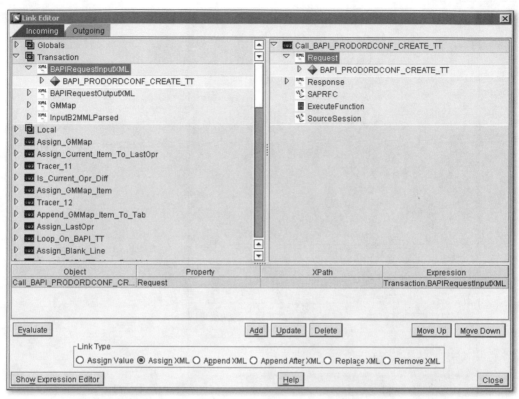

Figure 9.11 Assigning BAPIRequestInputXML to the Input Structure of the SAP JCo Action block calling BAPI_PRODORDCONF_CREATE_TT

Now, when the BAPI is executed through the SAP JCo Interface action block, it should pass all the rows of the table parameter to the actual function module in the backend.

9.4.3 An Alternative Approach

You can eliminate the BAPIRequestInputXML local property altogether and directly add the BAPITimeTickets property to the input structure of the BAPI in the SAP JCo Interface. However, to do this, you need to remove the default row that exists in the structure when the metadata of any remote function module is imported. Do this using Link Type Remove XML, as shown in Figure 9.12.

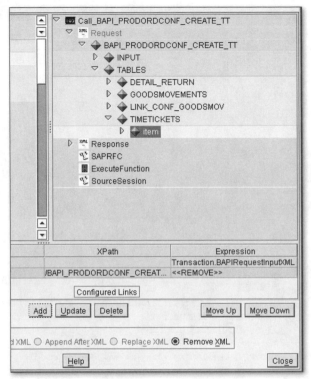

Figure 9.12 Using Remove XML for the Default Row of ITEM for the TIMETICKETS table of the BAPI_PRODORDCONF_CREATE_TT

In this section, you have learned how to use table input parameters for BAPI/RFC executed in BLS Transactions using the JCo/JRA action blocks. In the next section, you learn how to use the virtual server connectors to communicate between multiple SAP MII installations.

9.5 Using Virtual Servers for Communication Between SAP MII Servers

In an SAP MII implementation scenario with multiple plants, you will find it advisable to have one instance of SAP MII running per plant, with a separate instance at the corporate level. Ideally, the plant-level SAP MII server instances would talk and exchange data among themselves and the central instance, which would mainly serve the purpose of an analytics and reporting dashboard.

You can use virtual server connectors for integration scenarios that involve exchanging data by accessing the data servers of SAP MII server instances residing in different networks and time zones. Data servers not defined in a specific SAP MII server instance's network can still be accessed using virtual server connectors via the SAP MII server on which it is defined as a data server. The data server connector also provides an option for setting an offset to connect to servers in different time zones. This enables the retrieval of corresponding data from the target SAP MII server without changing the existing queries.

You have six types of virtual server connectors in SAP MII 12.0: VirtualAlarm, VirtualIDBC, VirtualOLAP, VirtualTAG, VirtualXML, and VirtualXacute. These correspond, respectively, to their Alarm, IDBC, OLAP, TAG, XML, and Xacute connectors, as explained in Section 3.1 Data Servers: Connecting to the Manufacturing Plant Floor, and behave in the exact same way. Therefore, using the virtual connectors enables you not only to connect to data server types such as IDBC, OLAP, or any tag-based data source, but also to invoke BLS Transactions from another SAP MII installation via the VirtualXacute connector. Using virtual connectors is faster in performance than the usual SOAP or HTTP calls, because it uses binary mode for data transfer.

To connect to the SAP MII data server using the virtual connector, you need to know the IP or machine name of the server, the user name and password of an SAP MII user who has appropriate rights to use the connector, and the name of the data server you are connecting to.

The next example demonstrates how interconnectivity can be achieved using the SAP MII virtual server connector. In this example, you try to connect to a SQL data server called PlasticResin, which has already been defined in the target SAP MII system using the IDBC connector. The first step is to define a virtual data server in the source SAP MII server to connect with this data server on the target system.

On the Data Server Configuration page, click New and select VirtualIDBC as the connector. The configuration parameters available are explained in Table 9.1.

Property	Description
DaysRetention	The number of days the entries of a buffered query should be retained in the buffer.
Description	A meaningful description of the connection.
IP	The IP address/machine name of the remote SAP MII server.
LegacyURL	Check this box to enable support for older SAP MII servers.
MaxRetryCount	Number of times to retry a connection if an attempt fails.
Port	The port to which the remote SAP MII server is listening.
Protocol	Default setting is "http"; however, this can be set to "https" if secure sockets layer (SSL) has been set up.
RemoteLoginName	The login name for the remote SAP MII server (not the remote data server) with proper access rights to the remote data source you want to access.
RemoteLoginPassword	The password for the remote SAP MII server.
RemoteServerName	The name of the data server that you want to access.
RetryInterval	Interval between retry attempts, in milliseconds.

Table 9.1 Virtual Server Configuration Properties

After you have configured the required parameters in the SAP MII server, click on Save to create a new virtual server called VirtualPlasticResin. This connects to the PlasticResin data source in the target system, as shown in Figure 9.13.

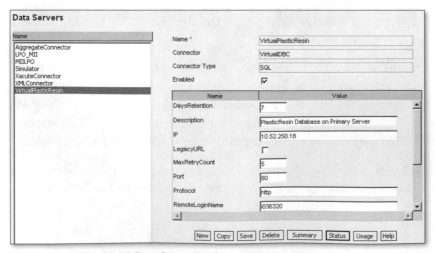

Figure 9.13 VirtualIDBC Data Server Configuration

The last step is to check whether the connection is actually working. Click on the Status button to check the server status.

You can now create data queries using the data server, which refers to another data server in a remote SAP MII installation. Launch the SAP MII Workbench and create a new SQL query template. In the Data Source View, VirtualPlasticResin should show up as an available data source. Select VirtualPlasticResin as the data source and the Mode as Query.

Shift to the SQL Query Details configuration, and, if a successful connection was made, all the tables from the remote data server should show up under the Available Tables list.

9.5.1 Troubleshooting

If the connection to the virtual server fails:

▸ Check whether the user name and password you have entered is correct. You should specify the user name and password of the remote SAP MII server, not of the remote data source.

▸ Check whether the target SAP MII server is accessible over the network.

▸ If you are accessing the remote server through a proxy server, verify whether the proxy server is configured: SYSTEM MANAGEMENT • SYSTEM ADMINISTRATION.

In this section, you have learned how to use virtual data server connectors to connect to data servers configured in remote SAP MII installations and how to create queries using these virtual servers. In the next section, you learn about the session variables available in SAP MII and how to use these variables in BLS Transactions and web reports.

9.6 Autobind and Session Variables in SAP MII

Session variables in SAP MII are used to store user- or session-specific data and can be accessed only in the current active session of the user. Other than the default session variables such as IllumLoginName, IllumLoginRoles, Machine, and so on, all custom attributes created and assigned to a user, or to a role to which the user belongs, are available as session variables in the login session of the user.

Autobind is a parameter of the Xacute connector, available in Data Services, which, when set, enables you to be automatically map session variables to Business Logic Transaction variables that have exactly the same name as the session variables. Therefore, you would need to enable Autobind on the Xacute connector to access the session variables of the logged-in user. To enable Autobind, check the Autobind checkbox in the XacuteConnector on the Data Servers configuration page and save the configuration (Figure 9.14).

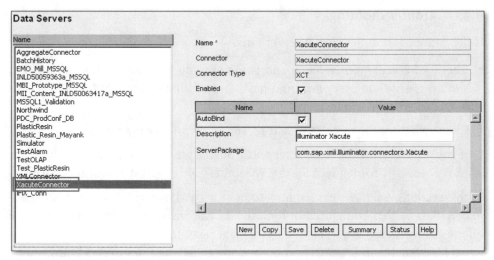

Figure 9.14 XacuteConnector Configuration with AutoBind Enabled

The question still remains as to when you would need to access session variables. One example is a case where you need to create a log file with logged-in names and date/timestamps for each logged-in user. You can retrieve the date/time values easily using the date/time functions of the BLS, but the best way of getting the logged-in user's user name would be by accessing the IllumLoginName session variable.

9.6.1 Example

Now we want to explore a very simple example that puts to use the concepts covered in this section. In the example, we create a Business Logic Transaction that prints out a simple greeting and displays the plant assignment of a logged-in user.

First you need to check out the list of session variables that are available for the logged-in user. The session variables listed in Table 9.2 are available for any user in SAP MII.

Session Variable	Description
Locale	The geographical location code of the place to where the user belongs.
UniqueName	The user name of the user.
FullName	Combination of the FirstName and LastName properties.
Machine	System from where the user is logged on to the server.
Accessibility	Indicates whether accessibility features are turned on.
Created_By	The administrator user who created this user's account.
Language	The localization language of the user.
LastName	The last name of the user.
IllumLoginName	The login name for the SAP MII Illuminator service. This is always equal to the UniqueName.
IllumLoginRoles	The UME roles assigned to this user.

Table 9.2 Common Session Variables and Their Description

Invoking *http://<servername>:<port>/XMII/PropertyAccessServlet?Mode=List* yields the result shown in Figure 9.15.

Name	Value
Color	Red
Locale	en
uniquename	i036320
FullName	Bhattacharjee, Abesh
Machine	10.52.170.106
Accessibility	false
CREATED_BY	Administrator
Language	en
lastname	Bhattacharjee
locale	en
Plant	1000
firstname	Abesh
IllumLoginName	i036320
IllumLoginRoles	'SAP_JAVA_NWADMIN_LOCAL','XMII Developers','XMII Administrators','SAP_JAVA_NWADMIN_LOCAL_READONLY','Everyone','XMII Users','SAP_JAVA_SUPPORT','Administrator','SAP_JAVA_NWADMIN_CENTRAL_READONLY','SAP_JAVA_NWADMIN_CENTRAL'

Figure 9.15 Session Variables for the Logged-In User.

In the preceding example, the custom attribute Plant, which has been mapped to the user, also shows up in the session variables list. To use the session variables in Business Logic Transactions, you need to define input or output properties having exactly the same name as that of the corresponding session variable. Now create a simple Business Logic Transaction with two transaction properties that have the same names as that of the session variables: IllumLoginName and Plant. Both would be of the string data type. You also need to create an output parameter called GreetingText of type string to hold the greeting text.

Insert an Assignment action block from LOGIC • ASSIGNMENT to the sequence and call it AssignSessionVars. The next step is to create the greeting text based on the transaction properties and assign it to the output variable GreetingText.

In the Link Editor for the AssignSessionVars action, select the Target XPath as Transaction.GreetingText and specify the value "Hello" and Transaction.IllumLoginName & "! You are assigned to Plant : " & Transaction.Plant & "." as the expression. Click on Add to create the assignment, as shown in Figure 9.16. Exit the Link Editor and save the transaction.

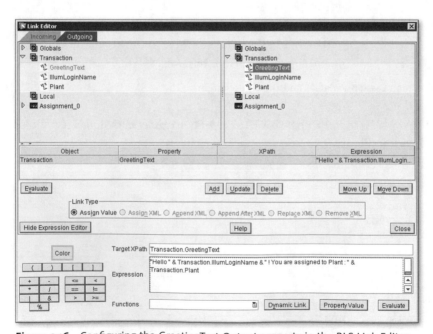

Figure 9.16 Configuring the GreetingText Output property in the BLS Link Editor

Please note that that the values of the session variables are mapped only at runtime when this transaction is invoked from a web page. Therefore, adding a Tracer Block to check the value of the transaction properties would not return any value. Do not set any values to the session variables in the Business Logic Transaction, because the values of those variables are assigned automatically by SAP MII runtime. You should use the session variables for read-only purposes.

The last step is to create an Xacute query from the transaction that you created previously. After the Xacute query has been saved, test the query. The output of the query shows that the session variables have been successfully mapped to the corresponding transaction properties at runtime, as shown in Figure 9.17.

GreetingText
Hello i036320 ! You are assigned to Plant : 1000

Figure 9.17 Output from the Xacute Query

Alternatively, you can use the session variables in an SAP MII Report (IRPT) page if required. The session variables are available to all reports, and can be accessed using the curly braces notation, for example, `{variablename}`, which is commonly used to access variables in SAP MII reports.

Now create a new SAP MII report and insert the following line of HTML in it:

```
<h5>Welcome {IllumLoginName} ! You are assigned to Plant : {Plant}.</
h5>
```

If you save and test the report, you should see exactly the same output as we saw in the previous example.

In this section, you have learned about the session variables and how to use them in BLS Transactions and IRPT web pages. In the next section, you learn how to dynamically pass data between SAP MII reports.

9.7   Dynamic Data Exchange Between SAP MII Web Pages

Composite applications developed in SAP MII generally do not consist of a single development object. Instead, they are spread over multiple development objects split according to the logical units of functionality each object is supposed to perform. A user interface of the composite application consists mainly of JavaScript (js) files, which contain the client-side scripting code, and HTML files, which are used to represent the data to the user in a visually appealing way. A composite application is thus the collaborative effort of development objects acting in harmony to exchange data and create a flow of information through seamless interaction.

9.7.1 Methods of Passing Variables Between Pages

Because HTML is a markup language that runs on the client side, it does not provide you with built-in methods of exchanging data between pages as other server-side technologies would. The only two ways of exchanging data in such a scenario are via session variables stored in session cookies on the client machine and by the use of SAP MII reports.

9.7.2 SAP MII Session Variables

To exchange data, SAP MII applets provide the methods `setPropertyValue` and `getPropertyValue`. The `setPropertyValue(PROPERTY_NAME,PROPERTY_VALUE)` method can be used to set a session variable with a name of `PROPERTY_NAME` and a value of `PROPERTY_VALUE`. This can be read from any HTML page in the same user session by calling the `getPropertyValue(PROPERTY_NAME)` method and passing the value of the `PROPERTY_NAME` on any applet present in that page. You can treat this as similar to setting a variable in code and then later retrieving the value of the variable.

Example

```
// SetBatch.html
.........
// set the value of the property "Batch" on the myGrid applet
document.myGrid1.setPropertyValue("Batch", "BATCH00001");
.........
<APPLET Name="myGrid1" CODEBASE="/XMII/Classes" CODE="iGrid"
ARCHIVE="illum8.zip" WIDTH="400" HEIGHT="200" MAYSCRIPT>
<PARAM NAME="QueryTemplate" VALUE="/SAPMIIESSENTIALS/Examples/Batch/
PlasticBottleBatchQT">
<PARAM NAME="DisplayTemplate" VALUE="/SAPMIIESSENTIALS/Examples/Batch/
PlasticBottleBatchDT">
</APPLET>
```

```
//GetBatch.html
.........
// get the value of the property "Batch"
var myBatch = document.myGrid2.getPropertyValue("Batch");

.........
<APPLET Name="myGrid2" CODEBASE="/XMII/Classes" CODE="iGrid"
ARCHIVE="illum8.zip" WIDTH="400" HEIGHT="200" MAYSCRIPT>
<PARAM NAME="QueryTemplate" VALUE="/SAPMIIESSENTIALS/Examples/Batch/
PlasticBottleBatchQT">
<PARAM NAME="DisplayTemplate" VALUE="/SAPMIIESSENTIALS/Examples/Batch/
PlasticBottleBatchDT">
</APPLET>

This would be equivalent to:
//Set the value of the variable "Batch"
var Batch = "BATCH00001";

.........
//Retrieve the value of the variable "Batch" into a new variable "my-
Batch";
var myBatch = Batch;
.........
```

Note that these session variables are accessible through pages on one session of the browser. That is, if you set a session variable and close the browser window (which destroys the session), the variable is not available for a new session when the browser window is reopened.

9.7.3   SAP MII Reports

SAP MII reports provide techniques to pass session variables between pages by HTTP GET or POST. These variables can then be accessed inside of a report (IRPT) by enclosing the name of the variable within curly braces {*variablename*}.

Example

```
//GetBatch.irpt

.........
<!-- Set the name of the Trend Chart -->
```

```
<H3>Trend for Batch: {Batch}</H3>
.........
```

You can call this page by passing the values in the URL (HTTP GET), for example, *http://<server>:<port> /CM/SAPMIIEssentials/GetBatch.irpt?Batch='BATCH00001'*

9.7.4   Weaving It All Together

We now present an example to put to use what you have learned in the previous sections. We use the PlasticBottleBatchDataQT and PlasticBottleTrendDataQT query templates and the PlasticBottleBatchDataDT and PlasticBottleTrendDataDT display templates to achieve this.

The PlasticBottleBatchDataQT returns a list of batches from the PlasticResinBatchData table in the PlasticResin database. PlasticBottleBatchDataDT displays the returned data in an iGrid applet.

The PlasticBottleTrendDataQT returns the trend data from the PlasticResinTrendData table in the PlasticResin database according to the batch that was passed as a parameter. The PlasticBottleTrendDataDT displays the trend of the data returned in an iChart applet.

To demonstrate the setPropertyValue and getPropertyValue of the applets, we script the iGrid to open a pop-up window displaying the trend of the selected batch, where the values are dynamically passed between pages.

Example

```
// DisplayBatchData.html
<!--Define the "BatchGrid" iGrid and add a handler called "batchSe-
lected" to the selection event.-->
<APPLET NAME="BatchGrid" WIDTH="600" HEIGHT="50" CODE="iGrid" CODE-
BASE="/Illuminator/Classes" ARCHIVE="illum8.zip" MAYSCRIPT>
<PARAM NAME="QueryTemplate" VALUE="SAPMIIEssentials/PlasticBottle-
BatchDataQT">
<PARAM NAME="DisplayTemplate" VALUE=" SAPMIIEssentials/PlasticBottle-
BatchDataDT">
<PARAM NAME="SelectionEvent" VALUE="batchSelected">
</APPLET>
```

```
.........
<SCRIPT>

//Implement the "batchSelected" handler to display a pop-up window
with the trend for the selected batch.
function batchSelected(){
var BatchNo = document.BatchGrid.getGridObject().getSelectedCell-
Value(1);
if (BatchNo == "") {
alert ("Please select a Batch !");
} else {
//Pass the Batch Number as a session variable to the pop-up window
document.BatchGrid.setPropertyValue("BatchNo", BatchNo);
window.open ("DisplayBatchTrend.html",null,"height=350,width=700,stat
us=yes,toolbar=no,menubar=no,location=no");
}
}

.........
</SCRIPT>
```

This example implements a handler for the Selection event of the iGrid, which passes the value of the selected batch as a session variable to the pop-up window. The implementation of the pop-up window is as follows:

Example

```
// DisplayBatchTrend.html

<!-- Define the "TrendChart" iChart and add a handler called "dis-
playTrend" to the "FirstUpdate" event. -->

<APPLET NAME="TrendChart" WIDTH="600" HEIGHT="300" CODE="iChart"
CODEBASE="/Illuminator/Classes" ARCHIVE="illum8.zip" MAYSCRIPT>

<PARAM NAME="QueryTemplate" VALUE="SAPMIIEssentials/PlasticBottle-
TrendDataQT">

<PARAM NAME="DisplayTemplate" VALUE=" SAPMIIEssentials/PlasticBottle-
TrendDataDT">

<PARAM NAME="CreationEvent" VALUE="displayTrend">

</APPLET>

.........

<SCRIPT>
```

```
function displayTrend(){
//Retrieve the value of the Batch from the session variable
var BatchNo = document.TrendChart.getPropertyValue("BatchNo");
document.TrendChart.getQueryObject().setParam(1,BatchNo);
document.TrendChart.getChartObject().setTitle("Trend for Batch : " +
BatchNo);
document.TrendChart.updateChart(true);
}
</SCRIPT>
```

The displayTrend function is triggered as soon as the iChart applet is initialized. It sets the parameter of the query template to the batch that has been passed from DisplayBatchData.html and updates the iChart applet with the graph for the required batch.

Now take a look at how you can achieve the same results using an SAP MII report. Here, instead of a grid, we manually pass the data using a form and generate the chart using a report (IRPT page). This is done using both HTTP GET and POST.

Example

```
// BatchInput.html
<!-- Form for passing the Batch value by HTTP GET -->
<form method="GET" action="DisplayBatchTrend.irpt">
Batch No : <input type="text" name="BatchNo" size="20">
<p><input type="submit" value="Submit Batch No. By GET"></p>
</form>
.........
<!-- Form for passing the Batch value by HTTP POST-->
<form method="POST" action=" DisplayBatchTrend.irpt">
Batch No : <input type="text" name="BatchNo" size="20">
<p><input type="submit" value="Submit Batch No. By POST"></p>
</form>
.........
```

This displays an HTML page with two input fields to pass the value of the batch to the DisplayBatchTrend.irpt page using both the GET and POST methods. The GET method is similar to clicking a link with the values passed as URL parameters, whereas the POST method generally submits form data.

Example

```
// DisplayBatchTrend.irpt

<APPLET NAME="TrendChart" WIDTH="670" HEIGHT="320" CODE="iChart"
CODEBASE="/Illuminator/Classes" ARCHIVE="illum8.zip" MAYSCRIPT>
<PARAM NAME="QueryTemplate" VALUE="Abesh/PlasticBottleTrendQT">
<PARAM NAME="DisplayTemplate" VALUE="Abesh/PlasticBottleTrendDT">

<!--Set the value of the Query Template Parameter using the value of
the batch passed.-->
<PARAM NAME="Param.1" VALUE="{BatchNo}">

<!--Set the title of the Chart using the value of the batch
passed.-->
<PARAM NAME="Title" VALUE="Trend for: {BatchNo}">
</APPLET>

.........
```

Depending on the values of the batch passed as a URL parameter, the trend chart should now be displayed on the report. This should work for both GET and POST.

In this section, you have learned how to use the session variables in SAP MII web pages to pass data dynamically between pages in a single session. In the next section, you learn how to implement role-based access to SAP MII web pages.

9.8 Implementing Role-Based Access to SAP MII Web Pages

Though the SAP MII portal supports role-based navigation, you have no way to ensure a role-based access to a particular HTML/IRPT page if the user knows the URL to it. You can restrict users from accessing a page only by checking the role to which they are assigned is permitted to view the page. To check the IllumLoginRoles session variable for the current role, you can create a Java Server Pages (JSP) page with the necessary code to check the user roles from the session variable IllumLoginRoles, as explained in the following example. This example checks the current user role at the server side and won't display the page if the role is not permitted.

Example

```
<html>
<head>
<title>Simple JSP Role Based Access</title>
</head>
<body>
<%
/* The UME Role required to access the page */
String roleToAccess = "GRANT_ME_ACCESS";

/* Retrieve the list of roles from the session variable IllumLogin-
Roles */
String myRoles = (String)session.getAttribute("IllumLoginRoles") ;

/* Check for the existence of the required role */
if (myRoles.indexOf(roleToAccess) != -1 ){

/* Role present, grant access */
out.println("<h3>Access Granted !</h3>");
}else{

/* Role absent, deny access */
out.println("<h3>Access Denied !</h3>");
}
%>
</body>
</html>
```

In this section, you have learned how to implement role-based access in SAP MII web pages. In the next section, you learn about the SAP MII HTTP services, which enable you to retrieve system and user information.

9.9   SAP MII Services: The Power Behind SAP MII

SAP MII services, also called Illuminator services, are a set of HTTP services that provide some of the core functionalities of the SAP MII application. You can invoke these services externally by XML message exchange. SAP MII services are the power behind SAP MII because they provide the functionalities of query templates, display templates, schedulers, security and system information, and more, all of which are used by the different modules in SAP MII.

Access to these services is configured in the SECURITY SERVICES • SYSTEM SECURITY menu, as explained in Section 2.3.1 System Security. Some of these services have input and output parameters and can be invoked externally as an HTTP services by a URL, whereas others are more internal to the system and should not be called externally. These services accept the input parameter values as query string parameters in the URL and return the required information in SAP MII XML messages format.

Each Illuminator service has a service name and one or more modes, which are like operations of a service. When you are executing the services, you must specify both the service name and modes; you must also specify the input parameters, if there are any. Most of the services have a mode called modeList, which returns the list of modes available for that service. The services can be called programmatically by sending HTTP requests, or just tested in a web browser by its URL. These services can be executed from web pages (using AJAX) or from Business Logic Services (using the HTTP POST action block), and the response XML can be parsed accordingly. You can use them in the SAP MII composite applications for various purposes, for example, checking user roles or profile information, getting server information, or manipulating the SAP MII scheduler.

The services are executed by a URL of the following pattern:

http://<server>:<port>/XMII/Illuminator?service=<servicename>&mode=<modename>& content-type=text/xml

Some of the useful services available in SAP MII 12.0 are as follows:

▸ Admin

▸ Scheduler

▸ SystemInfo

We now discuss the list of modes available in each of these services.

9.9.1 Admin Service

You use the Admin Service to retrieve the administrative and security information of the SAP MII server. The modeList mode (*http://<server>:<port>/XMII/Illuminat or?service=admin&mode=modelist&content-type=text/xml*) specifies the list of modes available for this service. These are as follows:

▸ **ContentList:** Retrieves the list of navigation links and their details created in the Navigation Services • Link Editor menu (*http://<server>:<port>/XMII/Illu minator?service=admin&mode=ContentList*).

▸ **CurrentProfile:** Retrieves the user profile of the current user, which includes user name, full name, roles, email ID, and navigation items and links (*http://<server>:<port>/XMII/Illuminator?service=admin&mode=CurrentProfile*).

▸ **DBInit:** Re-initializes the delivered database content of the SAP MII server. Additional parameter Type=All can be used in the URL, which re-initializes both the profiles and projects. Otherwise, it just updates the original projects delivered with the system. This should not be used unless the re-initialization is required (*http://<server>:<port>/XMII/Illuminator?service=admin&mode=DBInit*).

▸ **FullProfile:** Retrieves the full profile of the role or user specified in the additional parameter Group (*http://<server>:<port>/XMII/Illuminator?service=admin &mode=FullProfile&Group=<user or role>*), which includes roles and navigation items.

▸ **GetResource:** Retrieves string resources based on the resource file name and the specified language. These are typically required for translating the screen labels to different languages. Valid values for the resource file names are as follows: *UserStringResources, Messages, ErrorMessages and Applet. (http://<server>:<port>/ XMII/Illuminator?service=admin&mode=GetResource&language=<LanguageCode>& FileName=<ResourceFileName>*).

▸ **AddResource:** Adds a language resource file to the server specified by the File-Name parameter (*http://<server>:<port>/XMII/Illuminator?service=admin&mode= AddResource&language=<LanguageCode>&FileName=<UserStringResources>*).

▸ **Inspector:** Retrieves the list of methods supported by the applet class specified in the additional parameter Name (*http://<server>:<port>/XMII/Illuminator?service =admin&mode=Inspector&Name=<AppletClassName>*).

▸ **PermissionList:** Retrieves the security services and their mapping to different roles as configured in the Security Services • System Security menu (*http://<server>:<port>/XMII/Illuminator?service=admin&mode=PermissionList*).

▸ **ProfileEditor:** Used to modify the profile of user or role specified in the URL parameter Group. The user profile data has to be passed in the parameter Payload. The service is invoked by the following URL: *http://<server>:<port>/XMII/Illumin ator?service=admin&mode=ProfileEditor&Group=<user/role>&Payload=<XMLdata>*.

▶ **RoleAttribList:** Retrieves the attributes of a role or user specified by the additional parameter Group (*http://<server>:<port>/XMII/Illuminator?service=admin&mode=RoleAttribList&Group=<role/username>*).

▶ **RoleList:** Retrieves the list of roles available for the user or group specified in the Group parameter (*http://<server>:<port>/XMII/Illuminator?service=admin&mode=RoleList&Group=<role/username>*).

▶ **RoleProfile:** Retrieves the profile details (that is, navigation items assigned to the role specified in the Group parameter) (*http://<server>:<port>/XMII/Illuminator?service=admin&mode= RoleProfile&Group=<GroupName>*).

▶ **SessionList:** Retrieves the current logged-in user session details, which include user name, full name, and session expiration time (*http://<server>:<port>/XMII/Illuminator?service=admin&mode=SessionList*).

▶ **SystemList:** Retrieves the system properties of the SAP MII server configured in the SYSTEM MANAGEMENT • SYSTEM ADMINISTRATION menu (*http://<server>:<port>/XMII/Illuminator?service=admin&mode=SystemList*).

▶ **UserAttribList:** Retrieves the attributes with their values of the current logged-in user, or the user specified by the additional parameter Mask (*http://<server>:<port>/XMII/Illuminator?service=admin&mode=UserAttribList&Mask=<MaskName>*).

▶ **UserList:** Retrieves the list of users available in the system or as specified in Group parameter. The Group parameter accepts the name of a Role or Group as values (*http://<server>:<port>/XMII/Illuminator?service=admin&mode=UserList&Group=<Role/GroupName>*).

▶ **UserProfile:** Retrieves the profile attributes of the specified user in the Group parameter (*http://<server>:<port>/XMII/Illuminator?service=admin&mode=UserProfile&Group=<GroupName>*).

▶ **Who:** Retrieves the user name of the current logged-in user (*http://<server>:<port>/XMII/Illuminator?service=admin&mode=Who*).

9.9.2   Scheduler Service

You use the Scheduler service to programmatically control the SAP MII scheduler by HTTP calls. The modeList mode (*http://<server>:<port>/XMII/Illuminator?service=Scheduler&mode=modelist&content-type=text/xml*) specifies the list of modes available for this service. These are as follows:

▶ **Start:** Starts the SAP MII scheduler. (*http://<server>:<port>/XMII/Illuminator? service=Scheduler&mode=Start*).

▶ **Run:** Runs a scheduled job at the current instance. The Job ID needs to be specified using the additional parameter ID. (*http://<server>:<port>/XMII/Illuminator ?service=Scheduler&mode=Run&ID=<JobID>*).

▶ **Stop:** Stops the SAP MII scheduler (*http://<server>:<port>/XMII/Illuminator?service =Scheduler&mode=Stop*).

▶ **List:** Retrieves the list of scheduled jobs in the scheduler (*http://<server>:<port>/ XMII/Illuminator?service=Scheduler&mode=List*).

▶ **Import:** Imports scheduled job details from an XML file that has been exported from another SAP MII server. The XML file should be passed as the HTTP message payload (*http://<server>:<port>/XMII/Illuminator?service=Scheduler&mode= Import*).

▶ **Export:** Exports the details of a scheduled job in the scheduler in XML format. The Job ID needs to be specified in the additional parameter ID (*http://<server>: <port>/XMII/Illuminator?service=Scheduler&mode=Export&ID=<JobID>*).

▶ **History:** Retrieves the run history of a specific job specified by the ID parameter (*http://<server>:<port>/XMII/Illuminator?service=Scheduler&mode=History&ID=< JobID>*).

▶ **Enable:** Enables a scheduled job specified by the ID parameter (*http://<server>: <port>/XMII/Illuminator?service=Scheduler&mode=Enable&ID=<JobID>*).

▶ **Disable:** Disables a scheduled job specified by the ID parameter (*http://<server>:<port>/XMII/Illuminator?service=Scheduler&mode=Disable&ID=< JobID>*).

▶ **Delete:** Deletes a scheduled job specified by the ID parameter (*http://<server>: <port>/XMII/Illuminator?service=Scheduler&mode=Delete&ID=<JobID>*).

9.9.3   SystemInfo Service

You use the SystemInfo service to get the system-related information of SAP MII, which includes a list of data servers, SAP servers, host information, and uptime. The modeList mode (*http://<server>:<port>/XMII/Illuminator?service=SystemInfo&m ode=modelist&content-type=text/xml*) specifies the list of modes available for this service. These are as follows:

▸ **Configuration:** Retrieves the system properties of the SAP MII server configured in the SYSTEM MANAGEMENT • SYSTEM ADMINISTRATION menu (*http://<server>:<port>/XMII/Illuminator?service=SystemInfo&mode=Configuration*).

▸ **CurrentProfile:** Retrieves the profile of the current logged-in user, which includes the roles and navigation item details assigned to the user (*http://<server>:<port>/ XMII/Illuminator?service=SystemInfo&mode=CurrentProfile*).

▸ **HostInfo:** Retrieves the hostname and IP address of the current system (*http://<server>:<port>/XMII/Illuminator?service=SystemInfo&mode=HostInfo*).

▸ **JavaRunFinalizer:** Runs the finalization methods of any objects pending for finalization in the Java virtual machine (JVM) of the server. Executing the finalization method suggests that the JVM should try running the finalize methods of objects that have been found to be discarded, but whose finalize methods have not yet been run. When control returns from the method call, the virtual machine has made a best effort to complete all outstanding finalizations (*http://<server>:<port>/XMII/Illuminator?service=SystemInfo&mode–JavaRunFinalizer*).

▸ **JavaRunGC:** Runs the Java garbage collector in the server. Executing the GC function suggests that the JVM should try recycling unused objects to make the memory they currently occupy available for quick reuse. When control returns from the method call, the virtual machine has made its best effort to recycle all discarded objects (*http://<server>:<port>/XMII/Illuminator?service=SystemInfo& mode= JavaRunGC*).

▸ **JavaRunTimeStatus:** Retrieves the current status of the JVM in the server, which includes memory status, number of processors, and so on (*http://<server>:<port>/ XMII/Illuminator?service=SystemInfo&mode=JavaRunTimeStatus*).

▸ **JavaThreadStatus:** Retrieves the list of current runtime threads in the JVM of the server (*http://<server>:<port>/XMII/Illuminator?service=SystemInfo&mode=Java ThreadStatus*).

▸ **RoleList:** Retrieves the list of roles available in the server (*http://<server>:<port>/ XMII/Illuminator?service=SystemInfo&mode=RoleList*).

▸ **SAPServerInfo:** Retrieves information about a specific SAP server alias configured in the DATA SERVICES • SAP SERVER EDITOR menu. The SAP server alias name is specified in the Name parameter (*http://<server>:<port>/XMII/Illuminat or?service=SystemInfo&mode=SAPServerInfo&Name=<SAPServername>*).

▶ **ScheduleList:** Retrieves the list of time period schedules configured in the DATA SERVICES • TIME PERIOD SCHEDULES menu (*http://<server>:<port>/XMII/Illuminat or?service=SystemInfo&mode=ScheduleList*).

▶ **ScheduleAttribList:** Retrieves the list of time period schedules configured in the system along with their time periods (*http://<server>:<port>/XMII/Illuminator? service=SystemInfo&mode=ScheduleAttribList*).

▶ **ScheduleDetailList:** Retrieves the details of time period schedules specified by the Group parameter (*http://<server>:<port>/XMII/Illuminator?service=SystemInfo &mode=ScheduleDetailList&group=<schedulename>*).

▶ **ServerList:** Retrieves the list of data servers configured in the DATA SERVICES • DATA SERVERS menu. You specify the status of the server to be retrieved by the Mask parameter (*http://<server>:<port>/XMII/Illuminator?service=SystemInfo& mode=ServerList&Mask=<Enabled|Disabled|All>*).

▶ **ServerAttribList:** Retrieves the list of data servers and their configuration details available in the system (*http://<server>:<port>/XMII/Illuminator?service=System Info&mode=ServerAttribList&&Group=<servername>&Mask=<Enabled|Disabled| All>*).

▶ **ServerInfo:** Retrieves the list of data servers and their configuration details available in the system. This mode is similar to the ServerAttribList mode, except that this mode returns the server attribute details in the form of key value pairs, unlike the other, which returns the information in predefined XML metadata. The data server name is specified in the Name parameter (*http://<server>:<port>/ XMII/Illuminator?service=SystemInfo&mode=ServerInfo&Name=<servername>*).

▶ **ServiceList:** Retrieves the list of services available in the system security, which can be configured in the SECURITY SERVICES • SYSTEM SECURITY menu (*http://<server>:<port>/XMII/Illuminator?service=SystemInfo&mode=ServiceList*).

▶ **Status:** Retrieves the status of the data server available in the system, which includes the number of connections used, available connections, maximum connections used, and maximum wait time (*http://<server>:<port>/XMII/Illumin ator?service=SystemInfo&mode=Status*).

▶ **TimePeriodList:** Retrieves the list of time periods available in the system configured in the DATA SERVICES • TIME PERIODS menu (*http://<server>:<port>/XMII/ Illuminator?service=SystemInfo&mode=TimePeriodAttribList*).

- ▶ **TimePeriodAttribList:** Retrieves the list of time periods with their details available in the system (*http://<server>:<port>/XMII/Illuminator?service=SystemInfo&mode=TimePeriodList*).

- ▶ **UpTime:** Retrieves the information about the uptime of the SAP MII server, which includes the time when the server was last started and the time between the current time and the last startup (*http://<server>:<port>/XMII/Illuminator?service=SystemInfo&mode=UpTime*).

- ▶ **UserList:** Retrieves the list of users available in the system (*http://<server>:<port>/XMII/Illuminator?service=SystemInfo&mode=UserList*).

Using these services, you can access various system and user information that can be used in Business Logic Transactions or web pages.

9.10 Summary

In this chapter, you have learned some advanced tips and tricks to optimize and develop better solutions in SAP MII composite applications. In the next chapter, you will learn about the implementation architectural scenarios, along with various implementation considerations, troubleshooting tips, and best practices.

This chapter explains the different SAP MII implementation scenarios, including the solution architectures and best practices to follow for development and implementation.

10 Implementing SAP MII Composite Applications

SAP MII is a solution development platform and an integration and intelligence platform, mostly suitable for manufacturing plant floors. As such, you need to know about the various possible solution architectures, development best practices, troubleshooting tips, and implementation scenarios, all of which are important for implementing SAP MII in an enterprise. We cover all of these points in this chapter to help architects, consultants, and developers deliver better solutions.

In the following section, you learn about the steps and best practices you can follow for specifying, designing, and developing SAP MII composite applications.

10.1 Specifying and Designing SAP MII Composite Applications

Applications or solutions developed in SAP MII are composite applications that integrate different enterprise business systems (such as SAP Enterprise Resource Planning (ERP) or SAP Business Intelligence (BI)) with manufacturing plant-floor systems (such as Laboratory Information Management System (LIMS), Supervisory Control And Data Acquisition (SCADA), Manufacturing Execution System (MES), or Historian) and provide analysis dashboards for manufacturing personnel. When you are defining or analyzing an SAP MII implementation project, you need to understand the existing system landscape and high-level requirement scenarios involved.

10.1.1 Collecting Information Using a Pre-Implementation Questionnaire

In most of the SAP MII implementation projects, the initial definition phase might start with a mission statement: "…integrating the manufacturing plant floor with the enterprise." However, this is a broad statement, and it is a good idea to start collecting more specific information using a pre-implementation questionnaire. The objective of the questionnaire is to gain a better understanding of the existing systems with which SAP MII is to interact and the high-level business scenarios to be addressed in the project. This information helps you perform the gap analysis. You might collect the information under the following categories:

▶ **SAP NetWeaver Platform:** This might decide the release of SAP MII that can be implemented (for example, SAP MII 11.5 for pre-SAP NetWeaver 7.0 or non-SAP platforms; SAP MII 12.0 for SAP Netweaver 7.0).

▶ **Enterprise Systems:** This gives you an idea about what enterprise systems (for example, SAP ERP, SAP BI, legacy applications, and so on) are relevant for the project.

▶ **Manufacturing Systems:** This gives you an idea about the manufacturing systems (for example, MES, LIMS, SCADA, legacy, and so on) that are integrated with SAP MII, the data connectors available, and more. Check SAP Note 943237 for the list of connectors and systems supported by SAP MII.

▶ **Business Scenarios:** This gives you an idea about the high-level requirements and business processes that need to be implemented. Some of the most common requirements addressed by SAP MII implementation projects are as follows:

  ▶ Manufacturing Order Synchronization

  ▶ Manufacturing Order Confirmation

  ▶ Material Batch Management

  ▶ Inventory Synchronization

  ▶ Inventory Replenishment Requests

  ▶ Goods Movement (Receipt/Issue)

  ▶ Quality Inspection

  ▶ Plant Maintenance Notification

  ▶ Machine Downtime Capturing and Analysis

- ▶ **Report/Analysis:** This gives you an idea about the user interfaces and the analysis dashboards to be developed. You can include the following common categories:

  - ▶ Data Report (Grid)

  - ▶ Charts (Bar, Pie, Line, Area, Linear Regression, Gauge, Polar)

  - ▶ SPC Analysis/Histogram

  - ▶ Real-Time Monitoring Dashboard

Apart from the preceding points, information about the estimated data transaction rate through SAP MII, the number of manufacturing plant-floor systems, number of deployment sites, and whether or not seamless connectivity available between enterprise and plants can also be collected. This helps in determining the performance and architectural approach.

10.1.2 Specifying the SAP MII Implementation Requirements

In the next phase, specify the business requirements in detail by preparing the functional specification documents. You can use the following steps to specify the requirements:

- ▶ Identify the specific business processes that need to be implemented, with detailed explanations of the process steps.

- ▶ Identify the business services derived from the process steps.

- ▶ Identify the applications and systems providing those business services. This can include the existing applications and new applications.

- ▶ Determine whether or not to build or buy the new applications. If the services are generalized or specific to a domain, they can be addressed by specialized applications available. Otherwise, for specific custom requirements, you can use SAP MII as a development and deployment platform.

- ▶ Identify the integration scenarios to be addressed by SAP MII. Typically, these scenarios can include integrating Level 2 and Level 3 applications and systems (MES, Historian, LIMS, and so on) with the manufacturing plant floor and the enterprise applications (ERP, BI, and so on).

- ▶ Identify the human activities (for example, user interfaces for reports, dashboards, and so on).

10.1.3 Designing the SAP MII Implementation Solutions

In the next phase, design the SAP MII solutions. Start with the identified business processes and identify the following:

▶ **Data Sources:** Identify the available data sources and their corresponding connector type. Typically, these can be the Level 2 and Level 3 systems (LIMS, SCADA, MES, and so on) and the enterprise systems (ERP, BI, and so on). At this phase, also identify the custom data sources, if any. The custom data sources can be databases that can be used by the solution developed on SAP MII.

▶ **Data Queries:** Identify the query templates to be used to retrieve or write data from and to the data sources identified previously. Typically, these should include the data queries for the Level 2 and Level 3 systems and the custom data sources.

▶ **Business Logic Services:** Identify the BLS Transactions that need to be developed. You can identify the BLS Transactions from the services identified in the specification phase, which might include executing one or more data queries, parsing data, and executing SAP interfaces.

▶ **Visualization Templates:** Identify the display templates and animated objects used for raw data and chart display. These can be derived from the report and chart requirements and the real-time monitoring scenarios specified in the functional specification.

▶ **User Interfaces:** Identify the web pages needed to integrate the visualization templates and present them to the end users. Specify the scripting required to manipulate the visualization applets. Also, identify the enterprise portal content you need to integrate the web pages as URL iViews and the corresponding pages, worksets, and roles.

10.1.4 Best Practices for Developing SAP MII Solutions

When you are developing the SAP MII composite application, you can implement the following best practices to ensure quality and uniformity:

▶ Use a well-defined naming convention for all development objects (for example, use the prefix QT for query templates, DT for display templates, and BLS or BLT for BLS Transactions).

▶ Use a consistent style sheet in the created web pages. This ensures uniformity in the application.

▶ Design and develop the BLS Transactions so that they are as modular as possible; this enables you to reuse them when required.

▶ Instead of having the JavaScript functions defined in the same web page, define them in a separate js (JavaScript) file and include it in the web page.

▶ Use XPath expressions wherever possible in BLS Transactions for data filtering, row count, and so on to optimize performance and logic.

▶ Use JRA actions instead of JCo actions for executing RFC/BAPI from SAP systems in BLS Transactions. JRA is the recommended technology for executing RFC, and it enables you to use the data buffer feature of SAP MII also for network connectivity issues when you are performing asynchronous data updates.

▶ Use the XML Tracer action for creating custom application logs, and the Event Tracer for adding trace messages to the NetWeaver log.

▶ When you are executing any iCommand applet from a web page, use the getLastError() JavaScript method to check for any errors that can be displayed to the user by alert messages. Use the Event Tracer action block in the BLS Transactions to log error messages in the WebAS log. Use the Tracer action blocks for design-time debugging of BLS Transactions, but remove them at production.

▶ Do not hard code any hostname, IP, URL, or folder location in the action block configurations. Instead, create transaction or local properties to store the action block's Link Configuration values.

▶ Use the SAP MII Script Assistant to generate the applet JavaScript code to be used in the web pages.

▶ Add documentation as HTML and JavaScript comments in web pages, and as action blocks' documentation in BLS Transactions.

▶ When you are passing array values as input parameters to a BLS Transaction from web pages, the best way to do this would be to pass the values in a delimiter-separated string. In the BLS Transaction, you can use a String to XML Parser action block to splice out the values in the XML format and a Repeater action block to loop through these values and perform the necessary business logic. This is far more efficient than using JavaScript to call a BLS Transaction in a loop from the calling HTML/IRPT page. Do not use a blank character as the delimiter.

In this section, you have learned about the steps and best practices for specifying, designing, and developing SAP MII composite applications. In the next section, you learn about the various possible solution architecture scenarios for implementing SAP MII.

10.2 Solution Architecture of SAP MII Implementations

Typically, you can categorize a manufacturing enterprise into the following hierarchical levels:

- **Level 0:** The physical manufacturing machines and process that defines the actual physical processes.
- **Level 1:** Intelligent devices for sensing and manipulating the physical processes, for example, process sensors, analyzers, actuators, and related instrumentation.
- **Level 2:** Control systems for supervising, monitoring, and controlling the physical processes. These are real-time controls and software applications such as Distributed Control System (DCS), Human Machine Interface (HMI), and Supervisory Control And Data Acquisition (SCADA) software.
- **Level 3:** Manufacturing operations systems for managing production work flow to produce the desired products, for example, batch management; Manufacturing Execution/Operations Management Systems (MES/MOMS); laboratory, maintenance, and plant performance management systems; and data Historians and related middleware. Time frames considered are shifts, hours, minutes, and seconds.
- **Level 4:** Business Logistics Systems for managing the business-related activities of the manufacturing operations. Enterprise Resource Planning (ERP) is the primary system that establishes the basic plant production schedule, material use, and shipping and inventory levels. Periods considered are months, weeks, days, and shifts.

As an integration and analytics platform for manufacturing plant-floor integration, SAP MII is typically positioned between the Level 2 or Level 3 and Level 4 applications in an enterprise context. Though SAP MII has connectors and provides integration features for Level 2 shop-floor automation control systems (such as SCADA, Historian, DCS, and so on), we recommended that you position SAP MII between the MES and ERP to enable the connectivity layer between them. For enterprises or scenarios where solutions gaps are present in the existing MES or legacy Level 3 systems, you can position SAP MII between Level 2 and Level 4 to enable the connectivity and can address the solution gaps of Level 3 with custom-developed content.

Figure 10.1 shows the positioning of SAP MII in the enterprise context based on the preceding discussion.

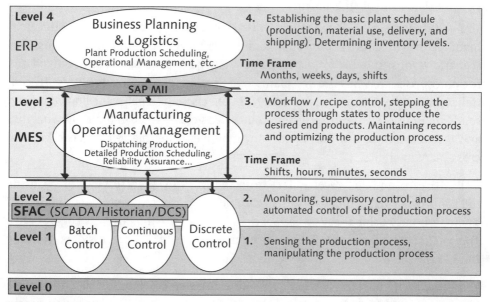

Figure 10.1 SAP MII Positioning in Enterprise Context

Though most of the standard MES packages provide connectivity to enterprise systems such as SAP ERP and integration and analytics capability over the manufacturing plant-floor applications, you can still use SAP MII to address the solution gaps by developing content for business logic, connectivity, or visualizations.

For scenarios where no standard MES package is available, SAP MII can play a very important role — especially for manufacturing plant-floor systems where the Level 2 systems need to be integrated with the enterprise systems. SAP MII can serve as an integration platform for all systems and can provide visualization and analytics of data for both plant-floor personnel and business users at the corporate level.

10.2.1 Implementation Architecture of SAP MII

Based on the scale and need of the specific manufacturing sites, you can consider different architectural scenarios for implementing SAP MII. We describe some of the most common scenarios in the sections that follow.

Central Deployment of SAP MII

You can deploy SAP MII at the corporate level and aggregate data from different manufacturing plants by connecting to the MES layer of the individual plants. This scenario is most suitable for plants that already have MES packages deployed and for enterprises that have fewer plants and smaller production facilities. In centralized deployment, the central SAP MII collects individual plant-floor data and sends them to the enterprise systems (and vice versa). You can build the analytics and visualization in SAP MII mainly for manufacturing plant-floor visibility and cross-plant analytics.

SAP MII can send and receive data from the MES by Web services or by using the proprietary data connectors as applicable. MES can also send data to SAP MII asynchronously using the Message Services. You can use the Business Logic Service Transactions to execute the Web services and aggregate and process data from the MES at the plant floor.

You can directly interface SAP MII with enterprise systems, or you can do so via a middleware or an Enterprise Service Bus (ESB) such as SAP PI. It has action blocks in BLS Transactions for sending messages to SAP PI using the SOAP or HTTP adapter. SAP PI can also send messages to SAP MII by executing the BLS Transactions having XML input parameters as Web or HTTP services synchronously, or asynchronously using the Message Services. Using SAP PI to integrate the enterprise systems with SAP MII and the plant-floor applications adds an abstraction and middleware layer in between them, which might be useful for various reasons (such as asynchronous and high-volume message transfers, message monitoring, and so on).

Figure 10.2 shows the architecture overview of the centralized deployment of SAP MII as discussed previously.

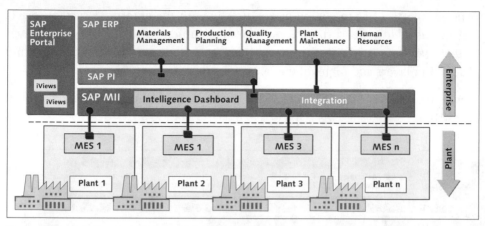

Figure 10.2 Solution Architecture of Central Deployment of SAP MII

Multi-Plant Deployment of SAP MII

You can deploy SAP MII at individual plant sites, which enables you to integrate the Level 2 and Level 3 systems with the enterprise systems and produce visualization for manufacturing plant-floor personnel. This solution is most suitable for scenarios where no standard MES package is available, or where the MES package available is not capable of acquiring all the required data from the manufacturing systems and providing the end-to-end visualization. This is also a suitable use case for an enterprise having multiple plants and larger production facilities.

SAP MII deployed at the individual plants can connect directly to plant-floor systems using data connectors for bi-directional access to the plant-floor data. This architecture is also suitable for plants having multiple legacy systems. Additionally, you can use SAP MII to provide visualization and transactional dashboards for the plant floor, through which the manufacturing personnel can visualize and analyze the plant-floor Key Performance Indicators (KPIs) and record process information such as quality inspection, order confirmation, and goods movement, which get updated to the enterprise system finally.

To integrate enterprise systems with plants, you can have another SAP MII installation present at the corporate level. This installation can integrate data from the plant level with the enterprise systems, either via SAP PI or directly. You can use the corporate level SAP MII for cross-plant analytics and plant data aggregation. Alternatively, you can bypass the corporate-level SAP MII installation, and the plant-level SAP MII can communicate directly with the enterprise systems or via SAP PI (installed at the corporate level). We recommend using an integration layer at the corporate level, because it provides important features for queuing and abstraction layers and high-volume message support.

Figure 10.3 shows the high-level architecture of the plant-based deployment of SAP MII.

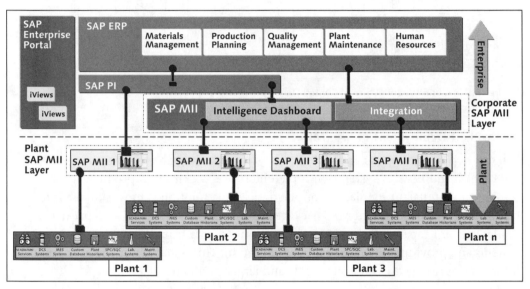

Figure 10.3 Solution Architecture of Plant-Based or Decentralized Deployment of SAP MII

10.2.2 Application Architecture of SAP MII Composite Applications

For composite applications developed in SAP MII, you need to consider certain architecture and design considerations from the application point of view. You should use SAP MII as the integration and analytics platform for manufacturing to enterprise integration and not as a planning or scheduling system such as MES. SAP MII is best suited for aggregating data from the plant systems in real time using the data servers and data queries, manipulating them using the BLS Transactions, and finally presenting them to the end users in the analysis dashboards by different types of charts and intelligent reports and updating in the enterprise system. Typically, in a SAP MII implementation project you might develop the following objects:

▶ **Query Templates:** Acquiring data from plant systems and legacy databases.

▶ **Display Templates:** Charts and grid reports for analysis dashboards.

▶ **Business Logic Service Transactions:** Business logic to process data, execute queries, read or update data to and from SAP systems, generate dynamic dashboard components such as animated objects, and so on.

▶ **HTML/IRPT Web Pages:** Web pages developed to present the analytics and the transaction dashboards to the end users via the SAP MII portal or SAP Enterprise Portal.

An important consideration here is to decide on the local data persistency option in SAP MII. The composite applications developed in SAP MII might need some local data persistency to store configuration and some transactional data temporarily. You can achieve this by using an external database such as MS SQL Server, Oracle, or DB2 and then using the IDBC Data Server connector to connect to it with SQL queries. Alternatively, you can use the database of the SAP NetWeaver Java WebAS, on which SAP MII is deployed, and connect to it by the DataSource or IDBC connectors. In both cases, you need to create custom application–specific database schemas and tables in the database. Though we do not recommended that you permanently persist any data in the local custom database that is also persisted in the enterprise systems, sometimes you need to for reasons involving temporary persistence or performance improvement. If you use local persistence for enterprise master data, make sure the data does not change often in the original system. You can also provide the option to synchronize the data as required by using the Message Services; SAP MII also enables local buffering of data to be sent asynchronously to the enterprise or plant systems in case of connection failure.

SAP MII systems can access data sources configured in other SAP MII servers using the virtual connectors, as explained in detail in Chapter 9 Advanced Techniques for SAP MII Composite Application Development. If an implementation of SAP MII installed in one plant needs to access the data sources of another SAP MII installation, or if you need to connect the corporate instance of SAP MII with the plant instances of SAP MII, using virtual connector is the best way to do this from a performance point of view.

You should design integration with enterprise systems using BAPI or Enterprise services. It is always better to use the JRA action blocks if BAPI or RFC is used, and you can use Message Services for asynchronous data transfer from enterprise systems to SAP MII. For retrieving BI data, use the OLAP connector along with OLAP queries, whereas for updating data, use an RFC. If you have high data volume from enterprise systems, consider using SAP PI as an integration broker or middleware between corporate to plant levels. SAP MII provides built-in action blocks in BLS Transactions for sending messages to SAP PI, and in Message Services for asynchronously receiving HTTP messages from SAP PI.

Figure 10.4 shows the high-level application architecture of SAP MII implementation as discussed previously.

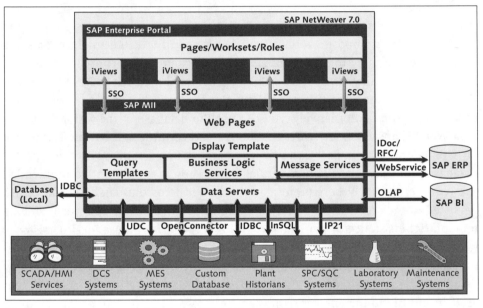

Figure 10.4 Application Architecture of SAP MII Composite Applications

In this section, you have learned about the various solution, implementation, and application architecture scenarios of SAP MII composite applications. In the next section, you learn about some of the useful troubleshooting tips you can use when you are developing and running SAP MII composite applications.

10.3 Troubleshooting of SAP MII Composite Applications

You might find it is useful to master some troubleshooting tips for SAP MII composite applications. First, it is a good practice to check the server trace when any abnormal situation happens. The default trace of the SAP NetWeaver Java WebAS contains the trace for the SAP MII application (explained in Section 2.1 User Management and WebAS Administration in SAP MII). Many times the entry in the default trace might point to the exact cause of the error. Additionally, see the pointers that follow:

▶ **Communication failure for external services:** If a communication failure happens while you are executing external Web services from SAP MII, check if the proxy setting has been maintained in the SYSTEM MANAGEMENT • SYSTEM ADMINISTRATION menu. For JCo or JRA communications, check the configurations in SAP Server Editor and Visual Administrator, if required.

▶ **Data Server connection failure:** For connection failure issues of Data Servers, check whether the security permission for that data server is configured for the user role in the Data Access menu present under Security Services menu category. For SQL data sources check if the correct JDBC driver is uploaded and deployed and the correct authentication with ValidationQuery and database driver classname (database-specific) are specified in the Data Server configuration. For Universal Data Connector (UDC)–based data sources check if the UDS instance for the Data Server is running.

▶ **Passing blank value in RFC calls:** If an input value of the structure or table type or multi-cardinality element need to be passed as null when you are executing RFC or Enterprise service from BLS Transactions, do not leave that parameter without any link mapping. Select the parameter on the right pane of the Link Editor and assign Remove XML. That removes the selected XML element itself from the RFC input XML.

▶ **Formatting object IDs with leading zeros:** When you are executing a BAPI/RFC or Enterprise service in SAP, you might need to format IDs with leading zeros. Otherwise, they might not be recognized as correct values in the SAP system. Using Link Configuration and the Expression Editor, you can format IDs in any of the following ways:

  ▶ format(Transaction.OrderNumber, "000000000000")

  ▶ stringright("000000000000"&Transaction.OrderNumber, 12)

▶ **Auto-commit in JCo action block:** Use the auto-commit option in the JCo action block when you are executing any RFC that might change data in the backend system. However, note that it is better to use the JRA or JCo Session action blocks for this.

▶ **Applet display issues:** Developers and end users often face the problem of an incorrectly displayed Java applet. If you encounter this problem, check the Java Runtime available in the client system. The minimum Java Runtime Environment (JRE) required in the client machines is 1.4.2_07 or higher, but not 1.5.0_07, 1.5.0_08, and 1.5.0_09. Moreover, check if the Use JRE <JREVersion> for Applets option is checked in the Internet Explorer TOOLS • INTERNET OPTIONS • ADVANCED menu. If a display or query template is changed, you must clear the Java Classloader Cache from the Internet Explorer TOOLS • SUN JAVA CONSOLE menu by pressing "x" and then refreshing the page. A useful method of debugging applets is to activate applet debugging from the SYSTEM MANAGEMENT • APPLET DEBUGGING menu.

▶ **Executing a JavaScript function on page onLoad event:** If a JavaScript function is executed on <body onLoad> event of the web page, make sure no applet is accessed there. This might sometimes create issues because the applet loading might take some time. When the JavaScript function is executed at the onLoad event of the page, the applet might not yet be loaded fully to execute. It is better to execute the JavaScript function on the CREATIONEVENT of the applet.

▶ **All data records not available in Query output:** If you do not see all the relevant data records available in the data source when you execute a query via a query template, it might be because the default value for RowCount set in a query template is 100. Unless you manually change that value, you get only the first 100 rows in the output.

▶ **Refreshing RFC interface:** While using custom RFC with JCo action block in BLS Transaction, if the RFC metadata is changed in the ABAP system, sometimes it might not get refreshed automatically in the JCo action block in BLS. You can clear the JCoProxy cache using the following URL: *http://<server>:<port>/XMII/JCOProxy?Mode=Reset.*

In this section, you have learned some of the useful troubleshooting tips for developing and running SAP MII composite applications. In the next section, you learn how you can implement ISA95/B2MML integration between enterprise and plant-floor systems.

10.4 Implementing ISA-95/B2MML in SAP MII

ANSI ISA-95 is an industrial standard for manufacturing industries that establishes data interfaces between the manufacturing plant floor and the enterprise. In other words, the purpose of this standard is to create data synchronization between the production control in plants and the enterprise business and planning operations on the corporate level. The most common and widely used implementation of this standard is that developed by the XML working group of World Batch Forum (*http://www.wbf.org*) as Business to Manufacturing Markup Language (B2MML), which uses XML schemas to implement the data models specified in the ISA-95 standard. You can download the latest version of these schemas for the B2MML messages from their website.

Now we want to delve deeper into how you can implement this standard for the manufacturing plant floor and enterprise integration. First, you need an ISA-95/ B2MML–compliant MES on the manufacturing plant floor; SAP MII serves as the enabler of the B2MML message exchange between the MES and the ERP. An example scenario is downloading real-time manufacturing planning data from the ERP to the MES, and uploading real-time production data from the MES to the ERP.

SAP MII already provides various ways and means of retrieving data from the enterprise systems. For newer SAP ERP releases such as SAP ERP 2005, invoking a BAPI/RFC using JCo Interface action blocks or Enterprise services (through the WebService action block in SAP MII) should suffice. However, for older R/3 4.6C or R/3 4.7 Enterprise releases, which might not have some of the required BAPIs/ RFCs, you can use IDocs or RFCs and the Message Services of SAP MII to store data asynchronously pushed out of R/3.

After the data is retrieved from ERP, use the Reference Schema Loader action block in BLS Transaction to load the B2MML schema corresponding to the message that you want to send to the manufacturing plant-floor system. To map the data retrieved from the ERP to the structure specified by the B2MML schema, define the XML structure of a transaction or local property using the Reference Document as a B2MML message and create the necessary logic in the BLS Transaction. You can then send this B2MML message over to the MES by the use of any other standard means of communication like Web services or an HTTP Post. If the data has been sent to MII asynchronously and has been stored in the Messaging Services buffer, you can retrieve the data using the Message Services action blocks, explained in Section 6.4.7 Web Service before mapping them onto a B2MML schema and consequently sending them over to the MES system.

It is easier to load a B2MML schema using the Reference Document loader action block and then model complicated logic in the transaction to generate the mapped B2MML message. Using an XSL transformation through the XSL Transformation action block would yield better performance in case of high message volume, but would also decrease legibility and maintainability of the resulting transactions.

The MES-to-ERP data transfer scenario is similar in execution to the data being received from MES as B2MML messages. You can achieve this scenario by using HTTP Post to deliver the XML message to the SAP MII Message Services from MES. Alternatively, the MES can invoke SAP MII transactions as Web or HTTP services and directly pass on the B2MML message as an input parameter. In this case, you need to map the data in the B2MML message to the input of the corresponding ERP interfaces, thus sending that data over to ERP. For example, you can download Production Orders to the MES using the ProductionSchedule B2MML message, whereas you can upload the ProductionPerformance B2MML message to the ERP as Production Confirmation (from the manufacturing plant floor). You can use the SAP MII Scheduler, explained in Section 2.2.3 Scheduler, to schedule these transactions at regular intervals to sync data from ERP to MES (and vice versa). This maintains a seamless connectivity between the manufacturing plant floor and the enterprise. In case of a network connection failure between MII and ERP, the Data Buffering features of SAP MII come into play, when you are updating data from SAP MII to SAP ERP asynchronously. Data Buffering guarantees delivery by ensuring that the data sent to ERP using synchronous RFC calls is executed whenever the connectivity is available.

Figure 10.5 illustrates the ISA95 implementation scenario using SAP MII.

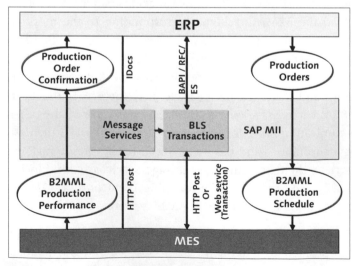

Figure 10.5 ISA95 Implementation Using SAP MII

In this section, you have learned the basic concepts of implementing ISA95/ B2MML standard in SAP MII so you can integrate the enterprise business with the manufacturing plant floor in a standard-based messaging method. In the next section, you can see the various implementation scenarios in the manufacturing industries where SAP MII often plays an important role.

10.5 Implementation Scenarios of SAP MII in Manufacturing Industries

As a flexible platform for developing manufacturing composite applications, you can use SAP MII to increase operational excellence in various types of manufacturing industries. Broadly, SAP MII can address three major types of scenarios:

▶ Performance management

▶ Manufacturing analytics

▶ Manufacturing data synchronization

Performance management scenarios mostly deal with monitoring and improving key drivers for the business. SAP MII addresses this via KPIs and alerts and provides standard features for both of these functions to update KPI and create alerts using the corresponding action blocks available in BLS Transactions. Via the KPI Watch List in the SAP Enterprise Portal, you can monitor KPIs from the Plant Manager 2.0 role. You can access alerts through the alert inbox, UWL, or other supported channels, such as mobile devices or emails. Additionally, you can configure SAP MII charts and visualizations to display and monitor different KPIs, such as OEE, production rate, hazardous waste, and material stock. You can use the BLS Transactions to calculate the KPIs and prepare intelligent visualization and reports. The real-time data collection capability and dynamic visualizations of SAP MII provide you with the ability to take immediate actions based on different operational events.

Manufacturing analytics is another powerful feature of SAP MII, because it delivers both current and historical analysis of the production process. It also enables you to integrate data from the plant floor and enterprise and provides analysis dashboards using display templates. SAP MII provides SPC charts to monitor process maturity, enables $3\text{-}\sigma$ or $6\text{-}\sigma$ analysis on various process parameters, and facilitates process trends analysis via trend charts. You can also use the SAP MII reporting framework for easy and quick deployment of custom reports about production data.

Manufacturing data synchronization is one of the most common scenarios for which manufacturing industries use SAP MII. Using the different plant-floor connectors such as Universal Data Connector, IDBC, OpenConnector, IP21, and InSQL, you can retrieve data from different sources such as MES and Plant Historians. You can then parse and aggregate this data using the Business Logic Services and update it in the SAP ERP or other enterprise systems. Integrating plant-floor and enterprise data and events in almost real time enables real-time visibility and operational excellence.

In the following sections, we explain some examples of common implementation scenarios of SAP MII in manufacturing industries.

10.5.1 Simpler User Interface and Enterprise Integration

Because of the complexity of transactions and user interfaces in the enterprise systems, you often need to create a simpler and customized user interface for plant workers. SAP MII accomplishes this via dashboards and web-based user interfaces; some typical examples include production order confirmation dashboards, quality inspection recording and analysis dashboards, batch tracking dashboards, and machine downtime recording dashboards, which you can develop using SAP MII. Using these dashboards, users can view and update data from and to the enterprise systems.

You can develop these scenarios by executing RFCs, Enterprise services, or OLAP queries to retrieve or update relevant data. You can also use custom databases in SAP MII to persist additional information required for the applications. Additionally, it is common to use the custom database for temporarily caching the data, which can then be updated at a later point. This is a useful scenario when the enterprise-to-plant network connectivity is not very strong or is not continuously available. Using temporary caching and local persistency in SAP MII, you can download relevant data to the plants at one specific time (perhaps at the start of the day or shift). Then you can temporarily persist the data, which can be updated once or twice daily. Instead of creating complex database to temporarily store these data, you can use the Message Services to buffer the data as XML messages and maintain the basic header information and the message ID of the buffered message in a simple database table. To retrieve the detail information when required, you can read the corresponding message from the message buffer using the Read Message action block in BLS Transaction by the corresponding message ID and parse the XML using the XML function and logic action blocks available there.

The analysis dashboards are typically charts used for quality inspection analysis, yield analysis, or batch characteristics. You can display reports through the iGrid display template or SAP MII Reports.

10.5.2 Plant Systems Integration and Manufacturing Dashboards

In manufacturing plants where multiple systems are present for manufacturing execution and data acquisition, SAP MII can play a very important role. For example, you can use SAP MII to connect to the Historian, LIMS, SCADA, MES, and so on for collecting the production data such as workcenter interruptions, quality inspection results, goods movement requests, or batch characteristics information using the Tag and SQL queries or Web services. You can update this data using the JCo/JRA action blocks or Web services in SAP ERP or SAP BI, via the BLS Transactions. In addition, user interfaces and visualizations created in SAP MII can provide useful dashboards for plant workers. You can fetch the data online and update them in the enterprise systems, display the data in dashboards in real time, or persist the data in a custom database.

SAP MII enables you to develop user interfaces for taking inputs and visualizations such as trend charts. You can also model custom business processes not supported by existing systems. Animated objects and display template applets with auto-refresh providing real-time visibility of the manufacturing plant floor.

10.5.3 Enterprise Services for the Manufacturing Plant Floor

Another common use of SAP MII is to expose Enterprise services so that manufacturing plant-floor applications can retrieve and update the enterprise data directly from the plant floor using these services via SAP MII. SAP MII Business Logic Services can execute Web services and RFCs provided by the enterprise systems and expose the output and input parameters hiding the complexity of the enterprise services or APIs. Also, you can combine multiple RFC/Web service calls to the enterprise systems in a single transaction to be executed by the plant systems. This makes it easier for the manufacturing applications to call the services. Any BLS Transaction created in SAP MII automatically becomes a Web service that you can execute as a SOAP Web service or simple HTTP XML service. Moreover, from the

BLS Transaction itself, you can push data to the plant systems by executing queries, Web services, or file transfers.

Though the possibilities of SAP MII are limitless, here we have given just a few pointers on the common scenarios and solution architectures that you might find useful.

10.6 Summary

In this chapter, you have learned about the development steps and best practices for SAP MII composite applications, and some useful troubleshooting tips that you can use when you are developing or running the applications. You have also learned about the various solution architectures of SAP MII composite applications and common implementation scenarios. You can use this knowledge when you are developing or implementing SAP MII composite applications for an enterprise.

Appendices

This chapter briefly explains the new features that are available in SAP MII 12.1.

A   New Features in SAP MII 12.1

SAP MII 12.1 has just recently been released, and at the time of writing this book, it is in its ramp-up. Because SAP MII 12.1 is the successor of SAP MII 12.0, on which this book is based, you might find it helpful to get an overview of the new features available in the next version. The new and enhanced features of SAP MII 12.1 can be grouped into the following categories:

▸ **Platform:** Runs on SAP NetWeaver CE 7.1.1(CE 7.1 EhP1) Java WebAS, based on Java EE 1.5.

▸ **UI Enhancements:** Java AWT applets for display templates have been replaced with Java Swing applets. Java Swing applets are lightweight compared to the AWT applets and have full accesibility support. No legacy functionality has been deprecated, and new enhancements such as validation of input parameters used in the JavaScript function calls, consistent floor plans, and message/information areas in applets have been added. Also now you can configure the logging options per applet to display information on a Java console, and you can specify auto-refresh rate for iGrid, iChart, and iSPCChart at runtime as well. The x-axis labels can be rotated to any angle and multiple y-axis can be also configured.

▸ **BLS Enhancements:** BLS runtime performance has been enhanced to a great extent by a redesign of the BLS runtime engine. New action blocks such as JMS, dynamic transaction call, qRFC, XML validation, and so on have been provided. Also new data types such as long, map, list, password, byte, binary, and so on are supported in this release as transaction and local properties data types. XML schema–based interface definition for transaction properties of Xml data type has been added in BLS Transactions. Also added, you can create Shared Properties for use in SAP MII Transactions and configure them from the SAP MII configuration screen for user-defined values without changing any BLS Transactions. For example, you can use these Shared Properties to configure the URL of an Enterprise service that might vary from the development to the production landscape. You can now create localization at the Project Level and export with the Project ZIP file. Data buffer is also supported for Web service, SAP XI, and SAP JCo action blocks and a separate log is provided to view the details of the BLS Transactions executed.

▶ **Security:** A new credential store has been added to manage user ID and passwords centrally, which can be reused in all authentications for BLS Transaction actions such as JCo, Web service, XI, Email, and so on and for Data Servers. Also, a password encryption feature has been added that you can use by configuring the encryption algorithms.

▶ **Content Management:** A Development Time Repository (DTR) has been integrated with the SAP MII Workbench with transport management using NetWeaver Development Infrastructure (NWDI) for managing all content developed in SAP MII. This provides the features of version management and controlled access to the content by a check-in/check-out facility. Also, Component Build Services (CBS) and Component Management Services (CMS) have been integrated. This means that content you create in Workbench can be built to create an SDA and deployed on a different MII Server using either (Java Support Package Manager (JSPM) or the NetWeaver Developer Studio. This approach is better than importing Project ZIP files because it maintains versions and does not allow changes of deployed content.

▶ The productivity wizards such as the Script Assistant and Content Publishing wizard have been integrated with the Workbench.

B   The Authors

Dipankar Saha works for IBM India as an Advisory System Analyst on SAP MII and SAP Composite Application development and architecture. He has experience in leading several SAP MII implementation projects globally. Dipankar has written several popular technical blogs and articles in SAP Community Network on SAP MII and related topics. Previously he worked for SAP Labs India, and was involved in the design and development of SAP MII 12.0 and developing composite applications using SAP MII with several manufacturing partners and customers of SAP. Dipankar is a SAP Certified Associate Enterprise Architect. He has over seven years of experience in the IT industry and has a Bachelors of Technology Degree in Chemical Engineering. He is also an SAP Mentor.

Abesh Bhattacharjee has over five years of experience in the IT industry and a year of manufacturing shopfloor experience. He has also worked as an Oracle DBA. He is currently employed with SAP Labs India Pvt. Ltd. as a Principal Software Engineer and has been working on SAP MII for the last three and a half years. His interests include SOA, BPM, Web 2.0, Enterprise 2.0, and RIAs. Abesh has authored several popular blogs, articles and e-courses around these topics. He is a Mechanical Engineer from NIT Trichy, and a Moderator in the SAP Community Network and an SAP Mentor.

Index

D

T

Y

Z

Learn the essentials of MDX as implemented in NetWeaver BI and Business Objects

Explore examples of common business problems solved with MDX using Business Objects, and other third-party tools

Design MDX-friendly InfoCubes, including characteristics (MDX dimensions) enabled with external hierarchies

Larry Sackett

MDX Reporting and Analytics with SAP NetWeaver BW

An Up-to-Date Guide for Business Intelligence Reporting and Analytics with SAP

This is the first book to provide a detailed guide of how MDX works in the SAP NetWeaver BI and Business Objects environments. Readers will learn the concepts behind MDX querying, how to design MDX-friendly InfoCubes, and how to apply the knowledge in solving business problems and creating reports efficiently.

approx. 350 pp., 69,95 Euro / US$ 69.95
ISBN 978-1-59229-249-3, Sept 2009

>> www.sap-press.de/1991

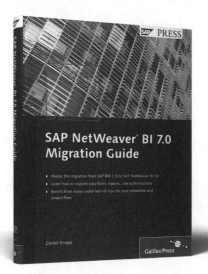

Master the functional professional migration of SAP BW 3.5 to SAP NetWeaver BI 7.0

Find out how to migrate data flows, reports, and authorizations

Use the many valuable tips from real-life projects on effort estimating and project progression

Daniel Knapp

SAP NetWeaver BI 7.0 Migration Guide

SAP PRESS Essentials 50

SAP NetWeaver BI 7.0 includes major changes from earlier releases, making migrations a challenging task, but with this book, consultants, developers, power users, and project teams will find the knowledge needed for technical and functional NetWeaver BI 7.0 migrations. Using real-life examples and highlighting SAP-recommended approaches, you'll work through data, authorizations, report migration and more. Both the automatic and manual aspects of report migration are highlighted, with particular attention to the radically revised Web reporting.

181 pp., 2008, 68,– Euro / US$ 85
ISBN 978-1-59229-228-8

>> www.sap-press.de/1852

Get a highly detailed overview of BEx tools and functionalities

Understand exactly how BEx works and how it impacts business

Learn from proven report design strategies, tips, tricks and more

Up to date for SAP NetWeaver BI 7.0

Peter Scott

SAP BEx Tools

SAP Business Explorer (BEx) Tools teaches users exactly what they need to know to perform effective BEx reporting, with no frills or extra information, with sample scenarios and practical examples included throughout the book. This new edition features completely updated terminology and technology, and explains how to update everything using the new interfaces. A newly added chapter covers advanced topics on the new tools, and includes an FAQ section that answers common questions and best practices information.

approx. 172 pp., 2. edition, 68,– Euro / US$ 85
ISBN 978-1-59229-279-0, June 2009

>> **www.sap-press.de/2058**

Understand all aspects of SAP
NetWeaver BI Information
Broadcasting

Learn from actual implementation
steps and screen shots

Discover quick and easy
troubleshooting tips to common
Information Broadcasting problems

Muke Abdelnaby

Mastering Information Broadcasting with SAP NetWeaver BI 7.0

When, where, why, and how to use SAP NetWeaver BI 7.0 Information Broadcasting

Mastering Information Broadcasting with SAP NetWeaver BI 7 is a detailed how-to guide that teaches NetWeaver BI 7.0 customers how to use the Information Broadcasting capabilities to distribute BI information through the various distribution methods, such as, email, PDF, html, and Portal. Users will learn what Information Broadcasting is and where it fits into a reporting solution, with the main focus being on when, why, and how to use Information Broadcasting's many features (scheduling, alerts/exceptions, bursting) and the technology associated with it.

approx. 215 pp., 68,– Euro / US$ 85
ISBN 978-1-59229-276-9, Sept 2009

>> www.sap-press.de/2056